WORLD CRICKET FACTS & RECORDS

Copyright © Carlton Books Limited 2010

First published under the title of World Cricket Records 2011 in 2010
Reissued in text-only version in 2011

A CIP catalogue record for this book is available from the British Library

Carlton Books Limited
20 Mortimer Street
London W1T 3JW

ISBN: 978-1-84732-772-7

Editor: Martin Corteel
Design: Ben Durston
Production: Karin Kolbe

Printed in Great Britain

WORLD CRICKET FACTS & RECORDS

CHRIS HAWKES

CARLTON

CONTENTS

INTRODUCTION 6

PART 1: TEST CRICKET 8

Test Records by Team 65

Test Records by Series 115

PART 2:
ONE-DAY INTERNATIONAL CRICKET 234

PART 3: TWENTY20 CRICKET 300

PART 4: DOMESTIC CRICKET RECORDS 314

PART 5: OTHER CRICKET 342

INTRODUCTION

WELCOME to the first edition of a new venture in international cricket publishing – World Cricket Facts and Records. Ranging across the length and breadth of world cricket and including the men's game, women's cricket and youth cricket, the intention of this book is to explore, explain and intrigue the reader with the people, places and competitions that have made the game of cricket one of the most popular and widespread sports on the planet.

One of the enduring fascinations of the game of cricket, in all its forms (timed matches, limited-overs matches and the new kid on the block, Twenty20 cricket) is that the game can be broken down into the minutest of details. Every ball of every match played in the professional game over the years has been recorded for posterity, meaning that fans from all over the world can dip in and out of the game's records and ascertain any number of facts. Few other sports can be scrutinized to such an extent as cricket.

First and foremost, World Cricket Records 2011 is not a history book. It is a celebration of both the best and the worst of performances in Test cricket, one-day international cricket, the Twenty20 game, first-class domestic cricket, women's cricket and youth international cricket. It is an exposition of benchmarks – those to which every player in the game would wish to aspire and surpass as well as those that players would want to avoid. For every one of the game's most wanted records, there is a plethora of unwanted ones.. Such a book, of course, would not be possible without the considerable efforts of others. Cricket is blessed with numerous and comprehensive archives, with scorecards and statistics dating back to the game's earliest days in the 19th century. And all are available to the general public at the touch of a button. It has been a privilege to spend months trawling through these archives to find the hidden gems dotted throughout this book, to bring performances that could have been lost in the mists of time back to life and to introduce readers to the feats of players whose achievements could, otherwise, have been consigned to unopened books on dusty shelves. A sport can only be as rich as its history and, in that regard, cricket is blessed with considerable treasures.

Because cricket has become a 12-month sport, clearly there had to be a cut-off point. Fortunately, the 2011 ICC World Cup held in the Bangladesh, India and Sri Lanka meant that, for once, all of the world's major teams were in the same part of the world at the same time – a rarity in the modern game. As such, all statistics in the book are correct as of 6 February 2011, the day Australia and England finished their marathon post-Ashes seven-match one-day series. Particular thanks are also due to Martin Corteel, whose encouragement while putting a book of this type together is both morale-boosting and invaluable, to Jim Lockwood and Kate Painter for their keen eye for design, to David Ballheimer for his assiduous attention to the minutest of cricketing details and to Kate Pimm for her huge efforts with the book's production. This project would not have come together without their considerable input.

Chris Hawkes
London, March 2011

PART 1: TEST CRICKET

Cricket had been played in various countries around the world for decades, but when, on the morning of Thursday, 15 March 1877, England's Arthur Shaw bowled to Australia's Charles Bannerman in Melbourne, a new phenomenon was born: Test cricket. More than 130 years later, the game has spread around the world and has left an indelible mark wherever it has settled.

Nobody is quite sure how it got its name, but Test cricket is just that: a complete and total test of a player's technique, his mental surety and, particularly in the modern game, his physical prowess. Its enduring fascination to players and spectators, of course, is that it is many other things beyond that: it can be an epic battle between bat and ball; it is a game in which, at any point during the five days, the balance of power can shift in an instant – an awe-inspiring catch, an unplayable delivery, an ill-advised shot or a farcical, out-of-the-blue run-out all have the ability to trigger a magical chain of events that appeared outrageously improbable only moments earlier.

As one might expect, a section on Test cricket's all-time record-breakers contains a legion of the game's most revered names – Donald Bradman, Garfield Sobers, Sachin Tendulkar and Shane Warne to name but four – but there are also some more unusual, less heralded entrants. Who, for example, was the first bowler to take nine wickets in an innings, or which wicketkeeper holds the record for the highest score in Test cricket?

TEAM RECORDS

⊙ THE WEST INDIES BY A WHISKER

When Australia's off-spinner Tim May took 5 for 9 in 6.5 overs to help dismiss the West Indies for 146 in the Fourth Test at Adelaide in January 1993, it left the home side needing a modest 186 runs for a victory that would hand them an unassailable 2–0 lead in the five-match series. Australia slipped to 144 for 9, before a rearguard action from May and Craig McDermott brought them within agonizing reach of the winning line. Then tragedy struck: a Courtney Walsh delivery found the edge of McDermott's bat; Junior Murray claimed the catch; and the West Indies had won one of the greatest Test matches in history by a single run – the smallest margin of victory (by runs) in Test history.

⊙ THE 40-YEAR WAIT

No country has been forced to endure a longer wait for a series victory than New Zealand. Between 1929 and 1969, they suffered 21 series defeats (with nine drawn) before a draw in the Third Test against Pakistan in Dacca in November 1969 secured a 1–0 series victory to end their 30 Test series without a victory.

RESULTS SUMMARY

Team	Span	Mat	Won	Lost	Tied	Draw	W/L	%W	%L	%D
Australia (1877–2011)		730	341	192	2	195	1.77	46.71	26.30	26.71
Bangladesh (2000–2010)		68	3	59	0	6	0.05	4.41	86.76	8.82
England (1877–2011)		908	321	261	0	326	1.22	35.35	28.74	35.90
ICC World XI (2005)		1	0	1	0	0	0.00	0.00	100.00	0.00*
India (1932–2011)		448	109	139	1	199	0.78	24.33	31.02	44.41
New Zealand (1930–2011)		364	68	147	0	149	0.46	18.68	40.38	40.94
Pakistan (1952–2011)		356	107	99	0	150	1.08	30.05	27.80	42.15
South Africa (1889–2011)		358	125	124	0	109	1.00	34.91	34.63	30.46
Sri Lanka (1982–2010)		198	61	70	0	67	0.87	30.80	35.35	33.83
West Indies (1928–2009)		468	152	154	1	161	0.98	32.47	32.90	34.40
Zimbabwe (1992–2005)		83	8	49	0	26	0.16	9.63	59.03	31.32

* An ICC World XI played a one-off "Super" Test against Australia in 2005 – the match was given official status by the ICC and so appears in all Test records.

⊙ ENGLAND CRUSH SORRY AUSTRALIA

England, inspired by 22-year-old Len Hutton (who made a then world record 364), put on a batting masterclass for two-and-a-half days of the final Test of the 1938 Ashes series, played at The Oval. Trailing 1–0 in the series, the home side compiled a massive 903 for 7 in their first innings to leave Australia with a daunting mountain to climb. They failed miserably, falling to 201 all out in their first innings and to 123 all out in their second. The margin of defeat – an innings and 579 runs – is the largest (by an innings) in Test history.

⊙ ENGLAND OFF TO A FLYER

A fine innings of 169 by Patsy Hendren helped England to a commanding first-innings score of 521 all out in the first Test of the 1928–29 Ashes series, played at Brisbane. In reply, Australia – featuring debutant Donald Bradman – limped to 122 all out, 399 runs in arrears. England, declining to enforce the follow-on, piled on the pressure, hitting 342 for 8 in their second innings to set Australia an unlikely victory target of 742. The home side wilted under the pressure, subsiding to 66 all out in 25.3 overs to lose by 675 runs – the largest losing margin (by runs) in Test history.

⊙ THE FIRST TIED TEST MATCH

In December 1960, in the First Test against the West Indies at Brisbane, the Australians, after holding a 52-run first-innings lead, were set 233 runs to win. They slipped to 92 for 6 before a record-breaking 134-run seventh-wicket stand between Alan Davidson (who became the first player to score 100 runs and take 10 wickets in a Test match) and captain Richie Benaud brought them to within six runs of victory. Then disaster struck: Davidson was run out for 80 and Benaud (52) followed two runs later. Panic set in and Australia lost their last two wickets – both run-outs – for only four runs. The match had ended in a tie: the first of only two instances of a tied match in Test cricket.

⊙ LONGEST UNBEATEN STREAK

With a battery of fast bowlers capable of intimidating any opposition line-up and an array of batting talent to rival any in the game, the West Indies side of the 1980s and early 1990s was the most formidable in modern cricket and, for a period, they were virtually unbeatable. Following their 1–0 series win over England in 1980, the Caribbean side did not lose a series over a 15-year period (in which they lost only 15 Test matches) before finally losing to Australia at home (2–1), in May 1995.

⊙ FIRST FIVE-TEST SERIES WHITEWASH

The 1920–21 Ashes series was nothing short of a nightmare for England. They were trounced by 377 runs in Sydney, by an innings and 91 runs in Melbourne, by 119 runs in Adelaide, by eight wickets back in Melbourne, and by nine wickets back in Sydney to become the first team in history to suffer a "whitewash" in a five-Test series.

⊙ PICK AND MIX FOR ENGLAND

England simply could not find a winning formula in the 1921 home Ashes series. Defeat by ten wickets at Trent Bridge prompted six changes for the Second Test at Lord's; Australia won the match by eight wickets. Seven changes ensued for the Third Test at Headingley, as well as the appointment of Lionel Tennyson as captain; Australia won by 219 runs. Six changes were made at Old Trafford (match drawn) and a further two at The Oval (match drawn), and in all England used 30 different players, a record for a five-match series.

⊙ THE TAMING OF THE TIGERS

Having attained Test status in June 2000, Bangladesh's cricketers struggled to establish themselves in the highest echelon of the game. After losing their first-ever Test match (and series) to India, the Tigers went a further 36 Tests and a record-breaking 16 series before recording their first series victory. When it finally happened – following a 1–0 series win against Zimbabwe in January 2005 – it sparked mass celebrations on the streets of cricket-mad Bangladesh.

⊙ HONOURS EVEN

When England dismissed Zimbabwe second time round for 234 at Bulawayo in December 2006 – the first-ever Test match played between the two countries in Zimbabwe – it left them with a simple equation: they needed 205 runs off 37 overs to secure a 1–0 lead in the two-match series. Often up with the rate, but never comfortably ahead of it, England eventually needed three runs off the final delivery (from Heath Streak) for victory. Nick Knight only managed two and the match – with England on 204 for 6 – ended in a draw. On two occasions a Test has been tied (the side batting last having been bowled out), but this remains the only Test match in history to end in a draw with the scores level.

⊙ A COME-FROM-BEHIND VICTORY

Being forced to follow on in the opening Test of the 1894–95 Ashes series, at Sydney, could have left England floundering, but instead it inspired them. Trailing by 263 runs, a fine 117 from Albert Ward was the basis of a fighting second-innings total of 437, before Bobby Peel took 6 for 67 to help England dismiss Australia for 166, 11 runs short of their victory target. It was the first of only three instances in Test cricket of a side coming back to win the match after being forced to follow on.

HIGH INNINGS TOTALS: TOP 10

	Score	Team	Inns	Opposition	Venue	Match Start
1	952/6d	Sri Lanka	2	India	Colombo	2 Aug 1997
2	903/7d	England	1	Australia	The Oval	20 Aug 1938
3	849	England	1	West Indies	Kingston	3 Apr 1930
4	790/3d	West Indies	2	Pakistan	Kingston	26 Feb 1958
5	765/6d	Pakistan	2	Sri Lanka	Karachi	21 Feb 2009
6	760/7d	Sri Lanka	2	India	Ahmedabad	16 Nov 2009
7	758/8d	Australia	2	West Indies	Kingston	11 Jun 1955
8	756/5d	Sri Lanka	2	South Africa	Colombo	27 Jul 2006
9	751/5d	West Indies	1	England	St John's	10 Apr 2004
10	749/9d	West Indies	2	England	Bridgetown	26 Feb 2009

⊙ WHEN TEN DAYS WERE NOT ENOUGH

Before the 1938–39 series, England and South Africa had agreed to make the Fifth Test, at Durban, "timeless" – played to a conclusion – if the scores going into the final match were level or if either side was one up in the series. England led 1–0. Play got under way on a bright, sunny morning on 3 March 1939. The batsmen had a field day. Ten days later, with the pitch showing few discernible signs of wear, England, chasing 696 for victory, had battled their way to 654 for 5 before play was abandoned at tea on 13 March to allow the England players time to undertake a two-day journey to Cape Town to catch the mail boat home. It remains the highest fourth-innings score in history.

⊙ INDIA'S BATSMEN PROSPER

For six Test matches, between October 1986 and February 1987, all played on Indian soil, India's batsmen were on fire, notching up an all-time record six consecutive scores of 400-plus – with a highest of 676 for 7 declared, including centuries for Mohammad Azharuddin (199), Sunil Gavaskar (176) and Kapil Dev (163) against Sri Lanka at Kanpur – before the run finally came to an end after they declared their second innings on 181 for 3 in the drawn Second Test against Pakistan at Kolkata in February 1987.

⊙ DIGGING DEEP

Faced with a mighty West Indies first-innings total of 575 for 9 declared in the First Test at Bridgetown, Barbados, in January 1958, Pakistan produced a woeful reply, limping to a paltry 106 all out in 42.2 overs. To their great credit, however, they dug deep in spectacular fashion second time round, thanks in no small part to Hanif Mohammad's massive 337, to score 657 for 8 and hold out for a remarkable draw. The difference in runs between the two innings, 551, is the largest in history.

⊙ INDIAN WICKETS TUMBLE

Already two matches down to England in a four-match series, India travelled to Old Trafford in July 1952 in understandably low spirits. And it showed. After watching England compile a steady 347 for 9 declared over the course of two rain-interrupted days, they slipped to 58 all out on the third day and, following on, 82 all out to lose by a mighty innings and 207 runs and become the first side in Test history to lose all 20 wickets in a single day. Fred Trueman, Alec Bedser and Tony Lock took nine, seven and four wickets, respectively for England.

⊙ THE SHORTEST MATCH

Much to the West Indies Cricket Board's chagrin, just ten deliveries, 1.4 overs, of the Second Test between the West Indies and England at the Sir Vivian Richards Stadium in Antigua in February 2009 were enough to establish that the sandy outfield was unsafe for bowlers and the match, amid much embarrassment and blame, was abandoned as a draw. The fiasco did produce one record, however: it remains the shortest completed Test match in history.

⊙ HISTORY-MAKING RUN-CHASE

Australia may have slipped from 242 for 0 to 417 all out in their second innings in the Fourth Test against the West Indies at St John's, Antigua, in May 2003, but they would still have fancied their chances of winning the match and securing a 4–0 series victory. The West Indies batsmen had other ideas, however. Chasing 418 – the scores were level after completion of the first innings – and helped by centuries from Ramnaresh Sarwan (105) and Shivnarine Chanderpaul (104), the home side cantered to the target with three wickets to spare. It remains the highest successful run-chase in Test history.

⊙ BLINK AND YOU'VE MISSED IT

South Africa's 1924 tour to England got off to a dreadful start at Edgbaston. After England had compiled 438 all out, South Africa subsided to a meagre 30 all out in just 12.3 overs – at 75 balls, it remains the shortest completed innings in Test history. They did better second time around (scoring 390), but England still went on to win the game by an innings and 18 runs.

LOWEST TOTALS: TOP 10

	Score	Team	Inns	Opposition	Venue	Match Start
1	26	New Zealand	3	England	Auckland	25 Mar 1955
2	30	South Africa	4	England	Port Elizabeth	13 Feb 1896
=	30	South Africa	2	England	Birmingham	14 Jun 1924
4	35	South Africa	4	England	Cape Town	1 Apr 1899
5	36	South Africa	1	Australia	Melbourne	12 Feb 1932
=	36	Australia	2	England	Birmingham	29 May 1902
7	42	New Zealand	1	Australia	Wellington	29 Mar 1946
=	42	Australia	2	England	Sydney	10 Feb 1888
=	42	India	3	England	Lord's	20 Jun 1974
10	43	South Africa	3	England	Cape Town	25 Mar 1889

⊙ THE LONGEST WAIT FOR VICTORY

Following an eight-wicket defeat by England in their first-ever Test match, at Christchurch in January 1930, life was tough for New Zealand cricketers. For the next 26 years, over a period of 44 Test matches (a record), New Zealand failed to produce a single Test victory. The magic moment, which saw local offices close and crowds stream into Eden Park in Auckland, finally arrived on 13 March 1956, as New Zealand, already three down in the four-match series, bowled out the West Indies for 77 in the second innings to record their first-ever Test victory, by 190 runs.

⊙ BANGLADESH JUST CAN'T SHAKE THAT LOSING FEELING

The argument that a team can only improve by pitting themselves against the best in the business was sorely tested when Bangladesh were granted Test status in June 2000. The country may have been a mine of untapped talent, but the Tigers' initial forays into Test cricket were nothing short of disastrous. Between 15 November 2001 and 19 February 2004, Bangladesh crashed to a record 21 consecutive defeats (12 of them by an innings or more) before the run came to an end following a rain-hit draw against Zimbabwe in Bulawayo in March 2004.

⊙ FORCING A RESULT

Having a rich, deep seam of talent at their disposal may have been the principal factor, but a large, and much heralded, part of Australia's success in world cricket in recent times was the positive manner in which they approached the game. Their philosophy was one based on attack: to score runs as quickly as possible to give themselves time to bowl out an opponent and force a result. As a consequence, it comes as little surprise that, between October 1999 and August 2001, Australia played out 23 Test matches (20 wins, three defeats) – an all-time record – without recording a single draw.

⊙ MOST MISSABLE DAY'S PLAY

The most turgid five-and-a-half hours' play in Test cricket? Look no further than the first day's play of the first-ever Test match between Pakistan and Australia, played at Karachi between 11 and 17 October 1956. Australia won the toss, elected to bat and, mesmerized by the guile of opening bowlers Fazal Mahmood (who took 6 for 34 off 27 overs) and Khan Mohammad (4 for 43 off 26.1 overs), produced a 53.1-over crawl to 80 all out. By the close of play, Pakistan had reached 15 for 2 and the day had produced a meagre 95 runs.

⊙ MOST CONSECUTIVE DRAWS

In recent times, pitches throughout the Caribbean have come under fire for their inability to produce a result, but this is no new phenomenon. It seems that wickets in the islands were equally lifeless back in the 1970s. Between the last three Tests of the West Indies' five-match series against India in 1970–71, a drawn five-match series against New Zealand in 1971–72 and the first two Test matches of the 1972–73 series against Australia, the West Indies played out ten consecutive draws (all of them at home). The record drawing streak finally came to an end in the Third Test against Australia at Port of Spain in March 1973, which the West Indies lost by 44 runs.

⊙ TAKING THE POSITIVE APPROACH

During the 1902–03 Test series in South Africa, Australia's reply to South Africa's first-innings total of 454 in the First Test, played at the Old Wanderers ground in Johannesburg, was all-out attack. And, although they fell for 296 – to trail by 158 runs – and were forced to follow on, they had compiled their total at a record rate of 5.80 runs per over (a record that stands to this day). Australia rallied in their second innings, hitting 372 for 7 – at a more leisurely rate of 4.76 runs per over – to force a draw.

⊙ HITTING AN ALL-TIME LOW

Just when New Zealand cricket fans thought things could not get much worse – their side had remained winless in 32 matches since the country's first-ever Test match, against England in 1930 – their players hit an all-time low. Facing a meagre first-innings deficit of 46 against England at Auckland in March 1955, and very much in with a chance of getting something out of the match, they capitulated to an all-time Test low score of 26 all out – compiled at an all-time low run-rate of 0.96 runs per over – to hand England victory by an innings and 20 runs.

⊙ ALL IN A DAY'S PLAY

There has been no harder day to bat in Test history than on 16 July 1888, the second day of the First Test (of three) between England and Australia, at Lord's. Resuming on 18 for 3 on the second morning, after a rain-affected first day had seen Australia amass a less than confident 116 all out, England limped their way to 53 all out. Australia made 60 in their second innings to set England an achievable 124 runs for victory, but the home side did not come close, slipping to 62 all out to lose the match by 61 runs. A total of 27 wickets fell on the second day, which remains an all-time record in Test cricket.

⊙ RECORD-BREAKERS

With a heady mix of batting talent, a world-class wicketkeeper-batsman and a bowling attack (including Glenn McGrath and legendary leg-spinner Shane Warne) as complete as any the game has ever seen, Australia dominated world cricket in the late 1990s and the first decade of the new millennium. Twice during that period (between October 1999 and February 2001, and again between December 2005 and January 2008) they put together a sequence of 16 consecutive victories. It is an all-time record in Test cricket.

⊙ BEAT US IF YOU CAN

For a period in the early 1980s, the West Indies – powered with the bat by Viv Richards, Gordon Greenidge, Desmond Haynes and co at their peak and with the ball by the most fearsome attack in the game's history – were literally unbeatable. From January 1982 (a drawn match against Australia at Sydney) to December 1984 (a draw against the same opposition in Melbourne), the men from the Caribbean did not lose a single one of their 26 matches. It remains the longest unbeaten streak in Test history.

MOST RUNS IN A DAY: TOP 10

	Runs	Team	Opposition	Day	Wkts	Venue	Date
1	588	England	India	2	6	Manchester	25 Jul 1936
2	522	England	South Africa	2	2	Lord's	28 Jun 1924
3	509	Sri Lanka	Bangladesh	2	9	Colombo	21 Jul 2002
4	508	England	South Africa	3	8	The Oval	17 Aug 1935
5	496	England	Pakistan	2	4	Nottingham	1 Jul 1954
6	494	Australia	South Africa	1	6	Sydney	9 Dec 1910
7	492	England	South Africa	2	8	The Oval	17 Aug 1935
8	491	England	New Zealand	3	7	Leeds	11 Jun 1949
9	482	Australia	India	3	10	Sydney	2 Jan 2000
10	475	England	Australia	1	2	The Oval	18 Aug 1934

⊙ SIXES GALORE

Aided in no small part by Matthew Hayden's then world record contribution of 380, Australia's massive first-innings total of 735 for 6 declared (the 11th highest innings total of all time) against Zimbabwe at Perth in October 2003 contained a single-innings record 17 sixes – Hayden struck 11 of them, Steve Waugh and Darren Lehmann hit one each, and wicketkeeper-batsman Adam Gilchrist plundered the other four.

MOST SIXES IN A MATCH : TOP 10

	6s	Team 1	Team 2	Match winner	Venue	Match start
1	27	Pakistan	India	drawn	Faisalabad	21 Jan 2006
2	23	New Zealand	England	England	Christchurch	13 Mar 2002
3	22	Pakistan	New Zealand	drawn	Karachi	30 Oct 1976
=	22	West Indies	South Africa	drawn	Basseterre	18 June 2010
5	19	West Indies	England	West Indies	St John's	11 Apr 1986
=	19	India	Pakistan	drawn	Chennai	3 Feb 1987
=	19	India	Australia	India	Chennai	18 Mar 2001
=	19	Australia	Zimbabwe	Australia	Perth	9 Oct 2003
=	19	New Zealand	South Africa	New Zealand	Auckland	18 Mar 2004
=	19	Pakistan	England	drawn	Faisalabad	20 Nov 2005
=	19	New Zealand	Bangladesh	New Zealand	Hamilton	15 Feb 2010

⊙ MOST DUCKS IN A SINGLE INNINGS

The record for the most ducks in a single innings is six, an event that has occurred on three occasions, all in the subcontinent. First in December 1980, when Pakistan slipped to 128 all out against the West Indies in the First Test in Karachi; second when South Africa collapsed to 105 all out and defeat in their fourth innings against India in Ahmedabad in November 1996; and third when Bangladesh slumped to 80 all out in their second innings against the West Indies in Dacca in December 2002 to lose by a mighty innings and 310 runs.

⊙ CHIPPING IN FOR THE CAUSE

Facing a first-innings deficit of 48 (which could have been far worse given that they were all out for 75 on the first day), England required a more fruitful second innings in the second Test against Australia at Melbourne in December 1894 if they wanted to maintain or extend their 1–0 series lead. Their 475 all out was significant for two reasons: it helped them seal a 2–0 Ashes series lead and was the first instance of 11 in Test history of all 11 batsmen making double figures in a single innings.

⊙ FINDING THE BOUNDARY ROPE

High-scoring draws are not always the most palatable affairs for spectators, but the drawn Fourth Test match between Australia and India at Sydney in January 2004 was notable for more than the consistently high standard of batting on display. Of the 1,747 runs scored in the match, 952 of them came from 238 fours – the most in Test history.

⊙ ALL 11 FAIL TO MAKE A MARK

South Africa's sorry 75-ball capitulation to 30 all out against England in the First Test in June 1924, at Edgbaston – the shortest completed innings (by balls) in history – was significant for another reason: it remains the only instance in Test history in which all 11 batsmen failed to make a double-figure score (extras were the top scorer with 11).

⊙ RECORD-SHATTERING PERFORMANCE

Memorable principally for being the highest innings total and containing the highest partnership in Test history (Mahela Jayawardene and Kumar Sangakkara's epic second-wicket stand of 624), Sri Lanka's colossal first-innings total of 952 for 6 declared in the First Test against India, at Colombo, in July 2006 also broke the record for the most fours scored in a single innings (109). In addition, it set a new record for the most runs scored in an innings from fours and sixes (448).

⊙ RUNNING RIOT

There have been two instances in Test cricket of five batsmen scoring a century in a single innings. The first came at Kingston, Jamaica, in June 1955, when Australia's Colin McDonald (127), Neil Harvey (204), Keith Miller (109), Ron Archer (128) and Richie Benaud (121) all passed three figures against the West Indies in the Fifth Test. The second came at Multan, Pakistan, in August 2001, when the home side's Saeed Anwar (101), Taufeeq Umar (104), Inzamam-ul-Haq (105), Mohammad Yousuf (102 not out) and Abdul Razzaq (110 not out) ran riot against an inexperienced Bangladesh attack in the First Test.

⊙ COMBINING TO GREAT EFFECT

Remembered as the match in which Arthur Morris (182) and Don Bradman (173) combined with devastating effect in the fourth innings to chase down a then world record victory target of 404 to secure an unassailable 3–0 lead in the 1948 Ashes series, the Third Test at Headingley – in which England, despite defeat, scored a commendable 861 runs – also saw the record for the most century partnerships in a single Test match (eight – five by England and three by Australia).

⊙ GETTING OFF TO A GOOD START

The maxim that the foundations of a good innings are more than often based on a solid opening partnership has been around for many years, but it wasn't until August 1899 – 22 years and 63 matches after the first-ever Test match – that two openers from the same team both scored a century in the same innings in a Test match. Stanley Jackson (118) and Tom Hayward (137) got England off to a flying start against Australia in the Fifth Test at The Oval, posting an opening partnership of 185. England could not capitalize on the situation, however, the match ended in a draw and Australia clinched the series 1–0.

⊙ A RUN-FEST IN ANTIGUA

Already holding an unassailable 2–0 lead in the four-Test series, South Africa would have been more than happy with their first-innings total of 588 for 6 – including centuries for A.B. de Villiers (114), Graeme Smith (126), Jacques Kallis (147) and Ashwell Prince (131) – in the Fourth Test at St John's, Antigua, in April–May 2005. But rather than capitulating, the West Indies batsmen dug deep and carved out a magnificent 747 in reply, with Chris Gayle (317), Ramnaresh Sarwan (127), Shivnarine Chanderpaul (127) and Dwayne Bravo (107) all passing three figures. The eight centuries scored in the match (which ended in a draw) is an all-time record.

⊙ TWO-MAN ATTACK

Monty Noble (7 for 17 and 6 for 60) and Hugh Trumble (3 for 38 and 4 for 49) were the scourge of England's batsmen in the Second Test at Melbourne in January 1902, combining to devastating effect as Australia won the match by 229 runs to level the Ashes series at 1–1. It was the first of six instances in Test cricket in which two bowlers have taken all 20 wickets in a match.

⊙ GIVING EVERYONE A GO

With the game long since destined for a draw, the Third Test (of five) between South Africa and England, at Cape Town in January 1965, produced a cricket peculiarity. During South Africa's second innings, which put the result beyond doubt, all ten England fielders had bowled. Then, with England needing an impossible 406 runs to win off eight overs, South Africa's captain Trevor Goddard elected to bowl the four members of his side who had not bowled in the first innings. For the first and only time in Test history, all 20 fielders had bowled in the match.

⊙ MOST WIDES IN A MATCH

The opening second-innings stand of 223 between Phil Jacques (108) and Simon Katich (157), which effectively batted the West Indies out of the game, took all the plaudits as Australia won the Third and final Test match by 87 runs at Bridgetown, Barbados, in June 2008 to win the series 2–0. Newspaper reports at the time failed to point the finger of blame at the West Indies' bowling attack, but perhaps they should have done, as during the match they bowled an all-time record 34 wides.

⊙ UNWANTED RECORD FOR MAKESHIFT KEEPER

In the final Test at The Oval in 1934, with the Ashes series locked at 1–1, England went in to bat facing a massive Bradman- and Ponsford-inspired Australian first-innings total of 701. Things really started to unravel for the home side after their wicketkeeper Les Ames was forced to retire hurt with a strained back and took no further part in the game. England fell to 321 all out. Australia, electing not to enforce the follow-on, batted again, scoring 327 – an innings that saw 47-year-old Frank Woolley take over the gloves for England (and concede a world record 37 byes) – to set England an improbable 708 runs for victory. They did not come close to the target, capitulating to 145 all out as Australia won by 562 runs to regain the Ashes.

⊙ RUN-OUT MADNESS

The run-out is possibly the most demoralizing dismissal in cricket; a basic misjudgement that leads to the cheap loss of a wicket. Losing one player to a run-out in an innings may be bad enough, but over the years there have been four run outs in a single innings on two occasions: India against Pakistan at Peshawar in February 1955; and Australia against the West Indies at Adelaide in January 1969. On both occasions the match ended in a draw.

⊙ COMBINING TO GREAT EFFECT

It is a captain's dream: not one but two of his bowlers firing on all cylinders to send an opponent packing. There are 52 instances in the history of Test cricket of two bowlers taking five wickets in the same innings, the first of which occurred in February 1887 when Australia's J.J. Ferris (5 for 71) and Charlie Turner (5 for 41) combined to dismiss England for 151 in their first innings at Sydney. Not that the pair's effort changed the course of the match, however. England's George Lohmann took 10 wickets of his own (for 87 runs) as the visitors won the match by 71 runs to take a 2–0 series lead.

⊙ MOST PLAYERS OUT CAUGHT

A more common phenomenon than one might think, there have been 57 instances in Test cricket – the first happening in the Second Test between Australia and England at Melbourne in January 1904 – in which all ten batsmen have been out caught in the same innings. The record for the most players caught in a match is 33, in the Fifth Test between Australia and India at Perth in February 1992.

⊙ FINDING THE TARGET

It may be that batsmen's techniques have improved over the years or that modern-day cricketers simply do not bowl straight enough, but both instances in Test history of nine players being bowled out in the same innings occurred in the 19th century. First at Cape Town in March 1889, when England bowled out South Africa for 43 in their second innings; and then in August 1890, when England dismissed Australia for 102 in the second innings of the Second Test, played at The Oval.

⊙ AN INCIDENTAL RECORD

The Third Test between England and South Africa at Edgbaston in July–August 2008 will best be remembered for the ruthless manner in which South Africa, inspired by captain Graeme Smith's unbeaten 154, chased down a victory target of 281. The five-wicket win saw South Africa take an unassailable 2–0 lead in the four-match series, prompting the tearful resignation of long-standing England captain Michael Vaughan. It is South Africa's first-innings total of 314 all out that makes the record books, however, as it contained a world record 35 leg-byes.

⊙ MOST PLAYERS OUT LBW IN A SINGLE TEST MATCH

Umpires Dickie Bird and Steve Bucknor had never been busier than during the First Test between the West Indies and Pakistan at Port of Spain in April 1993. During the match, which the West Indies won by 204 runs to take a 1–0 lead in the three-match series, the pair combined to give 17 players out lbw – a record for a Test match. The record for the most batsmen out lbw in a single Test innings is seven, an event that has occurred on two occasions: Zimbabwe, in their first innings of 94 against England at Chester-le-Street in June 2003; and New Zealand, as they were skittled for 131 in the second innings against Australia at Christchurch in March 2005.

⊙ OVERSTEPPING THE MARK

The First Test of the five-match series between the West Indies and Pakistan in 1976–77 got off to an exhilarating start at the Kensington Oval, Bridgetown, Barbados. In a high-scoring match, the home side – set 306 runs for victory – clung on for a hard-fought draw. The game has forced its way into the record books for another reason, however. As bowlers strained every sinew to force a breakthrough, no-balls blighted the game, a staggering 103 of them, an all-time record. The total number of extras conceded in the match – 173 (b37, lb31, w2, nb103) – is also a record.

MOST EXTRAS IN AN INNINGS: TOP 10

	Extras	(b, lb, w, nb)	Team	Opposition	Venue	Match start
1	76	(35, 26, 0, 15)	Pakistan	India	Bangalore	8 Dec 2007
2	74	(35, 12, 11, 16)	West Indies	England	Port of Spain	6 Mar 2009
3	71	(21, 8, 4, 38)	Pakistan	West Indies	Georgetown	2 Apr 1988
4	68	(29, 11, 0, 28)	Pakistan	West Indies	Bridgetown	18 Feb 1977
5	65	(10, 18, 1, 36)	Zimbabwe	Sri Lanka	Harare	11 Oct 1994
6	64	(4, 18, 6, 36)	South Africa	Pakistan	Johannesburg	19 Jan 1995
=	64	(18, 11, 1, 34)	England	West Indies	Manchester	27 Jul 1995
=	64	(12, 25, 0, 27)	India	West Indies	Kolkata	26 Dec 1987
=	64	(25, 21, 5, 13)	South Africa	England	Lord's	31 Jul 2003
10	62	(16, 10, 5, 31)	South Africa	Sri Lanka	Johannesburg	8 Nov 2002
=	62	(25, 21, 3, 13)	England	New Zealand	Leeds	3 Jun 2004
=	62	(19, 24, 9, 10)	South Africa	Australia	Cape Town	19 Mar 2009

BATTING RECORDS

⊙ GILLESPIE SHOWS THE WAY

Under normal circumstances, the most one could expect from a nightwatchman would be to see out the last few overs of a day and then to add a few quick runs the following morning before leaving the serious business of batting to the batsmen. But after successfully negotiating the final 6.4 overs of the first day (5 not out overnight) of the Second Test against Bangladesh at Chittagong in April 2006, and adding a further 14 runs on a rain-affected second day, Australia's nightwatchman Jason Gillespie had other ideas. On day three, the Australian fast bowler collected a further 83 runs to record his first Test century; on the fourth day, incredibly, he had reached 201 not out before Australia's declaration. It is the highest-ever score by a nightwatchman in Test cricket.

⊙ THE DON PLUNDERS THE ENGLAND ATTACK

That Australia recovered from losing the opening match of the 1930 series against England to regain the Ashes had much to do with the formidable talent of Donald Bradman. Not that the New South Wales batsman could have been blamed in any way for the 93-run defeat at Trent Bridge, scoring as he did 195 of Australia's 479 runs. His good form continued at Lord's, where his first-innings 254 did much to secure an Australian seven-wicket victory. At a drawn match at Headingley, the Don plundered a then world record score of 334 (including a record 309 runs on the first day). He failed in the rain-affected Fourth Test at Old Trafford, but resumed normal service with a sublime 232 runs in the deciding Test at The Oval; the innings was a major factor in Australia's innings-and-39-run victory. Bradman's 974 runs in the series (at an average of 139.14) is an all-time record.

⊙ PROSPERING ON HOME TURF

It would be safe to assume that the Sinhalese Sports Club ground in Colombo is the former Sri Lanka captain Mahele Jayawardene's favourite venue. Since playing there for the first time in 1997, the right-hander has scored ten centuries and seven 50s at the ground (with a highest score of 374 against South Africa in July 2006) and amassed 2,646 runs (at an average of 80.18). It is the highest amount of runs scored by a player at a single ground in Test history.

MOST CAREER RUNS: TOP 10

Pos	Runs	Player (Span)
1	14,692	Sachin Tendulkar (India, 1989–2011)
2	12,363	Ricky Ponting (Australia, 1995–2010)
3	12,063	Rahul Dravid (ICC/India, 1996–2011)
4	11,953	Brian Lara (ICC/West Indies, 1990–2006)
5	11,947	Jacques Kallis (ICC/South Africa, 1995–2011)
6	11,174	Allan Border (Australia, 1978–94)
7	10,927	Steve Waugh (Australia, 1985–2004)
8	10,122	Sunil Gavaskar (India, 1971–87)
9	9,527	Mahela Jayawardene (Sri Lanka, 1997–2011)
10	9,063	Shivnarine Chanderpaul (West Indies, 1997–2010)

⊙ GOOCH'S INDIAN SUMMER

Graham Gooch, the 11th-highest run-scorer of all time in Test cricket, reached the peak of his considerable powers in the First Test (of three) against India, at Lord's, in 1990. Leading by example, the England captain smashed 333 in the first innings and plundered a 113-ball 125 in the second as England romped to victory by 247 runs. The Essex man's 456 runs in the match is an all-time Test record.

⊙ A YEAR TO REMEMBER

In 2006, Mohammad Yousuf produced the best 12 months of batting form Test cricket has ever seen. He started the year with a century (173 against India in Lahore) and ended it in the same fashion (with a match-winning 124 against the West Indies in Karachi). In between times, the Pakistan right-hander registered nine centuries (a record for a calendar year), with a highest of 202 against England at Lord's, and amassed 1,788 runs – an all-time Test record for runs scored in a calendar year.

⊙ TEST CRICKET'S MOST PRODUCTIVE OVER

While six sixes in an over have been achieved in one-day international cricket (Herschelle Gibbs), Twenty20 international cricket (Yuvraj Singh) and first-class cricket (Garfield Sobers and Ravi Shastri), to date no one has completed the feat in Test cricket, where the most runs scored off one over is 28 (4,6,6,4,4,4) by Brian Lara off South Africa's slow left-armer Robin Peterson at Johannesburg in December 2003.

⊙ LONE RESISTANCE

It is not often that a batsman of a team that has just lost a Test match early on the fifth day takes all the plaudits, but the whole world knew that Sri Lanka's ten-wicket victory over the West Indies in the Third Test at Colombo in November–December 2001 would have been far greater had it not been for the efforts of Brian Lara. The Trinidad left-hander hit 221 (of 390) in the first innings and 130 (of 262) in the second. His 351 runs in the match are the most in Test history by any player to end up on the losing side.

⊙ FLOWER BLOOMS IN NAGPUR

If you had to pick one innings to confirm Zimbabwe wicketkeeper-batsman Andy Flower's credentials as a Test player of the highest quality, the obvious choice would be his second-innings performance against India in the Second Test at Nagpur in November 2000. Striding to the crease with his side in dire straits at 61 for 3, still 156 runs behind after following on, Flower dug deep for over nine hours, hitting an unbeaten 232 to take his side to 503 for 6 and safety. It is the highest individual score by a wicketkeeper in Test history.

⊙ LARA'S MOMENT OF MAGIC

England's bowlers had every reason to be sick of the sight of Brian Lara in the 1990s and after the turn of the century. In April 1994, at St John's, Antigua, the left-hander had plundered a world record 375 off their bowlers; a decade later at the same venue – having lost his record to Australia's Matthew Hayden (380 v Zimbabwe at Perth in October 2003) – the West Indies maestro did it again, smashing England's frustrated bowlers for 43 fours and four sixes en route to a world record score of 400 not out.

⊙ LINDSAY'S HEROICS HELP SOUTH AFRICA SINK AUSTRALIA

South Africa's epic 3–1 home series victory over Australia in 1966–67 created many legends – Graeme Pollock (with 537 runs) and Trevor Goddard (with 26 wickets) for example – but the real star of the series was South Africa wicketkeeper Denis Lindsay, whose 606 runs at an average of 86.57 (with three centuries, including an innings of 182 in the First Test at Johannesburg) remains the highest series total by a wicketkeeper in Test history.

⊙ FOSTER IN TIP-TOP FORM

One of seven brothers to represent Worcestershire before the First World War, Tip (Reginald Erskine) Foster was undoubtedly the most talented of them. The highlight of his brief eight-Test career came at Sydney, in the opening Test of the 1903–04 Ashes series, when he became the first player in Test history to pass the 250-run mark, hitting 287 – a figure that would remain as Test cricket's highest individual score for the next 26 years.

⊙ BOWING OUT IN STYLE

Often forced to play second fiddle to opening partner Jack Hobbs during his England career, Andy Sandham bowed out of Test cricket (after 14 Tests over nine years) with a truly headline-grabbing performance. As England piled on a massive 849 in their first innings against the West Indies at Kingston, Jamaica, in April 1930, Sandham, in his 40th year, batted for 10 hours, faced 640 balls and hit 28 fours en route to becoming the first player in Test history to score a triple-century. His innings of 325 remained a Test best for less than three months.

⊙ TOP OF THE CLASS

In the history of Test cricket, two players have scored a hundred in both innings of a Test match on three separate occasions: Sunil Gavaskar (124 and 220, India against the West Indies at Port of Spain in April 1971; 111 and 137, India against Pakistan at Karachi in November 1978; 107 and 182 not out, India against the West Indies at Kolkata in December 1978); and Ricky Ponting (149 and 104 not out, Australia against the West Indies at Brisbane in November 2005; 120 and 143 not out, Australia against South Africa at Sydney in January 2006; 103 and 116, Australia against South Africa at Durban in March 2006).

⊙ DRAMATIC DEBUTS

Five players have made a double-century in their first-ever Test match: Tip Foster (287 for England against Australia at Sydney in December 1903); Lawrence Rowe (214 for the West Indies against New Zealand at Kingston, Jamaica, in February 1972); Brendon Kuruppu (201 not out for Sri Lanka against New Zealand at Colombo in April 1987); Mathew Sinclair (214 for New Zealand against the West Indies at Wellington in December 1999); and Jacques Rudolph (222 not out for South Africa against Bangladesh at Chittagong in April 2003).

⊙ OFF TO A BLISTERING START

Test cricket did not have to wait long to witness the first-ever century. Indeed, the man who faced the first-ever ball in Test cricket, Australia's Charles Bannerman (against England at Melbourne in March 1877), went on to bat for a further four-and-three-quarter hours before retiring hurt on 165 (out of an Australian total of 245 all out). Australia went on to win the low-scoring match by 45 runs.

⊙ TWO HUNDREDS IN A MATCH

That Australia held out for a draw in serene fashion in the Fifth Test of the 1909 Ashes campaign at The Oval to complete a 2–1 series victory ha   d much to do with the history-making performance of their opener, Warren Bardsley. The New South Wales left-hander hit 136 in the first innings and 130 in the second to become the first player in Test history to score a century in both innings of a match, a feat since repeated on 67 occasions.

⊙ LEADING BY EXAMPLE

His country's finest batsman of the early 1880s and team captain, Billy Murdoch led the way as Australia put England's bowlers to the sword in the first innings of the Third Test at The Oval in August 1884. As the visitors compiled an accomplished 551 all out, Murdoch batted for 490 minutes, faced 525 balls and struck 24 fours en route to becoming the first player in Test history to score a double-century (211). England recovered well, however, to claim a draw and a 1–0 series win.

⊙ STARTING AS YOU MEAN TO GO ON

Hometown boy Lawrence Rowe made the most impressive start to an international career in Test history against New Zealand at Sabina Park, Kingston, Jamaica, in February 1972. Unleashing a barrage of trademark cuts and pulls, the elegant right-hander made 214 in the first innings of the match and an unbeaten century in the second; his 314 runs in the match are the most by any player on debut in Test history. Rowe went on to make 30 Test appearances for the West Indies over eight years.

⊙ FINISHING WITH A FLOURISH

Having seen his side reach an overwhelmingly dominant position in the Second Test against South Africa at Auckland in March 2004 – requiring just 54 runs for victory in their second innings – Kiwi captain Stephen Fleming decided to produce some fireworks. His 31 off 11 balls, which took his side past the winning line for the first time against South Africa on home soil, was hit at a rate of 281.81 runs per 100 balls – the highest strike-rate in an innings in Test history.

⊙ ENDING A 92-YEAR WAIT

In February 1969, at Sydney, Australia's Doug Walters made history. In the first innings of the Fifth Test against the West Indies he struck a majestic 242; he then crafted a patient 103 in the second innings to become, in the 646th Test match, the first player in 92 years of Test cricket to record a double-century and a century in the same match. Five players (Sunil Gavaskar, Lawrence Rowe, Greg Chappell, Graham Gooch and Brian Lara) have gone on to emulate the feat.

MOST HUNDREDS IN A CAREER: TOP 10

Pos	100s	Player (Team, Span)
1	51	Sachin Tendulkar (Ind, 1989–2011)
2	40	Jacques Kallis (ICC/SA, 1995–2011)
3	39	Ricky Ponting (Aus, 1995–2010)
4	34	Sunil Gavaskar (Ind, 1971–87)
=	34	Brian Lara (ICC/WI, 1990–2006)
6	32	Steve Waugh (Aus, 1985–2004)
7	31	Rahul Dravid (ICC/Ind, 1996–2011)
8	30	Matthew Hayden (Aus, 1994–2009)
9	29	Donald Bradman (Aus, 1928–48)
10	28	Mahela Jayawardene (SL, 1997–2011)

HIGHEST CAREER BATTING AVERAGE: TOP 10

Pos	Ave	Player (Team, Span)
1	99.94	Donald Bradman (Aus, 1928–48)
2	61.53	Jonathan Trott (Eng, 2009–11)
3	60.97	Graeme Pollock (SA, 1963–70)
4	60.83	George Headley (WI, 1930–54)
5	60.73	Herbert Sutcliffe (Eng, 1924–35)
6	59.23	Eddie Paynter (Eng, 1931–39)
7	58.67	Ken Barrington (Eng, 1955–68)
8	58.61	Everton Weekes (WI, 1948–58)
9	58.45	Walter Hammond (Eng, 1927–47)
10	57.78	Garfield Sobers (WI, 1954–74)

MOST HUNDREDS AGAINST ONE TEAM: TOP 10

Pos	100	Player	Opponent (Span)
1	19	Donald Bradman (Aus)	England (1928–48)
2	13	Sunil Gavaskar (Ind)	West Indies (1971–83)
3	12	Jack Hobbs (Eng)	Australia (1908–30)
4	11	Sachin Tendulkar (Ind)	Australia (1991–2008)
5	10	Garfield Sobers (WI)	England (1954–74)
=	10	Steve Waugh (Aus)	England (1986–2003)
7	9	Richie Richardson (WI)	Australia (1984–95)
=	9	Walter Hammond (Eng)	Australia (1928–47)
=	9	Brian Lara (ICC/WI)	Australia (1992–2005)
=	9	Greg Chappell (Aus)	England (1970–83)
=	9	David Gower (Eng)	Australia (1978–91)
=	9	Sachin Tendulkar (Ind)	Sri Lanka (1990–2010)

⊙ A GOOD MORNING'S WORK

There have been four instances in history of a player scoring a century before lunch on the first day of a Test match: Victor Trumper, 103 not out for Australia against England at Lord's in 1902; Charlie Macartney, 112 not out for Australia against England at Leeds in 1926; Donald Bradman, 105 not out for Australia against England at Leeds in 1930; and Majid Khan, 108 not out for Pakistan against New Zealand at Karachi in 1976.

⊙ SIX IN A ROW

When Donald Bradman passed three figures (103) in Australia's first innings against England at Headingley in July 1938, he achieved something that no player before or since has equalled. Starting with the Third Test match of the 1936–37 Ashes series at Melbourne, Bradman had recorded a century in six consecutive matches.

⊙ TEST CRICKET'S YOUNGEST CENTURION

In general, Bangladesh's early forays in the Test arena brought them nothing but disappointment, but there were some brighter moments, notably in September 2001 in the Second Test against Sri Lanka at Colombo. The record books may show that the home side cantered to an innings-and-137-run victory, but Bangladesh's second-innings score of 328 (after a pitiful 90 all out in their first innings) provided a moment of history. Playing in his first Test match, Mohammad Ashraful crafted a 212-ball 114 to become, aged 17 years 61 days, the youngest centurion in Test history.

⊙ THE DON LEADS THE WAY

If the mark of a good batsman is to push on once settled and register a big score, then there has been no finer exponent than Donald Bradman. The Australian maestro made an all-time record 12 double-centuries in his 20-year Test career – including a record three in a series against England in 1930 – and is one of only three batsmen in the game's history (along with Brian Lara and Virender Sehwag) to have passed 300 runs in a single innings twice in his Test career.

⊙ RICHARDS DESTROYS ENGLAND

With England already 4–0 down in the five-match series and facing a first-innings deficit of 164, West Indies captain Viv Richards strode to the crease with his side on 100 for 1 in the Fifth Test at St John's, Antigua, and decided to put on a batting masterclass for the home fans. By the time he declared his side's innings on 246 for 2, Richards had plundered an unbeaten 110 off 58 balls – he reached three figures off a mere 56 balls, to record the fastest century Test cricket has ever seen.

⊙ SOBERS STRIDES INTO THE HISTORY BOOKS

Garfield Sobers's first-innings score of 365 not out in the Third Test against Pakistan at Sabina Park, Kingston, Jamaica, in February–March 1958 was remarkable for a number of reasons. It was the highest-ever maiden century in the history of the game (in 16 previous Tests Sobers's highest score had been 80), it broke the world record for the highest individual score (Len Hutton's 364 against Australia in 1938) and meant that, at 21 years 213 days, Sobers had become the youngest player in Test history to score a triple-century.

⊙ FIVE IN FIVE FOR WEEKES

A fine second-innings knock of 141 by Everton Weekes in the Fourth Test against England at Kingston, Jamaica, in March 1948 did much to guide the West Indies to a ten-wicket victory and a 2–0 series win. Eight months later, the stocky right-hander picked up in the three-match series against India where he had left off against England, rattling off scores of 128 (in the First Test), 194 (in the Second Test) and 162 and 101 (in the Third Test) to become the first, and to date only, player in Test history to score five centuries in five consecutive innings.

⊙ THE OLDEST CENTURION IN TEST HISTORY

The 1928–29 Ashes series was an unqualified success for England, who won the first four Tests, but for Jack Hobbs (left) looking to bow out of his final overseas tour in style (21 years after making his Test debut), those matches had been a bitter disappointment – he had scored just 224 runs in seven innings. That all changed in Melbourne: in the first innings Hobbs hit a peerless 142 to become, aged 46 years and 82 days, the oldest centurion in Test history.

⊙ MAKING TEST CRICKET LOOK EASY

Mohammad Azharuddin's initial forays into Test cricket for India were the most spectacular in the game's history. Handed his debut in the Third Test against England at Kolkata in January 1985, the 21-year-old hit a sublime first-innings 110 before the match ended in a draw. Retaining his place for the Fourth Test at Chennai, he hit a second-innings 105, only to see India lose the match by nine wickets. His first-innings 122 in the drawn fifth and final Test at Kanpur meant he had become the first, and to date only, player in Test history to register three centuries in his first three matches.

⊙ RESILIENT IN DEFEAT

The West Indies may have crashed to a 3–0 loss in their home five-match series against Australia in the spring of 1955, but one of their defeated team could hold his head up high. Stylish right-hander Clive Walcott scored 698 runs in the series – including a series record five centuries in the five Tests (108 in the First, 126 and 110 in the Second and 155 and 110 in the Fifth) – at an average of 87.25.

⊙ MIANDAD MAKES HIS MARK

Javed Miandad's introduction to Test cricket was nothing short of remarkable. In his very first innings for Pakistan at the highest level of the game, he scored 163 against New Zealand at Lahore on 9–13 October 1976; three weeks later, in only his third Test – against the same opponents, in Karachi – he hit a brilliant 206 to become, aged 19 years 140 days, the youngest double-centurion in Test history.

⊙ THE LAHORE CRAWL

Pakistan's crawl to 407 for 9 over the first two-and-a-half days of the First Test against England at Lahore in December 1977 may have been painful to watch, but it did contain a moment of history. When opener Mudassar Nazar finally reached three figures – after 9 hours and 57 minutes of batting – he had recorded the slowest Test century in history.

MOST SCORES OF 50-PLUS IN A CAREER: TOP 10

Pos	50+	Player (Span)
1	110	Sachin Tendulkar (Ind, 1989–2011)
2	95	Ricky Ponting (Aus, 1995–2010)
3	94	Jacques Kallis (ICC/SA, 1995–2011)
4	90	Allan Border (Aus, 1978–94)
=	90	Rahul Dravid (ICC/Ind, 1996–2011)
6	82	Brian Lara (ICC/WI, 1990–2006)
=	82	Steve Waugh (Aus, 1985–2004)
8	79	Sunil Gavaskar (Ind, 1971–87)
9	77	Shivnarine Chanderpaul (WI, 1994–2010)
10	71	Inzamam-ul-Haq (ICC/Pak, 1992–2007)

⊙ GETTING OFF THE MARK

It is ironic given he was always seen as a nervous starter, but the record for the most consecutive innings in Test cricket without a duck is 119, set by England's David Gower between August 1982 and December 1990.

⊙ LEFT STRANDED ON 99

There are few more frustrating feelings for a batsman than being left stranded on 99 not out. The phenomenon has occurred five times in Test cricket: Geoffrey Boycott (England against Australia at Perth in December 1979); Steve Waugh (Australia against England at Perth in February 1995); Alex Tudor (England against New Zealand at Birmingham in July 1999); Shaun Pollock (South Africa against Sri Lanka at Centurion in November 2002); and Andrew Hall (South Africa against England at Headingley in August 2003). One player has been left stranded on 199 not out (Andy Flower, Zimbabwe against South Africa at Harare in September 2001), and one player on 299 not out (Donald Bradman, Australia against South Africa at Adelaide in January–February 1932).

⊙ ON A ROLL

The 12 months in which he truly established himself as an international batsman of genuine class, 1976 was a golden year for Viv Richards. The West Indian master-blaster swatted 1,710 runs (a record at the time for runs in a calendar year), blasted seven centuries (including a majestic 291 against England at The Oval) and laid the foundations for a record that has stood for over 30 years: between January 1976 and February 1977, Richards posted 50 or more in 11 consecutive matches.

⊙ MOST TIMES DISMISSED ON 99 IN TEST CRICKET

Five players have been dismissed on 99 twice in their Test careers: Richie Richardson (West Indies against India at Port of Spain in April 1989; West Indies against Australia at Bridgetown in April 1991); John Wright (New Zealand against Australia at Melbourne in December 1987; New Zealand against England at Christchurch in January 1992); Michael Atherton (England against Australia at Lord's in June 1993; England against South Africa at Headingley in August 1994); Greg Blewett (Australia against the West Indies at Adelaide in January 1997; Australia against New Zealand at Hobart in November 1997); and Sourav Ganguly (India against Sri Lanka at Nagpur in November 1997; India against England at Trent Bridge in August 2002).

⊙ TRUE GRIT

Trailing by 52 runs in the First Test of the 1958–59 Ashes series at Brisbane, England needed to dig deep in their second innings if they were going to post a remotely challenging victory target. And nobody dug deeper than Trevor Bailey. The Essex all-rounder limped to 50 off a record slow (by balls faced) 350 balls before falling for a commendable 68. Sadly for England, Bailey's efforts made little difference to the outcome of the match: Australia won by eight wickets.

⊙ FASTEST 50

A sorry mismatch between South Africa and Zimbabwe at Cape Town in March 2005, which the home side won by an innings and 21 runs inside two days, provided Jacques Kallis with a record-breaking opportunity. Coming to the crease with his side on a commanding 234 for 2 (already 184 ahead), Kallis reached his 50 off just 24 balls (ending on 54 not out): it is the fastest half-century (by balls faced) in Test history.

⊙ THE FIRST TO FALL SHORT

Lower-order resistance was the key to Australia's 229-run victory over England at Melbourne in the Second Test of the 1901–02 Ashes campaign, which saw the home side level the series at 1–1. Reggie Duff's battling 104 may have grabbed the majority of the headlines, but it was Clem Hill's innings that stole a place in the record books. The left-hander was out for 99; the first of 72 instances of such a feat.

⊙ MOST DUCKS IN A SERIES

Not only was the 1978–79 Ashes series one to forget for Australia, England having crushed them 5–1, it was also a record-breaking one for Alan Hurst. The renowned Victorian fast bowler batted 12 times during the campaign, scored a meagre 44 runs and recorded six ducks – an all-time record in a series.

⊙ OUT IN THE NERVOUS 90S

Two players hold the record for being out in the 90s the most times in a career: India's Rahul Dravid and Australia's Steve Waugh have both suffered the unfortunate fate on 10 occasions.

MOST DUCKS IN A CAREER: TOP 10

Pos	0	Player (Team, Span)
1	43	Courtney Walsh (WI, 1984–2001)
2	35	Glenn McGrath (Aus, 1993–2007)
3	34	Shane Warne (Aus, 1992–2007)
4	33	Muttiah Muralitharan (ICC/SL, 1992–2010)
5	29	Chris Martin (NZ, 2000–11
6	26	Mervyn Dillon (WI, 1997–2004
=	26	Curtly Ambrose (WI, 1988–2000)
8	25	Danish Kaneria (Pak, 2000–10)
9	24	Danny Morrison (NZ, 1987–97)
10	23	Bhagwath Chandrasekhar (Ind, 1964–79)

⊙ MR MAXIMUM

In all probability the finest wicketkeeper-batsman Test cricket has ever seen, Adam Gilchrist played for Australia on 96 occasions, scoring 5,570 runs (at an average of 47.60, including a highest score of 204 not out against South Africa in Johannesburg) and struck an all-time career Test record 100 sixes.

⊙ CONSECUTIVE FOURS

The record for the most consecutive fours is six. Three players have achieved the feat: Chris Gayle (off Matthew Hoggard, West Indies against England at The Oval in 2004); Ramnaresh Sarwan (off Munaf Patel, West Indies against India at St Kitts in 2006); and Sanath Jayasuriya (off James Anderson, Sri Lanka against England at Kandy in 2007).

⊙ STEALING THE LIMELIGHT

Seven players have batted on each day of a five-day match: Motganhalli Jaisimha (India against Australia at Kolkata in January 1960); Geoffrey Boycott (England against Australia at Trent Bridge in July 1977); Kim Hughes (Australia against England at Lord's in August 1980); Allan Lamb (England against the West Indies at Lord's in June 1984); Ravi Shastri (India against England at Kolkata in December 1984); Adrian Griffith (West Indies against New Zealand at Hamilton in December 1999); and Andrew Flintoff (England against India at Mohali in March 2006).

⊙ MOST FOURS IN AN INNINGS

A selector's dream – a technically gifted opening batsman who knew both his limitations and which ball to put away – John Edrich played 77 Test matches for England between 1963 and 1976, scoring 5,138 runs. The highlight of his career came against New Zealand at Headingley in July 1965, when he batted for eight minutes short of nine hours and faced 450 balls en route to compiling an unbeaten 310: the innings contained a world record 52 fours (and five sixes).

⊙ THE WORST OF STARTS

Two players share the record for being dismissed off the first ball of a Test match. India's Sunil Gavaskar (against England by Geoff Arnold at Birmingham in 1974, against Pakistan by Imran Khan in Jaipur in 1986–87, and against the West Indies by Malcolm Marshall in Kolkata in 1983–84) and Bangladesh's Hannan Sarkar (each time against the West Indies by Pedro Collins, at Dhaka in 2002–03, at Gros Islet in 2004 and at Kingston in 2004) have both suffered the ignominious feat on three occasions.

⊙ WAQAR'S UNUSUAL RECORD

One of the game's deadliest operators with the ball, where his ability to swing the ball late and at pace created havoc among opposition batsmen, Waqar Younis claimed 373 wickets in 87 Test matches between 1989 and 2003. His batting skills also found a place in the record books: with a highest score of 45, he remains the only player in history to score 1,000 career runs in Test cricket without scoring a single half-century.

HIGHEST SCORES BY BATTING POSITION

PosRuns		Player	Team	Opposition	Venue	Match start
1/2	380	Matthew Hayden	Australia	Zimbabwe	Perth	9 Oct 2003
1/2	364	Len Hutton	England	Australia	The Oval	20 Aug 1938
3	400*	Brian Lara	West Indies	England	St John's	10 Apr 2004
4	374	Mahela Jayawardene	Sri Lanka	South Africa	Colombo	27 Jul 2006
5	304	Donald Bradman	Australia	England	Leeds	20 Jul 1934
6	250	Doug Walters	Australia	New Zealand	Christchurch	18 Feb 1977
7	270	Donald Bradman	Australia	England	Melbourne	1 Jan 1937
8	257*	Wasim Akram	Pakistan	Zimbabwe	Sheikhupura	17 Oct 1996
9	173	Ian Smith	New Zealand	India	Auckland	22 Feb 1990
10	117	Walter Read	England	Australia	The Oval	11 Aug 1884
11	75	Zaheer Khan	India	Bangladesh	Dhaka	10 Dec 2004

UNUSUAL DISMISSALS

Player	Dismissal	Team	Opposition	Venue	Match start
Len Hutton	obstructing the field	England	South Africa	The Oval	16 Aug 1951
Russell Endean	handled the ball	South Africa	England	Cape Town	1 Jan 1957
Andrew Hilditch	handled the ball	Australia	Pakistan	Perth	24 Mar 1979
Mohsin Khan	handled the ball	Pakistan	Australia	Karachi	22 Sep 1982
Desmond Haynes	handled the ball	West Indies	India	Mumbai	24 Nov 1983
Graham Gooch	handled the ball	England	Australia	Manchester	3 Jun 1993
Steve Waugh	handled the ball	Australia	India	Chennai	18 Mar 2001
Marvan Atapattu	retired out	Sri Lanka	Bangladesh	Colombo	6 Sep 2001
Mahela Jayawardene	retired out	Sri Lanka	Bangladesh	Colombo	6 Sep 2001
Michael Vaughan	handled the ball	England	India	Bangalore	19 Dec 2001

⊙ CONSECUTIVE SIXES

The record for the most consecutive sixes in Tests is four. Three players have achieved the feat: Shahid Afridi (off Harbhajan Singh, for Pakistan against India at Lahore in 2006); Kapil Dev (off Eddie Hemmings, for India against England at Lord's in 1990); and A.B. de Villiers (off Andrew McDonald, for South Africa against Australia at Cape Town in 2008–09).

⊙ FASTEST TO 10,000 RUNS

Eight players in the history of the game have achieved the heady feat of accumulating over 10,000 Test runs. The fastest to do so were Brian Lara and Sachin Tendulkar, both of whom passed the milestone in their 195th Test innings.

⊙ THE LONGEST INDIVIDUAL INNINGS IN TEST HISTORY

Len Hutton's legendary innings of 364 against Australia at The Oval in August 1938 was not only the highest individual score in Test history at the time (Garfield Sobers broke it in 1958 with 365 not out against Pakistan), but it was, and also remains, the longest Test innings of all time. Hutton faced 847 balls.

⊙ MOST SIXES IN AN INNINGS

Wasim Akram showed his true credentials as a genuine all-rounder in spectacular fashion in the First Test against Zimbabwe at Sheikhupura in October 1996. The Pakistan captain smashed an imperious 257 off 363 balls (the highest innings by a No. 8 in Test history), an innings that included a world record 12 sixes.

⊙ DES STANDS HIS GROUND

Desmond Haynes holds the all-time Test record for carrying his bat (batting throughout his side's innings and remaining not out) on the most occasions. The right-handed opener stood firm while all around him capitulated three times during his Test career: 88 not out of the West Indies' 211 all out against Pakistan in Karachi in November 1986; 75 not out of the West Indies' 176 all out against England at The Oval in August 1991; and 143 not out of the West Indies' 382 all out against Pakistan at Port of Spain in April 1993.

⊙ HITTING THE MOST BOUNDARIES

No batsman in Test history has struck more fours than the sport's all-time leading run-scorer, Sachin Tendulkar. The Mumbai-born maestro has found the boundary on 1,892 occasions in 177 Tests since he made his debut for India against Pakistan in Karachi in November 1989.

BOWLING RECORDS

MOST WICKETS IN A CAREER: TOP 10

Pos	Wkts	Player (Span)
1	800	Muttiah Muralitharan (ICC/SL, 1992–2010)
2	708	Shane Warne (Aus, 1992–2007)
3	619	Anil Kumble (Ind, 1990–2008)
4	563	Glenn McGrath (Aus, 1993–2007)
5	519	Courtney Walsh (WI, 1984–2001)
6	434	Kapil Dev (Ind, 1978–94)
7	431	Richard Hadlee (NZ, 1973–90)
8	421	Shaun Pollock (SA, 1995–2008)
9	414	Wasim Akram (Pak, 1985–2002)
10	405	Curtly Ambrose (WI, 1988–2000)

⊙ THERE'S NO PLACE LIKE HOME

Despite being the leading wicket-taker (with 800 wickets) and the record-holder for the most five-wicket (67) and 10-wicket hauls (22) in Test history, the argument against Muttiah Muralitharan being the greatest bowler of all time is that he has the good fortune to play the majority of his games on the helpful wickets of Sri Lanka. And how he has prospered in his homeland: his 166 wickets at Colombo's Sinhalese Sports Club Ground, his 117 Test wickets at the Asgiriya Stadium in Kandy and his 111 Test wickets at Galle's International Stadium occupy the top three places on the all-time list for the most Test wickets taken by a player at a single ground.

⊙ WALSH FLATTENS KIWIS

New Zealand's batsmen could find no answers to the many questions posed to them by Courtney Walsh in the Second Test at Wellington in February 1995. The West Indies captain took 7 for 37 in the first innings and 6 for 18 in the second to lead his side to a colossal innings-and-322-run victory. Walsh's 13 for 55 are the best match figures by a captain in Test history.

⊙ LONE RESISTANCE

Javagal Srinath's commendable effort of taking 5 for 46 in the first innings and 8 for 86 in the second were not enough to prevent India from slipping to a 46-run defeat in the First Test against Pakistan in Kolkata in February 1999. The paceman's 13 for 132 are the best match figures by a player who has ended up on the losing side in Test history.

⊙ FIRST NINE-WICKET HAUL

The chief architect of England's comprehensive innings-and-197-run victory over South Africa at Johannesburg in March 1896 was George Lohmann. The Surrey man ripped the heart out of their batting line-up to take 9 for 28. It was the first instance (of 15) in Test history of a bowler taking nine wickets in an innings.

⊙ LAKER'S TEST

England's innings-and-71-run victory over Australia in the Fourth Test at Old Trafford in July 1956 to retain the Ashes will always be remembered as Jim Laker's Test. The Surrey off-break bowler took 9 for 37 in Australia's first innings and 10 for 53 in the second to become the first person in Test history to take ten wickets in an innings (a feat repeated only once, by Anil Kumble, who took 10 for 74 against Pakistan in 1999). Laker's match figures of 19 for 90 remain the best in Test history. It was also the first of six instances of a bowler dismissing all 11 batsmen in a match.

⊙ ENGLAND'S BRIGGS CASTS A SPELL ON SOUTH AFRICA

Dismissed for 292 in their first innings against South Africa in the Second and final Test at Cape Town in March 1889, England knew that, barring an outstanding performance with the ball, they would have to bat again. Cue Johnny Briggs. The Lancashire slow left-armer bewitched the hosts, taking 7 for 17 in the first innings and 8 for 11 in the second to secure an England victory by an innings and 202 runs and become the first player (of 12) in Test history to take 15 wickets or more in a match.

⊙ GOING OUT ON A HIGH

The star of England's 4–0 series win over South Africa in 1913–14 was S.F. Barnes. Despite playing in only four of the five Tests, the Staffordshire-born fast bowler was unplayable, taking an all-time record 49 wickets in the series, including seven five-wicket hauls – with a best of 9 for 103 in the Second Test at Johannesburg – and three ten-wicket match hauls. It turned out to be some swansong: these were the final Test matches of Barnes's career.

⊙ ALL IN VAIN

Nobody could point the finger of blame at Kapil Dev following India's 138-run defeat to the West Indies in the Third Test at Ahmedabad in November 1983. India's captain led from the front in the West Indies' second innings, taking 9 for 83: the best bowling performance in an innings by a captain and the best figures in an innings by a bowler who has ended up on the losing side in Test history.

⊙ FIERY FRED THE FIRST TO 300

No one will ever know how much more Fred Trueman could have achieved had not an insubordinate nature and a sharp tongue stood in his way. The Yorkshireman, a bowler with genuine pace, was selected for only 67 of a possible 118 Tests throughout his career, but when he played, he prospered. In his 65th Test, against Australia at The Oval in August 1964, he dismissed Neil Hawke to become the first bowler in history to take 300 Test wickets.

⊙ THE WORLD'S FIRST GREAT LEG-SPINNER

Clarrie Grimmett moved from New Zealand to Australia at the age of 17 to pursue a dream of playing Test cricket (New Zealand was not a Test-playing nation at the time), made his debut (against England) 16 years later and soon set about establishing his legend as the world's first great leg-spinner. Baffling batsmen around the world, he claimed his 200th Test wicket (the first player in history to do so) in only his 36th Test, the fewest in history.

⊙ GOLDEN YEAR

The legendary zip of his leg-spinner's action may have diminished over the years, but, by 2005, Shane Warne's experience, craft and guile were more than a match for his opponents. In the 15 Tests he played during that year, the spin wizard took 96 wickets – including a sensational 40 in a losing Ashes campaign – to set the record for the most Test wickets in a calendar year.

BEST ECONOMY RATE IN AN INNINGS: TOP 10
(minimum of 10 overs)

Pos	Econ	Player	Team	Opposition	Venue	Match start
1	0.15	Bapu Nadkarni	India	England	Chennai	10 Jan 1964
2	0.21	Garfield Sobers	West Indies	New Zealand	Wellington	3 Mar 1956
=	0.21	Bapu Nadkarni	India	England	Mumbai	21 Jan 1964
4	0.30	Majid Khan	Pakistan	West Indies	Port of Spain	1 Apr 1977
=	0.30	Bob Wyatt	England	South Africa	Durban	21 Jan 1928
=	0.30	Hedley Verity	England	South Africa	Leeds	13 Jul 1935
7	0.37	Jim Laker	England	South Africa	Cape Town	1 Jan 1957
8	0.40	Jim Burke	Australia	South Africa	Johannesburg	7 Feb 1958
9	0.41	Hedley Verity	England	South Africa	Leeds	13 Jul 1935
10	0.41	Pervez Sajjad	Pakistan	New Zealand	Rawalpindi	27 Mar 1965

⊙ THE MEAN MACHINE

Few players in the history of the game have frustrated batsmen as much as William Attewell, a bowler of metronomic accuracy who relied on the principle of bowling the ball at the off stump and setting an off-side field. In ten Tests between 1884 and 1894, the Nottinghamshire medium-pacer bowled 2,850 balls in Test cricket (taking 28 wickets) at an economy rate of 1.31 runs per over. Of the bowlers to have bowled 2,000 balls or more in Test cricket, it is the lowest economy rate in the game's history.

⊙ LEAN TIMES WITH THE BALL

Now considered one of his country's finest umpires, Asoka de Silva did not enjoy the best of careers as a player. Capped ten times for Sri Lanka between 1985 and 1991, the left-arm googly bowler set two dubious records: of the bowlers to have bowled 2,000 balls or more, he has the worst career bowling average (129.00 – 8 wickets for 1,032 runs) and the worst career strike-rate (a wicket every 291.0 balls).

⊙ ON A HOT STREAK

Although Australia lost the 1888 Ashes series 2–1 to England, none of the team's detractors would have apportioned any blame to Charlie Turner. Despite the loss, the fast-medium bowler was in inspired form with the ball, taking 5 for 44, 7 for 43, 5 for 27, 5 for 36, 6 for 112 and 5 for 86 to become the only player in Test history to claim five-wicket hauls in six consecutive innings.

⊙ THE BEST BOWLER IN HISTORY?

The first bowler to take nine wickets in an innings and the fastest to the 100-wicket milestone in Test history, on statistics alone George Lohmann has a rightful claim to being the greatest bowler in the game's history. In 18 Test matches between 1886 and 1896, the medium-pacer took 112 wickets at 10.75 (the lowest average in history) at a strike-rate of a wicket every 34.1 balls (also the lowest in history).

⊙ BEST STRIKE-RATE IN AN INNINGS

It took just 19 balls in India's first innings of the First Test at Brisbane in November–December 1947 for Australia's Eddie Toshack to claim a place in the record books. The left-arm medium-pace bowler took five wickets for two runs in 2.3 eight-ball overs to help reduce India to 58 all out. At 3.8 balls per wicket, it is the best strike-rate in Test history of any bowler who has taken four or more wickets in an innings.

⊙ INTO THE LION'S DEN

Fast-tracked into the Bangladesh Test side as an 18-year-old in 2005 after being discovered at a talent-spotting camp, fast bowler Shahadat Hossain found his early forays in international cricket to be a chastening experience. He claimed 60 wickets in 27 matches, but, of all the bowlers to have bowled 2,000 or more balls in Test cricket, he holds the record for the worst career economy rate (4.15 runs per over) and for the worst economy rate in an innings (8.41 – against England at Lord's in May 2005, when his figures were 12-0-101-0).

⊙ LACKING A CUTTING EDGE

A standout performer at youth international level, Roger Wijesuriya failed to make his mark in Test cricket. In four Tests for Sri Lanka between 1982 and 1985, the slow left-armer bowled 97.4 overs, conceded 294 runs and claimed just one Test victim (Pakistan's Abdul Qadir). His career bowling average of 294.0 is the worst, without qualification, in Test history.

⊙ MAKING AN EARLY MARK

With Australia already 2–0 down in the 1894–95 Ashes series, it was time to make changes for the Third Test at Adelaide. In came Albert Trott, and the Victoria slow bowler got off to a blistering start, taking a match-winning 8 for 43 in England's second innings to lead Australia to a 382-run victory. They are the best single-innings figures by a player on debut in the game's history.

⊙ YOUNGEST AND OLDEST

The youngest player to take five wickets in an innings is Nasim-ul-Ghani, who took 5 for 116 for Pakistan against the West Indies at Georgetown in March 1958 aged 16 years 303 days. The oldest player to achieve the feat is Bert Ironmonger, who took 6 for 18 for Australia against South Africa in Melbourne in February 1932 aged 49 years 311 days. The performance also saw Ironmonger become the oldest player to take ten wickets in a match.

⊙ TAKING THE BRUNT OF IT

Len Hutton and the rest of his England team-mates were not the only ones to enter the record books following their historic innings-and-579-run victory over Australia at The Oval in August 1938. The main victim of England's massive first-innings 903 for 7 declared was Australia's Chuck Fleetwood-Smith. The left-arm chinaman bowler delivered 87.0 overs and took just one wicket; his strike-rate of 522.0 is the worst in a single innings in Test history.

⊙ HIRWANI'S HEROICS

Drafted into the India team for the first time for the Fourth Test against the West Indies at Chennai in January 1988, Narendra Hirwani's introduction to Test cricket was the most spectacular in the game's history. The slow left-armer took 8 for 61 in the first innings and 8 for 75 in the second as India won by 255 runs to draw the series 1–1. Hirwani's match figures of 16 for 136 are a record for a Test debutant.

⊙ ALL-TIME LEADER

Unsurprisingly given his status as the leading Test wicket-taker of all time, Muttiah Muralitharan holds the record for the most wickets taken bowled (167 – 20.87 per cent of his wickets), the most wickets taken caught (435 – 54.37 per cent of his wickets) and for the most wickets by a stumping (47 – 5.87 per cent of his wickets).

MOST RUNS CONCEDED IN A CAREER: TOP 10

Pos	Runs	Player (Country, Span)
1	18,355	Anil Kumble (India, 1990–2008)
2	18,180	Muttiah Muralitharan (ICC/Sri Lanka, 1992–2010)
3	17,995	Shane Warne (Australia, 1992–2007)
4	12,867	Kapil Dev (India, 1978–94)
5	12,688	Courtney Walsh (West Indies, 1984–2001)
6	12,518	Harbhajan Singh (India, 1998–2011)
7	12,186	Glenn McGrath (Australia, 1993–2007)
8	11,724	Daniel Vettori (New Zealand, 1997–2011)
9	11,242	Makhaya Ntini (South Africa, 1998–2009)
10	10,878	Ian Botham (England, 1977–92)

⊙ HITTING THE RIGHT SPOT

Anil Kumble, India's legendary leg-spinner who, with 619 Test wickets, stands third on the all-time list of wicket-takers, may not have been the biggest turner of a cricket ball, but what he may have lacked in zip, he more than made up for with a nagging accuracy. The reward for his unremitting line-and-length policy was 156 lbw victims (25.2 per cent of his wickets) and 35 caught-and-bowled victims (5.65 per cent of his wickets). Both are all-time Test records.

⊙ MOST DELIVERIES

No bowler has bowled more deliveries in Test cricket than Muttiah Muralitharan. Sri Lanka's spinning legend, the all-time leading Test wicket-taker and the holder of numerous other records, including sending down an incredible 44,039 deliveries in 133 Test matches between 1992 and 2010.

⊙ SPOFFORTH'S STRIKES LEAVE ENGLAND REELING

Australia may already have been in dreamland after reducing England to 26 for 4 on the opening morning of the only Ashes Test of the tour, played at Melbourne in January 1879, but even better things were to follow. Fast bowler Fred Spofforth dismissed Vernon Royle, Francis Mackinnon and Tom Emmett in successive deliveries to leave England on a desperate 26 for 7 (a position from which they never recovered; Australia won the game by ten wickets) and record the first of 38 hat-tricks in Test history.

⊙ MOST WICKETS TAKEN HIT-WICKET

Australia's best fast bowler of the 1960s, Graham McKenzie had a languid action and surprising pace, which brought him 246 Test wickets in a ten-year career between 1961 and 1971. Uniquely, an all-time Test record four of those scalps were out hit-wicket.

⊙ TWO HAT-TRICKS IN A DAY

The triangular tournament between England, Australia and South Africa – held in England – in 1912 may have been an unusual occurrence in itself, but the match between Australia and South Africa at Old Trafford provided a unique moment in Test history. In South Africa's first innings, leg-break bowler Jimmy Matthews took the eighth hat-trick in Test history. Later in the day, with South Africa following on, he took another. Bizarrely they were the only wickets he took in the match, but Matthews remains the only man in history to have achieved the feat of taking two hat-tricks in a single Test match.

⊙ EARNING A CRUST

Trailing the West Indies by a massive 288 runs after the first innings in the First Test at Edgbaston in May–June 1957, England had to dig deep. And no one dug deeper than captain Peter May (285 not out) and Colin Cowdrey (154 not out) as the home side ground out a patient 583 for 4 declared off a mighty 258 overs; Sonny Ramadhin delivered 98 of those overs (588 deliveries) – a single-innings record – to take 2 for 179. The match ended in a draw.

⊙ FOUR WICKETS IN FIVE BALLS

There have been three instances in Test cricket of a bowler taking four wickets in five balls: Maurice Allom, W-WWW, on debut for England against New Zealand at Christchurch in 1929–30; Chris Old, WW-WW (the sequence was interrupted by a no-ball), for England against Pakistan at Birmingham in 1978; and Wasim Akram, WW-WW, for Pakistan against the West Indies at Lahore in 1990–91.

⊙ FINDING THE CORRIDOR OF UNCERTAINTY

The most successful fast bowler in the game's history and fourth on the all-time list of wicket-takers, Glenn McGrath used methods not based on express pace but on a metronomic ability to bowl the ball on the line of off stump or just outside. As a result, a record 152 of his 563 Test victims (26.99 per cent of his career haul) were out caught behind.

BOWLERS WITH MOST SUCCESS AGAINST A SINGLE BATSMAN

Pos	Wkts	Bowler	Batsman	Span
1	19	Glenn McGrath (Aus)	Michael Atherton (Eng)	1994–2001
2	18	Alec Bedser (Eng)	Arthur Morris (Aus)	1946–54
3	17	Curtly Ambrose (WI)	Michael Atherton (Eng)	1991–2000
=	17	Courtney Walsh (WI)	Michael Atherton (Eng)	1991–2000
5	16	Malcolm Marshall (WI)	Graham Gooch (Eng)	1980–91
6	15	Hugh Trumble (Aus)	Tom Hayward (Eng)	1896–1904
=	15	Curtly Ambrose (WI)	Mark Waugh (Aus)	1991–99
=	15	Glenn McGrath (Aus)	Brian Lara (ICC/WI)	1995–2005
=	15	Courtney Walsh (WI)	Ian Healy (Aus)	1988–995
10	14	Geoff Lawson (Aus)	David Gower (Eng)	1981–89
=	14	Shane Warne (Aus)	Alec Stewart (Eng)	1993–2002
=	14	Monty Noble (Aus)	Dick Lilley (Eng)	1899–1909

BOWLERS NO-BALLED FOR THROWING

Bowler	Team	Opposition	Venue	Year
Ernie Jones	Australia	England	Melbourne	1898
Tony Lock	England	West Indies	Kingston	1954
Geoff Griffin	South Africa	England	Lord's	1960
Haseeb Ahsan	Pakistan	India	Mumbai	1960
Ian Meckiff	Australia	South Africa	Brisbane	1963
Abid Ali	India	New Zealand	Christchurch	1968
Syed Kirmani	India	West Indies	Bridgetown	1983
David Gower	England	New Zealand	Nottingham	1986
Henry Olonga	Zimbabwe	Pakistan	Harare	1995
Muttiah Muralitharan	Sri Lanka	Australia	Melbourne	1995
Grant Flower	Zimbabwe	New Zealand	Bulawayo	2000

⊙ PLAYERS TO TAKE A HAT-TRICK ON TEST DEBUT

Three players in Test history have taken a hat-trick on debut:
Maurice Allom, for England against New Zealand at Christchurch
in 1929–30; Peter Petherick, for New Zealand against Pakistan
at Lahore in 1976–77; and Damien Fleming, for Australia against
Pakistan at Rawalpindi in 1994–95.

⊙ A SPECTACULAR INTRODUCTION

Picture the scene. A bowler is appearing in his first Test match. The captain has just thrown him the ball; he is standing at the end of his run-up, ball in sweaty hand; the crowd is hushed, and the nerves are jangling. But the debutant gets off to the perfect start: he takes a wicket with his first-ever ball. Thirteen players in Test history have enjoyed such an experience.

⊙ FASTEST TO 50

One of the best bowlers Australia has ever produced, Charlie Turner was a skilful right-arm fast-medium bowler with an effortless action. He made a blistering start to his Test career, reaching the 50-wicket milestone in only his sixth Test match and remains the fastest to achieve the feat in Test history.

⊙ THE MOST UNUSUAL HAT-TRICK

In the Second Test of the 1988–89 series between Australia and the West Indies, at Perth, Merv Hughes dismissed Gus Logie with the final ball of his 36th over of the first innings, and then Patrick Patterson with the first ball of his 37th over to end the West Indies' innings. When he trapped Gordon Greenidge lbw first ball in the West Indies' second innings, he had completed Test cricket's most unusual hat-trick.

⊙ FASTEST TO 150

The finest bowler of the early part of the 20th century, England's S.F. Barnes was one of the first bowlers to make use of a new ball's seam and, as a result, terrorized batsmen throughout his 13-year, 27-Test career. He claimed his 150th scalp in only his 24th Test – it is a record that stands to this day.

⊙ MORE MURALI RECORDS

Among Sri Lanka spin wizard Muttiah Muralitharan's many records is the speed at which he has reached various wicket milestones. He took his 350th Test wicket in a record low 66 matches; his 400th wicket in a record 72 matches; his 450th Test wicket in a record 80 matches; his 500th Test wicket in a record 87 matches; his 600th wicket in a record 101 matches; his 700th wicket in a record 113 matches; and, of course, he is the only player in history to have reached the 800 Test wicket milestone (in 133 matches).

⊙ THE FIRST HAT-TRICK IN TESTS TO BE SPLIT OVER TWO INNINGS

There have been two instances in Test history of a bowler taking a hat-trick split over two innings. In the First Test of the 1988–89 series between Australia and the West Indies at Brisbane, Courtney Walsh dismissed Tony Dodemaide with his final ball of Australia's first innings and Mike Veletta and Graeme Wood with his first two balls of the second to complete Test cricket's first "split" hat-trick. The second instance involved Merv Hughes.

⊙ NO NEED FOR CHANGE

For two bowlers to bowl unchanged throughout an innings is a rare event in Test cricket; there have been only 24 such occurrences in the game's history (and none since 1999). It usually occurs only when opening bowlers get into an unplayable groove and dismiss a side cheaply, but that is not always the case. In the first-ever instance of the feat, in the Second Test of the 1881–82 Ashes series, at Melbourne, Australia's Joey Palmer and Edwin Trott combined for an unchanged 115 (four-ball) overs in England's first innings.

BEST FIGURES IN AN INNINGS: PROGRESSIVE RECORD

Rank	Figures	Player	Match	Venue	Season
1	7–55	Tom Kendall (Aus)	Australia v England	Melbourne	1876–77*
2	7–44	Fred Spofforth (Aus)	England v Australia	The Oval	1882
3	7–28	Billy Bates (Eng)	Australia v England	Melbourne	1882–83
4	8–35	George Lohmann (Eng)	Australia v England	Sydney	1886–87
5	8–11	Johnny Briggs (Eng)	South Africa v England	Cape Town	1888–89
6	8–7	George Lohmann (Eng)	South Africa v England	Port Elizabeth	1895–96
7	9–28	George Lohmann (Eng)	South Africa v England	Johannesburg	1895–96
8	10–53	Jim Laker (Eng)	England v Australia	Manchester	1956

* Kendall took his 7 for 55 in the inaugural Test Match.

ALL-TIME LEADING TEST WICKETTAKER: PROGRESSIVE RECORD HOLDERS FROM THE START OF 20TH CENTURY

Record broken	Player	New record
1900	Johnny Briggs (England)	119
January 1904	Hugh Trumble (Australia)	141
December 1913	Sydney (S.F.) Barnes (England)	189
January 1936	Clarrie Grimmett (Australia)	216
July 1953	Alec Bedser (England)	236
January 1963	Brian Statham (England)	242
March 1963	Fred Trueman (England)	307
February 1976	Lance Gibbs (West Indies)	309
December 1981	Dennis Lillee (Australia)	355
August 1986	Ian Botham (England)	383
November 1988	Richard Hadlee (New Zealand)	431
January 1994	Kapil Dev (India)	434
March 2000	Courtney Walsh (West Indies)	519
May 2004	Muttiah Muralitharan (Sri Lanka)	520
July 2004	Shane Warne (Australia)	527*
August 2004	Muttiah Muralitharan (Sri Lanka)	532
October 2004	Shane Warne (Australia)	708
December 2007	Muttiah Muralitharan	792

* Warne equalled Muralitharan's record.

⊙ FASTEST TO 250 AND 300

After breaking on to the international scene in the early 1970s, with his fearsome pace and legendary stamina it did not take Dennis Lillee long to win the hearts of Australian cricket fans or to strike terror into batsmen around the world. As the fans chanted his name, Lillee responded in style: no player has taken 250 (48 matches) or 300 Test wickets (56 matches) in a shorter time.

WICKETKEEPING RECORDS

MOST DISMISSALS IN A CAREER: TOP 10

Pos	Dismissals	Player (Team, Span)
1	521	Mark Boucher (ICC/South Africa, 1997–2011)
2	416	Adam Gilchrist (Australia, 1999–2008)
3	395	Ian Healy (Australia, 1988–99)
4	355	Rodney Marsh (Australia, 1970–84)
5	270	Jeff Dujon (West Indies, 1981–91)
6	269	Alan Knott (England, 1967–81)
7	241	Alec Stewart (England, 1990–2003)
8	228	Wasim Bari (Pakistan, 1967–84)
9	219	Ridley Jacobs (West Indies, 1998–2004)
=	219	Godfrey Evans (England, 1946–59)

⊙ BORE DRAW BRINGS A RECORD

At first glance, the Second Test between the West Indies and New Zealand at St John's, Antigua, in April 1996 was an inspiring draw brought to life, briefly, by the West Indies' mini-collapse in the second innings, only for New Zealand to run out of time in their chase for victory. However, dig deeper and you will find that the match was a record-breaking one: the 1,299 runs scored in the match did not contain a single bye; it is the highest match aggregate with no byes conceded in Test history.

⊙ MOST DISMISSALS IN A SINGLE TEST MATCH

The Second Test between England and South Africa at Johannesburg in November–December 1995 was a memorable one for Jack Russell. The England wicketkeeper took six catches in the first innings and five in the second to set the all-time record for the most dismissals in a match (11). He then hung on grimly with the bat, facing 234 balls for an unbeaten 29 as England held out for an unlikely draw.

⊙ MOST DISMISSALS IN AN INNINGS

The record for the most dismissals in an innings by a wicketkeeper is seven, a feat that has been achieved on four occasions: Wasim Bari (7ct), Pakistan against New Zealand at Auckland in February 1979; Bob Taylor (7ct), England against India at Mumbai in February 1980; Ian Smith (7ct), New Zealand against Sri Lanka at Hamilton in February 1991; and Ridley Jacobs (7ct), West Indies against Australia at Melbourne in December 2000.

⊙ SETTING A SERIES BENCHMARK

The West Indies may have crashed to a 2–1 home series defeat against Australia in 1960–61, but it was not for any lack of effort by Gerry Alexander. The wicketkeeper-batsman not only topped the West Indies' batting averages, with 484 runs at an average of 60.50, he also excelled behind the stumps, taking 16 catches: it was the first time of 17 instances in history that a wicketkeeper has scored 300 runs and taken 15 dismissals in a series.

⊙ EVANS SETS A CAREER BENCHMARK

By the time Godfrey Evans finished his 91-match, 13-year England career in 1959 he was considered a true technician behind the stumps and one of the greatest wicketkeepers the game has ever seen. His career haul of 219 dismissals (173ct, 46st) and 2,439 runs became a target for other keepers to aim at. In modern times, 200 dismissals and 2,000 career runs is considered a fair benchmark by which to judge a wicketkeeper. Evans was the first of 19 players in Test history to achieve the feat.

⊙ MOST DISMISSALS IN A SERIES

Rod Marsh may not have made much of an impact with the bat during Australia's 2–1 Ashes victory over England in 1982–83 (scoring 124 runs at an average of 17.71), but he certainly shone behind the stumps. The Western Australian gloveman claimed 28 catches in the series – an all-time record.

⊙ SCANT CONSOLATION FOR TAIBU

Following an innings-and-240-run victory over Zimbabwe in the
First Test at Harare in May 2004, Sri Lanka's unerring march to 713
for 3 declared in the Second Test at Bulawayo merely confirmed
how far Zimbabwe cricket had fallen. However, for the home side's
wicketkeeper, Tatendra Taibu, there was a small crumb of comfort
to be had from the destruction: Sri Lanka's total remains the largest
in history in which no byes were conceded. Not that it made any
difference to the outcome of the match: Sri Lanka went on to win
by a colossal innings and 254 runs.

⊙ DUJON'S STANDOUT PERFORMANCES

The only wicketkeeper in Test history to score 300-plus runs and
take 15-plus dismissals in a series on three occasions is Jeff Dujon.
The West Indies keeper achieved the feat against India in 1983–84
(367 runs and 16 dismissals), against Australia in 1984–85 (341
runs and 19 dismissals) and against England in the 1988 series
(305 runs and 20 dismissals).

SCORING 100 AND FIVE DISMISSALS IN AN INNINGS

Player	Bat	Field	Team	Opposition	Venue	Match start
Denis Lindsay	182	6ct/ost	South Africa	Australia	Johannesburg	23 Dec 1966
Ian Smith	113*	4ct/1st	New Zealand	England	Auckland	10 Feb 1984
Amal Silva	111	5ct/ost	Sri Lanka	India	Colombo	6 Sep 1985
Adam Gilchrist	133	4ct/1st	Australia	England	Sydney	2 Jan 2003
Matt Prior	118	5ct/ost	England	Australia	Sydney	3 Jan 2011

FIELDING RECORDS

MOST CATCHES IN A CAREER: TOP 10

Pos	Catches	Player (Country/Span)
1	200	Rahul Dravid (ICC/India, 1996–2011)
2	181	Mark Waugh (Australia, 1991–2002)
3	178	Ricky Ponting (Australia, 1995–2010)
4	171	Stephen Fleming (New Zealand, 1994–2008)
5	166	Jacques Kallis (ICC/South Africa, 1995–2011)
6	165	Mahela Jayawardene (Sri Lanka, 1997–2010)
7	164	Brian Lara (ICC/West Indies, 1990–2006)
8	157	Mark Taylor (Australia, 1989–99)
9	156	Allan Border (Australia, 1978–94)
10	128	Matthew Hayden (Australia, 1994–2009)

⊙ MOST CATCHES IN AN INNINGS BY A FIELDER

The record for the most catches in an innings by a non-wicketkeeper is five, a feat that has occurred on five occasions: by Vic Richardson for Australia against South Africa at Durban in February 1936; by Yajurvindra Singh for India against England at Bangalore in January 1977; by Mohammad Azharuddin for India against Pakistan at Karachi in November 1989; by Kris Srikkanth for India against Australia at Perth in February 1992; and by Stephen Fleming for New Zealand against Zimbabwe at Harare in September 1997.

⊙ MOST CATCHES IN A MATCH

The record for the most catches in a match is seven, a feat that has been achieved on five occasions: by Greg Chappell for Australia against England at Perth in December 1974; by Yajurvindra Singh for India against England at Bangalore in January 1977; by Hashan Tillakaratne for Sri Lanka against New Zealand at Colombo in December 1992; by Stephen Fleming for New Zealand against Zimbabwe at Harare in September 1997; and by Matthew Hayden for Australia against Sri Lanka at Galle in March 2004.

⊙ MOST CATCHES IN A SERIES

There were many heroic Australian performances during their 5–0 whitewash of England in the 1920–21 series. Warwick Armstrong's three centuries and Arthur Mailey's 36 wickets in the series won the highest acclaim, but one perhaps more obscure performance entered the record books and has stood the test of time: Jack Gregory's 15 catches in the series has never been beaten.

⊙ SLIP-FIELDING ALL-TIME GREATS: MARK WAUGH (AUSTRALIA)

An elegant and gifted strokemaker with the bat (scoring 8,029 runs at an average of 41.81 for Australia in 128 Test matches between 1991 and 2002) and a talented off-spinner (with 59 Test wickets), Mark Waugh was equally at home in the hotbed of the slip cordon. By the time he finished his career, the younger of the Waugh twins had taken 128 catches, a mark that stood as a world record until Rahul Dravid broke it in April 2009.

⊙ FIELDING ALL-TIME GREATS: ROGER HARPER (WEST INDIES)

He was neither a world-beating off-spinner (25 Tests between 1983 and 1993 brought him a mere 46 wickets) nor a great batsman (he averaged 18.44 with the bat), but there have been few finer fielders in the game than Roger Harper. Just ask Graham Gooch. Batting for the MCC against the World XI at Lord's in 1987, the England opener drilled an on-drive off Harper's bowling and stepped out of his crease in anticipation, only to see Harper's telescopic arm reach down, grab the ball and throw down Gooch's stumps to run him out.

⊙ SLIP-FIELDING ALL-TIME GREATS: BOBBY SIMPSON (AUSTRALIA)

A first-rate opening batsman (he scored 4,869 runs at an average of 46.81 in 62 Tests for Australia between 1957 and 1978) and, with 71 Test wickets to his name, a handy leg-break bowler, Bobby Simpson also had electric reflexes – demonstrated in his youth when he used to catch flies with his bare hands to amuse his school-mates – that turned him into arguably the greatest slip fielder in the history of the game. He ended his career with 110 Test catches.

⊙ FIELDING ALL-TIME GREATS: COLIN BLAND (SOUTH AFRICA)

The hours spent honing his skills by throwing at a single stump certainly paid dividends for Colin Bland, who was born in Zimbabwe (then Rhodesia). Although a more than capable batsman (he scored 1,669 runs at an average of 49.08 for South Africa in a 21-Test career between 1961 and 1966), it was his speed, balance and powerful arm in the field that thrilled spectators and opponents around the world in equal measure. He was the world's first truly great fielder.

⊙ PROVING A POINT

Left out of the side and watching on from the sidelines as five of his team-mates went on to score centuries in the First Test against newcomers Bangladesh at Multan in August 2001, Pakistan's Younis Khan must have been kicking his heels. And when his chance to impress in the field finally came (on as a substitute for Inzamam-ul-Haq), he grabbed it with both hands, literally, taking an all-time record (for a substitute fielder) four catches in Bangladesh's second innings.

⊙ MOST CATCHES BY A SUBSTITUTE IN A MATCH

The record for most catches in a match by a substitute is four, a feat that has been achieved on three occasions: by Gursharan Singh for India against the West Indies at Ahmedabad in November 1983; by Younis Khan for Pakistan against Bangladesh at Multan in August 2001; and by Virender Sehwag for India against Zimbabwe at Nagpur in February 2002.

⊙ PERFECT PARTNERS

The most successful bowler-fielder combination in Test history is that of Sri Lanka's Muttiah Muralitharan and Mahela Jayawardene. The pair combined for a world-record 77 dismissals between 1997 and 2010.

ALL-ROUND RECORDS

ALL-ROUNDERS TO HAVE SCORED 3,000 RUNS AND TAKEN 200 TEST WICKETS (RANKED BY ORDER OF DEBUT)

Player (Span)	Runs	Wkts
Garfield Sobers (West Indies, 1954–74)	8,032	235
Imran Khan (Pakistan, 1971–92)	3,807	362
Richard Hadlee (New Zealand, 1973–90)	3,124	431
Ian Botham (England, 1977–92)	5,200	383
Kapil Dev (India, 1978–94)	5,248	434
Chris Cairns (New Zealand, 1989–2004)	3,320	218
Shane Warne (Australia, 1992–2007)	3,154	708
Chaminda Vaas (Sri Lanka, 1994–2009)	3,089	355
Shaun Pollock (South Africa, 1995–2008)	3,781	421
Jacques Kallis (ICC/Sourh Africa, 1995–2011)	11,947	270
Daniel Vettori (ICC/New Zealand, 1997–2011)	4,167	345
Andrew Flintoff (ICC/England, 1998–2009)	3,845	226

⊙ 100 RUNS AND TEN WICKETS IN A MATCH

Only three players in Test history have achieved the feat of scoring 100 runs and taking ten wickets in a Test match: Alan Davidson, 124 runs and 11 wickets for Australia against the West Indies at Brisbane in December 1960; Ian Botham, 114 runs and 13 wickets for England against India at Mumbai in February 1980; and Imran Khan, 117 runs and 11 wickets for Pakistan against India at Faisalabad in January 1983.

⊙ ALL-ROUND EXCELLENCE ALL IN VAIN

Working on the basic principle of hitting the ball as hard and bowling the ball as fast as he could, Jimmy Sinclair did much to put South African cricket on the map. The peak of his 15-year, 25-match career came against England at Cape Town in April 1899 when – despite an eventual 210-run win for England – he took 6 for 26 in England's first innings and then scored 106 to become the first of 26 players in history to score 100 and take five wickets in an innings in a Test match.

⊙ A CUT ABOVE THE REST

The only player in history to score 100 runs and take five wickets in an innings on five occasions is Ian Botham. The legendary England all-rounder achieved the feat against New Zealand at Christchurch in February 1978 (103 and 5 for 73); against Pakistan at Lord's in June 1978 (108 and 8 for 34); against India at Mumbai in February 1980 (114 and 6 for 58, then 7 for 48); against Australia at Headingley in July 1981 (149 not out and 6 for 95); and against New Zealand at Wellington in January 1984 (138 and 5 for 59).

⊙ THE FIRST GREAT ALL-ROUNDER

A fine batsman in defence, an excellent driver of the ball and a right-arm medium-pace bowler who relied on spin, guile and variations in flight and pace, Australia's George Giffen was Test cricket's first truly great all-rounder. In 31 Tests between 1881 and 1896, he became the first of 53 players in history to score 1,000 runs (1238) and take 100 wickets (103).

⊙ MAJOR CONTRIBUTIONS

A cornerstone of the England team for 58 Tests over 31 years from the turn of the 20th century, Wilfred Rhodes was the greatest slow left-armer of his day and a capable batsman (he once shared an opening stand of 323 with Jack Hobbs), who more than held his own in the field. He was the first of 22 players in history to score 1,000 runs (2,325), take 50 wickets (127) and snare 50 catches (60) in Test cricket.

⊙ THE FIRST OF THE FIELDING ALL-ROUNDERS

A superb batsman (scoring 7,249 runs for England at an average of 58.45, including 22 centuries), Walter Hammond ranks among the finest players ever to have played the game. A naturally gifted athlete, he also proved his worth in the field, taking 110 catches in his 20-year, 85-Test career to become the first of 59 players in history to score 5,000 runs and take 50 catches in Test cricket.

⊙ ALL-TIME GREAT ALL-ROUNDERS: IAN BOTHAM (ENGLAND)

Few players in the game's history have been able to galvanize a crowd like Ian Botham. A fast-medium swing bowler with an almost unique wicket-taking ability (by the time he ended his 15-year Test career in 1992 he was the world's leading wicket-taker with 383 wickets), Botham was also a hard-hitting batsman capable of turning a match on its head (few who saw it will ever forget his Ashes-turning 149 not out against Australia at Headingley in July 1981) and a world-class slip fielder, who bagged 120 catches in 102 matches.

⊙ ALL-TIME GREAT ALL-ROUNDERS: KAPIL DEV (INDIA)

Without doubt the finest fast bowler India has ever produced, Kapil Dev also made some hefty contributions to the Indian cause with the bat, plundering 5,238 runs – with a highest score of 163 against Sri Lanka at Kanpur in December 1986 – in a 16-year, 131-Test career between 1978 and 1994. However, it was Kapil Dev's relentless march to, and beyond, Richard Hadlee's then world record haul of 431 Test wickets that guaranteed his status among the game's all-time greats.

⊙ ALL-TIME GREAT ALL-ROUNDERS: GARFIELD SOBERS (WEST INDIES)

Garfield Sobers was the most complete cricketer in the game's history. In a 93-Test career for the West Indies spanning 20 years, he was a world-class performer with both bat (scoring 8,032 runs at an average of 57.78, including a then world record score of 365 not out against Pakistan at Kingston in February 1958), and ball (taking 235 wickets, as either a left-arm fast-medium or slow left-arm bowler). He also excelled in the field, taking 109 catches.

PARTNERSHIP RECORDS

HIGHEST PARTNERSHIPS BY WICKET: TOP 10

Wkt	Runs	Partners	Match	Venue	Date
1st	415	Neil McKenzie/Graeme Smith	SA v Bang	Chittagong	29 Feb 2008
2nd	576	Sanath Jayasuriya/Roshan Mahanama	SL v Ind	Colombo	2 Aug 1997
3rd	624	Kumar Sangakkara/Mahela Jayawardene	SL v SA	Colombo	27 Jul 2006
4th	437	Mahela Jayawardene/Thilan Samaraweera	SL v Pak	Karachi	21 Feb 2009
5th	405	Sid Barnes/Donald Bradman	Aus v Eng	Sydney	13 Dec 1946
6th	351	Mahela Jayawardene/Prasanna Jayawardene	SL v Ind	Ahmedabad	16 Nov 2009
7th	347	Denis Atkinson/Clairmonte Depeiaza	WI v Aus	Bridgetown	14 May 1955
8th	332	Jonathan Trott/Stuart Broad	Eng v Pak	Lord's	26 Aug 2010
9th	195	Mark Boucher/Pat Symcox	SA v Pak	Johannesburg	14 Feb 1998
10th	151	Brian Hastings/Richard Collinge	NZ v Pak	Auckland	16 Feb 1973
	151	Azhar Mahmood/Mushtaq Ahmed	Pak v SA	Rawalpindi	6 Oct 1997

⊙ GOLDEN PAIR SHOW AUSTRALIA THE WAY

Australia's Matthew Hayden (right) and Ricky Ponting (left) loved batting together in the 2005–06 season. Between 14 October 2005 and 9 April 2006 the pair batted together on 12 occasions, notching up seven century stands (the highest: 201 v South Africa in Durban) to amass 1,317 runs – a partnership record for a calendar year.

⊙ STUCK IN THE MIDDLE WITH YOU

It's a fielding side's worst nightmare. Pakistan were floundering on 176 for 9 chasing Sri Lanka's first-innings 273 in the First Test at Colombo in June 2000. Then Wasim Akram (78) and Arshad Khan (9 not out off 95 balls) held on for 257 balls (42.5 overs in three hours four minutes) to add 90 runs – it is the longest tenth-wicket stand (by balls faced) in Test history.

⊙ THE KARACHI KIDS

The best partnership in Test history (by average) not involving an opening pair is that of Pakistan's Javed Miandad and Shoaib Mohammad (both Karachi-born). The duo batted together 23 times between 1984 and 1993, hitting eight century and seven 50 partnerships and amassing 2,117 runs at a record average of 91.82 runs per partnership.

⊙ MAMMOTH EFFORT IS ALL IN VAIN

A valiant 363-run partnership between Pakistan's Mohammad Yousuf (192) and Younis Khan (173) on days two and three of the Third Test against England at Headingley in August 2006 ultimately counted for little. The home side went on to win the match by 167 runs to take an unassailable 2–0 lead in the four-Test series, and the pair's 83.5-over effort remains the highest partnership in a losing cause in Test history.

⊙ STANDING FIRM

The record for the most successful partnership in a series (868) is jointly held by England's great opening pair Jack Hobbs and Herbert Sutcliffe (against Australia in 1924–25, with four century stands) and Australia's Donald Bradman and Bill Ponsford (against England in 1934, including a then world record stand of 451 at Headingley).

⊙ THE BEST OPENING PAIR IN HISTORY

By some distance, the best opening partnership in Test history (in terms of average runs scored) was that of England's Jack Hobbs and Herbert Sutcliffe. The pair batted together on 38 occasions between 1924 and 1930, recording 15 century stands (highest of 283 v Australia at Melbourne in January 1925) at an average of 87.81 runs per innings – only one other pair in Test history (West Indies' Allan Rae and Jeffrey Stollmeyer) has averaged over 70.

⊙ SOLID AS A ROCK

The legend of the great West Indies sides of the late 1970s and '80s may have been built on a battery of formidable fast bowlers, but a crucial, if unheralded, factor in the success of those teams was the firm foundation provided by a rock-solid opening partnership. Gordon Greenidge and Desmond Haynes batted together on 148 occasions over 14 years and scored 6,482 runs – the most scored by any partnership in Test history.

⊙ LEADING FROM THE FRONT

Between 2 October 1964 and 14 May 1965, in ten Tests against India, Pakistan and the West Indies, Australia's Bill Lawry and Bobby Simpson averaged 66.94 runs when they batted together (with a highest of 382 v West Indies in Barbados), to become the first opening partnership to register 1,000 runs (1,205) in a calendar season.

⊙ PERFECT PARTNERS

Rahul Dravid and Sachin Tendulkar, who have formed the backbone of India's batting line-up for approaching 15 years, and in Tendulkar's case considerably more, hold the all-time Test record for the most century partnerships. The pair have added 100 runs or more together on 19 occasions between 1996 and 2010, with a highest effort of 249 (for the third wicket) in the Second Test against Zimbabwe at Nagpur in November 2000.

⊙ TEST CRICKET'S FIRST CENTURY PARTNERSHIP

Test cricket had to wait three years and four matches before witnessing the first century partnership. On the opening morning of the 1880 Oval Test against Australia, England's W.G. Grace (152) put on 91 for the first wicket with his brother, E.M. Grace, and then added 120 runs with Bunny Lucas (55) for the second wicket to lead England to a commanding first-innings score of 420 and an eventual five-wicket victory.

⊙ RESCUE ACT

Chasing South Africa's first-innings 169 in the First Test at Colombo on 27 July 2006, Sri Lanka had slipped to 14 for 2 when Mahele Jayawardene joined Kumar Sangakkara at the crease. 157 overs later, the pair – Sangakkara, 285; Jayawardene, 309 – had amassed a mighty 624-run partnership, smashing the partnership record for any wicket (576) set by compatriots Sanath Jayasuriya and Roshan Mohanama in 1997. Sri Lanka went on to win the match by an innings and 153 runs.

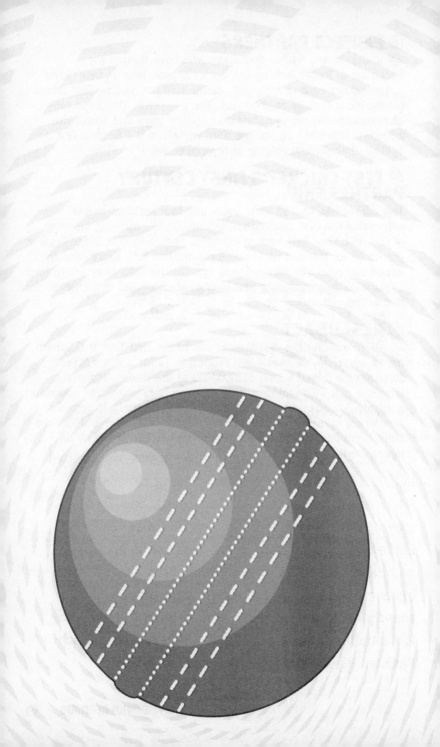

TEST RECORDS: BY TEAM

The spread of the game around the world was not instantaneous. Australia and England first locked horns in March 1877, but it took 123 years before we reached today's complement of ten Test-playing nations as South Africa (1889), West Indies (1928), New Zealand (1930), India (1932), Pakistan (1952), Sri Lanka (1982), Zimbabwe (1992, before losing their status in 2005) and Bangladesh (2000) joined the party. This section looks at the leading Test players on a country-by-country basis and tells you, among other things, who is Australia's all-time leading Test batsman and which Pakistan player has taken the most Test catches.

AUSTRALIA

One of international cricket's original two participants, Australia hosted the first-ever Test match, against England at Melbourne in March 1877. England have appeared in more matches than the other Test-playing nations, but no other country in the game's history has enjoyed as many Test wins (341) or as high a winning percentage (46.71) as Australia.

RESULT SUMMARY

Opposition (Span)	Mat	Won	Lost	Tied	Draw	W/L	%W	%L	%D
Bangladesh (2003–06)	4	4	0	0	0	–	100.00	0.00	0.00
England (1877–2011)	326	133	102	0	91	1.30	40.79	31.28	27.91
ICC World XI (2005)	1	1	0	0	0	–	100.00	0.00	0.00
India (1947–2010)	78	34	20	1	23	1.70	43.58	25.64	29.48
New Zealand (1946–2010)	50	26	7	0	17	3.71	52.00	14.00	34.00
Pakistan (1956–2010)	57	28	12	0	17	2.33	49.12	21.05	29.82
South Africa (1902–2009)	83	47	18	0	18	2.61	56.62	21.68	21.68
Sri Lanka (1983–2007)	20	13	1	0	6	13.00	65.00	5.00	30.00
West Indies (1930–2009)	108	52	32	1	23	1.62	48.14	29.62	21.29
Zimbabwe (1999–2003)	3	3	0	0	0	–	100.00	0.00	0.00

⊙ HITTING AN ALL-TIME LOW

Australia did not get off to the most convincing of starts in their 1902 Ashes-winning series. In the First Test, at Edgbaston, after England had reached 376 in their first innings, Australia, on a wicket affected by a heavy downpour, crashed to a cataclysmic 36 all out (the lowest total in the country's history), with only Victor Trumper (18) reaching double figures. The rain came back to save Australia, however, and the three-day match ended in a draw.

⊙ LARGEST VICTORIES

By an innings: by an innings and 360 runs against South Africa in Johannesburg in February 2002.
By runs: by 562 runs against England at The Oval in 1934.
By wickets: by ten wickets on 28 occasions.

⊙ SMALLEST VICTORIES

By runs: by three runs against England at Manchester in July 1902.
By wickets: by one wicket against the West Indies at Melbourne in December 1951.

⊙ HEAVIEST DEFEATS

By an innings: by an innings and 579 runs against England at The Oval in August 1938.
By runs: by 675 runs against England at Brisbane in November 1928.
By wickets: by ten wickets on ten occasions.

⊙ HAYDEN HITS THE HEIGHTS

By the end of the second day of the First Test between Australia and Zimbabwe at Perth in October 2003, the fact that Australia had amassed a mighty first-innings score of 735 for 6 – the highest total on Australian soil in 126 years of Test cricket – was all but forgotten. Every one of the following day's headlines would be reserved for one man: Matthew Hayden. The Queensland left-handed opener smashed a then world record 380 (off 437 balls); it remains the highest individual score by an Australian in Test history.

⊙ AUSTRALIA END CARIBBEAN TOUR ON AN ALL-TIME HIGH

After watching the West Indies compile 357 in their first innings of the Fifth Test at Kingston, Jamaica, in June 1955, Australia – already holding an unassailable 2–0 series lead – were determined to bow out of their first-ever tour to the Caribbean in style and put on a spectacular show. Centuries from Colin McDonald (127), Neil Harvey (204), Keith Miller (109), Ron Archer (128) and Richie Benaud (121) saw them reach an Australian record total of 758 for 8. They went on to win the match by an innings and 82 runs.

⊙ ALL-TIME GREAT: DONALD BRADMAN

Donald Bradman made his Test debut for Australia aged 20 against England in the 1928–29 Ashes series and registered the first of his 29 Test centuries in his second Test match. From that moment, he became the scourge of bowlers around the world. In the 1930 Ashes series, he plundered a record 974 runs (including a memorable and Test record-breaking knock of 334 at Headingley) at an average of 139.14 – it was the first of five times he would score 500-plus runs in a series. Going into his final Test, against England at The Oval in 1948, with his legend as the greatest batsman of all time confirmed, he needed a mere four runs to end with a career average of 100.00. Sensationally he was out for 0, but his career average of 99.94 still stands as the greatest of all time.

⊙ PONTING'S RECORD HAUL

Australia's best batsman of modern times and the heartbeat of one of his country's best-ever teams, Ricky Ponting has a talismanic approach to batting, in which every shot is played with a flourish of the bat, and it has brought him rich rewards. In 152 Tests for his country (69 of them as captain) he has plundered 12,363 runs (at an average of 53.51) with 39 centuries. Both are all-time national records.

⊙ STRUGGLING TO GET OFF THE MARK

The leading wicket-taker of all fast bowlers in Test history (with 563 wickets), Glenn McGrath may well have struck fear into opponents when he had the ball in his hand, but it was an altogether different story when he came out to bat. In 124 Test matches between 1993 and 2007, McGrath amassed just 671 runs (at an average of 7.36) and recorded an Australian record 35 ducks.

⊙ MAGICAL MAILEY DESTROYS DOWNBEAT ENGLAND

Already 3–0 up in the 1921 Ashes series, Australia went into the Fourth Test at Melbourne looking to ram home their advantage over England, and nobody did so more effectively than Arthur Mailey. The New South Wales leg-break bowler took 9 for 121 off 47 overs in England's second innings – the best-ever bowling figures in an innings by an Australian – as the home side went on to win the match by eight wickets to take a 4–0 series lead.

BOWLING – MOST WICKETS: TOP 10

Pos	Wkts	Player (Span)
1	708	Shane Warne (1992–2007)
2	563	Glenn McGrath (1993–2007)
3	355	Dennis Lillee (1971–84)
4	310	Brett Lee (1999–2008)
5	291	Craig McDermott (1984–96)
6	259	Jason Gillespie (1996–2006)
7	248	Richie Benaud (1952–64)
8	246	Garth McKenzie (1961–71)
9	228	Ray Lindwall (1946–60)
10	216	Clarrie Grimmett (1925–36)

⊙ FANTASTIC FERRIS

Of all the Australian bowlers to have bowled 2,000 or more deliveries in Test cricket, nobody has a better average than J.J. Ferris. In eight matches between 1887 and 1892, the left-arm swing bowler took 61 wickets – with a best return of 7 for 37 against South Africa in Cape Town in March 1892 (in his final appearance for his country) – at an amazing average of 12.70.

⊙ BURKE PRODUCES THE MOST MISERLY BOWLING SPELL

As South Africa battled in vain to avoid defeat against Australia at Johannesburg in the Fourth Test in 1957–58, Australian off-break bowler Jim Burke made history. His 15 (wicketless) overs cost a mere ten runs – the best economy rate in an innings by an Australian bowler in history (0.40).

⊙ BOB MASSIE'S MAGICAL DEBUT

With the exception of India's Narendra Hirwani, no bowler has enjoyed a more spectacular start to his Test career than Bob Massie. Playing at Lord's in the Second Test of the 1972 Ashes series, the fast-medium swing bowler destroyed England, taking 8 for 84 in the first innings and 8 for 53 in the second to help Australia to an eight-wicket win. His match figures of 16 for 137 are the best by an Australian bowler in Test history.

⊙ ALL-TIME GREAT: SHANE WARNE

From the moment at Old Trafford in June 1993 when Shane Warne ripped a massive leg-break from outside leg stump, past a bemused Mike Gatting's defensive push, and into the off stump with his first delivery in Ashes cricket, the world knew it was witnessing a bowler with supreme ability. His major tools may have changed over the years as a result of injuries – the frequency of the big-spinning deliveries was replaced with more craft and guile – but Warne's ability to hypnotize opponents continued unabated. By the time he finished his 145-match, 15-year Test career in 2007, Warne had taken more five-wicket hauls (37), more ten-wicket hauls (10) and more wickets (708) than any other Australian bowler in history.

WICKETKEEPER – MOST DISMISSALS: TOP 5

Pos	Dis	Player (Span)
1	416	Adam Gilchrist (1999–2008)
2	395	Ian Healy (1988–99)
3	355	Rodney Marsh (1970–84)
4	187	Wally Grout (1957–66)
5	130	Bert Oldfield (1920–37)

FIELDING – MOST CATCHES: TOP 5

Pos	Ct	Player (Span)
1	181	Mark Waugh (1991–2002)
2	178	Ricky Ponting (1995–2010)
3	157	Mark Taylor (1989–99)
4	156	Allan Border (1978–94)
5	128	Matthew Hayden (1994–2009)

⊙ MOST SUCCESSFUL CAPTAIN

A natural successor to Steve Waugh when he took over Australia's Test captaincy in 2004, Ricky Ponting has gone on to become the most successful captain in his country's history. In his 77 Tests in charge, Ponting has recorded 48 wins (seven more than Waugh) with a winning percentage of 62.33.

LONGEST-SERVING CAPTAINS: TOP 10

Pos	Mat	Player (Span)
1	93	Allan Border (1984–94)
2	77	Ricky Ponting (2004–10)
3	57	Steve Waugh (1999–2004)
4	50	Mark Taylor (1994–99)
5	48	Greg Chappell (1975–83)
6	39	Bobby Simpson (1964–78)
7	30	Ian Chappell (1971–75)
8	28	Richie Benaud (1958–63)
=	28	Kim Hughes (1979–84)
10	25	Bill Woodfull (1930–34)

⊙ MOST DISMISSALS: INNINGS/MATCHES/SERIES

Three players (Wally Grout, Rod Marsh and Ian Healy) hold the Australian record for the most dismissals in an innings with six. Adam Gilchrist holds the record for the most dismissals in a match with ten (all caught), achieved against New Zealand at Hamilton in March 2000, while Marsh holds the record for the most dismissals in a series, with 28 (all catches) in the 1982–83 Ashes series.

⊙ MOST CATCHES: INNINGS/MATCHES/SERIES

Vic Richardson holds the Australian record for the most catches in an innings with five, against South Africa at Durban in February 1936. Greg Chappell (against England at Perth in December 1974) and Matthew Hayden (against Sri Lanka at Galle in March 2004) hold the record for the most catches in a match, with seven; and Jim Gregory holds the record for the most catches in a series, having taken 15 against England in 1920–21.

ENGLAND

The home of cricket and the nation that gave the game to the world, England played in the first-ever Test match against Australia at Melbourne in 1877 and have since gone on to play in more Test matches than any other country (908). There have been many highs and lows along the way: England's 321 victories (second only to Australia) are balanced out by a record number of defeats (261).

RESULT SUMMARY

Opposition (Span)	Mat	Won	Lost	Tied	Draw	W/L	%W	%L	%D
Australia (1877–2011)	326	102	133	0	91	0.76	31.28	40.79	27.91
Bangladesh (2003–10)	8	8	0	0	0	–	100.00	0.00	0.00
India (1932–2008)	99	34	19	0	46	1.78	34.34	19.19	46.46
New Zealand (1930–2008)	94	45	8	0	41	5.62	47.87	8.51	43.61
Pakistan (1954–2010)	71	22	13	0	36	1.69	30.98	18.30	50.70
South Africa (1889–2010)	138	56	29	0	53	1.93	41.57	21.01	38.40
Sri Lanka (1982–2007)	21	8	6	0	7	1.33	38.09	28.57	33.33
West Indies (1928–2009)	145	43	53	0	49	0.81	29.65	36.55	33.79
Zimbabwe (1996–2003)	6	3	0	0	3	–	50.00	0.00	50.00

BATTING – MOST RUNS: TOP 10

Pos	Runs	Player (Span)
1	8,900	Graham Gooch (1975–95)
2	8,463	Alec Stewart (1990–2003)
3	8,231	David Gower (1978–92)
4	8,114	Geoffrey Boycott (1964–82)
5	7,728	Michael Atherton (1989–2001)
6	7,624	Colin Cowdrey (1954–75)
7	7,249	Walter Hammond (1927–47)
8	6,791	Len Hutton (1937–55)
9	6,806	Ken Barrington (1955–68)
10	6,744	Graham Thorpe (1993–2005)

⊙ LOW POINTS

There have been a few too many calamitous days for English cricket fans over the years – 46 all out against the West Indies at Port of Spain in March 1994; 51 all out against the same opposition at Bridgetown in January 2009 – but the lowest point in their history came in the first innings of the First Test of the 1886–87 Ashes series, at Melbourne, when they crashed to a miserable 45 all out. Astonishingly, however, England rallied to win the match by 13 runs.

⊙ LARGEST VICTORIES

By an innings: by an innings and 579 runs against Australia at The Oval in August 1938.
By runs: by 675 runs against Australia at Brisbane in November 1928.
By wickets: by ten wickets on 19 occasions.

⊙ SMALLEST VICTORIES

By runs: by two runs against Australia at Edgbaston in August 2005.
By wickets: by one wicket on three occasions: against Australia at The Oval in August 1902; against Australia at Melbourne in January 1908; and against South Africa in Cape Town in January 1923.

⊙ HEAVIEST DEFEATS

By an innings: by an innings and 332 runs against Australia at Brisbane in November 1946.
By runs: by 562 runs against Australia at The Oval in August 1934.
By wickets: by ten wickets on 19 occasions.

⊙ RECORDS TUMBLE IN ASHES FINALE AT THE OVAL

England's spectacular batting performance in the first innings of the Fifth Test against Australia at The Oval in August 1938, which led to them squaring the Ashes series 1–1, set several benchmarks for future generations of England cricketers to aspire to. The team total (903 for 7 declared) is the highest by an England team ever; Len Hutton's majestic innings of 364 has never been bettered by an Englishman; and the victory margin – by an innings and 579 runs – is the largest (by an innings) in England's history.

⊙ BEST OPENING PARTNERSHIP

Between 1924 and 1930 England were blessed with the greatest opening partnership in their history. During that seven-year span, Jack Hobbs and Herbert Sutcliffe batted together on 38 occasions and scored 3,249 runs with 15 century stands (only Gordon Greenidge and Desmond Haynes of the West Indies, with 16, have done better in Test history – taking 148 innings to achieve the feat). Hobbs and Sutcliffe's average partnership of 87.81 is the best in Test history.

⊙ ALL-TIME GREAT: WALTER HAMMOND

Without doubt one of the finest batsmen to play the game, Walter Hammond was also one of the first players to bring a real sense of dash to Test cricket. A naturally gifted athlete, he was quick on his feet, a dashing stroke player and a sweet timer of the ball who was equally dynamic off both the front and back foot, particularly when driving the ball. In 85 Tests for England between 1927 and 1947, Hammond scored 7,249 runs at an impressive average of 58.45. He also set the national record for the most centuries (22, equalled by Colin Cowdrey and Geoffrey Boycott) and for the most runs in a series (905 against Australia in 1928–29).

⊙ TROTT EXPLODES ONTO THE TEST SCENE

Jonathan Trott plied his trade in county cricket for nine years with Warwickshire before finally getting his chance with England, in the final Test of the 2009 Ashes series, and has gone on to become the No.3 batsman England have been craving for so long. In 18 Tests, he has scored 1,600 runs (with five centuries) at an average of 61.53 – the highest by an England batsman in Test history.

BOWLING – MOST WICKETS: TOP 10

Pos	Wkts	Player (Span)
1	383	Ian Botham (1977–92)
2	325	Bob Willis (1971–84)
3	307	Fred Trueman (1952–65)
4	297	Derek Underwood (1966–82)
5	252	Brian Statham (1951–65)
6	248	Matthew Hoggard (2000–08)
7	236	Alec Bedser (1946–55)
8	234	Andrew Caddick (1993–2003)
9	229	Darren Gough (1994–2003)
10	222	Steve Harmison (2002–09)

⊙ MOST DUCKS

The English record for the most ducks in Test cricket is 20, an unfortunate feat achieved by two players of contrasting batting ability: Steve Harmison (in 62 Tests between 2002 and 2009) and Michael Atherton (in 115 Tests between 1989 and 2001).

⊙ MOST FIVE-WICKET HAULS

A talismanic all-rounder with an uncanny ability to bring a crowd to its feet through his deeds with both bat and ball, Ian Botham ended his 15-year, 102-Test career in 1992 as the world's leading wicket-taker, with 383 wickets, including 27 five-wicket hauls. Both still stand as all-time England Test records.

⊙ TOILING IN THE SUMMER SUN

Not every day for Ian Botham was one to remember, however. As Pakistan prospered on a batsman-friendly surface in the Fifth Test at The Oval in August 1987, England's bowlers suffered, and none more so than Botham. The Somerset all-rounder's 52 overs eventually brought him three wickets, but they also cost 217 runs – the most ever conceded in a Test innings by an England bowler.

⊙ LAKER'S RECORD RETURN

No player in history, let alone one from England, has been able to match Jim Laker's amazing achievements with the ball during the Fourth Test against Australia at Old Trafford in July 1956. In an Ashes-retaining performance of sublime quality, the Yorkshire off-spinner took 9 for 37 in the first innings and an all-time best 10 for 53 in the second. His match figures of 19 for 90 are also an all-time record in Test cricket.

⊙ ALL-TIME GREAT: S.F. BARNES

England have produced some world-class bowlers over the years – Fred Trueman and Ian Botham to name but two – but none of them has struck as much fear into the hearts of opposing batsmen as the legendary S.F. Barnes, the greatest fast bowler of the early part of the 20th century. One of the first bowlers to make full use of the ball's seam and capable of swinging the ball both ways, at pace, Barnes took 189 wickets for England (including a national record seven ten-wicket match hauls) in 27 Tests between 1901 and 1914. In his final Test series, against South Africa, he took a world record 49 wickets in the series, in only four Tests.

⊙ MOST DISMISSALS: INNINGS/MATCHES/SERIES

The record for the most dismissals in an innings by an England wicketkeeper is seven by Bob Taylor (7ct) against India in Mumbai in February 1980. Jack Russell holds the record both for the most dismissals in a match – 11 catches in the Second Test of 1995–96 series against South Africa in Johannesburg – and for the most dismissals in a series – 27 (25ct, 2st) against South Africa in the 1995–96 series.

⊙ MOST SUCCESSFUL CAPTAIN

His sudden resignation following a five-wicket defeat to South Africa at Edgbaston in August 2008 prevented Michael Vaughan from surpassing Michael Atherton as England's longest-serving captain (51 Tests to Atherton's 54), but the history books will record that Vaughan was the most successful England captain in history, recording 26 wins. The highlight of his captaincy came in 2005, when England won the Ashes for the first time in 18 years.

⊙ MOST CATCHES: INNINGS/MATCHES/SERIES

The England record for the most catches in an innings is four, a feat achieved on 19 occasions; the record for the most catches in a match is six, a feat achieved on seven occasions; and the record for the most catches in a series is 12, a feat achieved on five occasions.

LONGEST-SERVING CAPTAINS: TOP 10

Pos	Mat	Player (Span)
1	54	Michael Atherton (1993–2001)
2	51	Michael Vaughan (2003–08)
3	45	Nasser Hussain (1999–2003)
4	41	Peter May (1955–61)
5	34	Graham Gooch (1988–93)
6	32	David Gower (1982–89)
=	32	Andrew Strauss (2006–11)
8	31	Ray Illingworth (1969–73)
=	31	Mike Brearley (1977–81)
10	30	Ted Dexter (1961–64)

INDIA

A Test-playing nation since 1932, India's rise towards the top of world cricket's ranks was gradual. First they became competitive at home, where overseas batsmen struggled against India's legion of spin bowlers on slow, low, turning wickets, and then, with the emergence of an array of batting talent, such as Sunil Gavaskar and Sachin Tendulkar, they started to make waves around the world.

RESULT SUMMARY

Opposition (Span)	Mat	Won	Lost	Tied	Draw	W/L	%W	%L	%D
Australia (1947–2010)	78	20	34	1	23	0.58	25.64	43.58	29.48
Bangladesh (2000–10)	7	6	0	0	1	–	85.71	0.00	14.28
England (1932–2008)	99	19	34	0	46	0.55	19.19	34.34	46.46
New Zealand (1955–2010)	50	16	9	0	25	1.77	32.00	18.00	50.00
Pakistan (1952–2007)	59	9	12	0	38	0.75	15.25	20.33	64.40
South Africa (1992–2011)	27	7	12	0	8	0.58	25.92	44.44	29.62
Sri Lanka (1982–2010)	35	14	6	0	15	2.33	40.00	17.14	42.85
West Indies (1948–2006)	82	11	30	0	41	0.36	13.41	36.58	50.00
Zimbabwe (1992–2005)	11	7	2	0	2	3.50	63.63	18.18	18.18

⊙ PLUMMETING TO NEW DEPTHS

A trip to Lord's is considered the pinnacle of many players' careers, but that was far from being the case when India played England at the home of cricket in June 1974. Forced to follow on in their second innings, still 327 runs behind, they crashed to a disastrous 42 all out to lose by an innings and 285 runs. It remains India's lowest-ever Test total.

⊙ STELLAR SEHWAG STEALS THE SHOW

After watching South Africa compile a handsome 540 all out in their first innings of the First Test at Chennai in March 2008, India needed a confident performance with the bat if they were to stay in the game. And Virender Sehwag duly obliged, batting for 8 hours and 50 minutes, facing 304 balls and hitting 42 fours and five sixes en route to a score of 319. It is the 16th highest score in Test history and the highest by an Indian batsman.

⊙ STARTING OFF IN STYLE

Sunil Gavaskar, India's first great batsman, burst on to the international scene in spectacular fashion against the West Indies, in the Caribbean, between February and April 1971. Handed his debut in the Second Test of the five-match series, the diminutive opener hit four centuries (with a highest score of 220 in the Fifth Test) and three half-centuries to help India to a sensational 1–0 series win. His haul of 774 runs in the series (at an average of 154.80) is an all-time Indian record.

⊙ LARGEST VICTORIES

By an innings: by an innings and 239 runs against Bangladesh in Dhaka in May 2007.
By runs: by 320 runs against Australia at Mohali in October 2008.
By wickets: by ten wickets on seven occasions.

⊙ SMALLEST VICTORIES

By runs: by 13 runs against Australia at Mumbai in November 2004.
By wickets: by one wicket against Australia at Mohali in October 2010.

BATTING – MOST RUNS: TOP 10

Pos	Runs	Player (Span)
1	14,692	Sachin Tendulkar (1989–2011)
2	12,040	Rahul Dravid (1996–2011)
3	10,122	Sunil Gavaskar (1971–87)
4	7,903	V.V.S. Laxman (1996–2011)
5	7,611	Virender Sehwag (2001–11)
6	7,212	Sourav Ganguly (1996–2008)
7	6,868	Dilip Vengsarkar (1976–92)
8	6,125	Mohammad Azharuddin (1984–2000)
9	6,080	Gundappa Viswanath (1969–83)
10	5,248	Kapil Dev (1978–94)

⊙ BATTING THEIR WAY TO A SERIES WIN

Already one-nil up in the three-match series and having seen Sri Lanka compile 393 all out in their first innings in the Third Test at Mumbai in December 2009, the equation for India was a simple one: to occupy the crease for as long as possible and bat Sri Lanka out of the game. They did so in record-breaking fashion, as a mighty innings of 293 from Virender Sehwag plus an unbeaten century from Mahendra Singh Dhoni saw them compile a massive 726 for 9 declared – the highest total in India's history – en route to an eventual innings-and-24-run victory and a 2–0 series win.

⊙ MANKAD AND ROY POWER INDIA TO SERIES WIN

One–nil up in the five-match series with one Test to go, at Chennai in January 1956, India won the toss, elected to bat and would have pinned their hopes of a series success on their batsmen batting New Zealand out of the game. Their openers, Vinoo Mankad (231) and Pankaj Roy (173), responded in spectacular fashion, putting on 413 for the opening wicket – the highest partnership in India's Test history. It provided the perfect foundation for India, who went on to win the match by an innings and 109 runs to take the series 2–0.

⊙ ALL-TIME GREAT: SACHIN TENDULKAR

Arguably the biggest icon the game has ever seen, Sachin Tendulkar is the most complete batsman of his age, capable of playing every shot in the coaching manual with equal aplomb and scoring heavily in every part of the world against any type of attack. A star from the moment he made his Test debut as a 16-year-old in 1989, Tendulkar made the first of his all-time record 51 Test centuries aged 17, against England in 1990, and has gone on to enjoy a spectacular career, achieving almost godlike status in cricket-mad India. In 2008 he surpassed Brian Lara as Test cricket's all-time leading run-scorer, and has now amassed 14,692 runs (at an average of 56.94).

⊙ HEAVIEST DEFEATS

By an innings: by an innings and 336 runs against the West Indies at Kolkata in December 1958.
By runs: by 342 runs against Australia at Nagpur in October 2004.
By wickets: by ten wickets on 15 occasions.

⊙ GENIUS WITH THE BALL, BUT A RABBIT WITH THE BAT

It would be safe to suggest that Bhagwath Chandrasekhar achieved fame more through his exploits with the ball than with the bat. His assortment of googlies, top-spinners and leg-breaks brought him 242 wickets in 58 Tests between 1964 and 1979, but with the bat he struggled, scoring a mere 167 runs in 80 innings and recording an all-time Indian record 23 ducks.

BOWLING – MOST WICKETS: TOP 10

Pos	Wkts	Player (Span)
1	619	Anil Kumble (1990–2008)
2	434	Kapil Dev (1978–94)
3	393	Harbhajan Singh (1998–2011)
4	271	Zaheer Khan (2000–11)
5	266	Bishan Bedi (1966–79)
6	242	Bhagwath Chandrasekhar (1964–79)
7	236	Javagal Srinath (1991–2002)
8	189	Erapalli Prasanna (1962–78)
9	162	Vinoo Mankad (1946–59)
10	156	Srinivas Venkataraghavan (1965–83)

⊙ RECORD-BREAKING ACHIEVEMENTS WITH THE BALL

The fourth and final day of the Second Test match between India and Pakistan at Delhi in February 1999 was a day to remember for Anil Kumble. With Pakistan set an unlikely 420 runs for victory, the leg-spinner became the first Indian, and only the second bowler in Test history, to take all ten wickets in an innings, finishing with 10 for 74 off 26.3 overs. The best match figures by an Indian bowler are 16 for 136, achieved by Narendra Hirwani against the West Indies at Chennai in January 1988.

⊙ A MISER WITH THE BALL

Renowned for his tireless efforts in practice, where he would spend hours bowling at a coin placed on a good length, Bapu Nadkarni was the most miserly bowler in Test history. The left-arm spinner holds the Indian record for both the best economy rate in an innings (0.15 against England at Chennai in January 1964, when his spell of 32-27-5-0 included 22 consecutive maidens) and the best economy rate in a career (his 1,527.3 overs cost him just 1.67 runs per over).

⊙ CHANDRASEKHAR TOO MUCH FOR ENGLAND

The star of India's 2–1 home series win over England in 1972–73 was, without doubt, Bhagwath Chandrasekhar. The leg-spinner bewitched England's batsmen throughout, taking four five-wicket hauls (with a best of 8 for 79 in the First Test at Delhi) and ended the series with 35 wickets to his name – an all-time record series haul by an Indian bowler.

⊙ ALL-TIME GREAT: ANIL KUMBLE

A determined performer who has probably won more matches for India than other bowler in history, Anil Kumble owed his success more to a high action that was capable of achieving both metronomic accuracy and an awkward bounce than an inherent ability to turn the ball. After making his debut against England at Old Trafford in 1990, the leg-spinner went on to break virtually every single Indian bowling record. In a 132-Test, 18-year international career he set records for the most wickets (619), the most five-wicket hauls in an innings (35) and the most ten-wicket hauls in a match (8).

⊙ A MASTER OF HIS ART

A left-arm spin bowler with a masterful control over flight, loop, spin and pace variation, Bishan Bedi was an outstanding performer for India from the moment he made his debut against the West Indies at Kolkata in December 1966. In a 67-Test career he took 266 wickets at 28.71 runs per wicket – the lowest average (with a minimum of 2,000 balls bowled) by an Indian in Test history.

⊙ INDIA'S MOST SUCCESSFUL CAPTAIN

Few players in modern times have split opinion as much as the forthright Sourav Ganguly, but there is little doubt he was the best captain India have ever had. When he assumed the captaincy from Sachin Tendulkar in 2000, the Kolkata batsman proved a shrewd and tough leader, and his team thrived under his stewardship. In 49 Tests with Ganguly in charge, India won 21 of them with a winning percentage of 42.85 per cent. Both are all-time Indian records.

⊙ MOST DISMISSALS IN A SERIES

The Indian record for the most dismissals by a wicketkeeper in a series is 19, held jointly by Naren Tamhane (12ct, 7st), against Pakistan in the 1954–55 series in Pakistan, and by Syed Kirmani (17ct, 2st) against Pakistan in 1979–80 in India.

⊙ MOST CATCHES: INNINGS/MATCHES/SERIES

The Indian record for the most catches in an innings is five, achieved on three occasions; the record for the most catches in a match is seven, by Yajurvindra Singh against England at Bangalore in January 1977; the record for the most catches in a series is 13, by Rahul Dravid against Australia in 2004–05.

⊙ MOST DISMISSALS: INNINGS/MATCHES/SERIES

The Indian record for the most dismissals in an innings is six, a feat achieved on two occasions: by Syed Kirmani (5ct, 1st) against New Zealand at Christchurch in February 1976; and by Mahendra Singh Dhoni (6ct) against New Zealand at Wellington in April 2009. The Indian record for the most dismissals in a match is eight, a feat achieved on four occasions – twice by Nayan Mongia and twice by Dhoni.

FIELDING – MOST CATCHES: TOP 5

Pos	Ct	Player (Span)
1	199	Rahul Dravid (1996–2011)
2	122	V.V.S. Laxman (1996–2011)
3	108	Sunil Gavaskar (1971–87)
4	106	Sachin Tendulkar (1989–2011)
5	105	Mohammad Azharuddin (1984–2000)

LONGEST-SERVING CAPTAINS: TOP 10

Pos	Mat	Player (Span)
1	49	Sourav Ganguly (2000–05)
2	47	Mohammad Azharuddin (1990–99)
=	47	Sunil Gavaskar (1976–85)
4	40	Nawab of Pataudi (1962–75)
5	34	Kapil Dev (1983–87)
6	25	Rahul Dravid (2003–07)
=	25	Sachin Tendulkar (1996–2000)
8	24	Mahendra Singh Dhoni (2008–11)
9	22	Bishan Bedi (1976–78)
10	16	Ajit Wadekar (1971–74)

NEW ZEALAND

New Zealand were granted Test status in 1929–30, but it took them 26 years and 44 Tests to record their first victory and 40 years before they could celebrate a first series win. However, the emergence of world-class all-rounder Richard Hadlee in the 1970s inspired a new generation of players to the extent that, today, New Zealand are one of the most competitive sides on the international circuit.

⊙ TURNER TRIUMPHS IN THE CARIBBEAN

Five consecutive draws between the West Indies and New Zealand in the 1971–72 series played in the Caribbean may not have made for the most entertaining of cricket viewing, but for New Zealand's Glenn Turner the tour was a triumphant one. The right-handed opener's haul of 672 runs in the series, including a highest score of 259 in the Fourth Test at Georgetown, Guyana, is an all-time New Zealand record.

⊙ LARGEST VICTORIES

By an innings: by an innings and 294 runs against Zimbabwe in Harare in August 2005.
By runs: by 204 runs against the West Indies at Bridgetown in June 2002.
By wickets: by ten wickets on four occasions.

⊙ HEAVIEST DEFEATS

By an innings: by an innings and 324 runs against Pakistan at Lahore in May 2002.
By runs: by 358 runs against South Africa in Johannesburg in November 2007.
By wickets: by ten wickets on 11 occasions.

⊙ SMALLEST VICTORIES

By runs: by 27 runs against the West Indies at Auckland in March 2006.
By wickets: by one wicket against the West Indies at Dunedin in February 1980.

RESULT SUMMARY

Opposition (Span)	Mat	Won	Lost	Tied	Draw	W/L	%W	%L	%D
Australia (1946–2010)	50	7	26	0	17	0.26	14.00	52.00	34.00
Bangladesh (2001–10)	9	8	0	0	1	–	88.88	0.00	11.11
England (1930–2008)	94	8	45	0	41	0.17	8.51	47.87	43.61
India (1955–2011)	50	9	16	0	25	0.56	18.00	32.00	50.00
Pakistan (1955–2011)	50	7	23	0	20	0.30	14.00	46.00	40.00
South Africa (1932–2007)	35	4	20	0	11	0.20	11.42	57.14	31.42
Sri Lanka (1983–2009)	26	9	7	0	10	1.28	34.61	26.92	38.46
West Indies (1952–2008)	37	9	10	0	18	0.90	24.32	27.02	48.64
Zimbabwe (1992–2005)	13	7	0	0	6	–	53.84	0.00	46.15

BATTING – MOST RUNS: TOP 10

Pos	Runs	Player (Span)
1	7,172	Stephen Fleming (1994–2008)
2	5,444	Martin Crowe (1982–95)
3	5,334	John Wright (1978–93)
4	4,702	Nathan Astle (1996–2006)
5	4,159	Daniel Vettori (1997–2011)
6	3,448	Bev Congdon (1965–78)
7	3,428	John Reid (1949–65)
8	3,389	Brendon McCullum (2004–11)
9	3,320	Chris Cairns (1989–2004)
10	3,124	Richard Hadlee (1973–90)

⊙ REARGUARD ACTION

Facing a 323-run first-innings deficit against Sri Lanka in the First Test at Wellington in January–February 1991, New Zealand needed a performance of epic proportions with the bat in their second innings merely to stay in the game. And they responded in style: led by Martin Crowe (299) and Andrew Jones (186), they compiled a mighty 671 for 4 declared – the highest total in New Zealand's history – to force a draw.

⊙ ALL-TIME GREAT: MARTIN CROWE

Born into a cricketing family (his father Dave played first-class cricket and his elder brother Jeff played 39 Tests for New Zealand), Martin Crowe was the most complete batsman his country has ever produced. A right-hander who possessed every shot in the book, and a seemingly limitless amount of time in which to play them, he scored 5,444 runs (at an average of 45.36) in 77 Tests for his country – including 17 centuries and a highest score of 299 (both national records) – before injury brought a premature end to his career in 1995.

⊙ MOST FIFTIES

A sweet timer of the ball and equally strong through the offside or off his pads, Stephen Fleming will enter the history books as one of New Zealand's best-ever batsmen. His sole weakness was an inability to convert good starts into big scores. In a 111-Test career for his country between 1994 and 2008, Fleming, New Zealand's most-capped player and all-time leading run-scorer, passed 50 on 55 occasions (a national record), but only managed to convert nine of them into three-figure scores – a conversion rate of just 16.36 per cent.

⊙ REID TOPS NEW ZEALAND AVERAGES LIST

John F. Reid may not have been as famous as his namesake John R. Reid (who scored 3,428 runs in 58 Tests for New Zealand between 1949 and 1965), but the left-hander still put together an impressive Test career. In 19 matches for his country between 1979 and 1986, he scored 1,296 runs (with a highest score of 180, against Sri Lanka in Colombo in March 1984) at an average of 46.28 – the highest by any New Zealand player in Test history.

⊙ PLUMBING THE DEPTHS

New Zealand, still chasing a first Test victory, were still very much in the match after both sides had completed their first innings in the Second Test at Auckland in March 1955, trailing England by just 46 runs. But what followed was the most dramatic collapse in Test history. New Zealand folded to a pitiful 26 all out – the lowest total in Test history – to lose by an innings and 20 runs.

⊙ A RABBIT WITH THE BAT

In a 61-Test career since making his debut for New Zealand against South Africa in November 2000, Chris Martin has taken a commendable 199 wickets, but his hapless performances with the bat are almost as remarkable as his feats with the ball. In 89 innings for his country, Martin has scored just 109 runs (at an average of 2.53), including a national record 29 ducks.

⊙ A TASTE FOR WICKETS

Among the fastest bowlers on the circuit before his retirement in 2010, Shane Bond's career has been blighted by a succession of injuries since he made his debut against Australia at Hobart in November 2001. When he was able to make it on to the pitch, however, he excelled. In 18 matches for the Blackcaps, Bond took 87 wickets at an average of 22.09 with a wicket every 38.7 balls – the best strike-rate by any New Zealand bowler in history.

⊙ BEST ECONOMY RATE: CAREER/INNINGS

Although Jeremy Coney's 52 Test matches brought him only a modest 27 wickets, no bowler (to have bowled more than 2,000 balls) in New Zealand's history can match his economy rate – a mere 2.04 runs per over. The best economy rate in an innings by a New Zealand bowler was achieved by Bev Congdon, whose 18 eight-ball overs against England at Christchurch in February 1978 went for just 14 runs (0.58 runs per over).

⊙ THE FIRST GREAT KIWI BOWLER

After Hadlee, the second best fast bowler New Zealand has ever produced, Jack Cowie played in all nine of New Zealand's Test matches between 1937 and 1949 (by which time he was 37 years old). He took 45 wickets (with best figures of 6 for 40 against Australia at Wellington in March 1946) at an average of 21.53 – the best by a New Zealand bowler in history.

⊙ PAKISTAN'S BATSMEN TAKE A LIKING TO BOOCK

As Pakistan, driven on by Javed Miandad's imperious 271, piled on the runs to reach 616 for 5 in the first innings against New Zealand in the Third Test at Auckland in February 1989, the Blackcaps' slow left-armer Stephen Boock found himself in the record books. His 70 overs in the innings, which brought him one wicket, cost an all-time New Zealand record 229 runs.

⊙ ALL-TIME GREAT: RICHARD HADLEE

Certainly the finest fast bowler his country has ever produced and one of the greatest all-rounders of all time, Richard Hadlee almost single-handedly changed New Zealand's cricket fortunes. In short, when Hadlee was firing on all cylinders with the ball, New Zealand had every chance of winning the game. By the time he ended his 86-match, 17-year Test career, he had taken 431 wickets (at the time an all-time record) and he still holds the New Zealand records for the best bowling in an innings (9 for 52 against Australia at Brisbane in November 1985), the best bowling in a match (15 for 123 in the same match), the most wickets in a series (33 against Australia in the 1985–86 series), the most five-wicket hauls in an innings (36) and the most ten-wicket hauls in a match (9).

BOWLING – MOST WICKETS: TOP 10

Pos	Wkts	Player (Span)
1	431	Richard Hadlee (1973–90)
2	344	Daniel Vettori (1997–2011)
3	218	Chris Cairns (1989–2004)
4	199	Chris Martin (2000–11)
5	160	Danny Morrison (1987–97)
6	130	Lance Cairns (1974–85)
7	123	Ewen Chatfield (1975–89)
8	116	Richard Collinge (1965–78)
9	111	Bruce Taylor (1965–73)
10	102	John Bracewell (1980–90)

WICKETKEEPER – MOST DISMISSALS: TOP 5

Pos	Dis	Player (Span)
1	201	Adam Parore (1990–2002)
2	176	Ian Smith (1980–92)
3	172	Brendon McCullum (2004–11)
4	96	Ken Wadsworth (1969–76)
5	59	Warren Lees (1976–83)

FIELDING – MOST CATCHES: TOP 5

Pos	Ct	Player (Span)
1	171	Stephen Fleming (1994–2008)
2	71	Martin Crowe (1982–95)
3	70	Nathan Astle (1996–2006)
4	64	Jeremy Coney (1974–87)
5	57	Daniel Vettori (1997–2011)

⊙ MOST CATCHES: INNINGS/MATCHES/SERIES

The New Zealand record for the most catches in an innings is five, achieved by Stephen Fleming against Zimbabwe at Harare in September 1999; he went on to take seven catches in the match (also a national record). Fleming also holds the record for the most catches in a series (10), a feat he achieved twice: against Zimbabwe in 1997–98 and against England in 1999.

⊙ MOST SUCCESSFUL CAPTAIN

Stephen Fleming proved an inspirational choice as New Zealand captain when, aged just 23 years and 321 days, he took over from Lee Germon in 1997. He went on to captain the Blackcaps on 80 occasions and recorded 28 wins – the most, by some distance, of any New Zealand captain in history.

⊙ MOST DISMISSALS: INNINGS/MATCHES/SERIES

The New Zealand record for the most dismissals in an innings is seven, achieved by Ian Smith (7ct) against Sri Lanka at Hamilton in February 1991. The New Zealand record for the most dismissals in a match is nine, set by Brendon McCullum (8ct, 1st) against Pakistan at Napier in December 2009. The record for the most dismissals in a series is 23, by Artie Dick (21ct, 2st) against South Africa in South Africa in 1961–62.

LONGEST-SERVING CAPTAINS: TOP 10

Pos	Mat	Player (Span)
1	80	Stephen Fleming (1997–2006)
2	34	John Reid (1956–65)
3	30	Geoff Howarth (1980–85)
4	27	Daniel Vettori (2007–10)
5	19	Graham Dowling (1968–72)
6	18	Ken Rutherford (1993–95)
7	17	Bev Congdon (1972–75)
8	16	Martin Crowe (1990–93)
9	15	Jeremy Coney (1984–87)
10	14	John Wright (1988–90)

PAKISTAN

Granted Test status in July 1952, following a recommendation from arch-rivals India, Pakistan are one of the most unpredictable Test teams: they can be world-beaters on one day and spectacularly ordinary on another. The country has produced some of Test cricket's all-time great players, such as Javed Miandad and Hanif Mohammad with the bat and Imran Khan and Wasim Akram with the ball.

⊙ SURRENDER IN SHARJAH

Forced to play their home series against Australia in October 2002 at neutral venues as a result of security fears in their own country, Pakistan looked like a fish out of water. In the Second Test at Sharjah (following a 41-run defeat in the First Test at Colombo) they capitulated in spectacular fashion, crashing to 59 all out in their first innings and 53 all out in their second – the two lowest scores in the country's history.

⊙ MAKING HAY AGAINST THE OLD ENEMY

There was little doubt as to who was the star of the show during Pakistan's triumphant and comprehensive 3–0 home series victory over arch-rivals India in 1982–83. Mudassar Nazar hit four centuries and one 50 (with a highest score of 231 in the Fourth Test at Faisalabad) to end the six-match series with an all-time Pakistan record haul of 761 runs at an impressive average of 126.83.

⊙ LARGEST VICTORIES

By an innings: by an innings and 324 runs against New Zealand at Lahore in May 2002.
By runs: by 341 runs against India at Karachi in January 2006.
By wickets: by ten wickets on ten occasions.

⊙ SMALLEST VICTORIES

By runs: by 12 runs against India at Chennai in January 1999.
By wickets: by one wicket on two occasions: against Australia at Karachi in September 1994; and against Bangladesh at Multan in September 2003.

⊙ HEAVIEST DEFEATS

By an innings: by an innings and 225 runs against England at Lord's in August 2010.
By runs: by 491 runs against Australia at Perth in December 2004.
By wickets: by ten wickets on nine occasions.

⊙ A RECORD-BREAKING RESPONSE

Any hopes of victory Sri Lanka had after compiling 644 for 7 declared in their first innings of the First Test against Pakistan, at Karachi in February 2009, soon turned to frustration. The home side, led by Younis Khan (313) and Kamran Akmal (158 not out), responded by posting 765 for 6 declared – the highest score in their history – as the match petered out into a draw.

RESULT SUMMARY

Opposition (Span)	Mat	Won	Lost	Tied	Draw	W/L	%W	%L	%D
Australia (1956–2010)	57	12	28	0	17	0.42	21.05	49.12	29.82
Bangladesh (2001–03)	6	6	0	0	0	–	100.00	0.00	0.00
England (1954–2010)	71	13	22	0	36	0.59	18.30	30.98	50.70
India (1952–2007)	59	12	9	0	38	1.33	20.33	15.25	64.40
New Zealand (1955–2011)	50	23	7	0	20	3.28	46.00	14.00	40.00
South Africa (1995–2010)	18	3	8	0	7	0.37	16.66	44.44	38.90
Sri Lanka (1982–2009)	37	15	9	0	13	1.66	40.54	24.32	35.13
West Indies (1958–2006)	44	15	14	0	15	1.07	34.09	31.81	34.09
Zimbabwe (1993–2002)	14	8	2	0	4	4.00	57.14	14.28	28.57

⊙ KANEIRA'S UNFORTUNATE RECORD

In his ten-year Test career Danish Kaneira has had considerable success with the ball – he has taken 261 wickets in 61 Tests for his country since making his debut in 2000 – but he has enjoyed few high points with the bat: he has been dismissed without scoring on 25 occasions, an all-time record for a Pakistan player.

⊙ ALL-TIME GREAT: JAVED MIANDAD

Far from conventional (he was one of the first players to perfect the reverse sweep) and often at the centre of controversy, Javed Miandad's greatest ability with the bat was his uncanny tendency to score runs at will under any conditions. He burst on to the international scene as a fresh-faced 19-year-old against New Zealand in 1976, scoring 504 runs in three Tests (including 203 in the Third Test to become the game's youngest-ever double centurion) and became a mainstay of Pakistan's batting line-up for the next 17 years. In 124 Tests he scored a Pakistan record 8,832 runs (including 23 centuries) at an average of 52.57 (also a record for a Pakistan player in Test cricket).

⊙ INZAMAM'S RECORD HAUL

Javed Miandad may have edged him out as his country's leading all-time run-scorer, but no Pakistan batsman in history has scored more hundreds or more 50s than Inzamam-ul-Haq. In 119 Tests for Pakistan between 1992 and 2007 the right-hander passed the half-century mark on 71 occasions and went on to reach three figures 25 times.

⊙ HANIF DIGS PAKISTAN OUT OF A HOLE

The first real star of Pakistan cricket, and the first player in Test history to be labelled "The Little Master", Hanif Mohammad showed star quality when his side really needed it in the First Test against the West Indies at Bridgetown in January 1958. With Pakistan forced to follow on in their second innings, still 473 runs in arrears, Hanif played the longest innings in Test history, taking 970 minutes to compile 337 – still the highest individual score by a Pakistan batsman – to help his side save the game.

⊙ THE PRINCE OF PAKISTAN

Wasim Akram may have been a fine all-rounder, but it was his performances with the ball that will leave an indelible mark in the history books. The most effective left-arm fast bowler Test cricket has ever produced, Wasim ended his 104-Test match career in 2003 as Pakistan's all-time leading wicket-taker (with 414 wickets), including a national record 25 five-wicket hauls (with a best of 7 for 119 against New Zealand at Wellington in March 1994).

BATTING – MOST RUNS: TOP 10

Pos	Runs	Player (Span)
1	8,832	Javed Miandad (1976–93)
2	8,829	Inzamam-ul-Haq (1992–2007)
3	7,530	Mohammad Yousuf (1998–2010)
4	5,768	Saleem Malik (1982–99)
5	5,617	Younis Khan (2000–11)
6	5,062	Zaheer Abbas (1969–85)
7	4,114	Mudassar Nazar (1976–89)
8	4,052	Saeed Anwar (1990–2001)
9	3,931	Majid Khan (1964–83)
10	3,915	Hanif Mohammad (1952–69)

⊙ KEEPING THINGS TIGHT

Pervez Sajjad holds the Pakistan record for the best economy rate in a career. In 19 matches for his country between 1964 and 1973, the slow left-armer took 59 wickets at an average of 23.89 and conceded just 2.04 runs per over. Majid Khan holds the record for the best economy rate in an innings. In the West Indies' second innings of the Fourth Test at Port of Spain in April 1977, the off-spinner bowled ten overs for just three runs (0.30 runs per over) with eight maidens.

⊙ THE WICKET MACHINE

Waqar Younis was the finest exponent of reverse-swing bowling Test cricket has ever seen. In 87 matches for his country between 1989 and 2003, the fast bowler took 373 wickets at 23.56 with a strike-rate of a wicket every 43.4 balls – the best by a Pakistan bowler, the eighth best of all time and the best by any bowler to have bowled more than 10,000 deliveries in Test history.

⊙ ON THE WRONG END OF A SOBERS PUMMELLING

While the Third Test of the 1957–58 series between the West Indies and Pakistan, at Kingston, Jamaica, was one to remember for Garfield Sobers (the 21-year-old hit a then world record score of 365 not out), it was certainly one to forget for two of Pakistan's bowlers. Khan Mohammad's 54 wicketless overs went for 259 runs (an all-time national record) while his team-mate Fazal Mahmood went for 247 runs off 85.2 overs – the second highest number of runs conceded in an innings by a Pakistan bowler.

⊙ ALL-TIME GREAT: IMRAN KHAN

With his good looks and limitless ability, Imran Khan did much to confirm cricket's status as the number-one sport in Pakistan from the moment he made his debut against England in 1971. He was worth a place in the Pakistan side for his ability with the bat alone (he scored 3,807 runs at an average of 37.69), but it was his bowling that made him a truly world-class performer, his bounding, athletic run, high-leaping delivery stride and a huge variety of deliveries – all produced at express pace – striking fear into the hearts of batsmen around the world. In 88 Tests for his country, 48 of them as captain, he set numerous national records: the best bowling figures in a match (14 for 116 against Sri Lanka at Lahore in March 1982), the most ten-wicket match hauls (6), the most wickets in a series (40 against India in Pakistan in 1982–83) and the best career average (22.81).

BOWLING – MOST WICKETS: TOP 10

Pos	Wkts	Player (Span)
1	414	Wasim Akram (1985–2002)
2	373	Waqar Younis (1989–2003)
3	362	Imran Khan (1971–92)
4	261	Danish Kaneria (2000–10)
5	236	Abdul Qadir (1977–90)
6	208	Saqlain Mushtaq (1995–2004)
7	185	Mushtaq Ahmed (1990–2003)
8	178	Shoaib Akhtar (1997–2007)
9	177	Sarfraz Nawaz (1969–84)
10	171	Iqbal Qasim (1976–88)

⊙ MOST DISMISSALS: INNINGS/MATCHES/SERIES

The Pakistan record for the most dismissals in an innings is seven, by Wasim Bari (7ct) against New Zealand at Auckland in February 1979. The record for the most dismissals in a match is nine, by Rashid Latif (9ct) against New Zealand at Auckland in February 1994 and by Kamran Akmal (9ct) against the West Indies at Kingston in June 2005. The record for the most dismissals in a series is 18 (17ct, 1st), by Rashid Latif against Bangladesh in 2003.

FIELDING – MOST CATCHES: TOP 5

Pos	Ct	Player (Span)
1	93	Javed Miandad (1976–93)
2	81	Inzamam-ul-Haq (1992–2007)
3	74	Younis Khan (2000–09)
4	66	Majid Khan (1964–83)
5	65	Saleem Malik (1982–99)
=	65	Mohammad Yousuf (1998–2010)

WICKETKEEPER – MOST DISMISSALS: TOP 5

Pos	Dis	Player (Span)
1	228	Wasim Bari (1967–84)
2	181	Kamran Akmal (2002–10)
3	147	Moin Khan (1990–2004)
4	130	Rashid Latif (1992–2003)
5	104	Saleem Yousuf (1982–90)

LONGEST-SERVING CAPTAINS: TOP 10

Pos	Mat	Player (Span)
1	48	Imran Khan (1982–92)
2	34	Javed Miandad (1980–93)
3	31	Inzamam-ul-Haq (2001–07)
4	25	Wasim Akram (1993–99)
5	23	A.H. Kardar (1952–58)
6	19	Mushtaq Mohammad (1976–79)
7	17	Intikhab Alam (1969–75)
=	17	Waqar Younis (1993–2003)
9	14	Zaheer Abbas (1983–84)
10	13	Moin Khan (1998–2001)

SOUTH AFRICA

A 21-year ban from Test cricket between 1970 and 1991 as a result of the South African government's oppressive apartheid policy may have stopped several potentially glittering international careers in their tracks, but since the country's return to the international fold, it has quickly resumed its position as one of the game's most competitive nations.

RESULT SUMMARY

Opposition (Span)	Mat	Won	Lost	Tied	Draw	W/L	%W	%L	%D
Australia (1902–2009)	83	18	47	0	18	0.38	21.68	56.62	21.68
Bangladesh (2000–08)	8	8	0	0	0	–	100.00	0.00	0.00
England (1889–2010)	138	29	56	0	53	0.51	21.01	40.57	38.40
India (1992–2011)	27	12	7	0	8	1.71	44.44	25.92	29.62
New Zealand (1932–2007)	35	20	4	0	11	5.00	57.14	11.42	31.42
Pakistan (1995–2010)	18	8	3	0	7	2.66	44.44	16.66	38.88
Sri Lanka (1993–2006)	17	8	4	0	5	2.00	47.05	23.52	29.41
West Indies (1992–2010)	25	16	3	0	6	5.33	64.00	12.00	24.00
Zimbabwe (1995–2005)	7	6	0	0	1	–	85.71	0.00	14.29

⊙ LARGEST VICTORIES

By an innings: by an innings and 229 runs against Sri Lanka at Cape Town in January 2001.
By runs: by 358 runs against New Zealand at Johannesburg in November 2007.
By wickets: by ten wickets on six occasions.

⊙ SMALLEST VICTORIES

By runs: by five runs against Australia at Sydney in January 1994.
By wickets: by one wicket against England at Johannesburg in January 1906.

⊙ HEAVIEST DEFEATS

By an innings: by an innings and 360 runs against Australia at Johannesburg in February 2002.
By runs: by 530 runs against Australia at Melbourne in February 1911.
By wickets: by ten wickets on 12 occasions.

⊙ LORDING IT AT THE HOME OF CRICKET

South Africa dominated England in crushing fashion in the Second Test at Lord's in July–August 2003. After dismissing the hosts for 173 in their first innings, the Proteas, led by captain Graeme Smith (259) and Gary Kirsten (108), amassed a mighty 682 for 6 declared – the highest score by a South Africa side in history – en route to an innings-and-92-run victory.

⊙ HITTING AN ALL-TIME LOW

South Africa have crashed to a sorry 30 all out on two occasions: in the First Test against England at Port Elizabeth in February 1896; and against the same opposition in the First Test at Birmingham in June 1924 (an innings in which extras was the highest scorer with 11).

⊙ ALL-TIME GREAT: JACQUES KALLIS

The history books will record that Jacques Kallis is one of the greatest batting all-rounders of all time. While his right-arm fast-medium bowling has brought him 270 wickets in a 145-match career, it is his performances with the bat that make him a truly outstanding performer. Not necessarily the most flamboyant of players, he shows a determined, limpet-like resolve at the batting crease that has brought him a national record 11,864 runs (only four players in history have scored more), 40 centuries and 54 half-centuries.

⊙ POLLOCK CUT SHORT IN HIS PRIME

One of a number of exceptional players whose international career was cut short by South Africa's expulsion from international cricket, Graeme Pollock was, with the exception of Garfield Sobers, arguably the best left-handed batsman Test cricket has ever seen. In 23 matches for his country between 1963 and 1970, he scored 2,256 runs (with a highest score of 274 against Australia at Durban in February 1970) at an average of 60.97, the highest by any South African player in history to have completed 20 innings.

⊙ DE VILLIERS HITS NEW HEIGHTS

With the two-match series locked at 0–0 after the drawn First Test, South Africa won the toss and elected to bat in the Second Test against Pakistan in Abu Dhabi in November 2010 and immediately ran into trouble, slipping to a worrying 33 for 3. And then A.B. de Villiers strode to the crease: he added 179 for the fourth wicket with Jacques Kallis (105) and by the time South Africa had reached an imposing 584 for 9 declared remained unbeaten on 278 – the highest individual score by a South Africa player in Test cricket. His efforts did not lead his side to victory, however. Pakistan replied with 434 and the match petered out into a draw.

⊙ MAKHAYA'S MISFORTUNE WITH THE BAT

The first black African cricketer to play for South Africa when he made his Test debut against Sri Lanka at Cape Town in March 1998, Makhaya Ntini has enjoyed considerable success with the ball in his 101-match career, taking 390 wickets. His performances with the bat have been less impressive, however. His tally of 21 ducks is an all-time South African record.

⊙ FAULKNER FLOURISHES AS SORRY SOUTH AFRICA FOLD

Few players in Test cricket have emerged with as much credit following a crushing series defeat as Aubrey Faulkner. As South Africa, struggling on fast, bouncy wickets, crashed to a 4–1 series defeat against Australia in 1910–11, only Faulkner stood tall, hitting 732 runs in the five Tests (a staggering 26.3 per cent of his team's total runs), with a highest score of 204 in the Second Test at Melbourne. His series haul remains a South African record to this day.

BOWLING – MOST WICKETS: TOP 10

Pos	Wkts	Player (Span)
1	421	Shaun Pollock (1995–2008)
2	390	Makhaya Ntini (1998–2010)
3	330	Allan Donald (1992–2002)
4	269	Jacques Kallis (1995–2011)
5	238	Dale Steyn (2004–11)
6	170	Hugh Tayfield (1949–60)
7	134	Paul Adams (1995–2004)
8	123	Trevor Goddard (1955–70)
=	123	Andre Nel (2001–08)
10	116	Peter Pollock (1961–70)

BATTING – MOST RUNS: TOP 10

Pos	Runs	Player (Span)
1	11,864	Jacques Kallis (1995–2011)
2	7,445	Graeme Smith (2002–11)
3	7,289	Gary Kirsten (1993–2004)
4	6,167	Herschelle Gibbs (1996–2008)
5	5,295	M.V. Boucher (1997–2011)
6	4,741	A.B. de Villiers (2004–11)
7	4,554	Darryl Cullinan (1993–2001)
8	3,897	Hashim Amla (2004–11)
9	3,781	Shaun Pollock (1995–2008)
10	3,714	Hansie Cronje (1992–2000)

⊙ SUPER STEYN'S GREED FOR WICKETS

Fast-tracked into the South African side to face England in 2004 little more than a year after making his first-class debut, Dale Steyn's lack of experience was exposed in his early forays in Test cricket, but, once he had found his feet, he demonstrated just how effective he could be. He is genuinely fast, with aggression to match; his 46 matches to date have brought him 238 wickets, and his strike-rate of a wicket every 39.9 deliveries is the best by any South Africa bowler in history.

⊙ ALL-TIME GREAT: SHAUN POLLOCK

Born into a South African cricketing dynasty – his father Peter and uncle Graeme both starred for the country in the 1960s – Shaun Pollock made his Test debut against England in 1996, went on to form an effective new-ball partnership with Allan Donald and soon established himself as an international cricketer of the highest class. His meticulous line-and-length bowling saw him become the first, and to date only, South African bowler to pass the 400-wicket milestone, and he ended his 108-Test match career (26 of them as captain) with 421 scalps to his name.

⊙ MAKHAYA GOES INTO THE RECORD BOOKS

With an action based on that of Malcolm Marshall, Makhaya Ntini has enjoyed considerable success for South Africa. One of only three of his countrymen to have taken more than 300 Test scalps, the right-arm fast bowler holds the national record for the best figures in a match (13 for 132 against the West Indies at Port of Spain in April 2005) and shares the record for the most ten-wicket match hauls (four) with Dale Steyn.

⊙ ADCOCK'S RECORD AVERAGE

Picked for South Africa to play against New Zealand in December 1953 with only eight first-class matches under his belt, Neil Adcock rewarded the selectors' faith in him in spectacular style. Exploiting his height to create an awkward, sharp-lifting bounce, the fast bowler went on to become the first South Africa bowler in history to take 100 Test wickets, ending his nine-year, 26-match career with 104 wickets at an average of 21.10 – the lowest by any South African bowler to have bowled 2,000 balls or more in Test cricket.

⊙ WHITE LIGHTNING STRIKES

The first genuinely world-class South Africa player since the country's readmission to the international fold in 1992, Allan Donald's searing pace was enough to send shivers down the spines of opposing batsmen. In 72 Tests for his country before his retirement in 2002, the man known as "White Lightning" became the first South Africa bowler in history to claim 300 Test wickets (he finished with 330), and he still holds the national record for the most five-wicket hauls (with 20).

⊙ MOST DISMISSALS: INNINGS/MATCHES/SERIES

The South Africa record for the most dismissals in an innings is six, a feat achieved by Denis Lindsay (6ct) against Australia at Johannesburg in December 1966 and by Mark Boucher on three occasions. The record for the most dismissals in a match is nine, by Dave Richardson (9ct) against India at Port Elizabeth in December 1992 and by Mark Boucher on three occasions. The most dismissals in a series is 26, set by John Waite (23ct, 3st) against New Zealand in 1960–61 and by Mark Boucher (25ct, 1st) against England in 1998.

⊙ MOST CATCHES: INNINGS/MATCHES/SERIES

The South African record for the most catches in an innings is four, a feat achieved on eight occasions. The record for the most catches in a match is six, by Bert Vogler against England at Durban in January 1910 and by Bruce Mitchell against Australia at Melbourne in December 1931; both went on to take 12 catches in the series, a national record equalled by Trevor Goddard against England in 1956–57.

⊙ SMITH SILENCES THE CRITICS

He may have been a surprise choice as South African captain following the Proteas' dismal showing at the 2003 ICC World Cup, but Graeme Smith, just 23 years old at the time of his appointment, has gone on to become the most successful captain in South Africa's history, winning 38 of his 82 Tests in charge between 2003 and 2011.

WICKETKEEPER – MOST DISMISSALS: TOP 5

Pos	Dis	Player (Span)
1	519	Mark Boucher (1997–2011)
2	152	Dave Richardson (1992–98)
3	141	John Waite (1951–65)
4	56	Denis Lindsay (1963–70)
5	51	Jock Cameron (1927–35)

FIELDING – MOST CATCHES: TOP 5

Pos	Ct	Player (Span)
1	162	Jacques Kallis (1995–2011)
2	116	Graeme Smith (2002–11)
3	94	Herschelle Gibbs (1996–2008)
4	83	Gary Kirsten (1993–2004)
=	83	A.B. de Villiers (2004–11)

LONGEST-SERVING CAPTAINS: TOP 10

Pos	Mat	Player (Span)
1	82	Graeme Smith (2003–11)
2	53	Hansie Cronje (1994–2000)
3	26	Shaun Pollock (2000–03)
4	18	Herbie Taylor (1913–24)
5	16	Kepler Wessels (1992–94)
6	15	Jack Cheetham (1952–55)
=	15	Dudley Nourse (1948–51)
8	14	Jackie McGlew (1955–62)
9	13	Trevor Goddard (1963–65)
=	13	Percy Sherwell (1906–11)

SRI LANKA

Sri Lanka were granted Test status in 1981 to become the eighth Test-playing nation and made such strides that, by the mid-1990s, they were considered a major force in international cricket. Their success has been founded on the emergence of a host of world-class batsmen and, in Muttiah Muralitharan, the leading Test wicket-taker of all time.

RESULT SUMMARY

Opposition (Span)	Mat	Won	Lost	Tied	Draw	W/L	%W	%L	%D
Australia (1983–2007)	20	1	13	0	6	0.07	5.00	65.00	30.00
Bangladesh (2001–09)	12	12	0	0	0	–	100.00	0.00	0.00
England (1982–2007)	21	6	8	0	7	0.75	28.57	38.09	33.33
India (1982–2010)	35	6	14	0	15	0.42	19.14	40.00	42.85
New Zealand (1983–2009)	26	7	9	0	10	0.77	26.92	34.61	38.46
Pakistan (1982–2009)	37	9	15	0	13	0.60	24.32	40.54	35.13
South Africa (1993–2006)	17	4	8	0	5	0.50	23.52	47.05	29.41
West Indies (1993–2010)	15	6	3	0	6	2.00	40.00	20.00	40.00
Zimbabwe (1994–2004)	15	10	0	0	5	–	66.66	0.00	33.33

⊙ CAPITULATION IN KANDY

Trailing 1–0 in the series going into the Third and final Test against Pakistan at Kandy in August 1994, Sri Lanka got off to the worst possible start. After losing the toss and being put in to bat, they wilted in the face of some excellent fast bowling from Wasim Akram (4 for 32) and Waqar Younis (6 for 34) and crashed to 71 all out in just 28.2 overs – the lowest total in their history. Pakistan went on to win the match by an innings and 52 runs.

⊙ MURALI'S STRUGGLES WITH THE BAT

While Muttiah Muralitharan holds virtually every Sri Lankan bowling record in the book, his performances with the bat have been less eyebrow-raising: in 132 Tests for his country between 1992 and 2010 he has scored 1,259 runs at an average of 11.87 including a national record 32 ducks.

⊙ BATTING FOR FUN

With India having amassed an impressive 537 for 8 declared in the first innings of the First Test in Colombo in August 1997, it was time for Sri Lanka to produce a batting masterclass of their own if they wanted to stay in the match. They did just that. Bolstered by centuries from Sanath Jayasuriya (340), Roshan Mahanama (225) and Aravinda de Silva (126), they reached 952 for 6 declared – the highest total in Test history.

⊙ JAYASURIYA PROSPERS AGAINST INDIA

An explosive performer in all formats of the game, Sanath Jayasuriya reserved his best performances in the Test arena for the two-match series against India in August 1997. In three innings he scored 340 (at the time a new national record), 32 and 199. His series haul of 571 runs (at an unbelievable average of 190.33) is an all-time Sri Lankan record.

⊙ LARGEST VICTORIES

By an innings: by an innings and 254 runs against Zimbabwe at Bulawayo in May 2004.
By runs: by 465 runs against Bangladesh at Chittagong in January 2009.
By wickets: by ten wickets on seven occasions.

⊙ SMALLEST VICTORIES

By runs: by 42 runs against Pakistan at Faisalabad in September 1995.
By wickets: by one wicket against South Africa at Colombo in August 2006.

⊙ HEAVIEST DEFEATS

By an innings: by an innings and 229 runs against South Africa at Cape Town in January 2001.
By runs: by 301 runs against Pakistan at Colombo in August 1994.
By wickets: by ten wickets on three occasions.

⊙ SUPER SANGAKKARA

Hauled into the Test side in 2000 at the age of 22 despite modest performances in first-class cricket, Kumar Sangakkara has more than repaid the faith the Sri Lankan selectors showed in him. In 94 Tests, the classy left-hander has scored 8,244 runs (with a highest score of 287 against South Africa at Colombo in July 2006) at an average of 57.25 – the highest by any Sri Lankan batsman in history.

⊙ ALL-TIME GREAT: MAHELA JAYAWARDENE

From the moment Mahela Jayawardene stepped into the Test arena, with his side on 790 for 4 against India at Colombo in August 1997, he knew the benchmark to which he must aspire. And he has not disappointed. A right-hand batsman with limitless concentration and application, Jayawardene has consistently delivered the goods and holds the Sri Lankan record for the most runs scored (9,527), the highest individual score (a stunning knock of 374 against South Africa at Colombo in July 2006, as part of an all-time record partnership of 624 with Kumar Sangakkara), the most centuries (28) and the most scores of 50 or over (66).

BATTING – MOST RUNS: TOP 10

Pos	Runs	Player (Span)
1	9,527	Mahela Jayawardene (1997–2010)
2	8,244	Kumar Sangakkara (2000–10)
3	6,973	Sanath Jayasuriya (1991–2007)
4	6,361	Aravinda de Silva (1984–2002)
5	5,502	Marvan Atapattu (1990–2007)
6	5,105	Arjuna Ranatunga (1982–2000)
7	4,545	Hashan Tillakaratne (1989–2004)
8	4,395	Thilan Samaraweera (2001–10)
9	3,990	Tillakaratne Dilshan (1999–2010)
10	3,089	Chaminda Vaas (1994–2009)

⊙ MR ECONOMY

Don Anurasiri found it difficult to cement a permanent place in the Sri Lanka side after making his Test debut at the age of 20 against Pakistan in Colombo in March 1986 (he played just 18 times for his country over a 12-year period), but when the slow left-armer did play, he was the epitome of both accuracy and economy. He holds the Sri Lanka record for both best career economy rate (2.33) and for the best economy rate in an innings – 0.60 (15-11-9-0) in the Third Test against Pakistan at Colombo in March 1986.

BOWLING – MOST WICKETS: TOP 10

Pos	Wkts	Player (Span)
1	795	Muttiah Muralitharan (1992–2010)
2	355	Chaminda Vaas (1994–2009)
3	101	Lasith Malinga (2004–2010)
4	98	Sanath Jayasuriya (1991–2007)
5	90	Dilhara Fernando (2000–2010)
6	85	Pramodya Wickramasinghe (1991–2001)
7	78	Rangana Herath (1999–2010)
8	73	Rumesh Ratnayake (1983–92)
9	69	Kumar Dharmasena (1993–2004)
10	64	Nuwan Zoysa (1997–2004)

⊙ SLINGA MALINGA

The fastest bowler Sri Lanka has ever produced, Lasith Malinga can be a batsman's worst nightmare. Generating genuine pace whether the ball is new or old, his low-slung, round-arm action can make him almost impossible to pick up and when he is fit – injuries kept him out of Test cricket between December 2007 and July 2010 – he is deadly: he has taken 101 wickets in 30 Test matches to date and has a strike-rate of a wicket every 51.5 deliveries, an all-time Sri Lankan record.

⊙ ALL-TIME GREAT: MUTTIAH MURALITHARAN

Predictably enough, Muttiah Muralitharan, Test cricket's all-time leading wicket-taker with 800 wickets, holds virtually every single Sri Lankan bowling record. He leads the way for the best bowling figures in an innings (9 for 51 against Zimbabwe at Kandy in January 2002), the best bowling figures in a match (16 for 220 against England at The Oval in August 1998), the best average of any Sri Lanka bowler to have bowled 2,000 or more balls in Test cricket (22.67), the most five-wicket hauls in an innings (67), the most ten-wicket hauls in a match (22) and the most runs conceded in an innings (224 against Australia in Perth in December 1995).

⊙ THE OTHER HAT-TRICK MAN

The only Sri Lanka bowler in Test history to take a hat-trick is Nuwan Zoysa. The left-arm fast-medium bowler dismissed Trevor Gripper (lbw), Murray Goodwin (caught behind) and Neil Johnson (lbw) in the first innings of the Second Test against Zimbabwe in Harare in November 1999 to create his own slice of Sri Lankan cricket history.

⊙ MOST DISMISSALS: INNINGS/MATCHES/SERIES

The Sri Lanka record for the most dismissals in an innings is six, by Amal Silva (6ct) against India at the Sinhalese Sports Club Ground in Colombo in August 1985. He went on to achieve nine dismissals in the match and repeated the feat in the following Test (8ct, 1s) at the P. Sara Oval ground in Colombo to end the series with a record 22 dismissals to his name.

⊙ MOST CATCHES: INNINGS/MATCHES/SERIES

The Sri Lanka record for the most catches in an innings is four, a feat achieved on ten occasions. The record for the most catches in a match is seven, by Hashan Tillakaratne against New Zealand in Colombo in December 1992. Mahela Jayawardene holds the Sri Lanka record for the most catches in a series, with ten against Bangladesh in 2007.

⊙ MOST SUCCESSFUL CAPTAIN

Certainly the most barnstorming batsman Sri Lanka has ever produced, Sanath Jayasuriya is also the most successful Sri Lankan captain in history. In 38 Tests in charge of his country between 1999 and 2002 he led his side to 18 wins with a win percentage of 47.36 per cent.

LONGEST-SERVING CAPTAINS: TOP 10

Pos	Mat	Player (Span)
1	56	Arjuna Ranatunga (1989–99)
2	38	Sanath Jayasuriya (1999–2002)
3	28	Mahela Jayawardene (2006–09)
4	19	Duleep Mendis (1982–87)
5	18	Marvan Atapattu (2002–05)
6	14	Kumar Sangakkara (2009–)
7	11	Hashan Tillakaratne (1999–2004)
8	6	Aravinda de Silva (1991–99)
9	4	Bandula Warnapura (1982)
10	2	Samachandra de Silva (1983)
=	2	Ranjan Madugalle (1988)

WEST INDIES

Granted Test status in 1928 to become the fourth Test-playing nation, the West Indies enjoyed only sporadic success until the late 1970s and early '80s, when a mix of dashing stroke players and fearsome fast bowlers took them to the top of the world game. In recent years, however, the men from the Caribbean have struggled to recapture the glorious successes of those golden years.

⊙ HARMISON BLOWS THE WINDIES AWAY

It was a collapse of spectacular proportions. Trailing England by just 28 runs after the first innings in the First Test at Kingston, Jamaica, in March 2004, the West Indies capitulated to 47 all out in 25.3 overs, with Steve Harmison doing most of the damage for England, taking 7 for 12. It remains the lowest total in the islanders' history.

⊙ LARGEST VICTORIES

By an innings: by an innings and 336 runs against India at Kolkata in December 1958.
By runs: by 425 runs against England at Manchester in July 1976.
By wickets: by ten wickets on 22 occasions.

⊙ SMALLEST VICTORIES

By runs: by one run against Australia at Adelaide in January 1993.
By wickets: by one wicket on two occasions – against Australia at Bridgetown in March 1999 and against Pakistan at St John's in May 2000.

⊙ HEAVIEST DEFEATS

By an innings: by an innings and 283 runs against England at Leeds in May 2007.
By runs: by 382 runs against Australia at Sydney in February 1969.
By wickets: by ten wickets on 15 occasions.

⊙ SOBERS AND HUNTE LEAD THE WAY AT KINGSTON

Garfield Sobers's then world record score of 365 not out in the Third Test against Pakistan at Kingston, Jamaica, in February–March 1958, coupled with Conrad Hunte's innings of 260 (the pair added 446 for the second wicket), provided the platform for the West Indies' highest-ever total – 790 for 3 declared. It is one of four 700-plus scores by the islanders.

⊙ ALL-TIME GREAT: BRIAN LARA

No player since Don Bradman has had such an appetite for building big scores and few players have broken as many records during their career as Brian Lara. Twice the left-hander broke the record for the all-time highest score in Test cricket, first with a brilliant knock of 375 against England at St John's, Antigua, in April 1994 and then with a blistering 400 not out against the same opponents at the same venue almost exactly a decade later. He finished his 131-Test, 16-year career in 2006 as the leading run-scorer of all time (his tally of 11,912 runs has since been broken by Sachin Tendulkar) and as the holder of several West Indian records: the most hundreds (34) and the most scores of 50 plus (82).

⊙ THE "BLACK BRADMAN"

The first of the great black batsmen to emerge from the islands at a time when the West Indies team comprised mostly white players, George Headley performed such feats with the bat that he was dubbed the "Black Bradman". In 22 Tests for the islanders between 1930 and 1954 he scored 2,190 runs, including 10 centuries (with a highest score of 270 not out against England at Kingston, Jamaica, in March 1935), at an average of 60.83 – the highest by any West Indian batsman in history.

BATTING – MOST RUNS: TOP 10

Pos	Runs	Player (Span)
1	11,912	Brian Lara (1990–2006)
2	9,063	Shivnarine Chanderpaul (1994–2009)
3	8,540	Viv Richards (1974–91)
4	8,032	Garfield Sobers (1954–74)
5	7,558	Gordon Greenidge (1974–91)
6	7,515	Clive Lloyd (1966–85)
7	7,487	Desmond Haynes (1978–94)
8	6,373	Chris Gayle (2000–10)
9	6,227	Rohan Kanhai (1957–74)
10	5,949	Richie Richardson (1983–95)

⊙ THE MASTER BLASTER RUNS RIOT

Viv Richards was at his swaggering best during the West Indies'
3–0 series win over England in 1976. In seven innings during the
five-match series – he missed the Second Test at Lord's through
injury – the master blaster smashed three centuries and two
half-centuries (with a highest score of 291 at The Oval in the Fifth
Test) en route to amassing 829 runs at an average of 118.42. It
remains the highest series haul by any West Indian batsman.

RESULT SUMMARY

Opposition (Span)	Mat	Won	Lost	Tied	Draw	W/L	%W	%L	%D
Australia (1930–2009)	108	32	52	1	23	0.61	29.62	48.14	21.29
Bangladesh (2002–09)	6	3	2	0	1	1.50	50.00	33.33	16.66
England (1928–2009)	145	53	43	0	49	1.23	36.55	29.65	33.79
India (1948–2006)	82	30	11	0	41	2.72	36.58	13.41	50.00
New Zealand (1952–2008)	37	10	9	0	18	1.11	27.02	24.32	48.64
Pakistan (1958–2006)	44	14	15	0	15	0.93	31.81	34.09	34.09
South Africa (1992–2010)	25	3	16	0	6	0.18	12.00	64.00	24.00
Sri Lanka (1993–2010)	15	3	6	0	6	0.50	20.00	40.00	40.00
Zimbabwe (2000–03)	6	4	0	0	2	–	66.66	0.00	33.3

BOWLING – MOST WICKETS: TOP 10

Pos	Wkts	Player (Span)
1	519	Courtney Walsh (1984–2001)
2	405	Curtly Ambrose (1988–2000)
3	376	Malcolm Marshall (1978–91)
4	309	Lance Gibbs (1958–76)
5	259	Joel Garner (1977–87)
6	249	Michael Holding (1975–87)
7	235	Garfield Sobers (1954–74)
8	202	Andy Roberts (1974–83)
9	192	Wes Hall (1958–69)
10	161	Ian Bishop (1989–98)

⊙ WHISPERING DEATH DESTROYS ENGLAND

Nicknamed "Whispering Death" for his graceful, stealth-like
approach to the bowling crease and an effortless action that
produced deliveries at a blistering pace, Michael Holding was one of
the most feared bowlers of his day. In 60 Tests for the West Indies
between 1975 and 1987 he took 249 wickets, with his best
performance coming against England at The Oval in August 1976.
He took 8 for 92 in the first innings and 6 for 57 in the second: his
match haul of 14 for 149 is an all-time West Indies record.

⊙ BRIEF BUT MIGHTILY EFFECTIVE FOR LAWSON

After bursting on to the international scene in December 2002, with 6 for 3 in only his third Test match, against Bangladesh at Chittagong, followed by a career-best 7 for 78 against the all-conquering Australians the following May, Jermaine Lawson's career started to unravel. As the ICC started to question the legitimacy of his action, he struggled to hold a place in the West Indies line-up and by 2005 his international career was over. However, his 51 wickets in 13 Tests came at a strike-rate of a wicket every 46.3 deliveries – an all-time record for a West Indies bowler.

⊙ KEEPING IT TIGHT

Gerry Gomez was the most economical bowler in West Indies cricket history. In 29 Tests for the islanders between 1939 and 1954, his 5,236 deliveries of medium-pace bowling went for just 1.82 runs per over. Garfield Sobers holds the national record for the best economy rate in an innings: he produced a spell of 14-11-3-1 against New Zealand at Wellington in March 1956 – an economy rate of just 0.21 runs per over.

⊙ ALL-TIME GREAT: MALCOLM MARSHALL

Of the battery of world-class fast bowlers to have emerged from the Caribbean islands over the years, Malcolm Marshall was the best of them. Relatively short for a fast bowler, standing at just 5ft 9in, he made up for any lack of height with express pace and an ability to swing the ball both ways. In 81 Tests for the West Indies between 1978 and 1991 he took 376 wickets and set national records for: the best average (20.94); the best strike-rate in an innings (6.5 – against Pakistan at Faisalabad in November 1990, where his figures were 4.2-0-24-4); the most five-wicket hauls (22, shared with Curtly Ambrose and Courtney Walsh); the most ten-wicket match hauls (4); and the most wickets in a series (35, against England in 1988).

⊙ BUCKING THE TREND

Given that the golden years of cricket in the Caribbean were based on a fearsome, four-pronged pace attack, it may seem strange that the best bowling figures ever recorded by a West Indian bowler were produced by an off-spinner. In only his second Test match, against India at Port of Spain, Trinidad, in March 1971, 35-year-old Jack Noreiga took 9 for 95. It remains the only nine-wicket innings haul in West Indies cricket history.

⊙ MOST DISMISSALS: INNINGS/MATCHES/SERIES

The West Indies record for the most dismissals in an innings is seven, achieved by Ridley Jacobs (7ct) against Australia at Melbourne in December 2000. Jacobs went on to take a national record nine dismissals in the match (8ct, 1st), equalling previous performances by David Murray (9ct) against Australia at Melbourne in December 1981 and by Courtney Brown against England at Nottingham in August 1995. Murray also holds the record for the most dismissals in a series, 24 (22ct, 2st) against England in 1963.

⊙ MOST CATCHES: INNINGS/MATCHES/SERIES

The West Indies record for the most catches in an innings is four, a feat achieved on 11 occasions. The record for most catches in a match is six, by Garfield Sobers against England at Lord's in August 1973 and by Jimmy Adams against England at Kingston in February 1994. Brian Lara holds the national record for the most catches in a series with 13, a feat he achieved on two occasions (against England in 1997–98 and against India in 2006).

⊙ GOLDEN TIMES UNDER LLOYD

Blessed no doubt by having a myriad of world-class talent at his disposal, Clive Lloyd is the most successful captain in the West Indies' long cricket history. Between 1974 and 1985 he captained the islanders on 74 occasions, notching up 36 wins with a winning percentage of 48.64.

LONGEST-SERVING CAPTAINS: TOP 10

Pos	Mat	Player (Span)
1	74	Clive Lloyd (1974–85)
2	50	Viv Richards (1980–91)
3	47	Brian Lara (1997–2006)
4	39	Garfield Sobers (1965–72)
5	24	Richie Richardson (1992–95)
6	22	John Goddard (1948–57)
=	22	Carl Hooper (2001–02)
=	22	Courtney Walsh (1994–97)
9	20	Chris Gayle (2007–10)
10	18	Gerry Alexander (1958–60)

BANGLADESH

Test cricket's newest incumbents – they were granted Test status in 2000, to become the game's tenth Test-playing nation – Bangladesh have struggled to find their feet in the hotbed of the Test arena. In over 60 matches to date, the Tigers have won just three times: once against struggling Zimbabwe and twice against a severely weakened West Indies outfit.

RESULT SUMMARY

Opposition (Span)	Mat	Won	Lost	Tied	Draw	W/L	%W	%L	%D
Australia (2003–06)	4	0	4	0	0	0.00	0.00	100.00	0.00
England (2003–10)	8	0	8	0	0	0.00	0.00	100.00	0.00
India (2000–10)	7	0	6	0	1	0.00	0.00	85.71	14.28
New Zealand (2001–10)	9	0	8	0	1	0.00	0.00	88.88	11.12
Pakistan (2001–03)	6	0	6	0	0	0.00	0.00	100.00	0.00
South Africa (2002–08)	8	0	8	0	0	0.00	0.00	100.00	0.00
Sri Lanka (2001–09)	12	0	12	0	0	0.00	0.00	100.00	0.00
West Indies (2002–09)	6	2	3	0	1	0.66	33.33	50.00	16.66
Zimbabwe (2001–05)	8	1	4	0	3	0.25	12.50	50.00	37.50

⊙ ASHRAFUL SHOWS TIGERS THE WAY FORWARD

The youngest centurion in Test history (he was aged just 17 years and 61 days when he struck 114 on his debut against Sri Lanka at Colombo in September 2001), Mohammad Ashraful is one of the few good-news stories to have emerged from Bangladesh's well-documented struggles in the Test arena. The flamboyant right-hander has posted five centuries for his country – a national record – including 158 not out against India at Chittagong, the highest score by any Bangladesh batsman in the country's short Test history.

⊙ LEADING GLOVEMAN

A regular behind the stumps for Bangladesh following their introduction to Test cricket, Khaled Mashud holds the national record for the most dismissals with 87 (78ct, 9st) in 44 Tests between 2000 and 2007.

⊙ ALL-TIME GREAT: HABIBUL BASHAR

One of the few Bangladesh players of genuine Test quality, Habibul Bashar carried his side's batting in their early days as a Test-playing nation. The Tigers' longest-serving captain (he led them on 18 occasions between 2004 and 2007) and one of only two Bangladesh players to have played in 50 Tests (Mohammad Ashraful is the other), the right-hander (and former captain) holds the national record for the most runs (3,026) and for the most scores of 50 or over (27).

⊙ BANGLADESHI BOWLING BESTS

Renowned more as a talented, hard-hitting batsman, Shakib Al Hasan showed his true all-round potential when he took 7 for 36 against New Zealand at Chittagong in December 2008 with his slow left-arm spin bowling. They are the best figures in an innings ever recorded by a Bangladesh bowler. Another slow left-arm bowler, Enamul Haque Jr, holds the record for the best figures in a match: his 12 for 200 against Zimbabwe at Dhaka in January 2005 did much to ensure his country's first-ever series win (during which he took a national record 18 wickets).

⊙ LEFT-ARMER RAFIQUE LEADS THE WAY WITH THE BALL

A slow left-arm bowler who relied on nagging accuracy rather than an ability to spin the ball sharply, Mohammad Rafique was a mainstay of Bangladesh's bowling attack between 2000 and 2008. In 33 Tests for his country, he became the first, and to date only, Tigers bowler in history to claim 100 Test wickets, taking his 100th and final wicket (that of South Africa's Robin Peterson) in his last Test against South Africa at Chittagong in February 2008.

ZIMBABWE

Zimbabwe became the ninth Test-playing nation in 1992 and were perennial strugglers in the longest format of the game until the turn of the century when, although never strong, they were at least competitive. Zimbabwe's political problems, however, have led to their expulsion from the Test arena since January 2006, and the future for international cricket in the country looks bleak.

⊙ LEADING FROM THE FRONT

Dave Houghton, Zimbabwe's first Test captain, led by example in the Second Test against Sri Lanka at Bulawayo in October 1994. Coming to the crease with his side precariously placed on 5 for 2, the right-hander batted for over 11 hours and faced 541 balls en route to amassing 266 runs – the highest score ever made by a Zimbabwe batsman.

⊙ BEST BOWLING IN AN INNINGS/MATCH

A leg-spinner with the full repertoire, Paul Strang is Zimbabwe's second most prolific wicket-taker of all time with 70 Test wickets to his name in 24 Tests between 1994 and 2001. He holds the record for the best bowling figures in an innings: 8 for 109 against New Zealand at Bulawayo in September 2000. Adam Huckle holds the record for the best match figures: the leg-spinner took 11 for 255 against New Zealand at Bulawayo in September 1997.

RESULT SUMMARY

Opposition (Span)	Mat	Won	Lost	Tied	Draw	W/L	%W	%L	%D
Australia (1999–2003)	3	0	3	0	0	0.00	0.00	100.00	0.00
Bangladesh (2001–05)	8	4	1	0	3	4.00	50.00	12.50	37.50
England (1996–2003)	6	0	3	0	3	0.00	0.00	50.00	50.00
India (1992–2005)	11	2	7	0	2	0.28	18.18	63.63	18.18
New Zealand (1992–2005)	13	0	7	0	6	0.00	0.00	53.84	46.15
Pakistan (1993–2002)	14	2	8	0	4	0.25	14.28	57.14	28.57
South Africa (1995–2005)	7	0	6	0	1	0.00	0.00	85.71	14.28
Sri Lanka (1994–2004)	15	0	10	0	5	0.00	0.00	66.67	33.33
West Indies (2000–03)	6	0	4	0	2	0.00	0.00	66.67	33.33

TEST RECORDS: BY SERIES

As some rivalries in cricket stretch back a century or more, it stands to reason that some series carry more weight than others. Take the English summer of 2005. In May, England trudged off the field after beating Bangladesh by an innings and 261 runs at a sparsely populated Lord's; two months later, at the same venue, England's players buzzed with tension in the dressing-room as vast crowds desperate to watch the first day of the 2005 Ashes series packed the pavement outside. In short, for players and the public alike, some matches mean more than others. The following section looks at records on a series-by-series basis.

AUSTRALIA v ENGLAND

It is the oldest and the most eagerly anticipated rivalry in world cricket. England and Australia have been locking horns on a cricket pitch since 1877, and matches between the two countries have become the stuff of legend. Australia lead the way with 133 wins, to England's 102 (with 91 draws), and matches between the game's oldest rivals remain the highlight of the cricket calendar.

⊙ PROVING THEIR POINT

In 1938, with any hopes of regaining the Ashes already dashed, England went into the final Test at The Oval 1–0 down in the series and determined to prove a point. They had a plan: to bat the Australians into submission. England won the toss, batted and, over the next two-and-a-half days, ground out a mammoth 903 for 7, a then world record score and still the highest team total in Ashes history. England went on to win the match by an innings and 579 runs (the largest victory margin in Ashes history).

⊙ A HERCULEAN EFFORT FROM 22-YEAR-OLD HUTTON

The main architect of England's Ashes record 903 for 7 and subsequent innings-and-579-run victory over Australia at The Oval in 1938 was Len Hutton. The Yorkshire opener faced 847 balls and batted for 13 hours and 17 minutes to compile an innings of 364 – breaking Walter Hammond's world record score of 336 not out (broken by Garfield Sobers in 1958) and setting an all-time Ashes record.

⊙ CAPTAIN FANTASTIC

The most successful captain in Ashes history? Allan Border. The Queensland batsman reluctantly took over the Australian captaincy in 1984–85, but led the side with great distinction to the top of the world game. He captained Australia in 29 Tests against England over five series between 1985 and 1993, winning three of them and an Ashes record 13 matches.

⊙ MARSH TOPS DISMISSALS LIST

An ever-present behind the stumps for Australia for over a decade, Rod Marsh is the most successful wicketkeeper in Ashes history. The combative Western Australian took 141 catches – c. Marsh b. Lillee became a part of cricket folklore Down Under – and seven stumpings in 42 Ashes Tests between 1970 and 1983.

OVERALL SERIES RECORDS
(326 Tests between 1877 and 2011)

	W	L	T	D	W/L	%W	%L	%D
Australia	133	102	0	91	1.30	40.80	31.29	27.91
England	102	133	0	91	0.76	31.29	40.80	27.91

First match: 15–19 March 1877, Melbourne Cricket Ground

MOST RUNS: TOP 10

Pos	Runs	Player (Team, Span)
1	5,028	Donald Bradman (Australia, 1928–48)
2	3,636	Jack Hobbs (England, 1908–30)
3	3,548	Allan Border (Australia, 1978–93)
4	3,269	David Gower (England, 1978–91)
5	3,200	Steve Waugh (Australia, 1986–2003)
6	2,945	Geoffrey Boycott (England, 1964–81)
7	2,852	Walter Hammond (England, 1928–47)
8	2,741	Herbert Sutcliffe (England, 1924–34)
9	2,660	Clem Hill (Australia, 1896–1912)
10	2,644	John Edrich (England, 1964–75)

MOST WICKETS: TOP 10

Pos	Wkts	Player (Team, Span)
1	195	Shane Warne (Australia, 1993–2007)
2	167	Dennis Lillee (Australia, 1971–82)
3	157	Glenn McGrath (Australia, 1994–2007)
4	148	Ian Botham (England, 1977–89)
5	141	Hugh Trumble (Australia, 1890–1904)
6	128	Bob Willis (England, 1971–83)
7	115	Monty Noble (Australia, 1898–1909)
8	114	Ray Lindwall (Australia, 1946–59)
9	109	Wilfred Rhodes (England, 1899–1926)
10	106	S.F. Barnes (England, 1901–12)
=	106	Clarrie Grimmett (Australia, 1925–34)

⊙ BEST IN THE BUSINESS

In 37 Tests between 1928 and 1948, Donald Bradman terrorized English bowling attacks and set numerous Ashes records along the way. No other batsman in history has scored more runs in Ashes encounters (5,028), no batsman has recorded a higher career average (89.78) and no one has scored more Ashes centuries (19) – his nearest rival on the all-time Ashes centuries list is England's Jack Hobbs, with 12.

⊙ MAKING HAY AT THE TOP OF THE ORDER

The most productive partnership in all Tests between Australia and England is that of England's Jack Hobbs and Herbert Sutcliffe. The legendary opening pair combined to score 2,452 runs in 30 innings between 1924 and 1930 at an average of 84.55, with 11 century partnerships and nine half-century partnerships.

⊙ AUSTRALIA GET OFF TO THE WORST OF STARTS

It was the first match of five in the 1902 Ashes series, at Edgbaston, and a chance for England to avenge the crushing 4–1 series defeat they had suffered in Australia just two months earlier. England batted first and scored 376. Australia, embarrassingly, subsided to a sorry 36 all out – the lowest score in Ashes history. Amazingly, however, because it was only a three-day game, they managed to hold out for the draw, and went on to win the series 2–1.

⊙ PONSFORD AND BRADMAN DASH ENGLAND'S HOPES

The outcome of the 1934 Ashes series was still hanging in the balance when the two teams arrived for the Fifth and final Test at The Oval locked at 1–1, but by the end of the first day's play, thanks to stunning performances from Bill Ponsford (266) and Donald Bradman (244), there was only going to be one winner. The pair combined to add an Ashes record 451 runs for the second wicket to propel Australia to a mighty first-innings total of 701 all out and an eventual series-clinching 562-run victory.

⊙ CHAPPELL CLAIMS THE MOST CATCHES

The outstanding Australian batsman of his generation and a fine captain (he led his country to Ashes success in 1982–83), Greg Chappell is also the most successful fielder in all matches between England and Australia, taking 61 catches in 35 Ashes Tests between 1970 and 1983.

SOUTH AFRICA v ENGLAND

The first fixture between the two sides took place in March 1889, making this the second-oldest fixture in Test cricket. England enjoyed an early supremacy over South Africa, but matches in recent times, particularly since the Proteas' readmission to international cricket in 1992, have been much closer affairs with South Africa claiming 11 wins to England's ten.

⊙ BEST PARTNERSHIP

Having battled to escape with a draw in the First Test against South Africa in the 1947 series, Bill Edrich (189) and Denis Compton (208) ensured that any momentum gained continued to swing in England's favour in the Second Test at Lord's. The pair added 370 for the third wicket – the highest partnership in all Tests between the two countries – as England compiled a first-innings total of 554 en route to a ten-wicket victory and a 1–0 series lead.

⊙ BRILLIANT BARNES TOO GOOD FOR SOUTH AFRICA

If statistics alone can be proof of greatness, then S.F. Barnes was the best fast bowler England has ever produced and he was at his electrifying best against South Africa during England's 1913–14 tour when, playing on matting wickets, he was virtually unplayable. In the Second Test at Johannesburg, which England won by an innings and 12 runs, he produced match figures of 17 for 159 (a record in Tests between the two countries) and ended the series (despite missing the fifth and final Test match) with 49 wickets to his name (an all-time Test record for a five-match series).

⊙ SMITH IS MOST SUCCESSFUL CAPTAIN

Graeme Smith has come a long way since he first assumed the South African captaincy in the wake of his country's disastrous showing at the 2003 ICC World Cup and has led his country with distinction to this day. He is the most successful captain in South Africa–England Tests, leading his side to six wins in 18 matches between 2003 and 2010.

⊙ COMPTON'S MAGICAL SERIES

Denis Compton's battling 163 in the second innings of the First Test against South Africa at Trent Bridge in 1947 not only helped England save the match (the home side had been forced to follow on still 325 runs in arrears), but also changed the course of the series. England went on to win the five-match series 3–0 with Compton's fine form continuing: he hit 208 at Lord's in the Second Test, 115 at Old Trafford in the Third Test and 113 in the Fifth and final Test at The Oval. The Middlesex star's series haul of 753 runs (at an average of 94.12) is an all-time record in matches between the two countries.

⊙ LOHMANN RIPS THROUGH SOUTH AFRICA

The South African batsmen had no answer to George Lohmann on the matting wicket at the Old Wanderers ground in Johannesburg in March 1896. The right-arm fast-medium bowler, who was renowned for his accuracy, took 9 for 28 in South Africa's first innings as England went on to win the match by an innings and 197 runs. Lohmann's effort remains the best bowling performance in an innings in matches between the two sides.

OVERALL SERIES RECORDS
(138 Tests between 1889 and 2010)

	W	L	T	D	W/L	%W	%L	%D
South Africa	29	56	0	53	0.51	21.01	40.57	38.40
England	56	29	0	53	1.99	40.57	21.01	38.40

First match: 12–13 March 1889, Port Elizabeth

⊙ KICKING ENGLAND WHEN THEY WERE DOWN

Following the sudden resignation of Nasser Hussain as England captain after a drawn First Test at Edgbaston in 2003, South Africa piled more misery on to England when the two sides reconvened at Lord's for the Second Test. First they skittled out the home side for 173, then, led by captain Graeme Smith (259) and Gary Kirsten (108), they compiled 682 for 6 declared – the highest total in all matches between the two sides – en route to completing a convincing innings-and-92-run victory.

⊙ NEW CAPTAIN SMITH ANSWERS HIS CRITICS IN STYLE

In the first innings of the First Test against England at Edgbaston in July 2003, South Africa's Graeme Smith, in only his third Test as captain, did much to silence the doubters who thought that, at 22 years of age, he was both too young and too inexperienced to lead his country into a new golden age. The left-handed opener smashed 277 off 373 balls (including 35 fours) – the highest individual score in all matches between the two countries.

⊙ EDRICH FINALLY MASTERS THE SOUTH AFRICANS

Having scored a meagre 21 runs in his first five innings against South Africa on the 1938–39 tour, it could be argued that a battling 219 in the Fifth "timeless" Test at Durban saved Bill Edrich's career. He was full of confidence when South Africa toured England in 1947, hitting two half-centuries in the First Test, 189 in the Second Test at Lord's and a brilliant 191 in the Third Test at Old Trafford. In 12 innings against South Africa, Edrich scored 792 runs at an average of 72.00, the highest average of any player to have batted ten times or more in Tests between the two countries.

⊙ MOST DISMISSALS

A standout performer for South Africa for over a decade, and one of the finest wicketkeeper-batsmen in history, Mark Boucher holds the all-time record for the most dismissals in Test matches between England and South Africa. The East London-born keeper has claimed 105 dismissals (103 catches and two stumpings) in 25 Tests against England between 1998 and 2010.

⊙ MOST PRODUCTIVE PARTNERSHIP

The most productive partnership in all Tests between England and South Africa is that between Len Hutton and Cyril Washbrook. In 19 innings between 1947 and 1949, the pair combined to score 1,371 runs at an average of 80.64.

⊙ MOST CATCHES

A stalwart of the South Africa side who appeared in 42 consecutive Tests for his country between 1929 and 1949, Bruce Mitchell was a fine batsman (scoring 1,380 Test runs at an average of 51.11) and an excellent fielder. He holds the record for the most catches by a player in Tests between England and South Africa, with 43 in 30 Tests between 1929 and 1949.

MOST WICKETS: TOP 10

Pos	Wkts	Player (Team, Span)
1	91	Shaun Pollock (South Africa, 1995–2005)
2	86	Allan Donald (South Africa, 1994–2000)
3	83	S.F. Barnes (England, 1912–14)
4	75	Hugh Tayfield (South Africa, 1955–60)
5	72	Cyril Vincent (South Africa, 1927–35)
6	70	Makhaya Ntini (South Africa, 1998–2009)
7	69	Brian Statham (England, 1951–65)
8	68	Aubrey Faulkner (South Africa, 1906–24)
9	63	Trevor Goddard (South Africa, 1955–65)
10	60	Bert Vogler (South Africa, 1906–10)

MOST RUNS: TOP 10

Pos	Runs	Player (Team, Span)
1	2,732	Bruce Mitchell (South Africa, 1929–49)
2	2,287	Herbie Taylor (South Africa, 1912–31)
3	2,205	Denis Compton (England, 1947–57)
4	2,188	Walter Hammond (England, 1927–39)
5	2,037	Dudley Nourse (South Africa, 1935–51)
6	1,879	Jacques Kallis (South Africa, 1995–2010)
7	1,779	Graeme Smith (South Africa, 2003–10)
8	1,608	Gary Kirsten (South Africa, 1994–2003)
9	1,564	Len Hutton (England, 1938–51)
10	1,562	Jack Hobbs (England, 1910–29)

SOUTH AFRICA v AUSTRALIA

Australia hold a dominating lead in all Tests between the two countries, with 47 wins to South Africa's 18, but in recent times clashes between the two sides have been close affairs, with the series-winning side often considered the best team on the planet.

OVERALL SERIES RECORDS
(83 Tests between 1902 and 2009)

	W	L	T	D	W/L	%W	%L	%D
South Africa	18	47	0	18	0.38	21.69	56.63	21.69
Australia	47	18	0	18	2.61	56.63	21.69	21.69

First match: 11–14 October 1902, Johannesburg

⊙ CLASSY GRIMMETT LEAVES SOUTH AFRICA IN A SPIN

South Africa's batsmen continually failed to come to terms with Clarrie Grimmett's mastery of leg-spin bowling. In ten Tests against the South Africans, the spin wizard claimed 77 scalps (35.65 per cent of his Test victims), including 14 for 199 in the Fourth Test at Adelaide in January–February 1932 (a record match haul in Tests between the two countries) and a series record 44 wickets in the home series in 1935–36.

⊙ PROLIFIC PONTING AN ALL-ROUND RECORD-BREAKER

Ricky Ponting has enjoyed some great moments against South Africa. He is the leading run-scorer in all Tests between the two countries (2,030 runs), the most successful captain (eight wins) and a member (along with Matthew Hayden) of the most productive partnership. He also holds the record for the most catches, with 30 in 21 Tests between 1997 and 2009.

⊙ AUSTRALIAN BATSMEN FIND THEIR FORM

The Australians made a huge statement of intent in the opening Test of their 2001–02 tour to South Africa at Johannesburg. Having won the toss and elected to bat they put South Africa's bowlers to the sword, with Adam Gilchrist (204), Damien Martyn (133) and Matthew Hayden (122) all making hefty contributions as Australia amassed the highest-ever total in all Tests between the two countries – 652 for 7 declared. Australia went on to win the match by an innings and 360 runs.

⊙ SOUTH AFRICA DOWN AND OUT

Already 4–0 down in the series, the South African tourists had any urge to continue the fight knocked out of them as they returned to Melbourne for the Fifth and final Test against Australia in February 1932. And how it showed. After winning the toss and choosing to bat, they collapsed to a miserable 36 all out in a little under 90 minutes – the lowest-ever total in matches between the two sides. Australia went on to win the Test by an innings and 72 runs to complete a series whitewash.

⊙ BRILLIANT BOUCHER LEADS THE WAY

The most prolific wicketkeeper in history, Mark Boucher leads the dismissals list in Tests between Australia and South Africa. In 18 Tests against the Aussies between 2001 and 2009, the South Africa gloveman has claimed 61 dismissals, with 59 catches and two stumpings.

⊙ BEST PARTNERSHIP

When Greg Blewett joined Steve Waugh with Australia on 174 for 4, still 128 runs behind South Africa in the First Test at Johannesburg in February–March 1997, the home side would have felt very much as though they were still in the game. Not for long, however. Over the next day and a half the pair – Waugh (160), Blewett (214) – combined to add an Australia–South Africa Test-best partnership of 385 runs to help Australia to 628 for 8 declared and an eventual innings-and-196-run victory.

⊙ MOST PRODUCTIVE PARTNERSHIP

The most productive partnership in all Tests between South Africa and Australia is that of Matthew Hayden and Ricky Ponting. The pair combined to score 1,136 runs in 14 innings between 2001 and 2009 at an average of 87.38.

⊙ MOST SUCCESSFUL CAPTAIN

The most successful Test captain of all time (with 46 wins), Ricky Ponting has enjoyed considerable success against South Africa. In 12 Tests against them between 2005 and 2009, the Tasmanian has led his side to a record eight wins.

⊙ THE DON'S BATTING MASTERCLASS

Having already posted scores of 226 and 112 in his first two Tests against South Africa, Donald Bradman reserved his best performance of the 1931–32 series for the Fourth Test at Adelaide, hitting a magnificent unbeaten 299 – the highest individual score in all matches between the two countries. Ironically, he was left stranded after running out No. 11 Pud Thurlow in a scrambled, and ultimately misguided, attempt to reach 300.

⊙ HARVEY'S HEROICS IN VAIN IN DRAWN SERIES

An electrifying batsman who thrilled crowds with his stunning strokeplay and frustrated opponents with his seemingly limitless powers of concentration, Neil Harvey was at his best during the scintillating 2–2 series draw against South Africa in 1952–53. The left-hander hit four centuries and three half-centuries (with a highest score of 205 in the Fifth Test at Melbourne) to end the series with 834 runs at an average of 92.66. His tally remains the highest series haul by any batsman in all Tests between the two countries. He also holds the record for the highest batting average of all batsmen to have batted in at least ten innings in matches between Australia and South Africa, scoring 1,625 runs at an average of 81.25 in 23 innings against South Africa between 1949 and 1958.

⦿ JOHNSON'S RECORD-BREAKING PERFORMANCE

Mitchell Johnson produced one of the most devastating spells of fast bowling in recent times in the First Test against South Africa at Perth in December 2008, taking five wickets for two runs in 21 balls to end with figures of 8 for 61 – the best in all matches between the two countries. His record-breaking efforts were all in vain, however, as the Proteas rallied to win the match by six wickets.

MOST RUNS: TOP 10

Pos	Runs	Player (Team, Span)
1	2,030	R.T. Ponting (Australia, 1997–2009)
2	1,625	R.N. Harvey (Australia, 1949–58)
3	1,581	J.H. Kallis (South Africa, 1997–2009)
4	1,486	M.L. Hayden (Australia, 1994–2009)
5	1,453	R.G. Pollock (South Africa, 1963–70)
6	1,149	E.J. Barlow (South Africa, 1963–70)
7	1,147	S.R. Waugh (Australia, 1994–2002)
8	1,135	M.E. Waugh (Australia, 1993–2002)
9	1,134	G. Kirsten (South Africa, 1993–2002)
10	1,090	T.L. Goddard (South Africa, 1957–70)

MOST WICKETS: TOP 10

Pos	Player (Team, Span)	Wickets
1	S.K. Warne (Australia, 1993–2006)	130
2	C.V. Grimmett (Australia, 1931–36)	77
3	H.J. Tayfield (South Africa, 1949–58)	64
4	M. Ntini (South Africa, 2001–09)	58
5	G.D. McGrath (Australia, 1994–2006)	57
6	T.L. Goddard (South Africa, 1957–70)	53
=	A.A. Donald (South Africa, 1993–2002)	53
8	R. Benaud (Australia, 1952–64)	52
=	P.M. Pollock (South Africa, 1963–70)	52
10	W.J. Whitty (Australia, 1910–12)	50
=	B. Lee (Australia, 2001–08)	50

ENGLAND v WEST INDIES

After the Ashes, this is the second most contested fixture in international cricket. Fortunes have wavered for both England and the West Indies since the two countries played a Test match for the first time in 1928, with both sides enjoying periods of dominance, none more extreme than when the West Indies went unbeaten in 29 straight Tests against England between June 1976 and February 1990.

⊙ LARA'S LOVE-IN AT ANTIGUA

Brian Lara seemed to reserve his greatest performances for matches against England at St John's, Antigua. In April 1994 he plundered the England attack for a then world record 375. A decade later he was at it again, this time amassing a new all-time Test record score of 400 not out (off 582 balls) with 43 fours and four sixes.

⊙ MURRAY THE MASTER BEHIND THE STUMPS

A regular behind the stumps for the West Indies for 17 years between 1963 and 1980, Deryck Murray holds the record for the most dismissals in Tests between England and the West Indies. In 28 matches against England, the Trinidad keeper claimed 94 scalps (90 catches and four stumpings).

⊙ MOST SUCCESSFUL CAPTAIN

Viv Richards had the good fortune to captain the West Indies during the islanders' golden era, and remains the most successful captain in Test matches between the two countries, leading his side to 13 wins in 19 Tests between 1980 and 1991.

⊙ MOST CATCHES

Brian Lara not only terrorized England with the bat between 1994 and 2004, he also caused havoc in the field. In 30 Tests against the English, the Trinidad star snared 45 catches, an all-time record for any player in Tests between the two countries.

⊙ MOST PRODUCTIVE PARTNERSHIP

The most productive partnership in all Tests between England and the West Indies is that between Gordon Greenidge and Desmond Haynes, who combined to score 1,862 runs in 37 innings at an average of 51.72.

⊙ THE MASTER BLASTER'S GOLDEN SUMMER

Viv Richards established himself as a player of true international class during the West Indies' 1976 tour to England. He hit 232 in the First Test at Trent Bridge, 135 in the Third Test at Old Trafford (after missing the Second Test through injury) and a magnificent 291 in the Fifth and final Test at The Oval. His series haul of 829 runs (at an average of 118.42) remains an all-time high in all matches between the two countries.

OVERALL SERIES RECORDS
(145 Tests between 1928 and 2009)

	W	L	T	D	W/L	%W	%L	%D
England	43	53	0	49	0.81	29.66	36.55	33.79
West Indies	53	43	0	49	1.23	36.55	29.66	33.79

First match: 23–6 June 1928, Lord's

⊙ COWDREY AND MAY RESCUE ENGLAND WITH RECORD-BREAKING PARTNERSHIP

With England trailing the West Indies by a mighty 288 runs after the completion of the first innings of the First Test at Edgbaston in May–June 1957, Colin Cowdrey and Peter May came to the rescue when their country truly needed them. The pair added a record 411 runs for the fourth wicket to lead England to 583 for 4 declared and the eventual safety of a draw.

⊙ HUTTON TOPS THE AVERAGES

One of the finest batsmen Test cricket has produced, Len Hutton enjoyed some particularly good times against the West Indies. In 13 matches against the islanders he hit five centuries – with a highest score of 202 not out at The Oval in August 1950 – and amassed 1,661 runs at an average of 79.09, the highest of any player to have batted in ten innings in matches between England and the West Indies.

⊙ WHISPERING DEATH MAKES HIS DEADLY MARK

Nicknamed "Whispering Death" because of his stealth-like approach to the bowling crease, Michael Holding truly found his stride in the Fifth Test against England at The Oval in August 1976. The Jamaican paceman took 8 for 92 in the first innings and 6 for 57 in the second to end up with match figures of 14 for 149: an all-time West Indian record and a record in all Tests between England and the West Indies.

⊙ ENGLAND PROSPER IN KINGSTON

With the 1929–30 series locked at 1–1, it was decided that the Fourth and final Test match, at Kingston, Jamaica, should be a timeless one. England won the toss, elected to bat and, led by Andy Sandham's 325, batted themselves into an impregnable position, amassing 849 all out. The score remains the highest total in all matches between the two countries, but it wasn't enough to win the match. After rain on days eight and nine prevented any further play, the two teams agreed on a draw.

⊙ MARSHALL PRODUCES HIS MENACING BEST

The sheer pace and consistent excellence that became the trademark of Malcolm Marshall's career proved too much for England's batsmen during the West Indies' comprehensive 4–0 series win in 1988. Using his unorthodox, open-chested action to swing the ball both ways at frightening pace, Marshall took 35 wickets in the series (an all-time record in Tests between the two countries) with a best of 7 for 22 in the Third Test at Old Trafford.

⊙ AMBROSE THE DESTROYER

English batsmen could find few answers to the hostile pace and bounce of Curtly Ambrose over a 12-year period between 1988 and 2000. In 34 Tests against England, the 6ft 7in Antiguan took 164 wickets (40.49 per cent of his career Test wicket haul) with a best of 8 for 45 (at Bridgetown, Barbados, in April 1990). Both are all-time records in Test matches between the two countries.

⊙ SORRY ENGLAND CAPITULATE IN TRINIDAD

Set just 194 runs to win the Third Test of the 1993–94 series at Port of Spain, Trinidad, England collapsed in spectacular and record-breaking style. The tone was set when they lost captain Michael Atherton to the first ball of the innings. Just 19.1 overs later, they had been dismissed for a paltry 46 all out – the lowest score in England–West Indies matches – with Curtly Ambrose (6 for 24) the chief destroyer.

MOST WICKETS: TOP 10

Pos	Wkts	Player (Team, Span)
1	164	Curtly Ambrose (West Indies, 1988–2000)
2	145	Courtney Walsh (West Indies, 1986–2000)
3	127	Malcolm Marshall (West Indies, 1980–91)
4	102	Garfield Sobers (West Indies, 1954–74)
5	100	Lance Gibbs (West Indies, 1963–74)
6	96	Michael Holding (West Indies, 1976–86)
7	92	Joel Garner (West Indies, 1980–86)
8	86	Fred Trueman (England, 1954–63)
9	80	Sonny Ramadhin (West Indies, 1950–60)
10	72	John Snow (England, 1966–76)

MOST RUNS: TOP 10

Pos	Runs	Player (Team, Span)
1	3,214	Garfield Sobers (West Indies, 1954–74)
2	2,983	Brian Lara (West Indies, 1994–2004)
3	2,869	Viv Richards (West Indies, 1976–91)
4	2,392	Desmond Haynes (West Indies, 1980–94)
5	2,318	Gordon Greenidge (West Indies, 1976–90)
6	2,267	Rohan Kanhai (West Indies, 1957–74)
7	2,205	Geoffrey Boycott (England, 1966–81)
8	2,197	Graham Gooch (England, 1980–91)
9	2,124	Shivnarine Chanderpaul (West Indies, 1994–2009)
10	2,120	Clive Lloyd (West Indies, 1968–84)

NEW ZEALAND v ENGLAND

It took New Zealand 47 Test matches more than 48 years before they finally managed to record their first-ever victory over England – at Wellington in February 1978 – but, helped by the emergence of several players of true international class, matches between the two countries have been more closely fought encounters in recent years.

⊙ MOST PRODUCTIVE PARTNERSHIP

The most productive partnership in all Tests between England and New Zealand is that between Michael Atherton and Alec Stewart. The England opening pair combined to score 809 runs in 14 innings at an average of 57.78 (with a highest partnership of 182 runs in the First Test at Auckland in January 1997).

⊙ STARTING AS YOU MEAN TO GO ON

There is no better time to make a statement of intent than in the first innings of the opening Test of a series and, in February 1975 at Auckland, England, recently arrived in New Zealand licking their wounds following a 4–1 thumping in the Ashes series, did just that. Helped by superb innings from Keith Fletcher (216) and captain Mike Denness (181), they compiled 593 for 6 declared – the highest innings total in all matches between the two countries – en route to winning the match by an innings and 83 runs.

⊙ LOCK'S SPELL IN THE LIMELIGHT

An aggressive left-arm spinner who for the most part had to play second fiddle to Jim Laker throughout his 49-Test match career, Tony Lock enjoyed a spell in the limelight against New Zealand in 1958. The Surrey left-arm spinner took 34 wickets in the series (with three five-wicket hauls and a best return of 7 for 35 in the Fourth Test at Old Trafford). No bowler has taken more wickets in an England–New Zealand series.

⊙ HAPPY DAYS FOR VAUGHAN

Michael Vaughan is the most successful captain in the history of Test cricket between England and New Zealand. The Yorkshire star led England to six wins over the Kiwis in eight Tests between 2004 and 2008.

⊙ MOST CATCHES

One of the most prolific slip catchers Test cricket has ever seen, Stephen Fleming has bagged more catches in England–New Zealand Test matches than any other player. The former Kiwi captain took 33 catches in 19 Tests against England between 1994 and 2008.

OVERALL SERIES RECORDS
(94 Tests between 1930 and 2008)

	W	L	T	D	W/L	%W	%L	%D
New Zealand	8	45	0	41	0.17	8.51	47.87	43.62
England	45	8	0	41	5.62	47.87	8.51	43.62

First match: 10–13 January 1930, Christchurch

⊙ THE EDRICH AND BARRINGTON SHOW

Already 2–0 up in the 1965 series going into the Third Test at Headingley in July 1965, England were able to build on their advantage over New Zealand thanks to the batting of John Edrich (310 not out) and Ken Barrington (163). Coming together in the first innings with the score on 13 for 1, the pair added 369 for the second wicket – an all-time record partnership in matches between the two countries – to propel England to a first-innings total of 546 for 4 declared and an eventual innings-and-187-run victory.

⊙ THE MOST SUCCESSFUL KEEPER? THAT'S PARORE

An able performer with the bat and, arguably, the most consistent wicketkeeper in world cricket in the 1990s, Adam Parore claimed more dismissals in England–New Zealand Test matches than any other keeper in history. In 15 matches against England between 1990 and 2002, the Auckland gloveman bagged 46 scalps (45 catches and one stumping).

⊙ DEADLY DEREK STRIKES AGAIN

Nicknamed "Deadly" by his team-mates because of his effectiveness on rain-affected pitches, Derek Underwood lived up to his reputation in the First Test match against New Zealand at Christchurch in February 1971. On a damp wicket, he took 6 for 12 in the first innings and 6 for 85 in the second to lead England to an eight-wicket victory. His match haul of 12 for 97 is an all-time record in matches between the two countries.

⊙ KIWIS OUT OF THEIR DEPTH

Early matches between England and New Zealand were a sorry mismatch and the Kiwis hit an all-time low in the Second Test of the 1954–55 series at Auckland. Trailing England by 46 runs after the completion of the first innings, they crashed to the lowest score in Test history: a miserable 26 all out in 27 overs.

⊙ UNDERWOOD SPINS ENGLAND TO A COMPREHENSIVE VICTORY

England's most successful spin bowler of all time, Derek Underwood produced a match-winning performance of star quality in the First Test against New Zealand at Lord's in July 1969. With New Zealand set an improbable 362 runs to win, the Kent left-arm spinner took 7 for 32 off 31 overs to propel England to a 230-run victory. They are the best single-innings figures in England–New Zealand Tests.

⊙ CLASSY HAMMOND THE PICK OF THE CROP

One of Test cricket's all-time great batsmen, Walter Hammond flourished against all opponents in the Test arena, but particularly against New Zealand. In the Second Test against the Kiwis in Auckland in March–April 1933, he struck a then world record score of 336 not out (still the highest individual score in all matches between the two countries), an innings that included ten sixes (a world record that stood for 63 years). He ended the series with 563 runs (another all-time high in England–New Zealand Tests) and finished his Test career averaging 112.77 against New Zealand (the highest average of any player to have completed ten or more innings in matches between the two countries).

MOST RUNS: TOP 10

Pos	Runs	Player (Team, Span)
1	1,518	John Wright (New Zealand, 1978–92)
2	1,421	Martin Crowe (New Zealand, 1983–94)
3	1,229	Stephen Fleming (New Zealand, 1994–2008)
4	1,148	Graham Gooch (England, 1978–94)
5	1,145	Alec Stewart (England, 1990–99)
6	1,143	Bev Congdon (New Zealand, 1965–78)
7	1,133	Colin Cowdrey (England, 1955–71)
8	1,088	Michael Atherton (England, 1990–99)
9	1,051	David Gower (England, 1978–86)
10	1,049	Bert Sutcliffe (New Zealand, 1947–65)

MOST WICKETS: TOP 10

Pos	Wkts	Player (Team, Span)
1	97	Richard Hadlee (New Zealand, 1973–90)
2	64	Ian Botham (England, 1978–92)
3	60	Bob Willis (England, 1971–84)
4	48	Richard Collinge (New Zealand, 1965–78)
=	48	Derek Underwood (England, 1969–75)
6	47	Tony Lock (England, 1958–59)
=	47	Chris Cairns (New Zealand, 1992–2004)
=	47	Andrew Caddick (England, 1997–2002)
9	45	Daniel Vettori (New Zealand, 1997–2008)
10	41	Ryan Sidebottom (England, 2008)

AUSTRALIA v WEST INDIES

This is the sixth-oldest fixture in international cricket and, over the years, one of the most closely contested. Australia lead the way with 52 wins to the West Indies' 32 and, in recent times, have enjoyed a period of dominance over the islanders, but that has not always been the case.

⊙ WALTERS'S WEST INDIAN LOVE AFFAIR

Renowned as much for his off-the-field antics as for his skills on a cricket pitch, Doug Walters liked nothing more than a battle and reserved some of his best performances for matches against the West Indies fast bowlers. In nine matches against the islanders between 1968 and 1973, the New South Wales stroke player hit six centuries (with a highest score of 242 in the Fifth Test at Sydney in February 1969) and scored 1,196 runs at an average of 92.00 – the highest of any player to have completed ten innings or more in matches between the two countries.

⊙ WEST INDIES CRASH TO A RECORD-BREAKING LOW IN CRUSHING DEFEAT

The golden years of West Indian dominance seemed like a distant memory in the First Test of the 1999 series against Australia at Port of Spain, Trinidad. Set 364 runs to win the opening rubber, the West Indies crashed in spectacular style to 51 all out in a paltry 19.1 overs and a crushing 312-run defeat. It is the lowest team total in all Tests between the two countries.

⊙ CAPTAIN LLOYD LEADS THE WAY

Clive Lloyd is the most successful of all captains in the history of Test matches between Australia and the West Indies. In 22 Tests against Australia between 1975 and 1985, Lloyd led the islanders to 12 victories.

⊙ LAWRY AND SIMPSON DIG DEEP

Having lost two of the first three matches of the 1964–65 series against the West Indies, Australia needed to show considerably more fight when the two teams arrived at Bridgetown, Barbados, for the Fourth Test in May 1965. And Bill Lawry (210) and captain Bobby Simpson (201) did just that, putting on 382 runs for the opening wicket – the best partnership in the history of Australia–West Indies Tests. Unfortunately for the tourists, the West Indies held out for a draw to secure a series victory.

⊙ BOWING OUT IN RECORD-BREAKING STYLE

In June 1955 Australia held an unassailable 2–0 lead going into the Fifth and final Test at Kingston, Jamaica, and with the series already in the bag, and the pressure off, the tourists put on a show. After watching the home side compile a steady 357 all out, five Australian batsmen passed three figures as they amassed a mighty 758 for 8 declared (the highest total in all Tests between the two sides) on the way to an innings-and-82-run victory.

⊙ MOST PRODUCTIVE PARTNERSHIP

The most productive partnership in all Tests between Australia and the West Indies is that of Gordon Greenidge and Desmond Haynes. The legendary opening batsmen combined to score 2,252 runs in 48 innings between 1978 and 1991 at an average of 53.61.

⊙ LONE DEFIANCE FROM WALCOTT

Rarely has a player prospered so much in a losing cause. Australia may have eased to a 3–0 victory over the West Indies in the 1954–55 series in the Caribbean, but they did so despite the best efforts of Clyde Walcott. The Bajan right-hander hit five centuries and two half-centuries (with a highest score of 155 in the Fifth Test at Kingston, Jamaica) to end the series with 827 runs at an average of 82.70. It remains the highest series run haul by any batsman in the history of Australia–West Indies matches.

⊙ MOST CATCHES

The possessor of one of the safest pairs of hands in Test history, Mark Waugh holds the record for the most catches in Test matches between Australia and the West Indies: the younger of the Waugh twins took 45 catches in 28 Test matches against the islanders between 1991 and 2001.

⊙ McKENZIE MAKES THE MOST OF HELPFUL CONDITIONS

Garth McKenzie took full advantage of both the bitterly cold Boxing Day conditions and the green tinge of the Melbourne wicket in the Second Test against the West Indies in December 1968. The Western Australian fast bowler took 8 for 71 – the best single-innings figures by any bowler in Australia–West Indies Tests – to help his side to an innings-and-30-run victory.

⊙ TRIO SHARE RECORD FOR MOST WICKETS IN A SERIES

Three bowlers hold the record for the most wickets in a series between Australia and the West Indies with 33: Clarrie Grimmett in Australia's 4–1 series victory in the Caribbean in 1930–31; Alan Davidson, in Australia's 2–1 home series win in 1960–61; and Curtly Ambrose, in the West Indies 2–1 series win in Australia in 1992–93.

⊙ LARA MAKES A NAME FOR HIMSELF

It was in the Third Test at Sydney, in January 1993, that Brian Lara announced himself to the world as a player of exceptional talent. With the West Indies under intense pressure following Australia's first-innings total of 503 for 9 declared, the Trinidad star produced a batting display of breathtaking quality, facing 372 balls and hitting 38 fours en route to compiling a magnificent 277 – the highest individual score in all matches between the two countries.

MOST RUNS: TOP 10

Pos	Runs	Player (Team, Span)
1	2,815	Brian Lara (West Indies, 1992–2005)
2	2,266	Viv Richards (West Indies, 1975–91)
3	2,233	Desmond Haynes (West Indies, 1978–93)
4	2,211	Clive Lloyd (West Indies, 1968–85)
5	2,192	Steve Waugh (Australia, 1988–2003)
6	2,175	Richie Richardson (West Indies, 1984–95)
7	2,052	Allan Border (Australia, 1979–93)
8	1,858	Mark Waugh (Australia, 1991–2001)
9	1,831	Ricky Ponting (Australia, 1996–2009)
10	1,819	Gordon Greenidge (West Indies, 1975–91)

OVERALL SERIES RECORDS
(108 Tests between 1930 and 2009)

	W	L	T	D	W/L	%W	%L	%D
Australia	52	32	1	23	1.62	48.15	29.63	21.30*
West Indies	32	52	1	23	0.61	29.63	48.15	21.30*

First match: 12–16 December 1930, Adelaide
One match tied

MOST WICKETS: TOP 10

Pos	Wkts	Player (Team, Span)
1	135	Courtney Walsh (West Indies, 1984–2001)
2	128	Curtly Ambrose (West Indies, 1988–99)
3	110	Glenn McGrath (Australia, 1995–2005)
4	103	Lance Gibbs (West Indies, 1961–76)
5	89	Joel Garner (West Indies, 1978–85)
6	87	Malcolm Marshall (West Indies, 1984–91)
7	76	Michael Holding (West Indies, 1975–85)
8	65	Shane Warne (Australia, 1992–2005)
9	64	Brett Lee (Australia, 2000–08)
10	62	Jeff Thomson (Australia, 1975–82)

⊙ BIG MERV BATTERS THE WINDIES AT PERTH

A lion-hearted fast bowler who played a major role in helping
Australia to climb to the top of world cricket, Merv Hughes was at
his menacing best in the Second Test against the West Indies at
Perth in December 1988. He took 5 for 130 in the first innings and
a magnificent 8 for 87 in the second to propel his side to a 169-run
victory. His match figures of 13 for 217 are the best by any bowler in
all Test matches between the two countries.

⊙ MOST DISMISSALS

Jeff Dujon heads the list of most successful wicketkeepers in
matches between Australia and the West Indies. The Jamaican
keeper claimed 86 scalps (85 catches and one stumping) in 23
matches against Australia between 1981 and 1991.

NEW ZEALAND v SOUTH AFRICA

A combination of New Zealand's geographical isolation and South Africa's ostracism from world cricket meant that Test matches between the two countries were few and far between for decades following the sides' first meeting in 1932. In recent times, however, they have met on a more regular basis and South Africa have dominated the encounters, winning 11 out of 18 Tests since 1995.

OVERALL SERIES RECORDS
(35 Tests between 1932 and 2007)

	W	L	T	D	W/L	%W	%L	%D
New Zealand	4	20	0	11	0.20	11.43	57.14	31.43
South Africa	20	4	0	11	5.00	57.14	11.43	31.43

First match: 27 February–1 March 1932, Christchurch, New Zealand

⊙ AMLA AND KALLIS CONQUER BATTING DEMONS IN JOHANNESBURG

After 22 wickets had fallen over the first day-and-a-half of the First Test between South Africa and New Zealand at Johannesburg in November 2007, Hashim Amla (176 not out) and Jacques Kallis (186) finally made batting look easy. The pair added 330 for the third wicket – an all-time high in Tests between the two countries – to help South Africa to a second-innings total of 422 for 3 declared and an eventual 358-run victory. Amla and Kallis have also enjoyed the most productive partnership in South Africa–New Zealand Tests, combining to score 752 runs in five innings at an average of 150.40.

⊙ WICKETKEEPER WAITE LEADS THE WAY

The best wicketkeeper in South Africa's history until the arrival of Mark Boucher in the 1990s, and the first South African player to win 50 caps, Johnny Waite is the most successful keeper in the history of Test matches between South Africa and New Zealand. In 15 Tests against the Kiwis between 1953 and 1964, he claimed 56 dismissals, with 47 catches and ten stumpings.

⊙ GOOFY BY NAME BUT NOT BY NATURE

A 6ft 5in fast bowler who relied more on hard work than on natural ability, Godfrey "Goofy" Lawrence appeared in only five Test matches for South Africa, but he more than made his mark in the second innings of the Second Test against New Zealand at Johannesburg in December 1961, taking 8 for 53 – the best single-innings figures in all Tests between South Africa and New Zealand. Unfortunately for Lawrence and South Africa, his performance did not turn out to be a match-winning one: the game petered out into a bore draw. Lawrence ended the series with 28 wickets to his name – another record in Tests between the two countries – but, owing to South Africa's limited Test schedule, never played for his country again.

⊙ MOST SUCCESSFUL CAPTAIN

Two South African captains have led their side to a record five wins over New Zealand: Jack Cheetham, in seven Tests between 1953 and 1954; and Graeme Smith, in eight Tests between 2004 and 2007.

⊙ MARVELLOUS MARTIN LEADS KIWIS TO MEMORABLE VICTORY

Chris Martin was a key figure for his country as New Zealand secured only their fourth-ever victory over South Africa, in the Second Test at Auckland in March 2004. The Kiwi paceman took 6 for 76 in the first innings and 5 for 104 in the second to help his side to a nine-wicket victory. His match haul of 11 for 180 is the best in all Tests between the two sides.

⊙ REID LEADS BY EXAMPLE

John Reid was the star of the show as New Zealand fought back to claim a 2–2 draw in the five-match series in South Africa in 1961–62. The New Zealand captain led from the front, hitting a total of four half-centuries and a century (142 in the Fourth Test at Johannesburg) to end the series with 546 runs – an all-time high in series between the two countries – at an average of 60.66

⊙ CULLINAN PROSPERS AGAINST NEW ZEALAND

Daryll Cullinan was the main beneficiary of Dion Nash's dubious decision to put South Africa in to bat in the First Test at Auckland in February–March 1999. The elegant No. 4 batsman put New Zealand's bowlers to the sword, hitting an unbeaten 275 (off 490 balls with 27 fours and two sixes), which is not only the highest individual score in matches between the two countries but also the highest score by a South African in Test cricket. Cullinan also holds the record for the highest average by any batsman to have completed ten or more innings in New Zealand–South Africa Tests: he scored 823 runs in 16 innings against New Zealand between 1994 and 2000 at an average of 68.58.

⊙ SOUTH AFRICA BENEFIT FROM POOR CAPTAIN'S CHOICE

South Africa's batsmen made New Zealand captain Dion Nash's decision to bowl first in the First Test at Auckland in February–March 1999 look like one of Test cricket's more regrettable choices when they put on 621 for 5 over the first two-and a-half days – the highest score in all Tests between the two countries. Fortunately for Nash, South Africa's bowlers also struggled on the lifeless pitch and the match ended in a draw.

MOST RUNS: TOP 10

Pos	Runs	Player (Team, Span)
1	1,356	Jacques Kallis (South Africa, 1999–2007)
2	1,100	Jackie McGlew (South Africa, 1953–62)
3	1,072	Stephen Fleming (New Zealand, 1994–2007)
4	951	Gary Kirsten (South Africa, 1994–2004)
5	914	John Reid (New Zealand, 1953–64)
6	823	Darryl Cullinan (South Africa, 1994–2000)
7	790	Herschelle Gibbs (South Africa, 1999–2007)
8	643	John Waite (South Africa, 1953–64)
9	625	Eddie Barlow (South Africa, 1961–64)
10	572	Roy McLean (South Africa, 1953–62)

⊙ NEW ZEALAND BATSMEN THROW AWAY SOLID POSITION

Having seen South Africa struggle to 243 all out on a damp wicket at Johannesburg in the Fourth Test of the 1953–54 series, New Zealand, 2–0 down in the series, would have felt confident of getting something out of the game. Instead, the wheels fell off in spectacular style: the Kiwis slipped to 79 all out – the lowest score in Tests between the two countries – and went on to lose the match by nine wickets.

MOST WICKETS: TOP 10

Pos	Wkts	Player (Team, Span)
1	46	Makhaya Ntini (South Africa, 2000–07)
2	44	Chris Martin (New Zealand, 2000–07)
3	43	Shaun Pollock (South Africa, 1999–2006)
4	37	John Reid (New Zealand, 1953–64)
5	36	Dale Steyn (South Africa, 2006–07)
6	33	Neil Adcock (South Africa, 1953–62)
7	32	Peter Pollock (South Africa, 1961–64)
8	31	Hugh Tayfield (South Africa, 1953–54)
9	29	Frank Cameron (New Zealand, 1961–64)
10	28	Goofy Lawrence (South Africa, 1961–62)

⊙ MOST CATCHES

Jacques Kallis, perhaps the most underrated all-rounder in Test history, is the leading fielder in Tests between South Africa and New Zealand. In 14 Tests against the Blackcaps between 1999 and 2007, the all-rounder has taken 14 catches.

ENGLAND v INDIA

Since the fixture was first contested in 1932, England have enjoyed the upper hand against India in home Test matches (winning 23 of the 48 matches played and losing just five), but contests on the slow, low, spin-friendly surfaces of the subcontinent have proved to be altogether closer affairs, with India leading the way with 14 wins to England's 11.

OVERALL SERIES RECORDS
(99 Tests between 1932 and 2008)

	W	L	T	D	W/L	%W	%L	%D
England	34	19	0	46	1.78	34.34	19.19	46.46
India	19	34	0	46	0.55	19.19	34.34	46.46

First match: 25–28 June 1932, Lord's

⊙ MOST SUCCESSFUL CAPTAINS
The most wins recorded by a captain in Test matches between England and India is three, a feat achieved by no fewer than eight players: Brian Close (England) in three Tests in 1967; Mike Denness (England) in three Tests in 1974; Tony Grieg (England) in five Tests between 1976 and 1977; Len Hutton (England) in four Tests in 1952; Douglas Jardine (England) in four Tests between 1932 and 1934; Peter May (England) in three Tests in 1959; Mohammad Azharuddin (India) in nine Tests between 1990 and 1996; and Ajit Wadekar (India) in 11 Tests between 1971 and 1974

⊙ GAVASKAR PROVES HIS WORTH IN THE FIELD
Not only is Sunil Gavaskar the leading run-scorer in Test matches between England and India (with 2,483 runs), he is also the most successful fielder. In 38 Tests against England between 1971 and 1986, the diminutive opening batsman took a record 35 catches.

⊙ THE LEADING WICKETKEEPER

Arguably the most complete wicketkeeper England has ever produced and without doubt the best when standing up to spin bowlers (his partnership with Derek Underwood for both Kent and England is legendary), Alan Knott is the most successful wicketkeeper in the history of England–India Test matches. In 16 Tests against India between 1971 and 1977 he claimed 54 dismissals, with 49 catches and five stumpings.

⊙ MOST PRODUCTIVE PARTNERSHIP

The most productive partnership in all Tests between England and India is that between Sourav Ganguly and Sachin Tendulkar, who combined to score 834 runs in nine innings between 1996 and 2007 at an average of 92.66.

⊙ THE VISWANATH AND SHARMA SHOW SECURES SERIES WIN

England, 1–0 down in the series going into the Sixth and final Test at Chennai in January 1982, won the toss and, in an attempt to force a result, put India in to bat. And when Dilip Vengsarkar retired hurt with the score (effectively) on 150 for 3, the tourists must have felt their chance to rip through India's middle order had arrived. Gundappa Viswanath (222) and Yashpal Sharma (140) had other ideas, however, adding 316 runs for the third wicket – an all-time partnership best in matches between the two countries – to help India to an eventual series-clinching draw.

⊙ GOOCH'S INDIAN SUMMER

Graham Gooch, England's all-time leading run-scorer, was in the form of his life in the 1990 series against India. In the First Test at Lord's he hit 333 in the first innings (the highest individual score in all Tests between the two countries) and 123 in the second – his match aggregate of 456 runs is the highest in Test history. The Essex man's rich vein of form continued in the Second Test at Old Trafford, where he made 116 and 7, and knocks of 85 and 88 in the third and final Test at The Oval meant that he finished the three-match series with an England–India series record 752 runs to his name at the impressive average of 125.33.

⊙ INDIA FOLD AT THE HOME OF CRICKET

Trailing England by 327 runs after the completion of the first innings in the Second Test at Lord's in June 1974, India were asked to follow on and then gave up the fight in sorry fashion, subsiding to an embarrassing 42 all out in just 17 overs – the lowest total in all Test matches between England and India – and losing the match by the massive margin of an innings and 285 runs.

⊙ BARRINGTON RESERVES HIS BEST FOR INDIA

A player who learnt to curb his natural attacking instincts to become one of the most obdurate batsmen England has ever produced, Ken Barrington enjoyed some particularly good times against India. In 14 matches against them between 1959 and 1967 he scored 1,355 runs (with three centuries and a highest score of 172 at Kanpur in December 1961) at an average of 75.27 – the highest of any batsman to have completed ten or more innings in Test matches between the two countries.

⊙ CHANDRA'S BOX OF TRICKS CONFOUNDS ENGLAND

One of the major factors behind India's 2–1 series victory over England in 1972–73 was the England batsmen's continued inability to unravel the secrets of leg-spinner Bhagwath Chandrasekhar's box of tricks. The Karnataka spin wizard used his dazzling array of leg-spinners, top-spinners, googlies and sliders to great effect, taking four five-wicket hauls in five Tests (with a best of 8 for 79 in the First Test at Delhi), and ended the series with 35 wickets to his name – a record for an England–India series.

MOST RUNS: TOP 10

Pos	Runs	Player (Team, Span)
1	2,483	Sunil Gavaskar (India, 1971–86)
2	2,150	Sachin Tendulkar (India, 1990–2008)
3	1,880	Gundappa Viswanath (India, 1971–82)
4	1,725	Graham Gooch (England, 1979–93)
5	1,589	Dilip Vengsarkar (India, 1977–90)
6	1,489	Rahul Dravid (India, 1996–2008)
7	1,391	David Gower (England, 1979–90)
8	1,355	Ken Barrington (England, 1959–67)
=	1,355	Kapil Dev (India, 1979–93)
10	1,278	Mohammad Azharuddin (India, 1984–96)

⊙ BEEFY BOTHAM ON FIRE IN MUMBAI

The Golden Jubilee Test, played at Mumbai in February 1980, was the Test match whichshowed the world that, in Ian Botham, England possessed an all-rounder of the highest quality. The Somerset man took 6 or 58 in India's first innings, helped himself to 114 runs when England batted, and then took 7 for 48 in India's second to become only the second player in history (Australia's Alan Davidson being the other) to score a century and take 10 wickets in a Test match. Botham's match haul of 13 for 106 remains an all-time record in England–India Tests.

MOST WICKETS: TOP 10

Pos	Wkts	Player (Team, Span)
1	95	Bhagwath Chandrasekhar (India, 1964–79)
2	92	Anil Kumble (India, 1990–2007)
3	85	Bishan Bedi (India, 1967–79)
=	85	Kapil Dev (India, 1979–93)
5	62	Derek Underwood (England, 1971–82)
=	62	Bob Willis (England, 1974–82)
7	59	Ian Botham (England, 1979–82)
8	54	Vinoo Mankad (India, 1946–52)
9	53	Fred Trueman (England, 1952–59)
10	45	John Lever (England, 1976–86)

⊙ RECORD-BREAKING ALL-ROUND EFFORT SECURES SERIES WIN

Holding a slender 1–0 lead going into the Third and final Test of the series at The Oval in August 2007, India produced the goods when it mattered, amassing a mighty 664 all out – the highest team total in all matches between the two countries.

⊙ FIERY FRED ROUTS INDIA

Batting on an already green wicket that had been further softened by rain, India's batsmen could find no answer to the pace and hostility of Fred Trueman in the Third Test of the 1952 series at Old Trafford. In 8.4 electrifying overs, the legendary Yorkshire fast bowler took 8 for 31 – the best single innings figures in all Tests between England and India – to propel England to an eventual innings-and-207-run victory.

NEW ZEALAND v AUSTRALIA

Given that New Zealand have been playing Test cricket since 1930, it seems strange that they had to wait 16 years before playing near-neighbours Australia for the first time – at Wellington, a match they ended up losing by an innings and 103 runs. And Australia have generally dominated the Kiwis from that moment on, winning 26 of the 50 Test matches played and losing only seven.

⊙ MOST PRODUCTIVE PARTNERSHIP
The most productive partnership in all Tests between New Zealand and Australia is that between Matthew Hayden and Justin Langer. The Aussie pair combined to score 961 runs in 13 innings between 2000 and 2005 at an average of 73.92.

⊙ MOST CATCHES
The seventh most prolific fielder in Test history (with 156 catches), Allan Border leads the fielding list in Australia–New Zealand clashes. The former Australian captain bagged 31 catches in 23 Tests against New Zealand between 1980 and 1993.

⊙ PONTING PROSPERS AGAINST NEW ZEALAND
Ricky Ponting is the most successful captain in the history of Tests between Australia and New Zealand. The Australian captain, the most successful skipper in Test history, has led his side to eight wins over New Zealand in nine Tests between 2004 and 2010.

⊙ AUSTRALIA SECURE SERIES WIN IN STYLE
Holding a 1–0 lead in the 1993–94 series going into the Third and final Test at Brisbane, Australia soon extinguished any hopes New Zealand might have had of squaring the series. First they dismissed New Zealand for 233; then, with Steve Waugh (147 not out) and Allan Border (105) starring, they batted their opponents out of the game, compiling a massive 607 for 6 declared – the highest team total in all matches between the two countries – en route to completing an innings-and-96-run victory.

⊙ MOST DISMISSALS

Rod Marsh heads the wicketkeeping list in all Tests between Australia and New Zealand. The Western Australian gloveman claimed 58 scalps in 14 Tests against New Zealand between 1973 and 1982 with 57 catches and one stumping.

⊙ BROTHERS IN ARMS

Coming to the wicket with Australia in trouble at 55 for 2 in the First Test against New Zealand at Wellington in March 1974, brothers Ian (right, 145) and Greg Chappell (left, 247 not out) combined to record-breaking effect, putting on 264 runs for the third wicket (an all-time record in Australia–New Zealand Tests) to help their side to 511 for 6 declared. The match eventually fizzled out into a draw.

⊙ GILCHRIST RESERVES BEST FORM FOR NEW ZEALAND

The finest wicketkeeper-batsman of his generation, Adam Gilchrist was at his destructive best with the bat in matches against New Zealand. In 11 Test matches against the Kiwis between 2000 and 2005, Gilchrist hit four centuries – with a highest score of 162 at Wellington in March 2005 – at an average of 76.91, the highest by any batsman to have completed ten or more innings in Test matches between the two countries.

MOST WICKETS: TOP 10

Pos	Wkts	Player (Team, Span)
1	130	Richard Hadlee (New Zealand, 1973–90)
2	103	Shane Warne (Australia, 1993–2005)
3	63	Daniel Vettori (New Zealand, 1997–2010)
4	56	Glenn McGrath (Australia, 1993–2005)
5	48	Craig McDermott (Australia, 1985–93)
6	44	Brett Lee (Australia, 2000–08)
7	39	Chris Cairns (New Zealand, 1989–2001)
8	38	Dennis Lillee (Australia, 1977–82)
=	38	John Bracewell (New Zealand, 1980–90)
10	37	Danny Morrison (New Zealand, 1987–93)

OVERALL SERIES RECORDS
(50 Tests between 1946 and 2010)

	W	L	T	D	W/L	%W	%L	%D
New Zealand	7	26	0	17	0.26	14.00	52.00	34.00
Australia	26	7	0	17	3.71	52.00	14.00	34.00

First match: 29–30 March 1946, Wellington, New Zealand

⊙ INAUSPICIOUS BEGINNINGS

New Zealand got off to the worst possible start in their first-ever Test match against Australia at Wellington in March 1946. Having won the toss and elected to bat, they capitulated to a sorry 42 all out in 39 overs – the lowest-ever total in Australia–New Zealand Test matches. The Kiwis fared little better in the second innings, limping to 54 all out to lose the match by an innings and 103 runs.

⊙ WALTERS DIGS AUSTRALIA OUT OF A CONSIDERABLE HOLE

With Australia struggling on 112 for 4 in the First Test against New Zealand at Christchurch in February 1977, they were in desperate need of a rescue act from one of their batsmen. And Doug Walters came to the party in style, hitting a magnificent 342-ball 250, the highest individual score in all Australia–New Zealand Tests, to help his side to 552 all out. It wasn't enough to win the match, however, as New Zealand eventually held on to force a draw.

⊙ CHAPPELL CASHES IN AGAINST THE KIWIS

Greg Chappell was the undoubted star of the show as Australia came back from 1–0 down to square the series against New Zealand in 1973–74. The middle-order batsman hit two centuries in three Tests, with a highest score of 247 not out in the First Test at Wellington, and ended the series with 449 runs – a record for Test matches between the two countries – at an average of 89.80.

MOST RUNS: TOP 10

Pos	Runs	Player (Team, Span)
1	1,500	Allan Border (Australia, 1980–93)
2	1,277	John Wright (New Zealand, 1980–93)
3	1,255	Martin Crowe (New Zealand, 1982–93)
4	1,196	Justin Langer (Australia, 1993–2005)
5	1,187	David Boon (Australia, 1985–93)
6	1,117	Steve Waugh (Australia, 1986–2001)
7	1,076	Greg Chappell (Australia, 1973–82)
8	977	Ricky Ponting (Australia, 1997–2010)
9	930	Nathan Astle (New Zealand, 1997–2005)
10	923	Adam Gilchrist (Australia, 2000–05)

AUSTRALIA v INDIA

Although Australia enjoyed a sustained period of dominance over India – they won six and drew one of the first seven series – since 1979 series wins on the subcontinent have almost proved as elusive as the Holy Grail for the men from Down Under. They have recorded only one victory (as opposed to India's six) in their last eight attempts on Indian soil.

⊙ MOST DISMISSALS

The history books will record that Adam Gilchrist was a hard-hitting batsman who had the ability to take a match away from the opposition in one innings, but he was also a more than capable wicketkeeper who enjoyed considerable success against India. In 18 Tests against them between 1999 and 2008 he claimed 75 scalps, with 73 catches and two stumpings – an all-time record in Tests between the two countries.

⊙ INDIA CHALLENGE AUSTRALIA'S DOMINANCE

It was decisive proof of just how much India's fortunes had improved on Australian soil. With the series tied at 1–1 going into the Fourth and final Test at Sydney in January 2004, India won the toss, elected to bat, and batted Australia out of the game. Stunning batting from Sachin Tendulkar (241 not out) and V.V.S. Laxman (178), helped them to compile a massive 705 for 7 over seven sessions of the match – the highest total in all Tests between the two countries. The match ended in a draw, ensuring that India retained the Border-Gavaskar trophy.

OVERALL SERIES RECORDS
(78 Tests between 1947 and 2010)

	W	L	T	D	W/L	%W	%L	%D
Australia	34	20	1	23	1.70	43.59	25.60	29.49
India	20	34	1	23	0.58	25.60	43.59	29.49

First match: 28 November–4 December 1947, Brisbane, Australia

⊙ BRILLIANT BRADMAN PUTS INDIA TO THE SWORD

Just as England, South Africa and the West Indies had discovered before them, India found out how good a player Donald Bradman was when Test cricket's greatest-ever batsman played his one and only series against them in 1947–48. Bradman struck four centuries in six innings, with a highest score of 201 in the Fourth Test at Adelaide, and ended the series with a haul of 715 runs (a record for an Australia–India series) at the astonishing average of 178.75.

⊙ PATEL POWERS INDIA TO HISTORIC VICTORY

Jasubhai Patel's sensational bowling performance in the Second Test at Kanpur in December 1959 was a major factor in India's first-ever Test victory over Australia. The off-spinner took 9 for 69, the best single-innings figures in Australia–India Test matches, in the first innings and 5 for 55 in the second as India won the match by 119 runs.

⊙ SHASTRI SHINES AGAINST AUSTRALIA

An obdurate batsman who enjoyed considerable success both as an opener and in the middle order, and a player of huge importance to India for over a decade, Ravi Shastri enjoyed particular success against Australia. In nine Tests against them between 1985 and 1992 he scored 622 runs, including two centuries (with a highest score of 206 at Sydney in January 1992) at an average of 77.75 – the highest of any player in history to have completed ten or more innings in all Tests between the two countries.

⊙ MOST SUCCESSFUL CAPTAIN

Australia's Bobby Simpson is the most successful captain in all Test matches between Australia and India. In ten Tests against the Indians between 1964 and 1978 (the year in which he emerged from retirement, aged 41, to lead an Australian side decimated by the departure of several players to World Series cricket), he led Australia to six wins.

⊙ MOST CATCHES

The safest pair of hands in Test history – with 193 catches he has taken more catches than any other player – Rahul Dravid also heads the Australia–India fielding list, taking 46 catches in 28 Tests against Australia between 1996 and 2010.

⊙ LAXMAN STUNS AUSTRALIA

It was the innings that turned a Test match on its head in the most spectacular style. With India trailing Australia by 274 runs after the completion of the first innings in the Second Test at Kolkata in March 2001, forced to follow on and in deep trouble, V.V.S. Laxman hauled his side back into contention with a stunning knock of 281 (the highest individual score in all Test matches between the two countries). Remarkably, India went on to win the match by 171 runs.

⊙ THE TURBANATOR TORMENTS AUSTRALIA

In March 2001, having sneaked a sensational come-from-behind victory to level the series in the Second Test at Kolkata, India carried their momentum into the Third and final Test of the series at Chennai, largely thanks to Harbhajan Singh. "The Turbanator" took 7 for 133 in Australia's first innings and 8 for 84 in the second – his match figures of 15 for 217 are the best in all matches between the two countries – to help India to a two-wicket win and a memorable series victory. Harbhajan's 32 wickets in the series is also a record in Australia–India Tests.

⊙ INDIA BEWILDERED IN BRISBANE

Unfortunate in many ways to be caught on a treacherous pitch in their first-ever Test match against Australia at Brisbane in November–December 1947, India's batsmen were horribly out of their depth. Having seen Australia compile 382 for 8 declared in the first innings, India collapsed to 58 all out in 21.3 (eight-ball) overs – the lowest-ever total in Australia–India Tests. Following on, they fared little better in the second innings, dismissed for 98 to lose the match by an innings and 226 runs.

MOST WICKETS: TOP 10

Pos	Wkts	Player (Team, Span)
1	111	Anil Kumble (India, 1996–2008)
2	90	Harbhajan Singh (India, 1998–2010)
=	79	Kapil Dev (India, 1979–92)
4	57	Erapalli Prasanna (India, 1967–78)
5	56	Bishan Bedi (India, 1968–78)
6	55	Shivlal Yadav (India, 1979–86)
7	53	Brett Lee (Australia, 1999–2008)
8	52	Richie Benaud (Australia, 1956–60)
9	51	Glenn McGrath (Australia, 1996–2004)
10	47	Garth McKenzie (Australia, 1964–69)

⊙ PARTNERS IN CRIME

V.V.S. Laxman inevitably grabbed most of the headlines for his innings of 281 against Australia in the Second Test at Kolkata in March 2001 that laid the foundations for India's sensational come-from-behind victory, but he was more than aided by Rahul Dravid. The pair added 376 for the fifth wicket – a record partnership in all Australia–India Tests – to take India into a dominant position. The pair also hold the record for the most productive partnership in all Tests between the two countries, combining to score 1,394 runs in 22 innings between 1998 and 2008 at an average of 66.38.

MOST RUNS: TOP 10

Pos	Runs	Player (Team, Span)
1	3,151	Sachin Tendulkar (India, 1991–2010)
2	2,279	V.V.S. Laxman (India, 1998–2010)
3	2,011	Ricky Ponting (Australia, 1996–2010)
4	1,949	Rahul Dravid (India, 1996–2010)
5	1,888	Matthew Hayden (Australia, 2001–08)
6	1,567	Allan Border (Australia, 1979–92)
7	1,550	Sunil Gavaskar (India, 1977–86)
8	1,538	Gundappa Viswanath (India, 1969–81)
9	1,513	Virender Sehwag (India, 2003–10)
10	1,403	Sourav Ganguly (India, 1996–2008)

INDIA v WEST INDIES

In the early days of this fixture, India's misfortunes were blamed on a lack of experience of playing on hard, bouncy surfaces against a battery of fast bowlers, but even in recent times India have struggled against the West Indies. Of their total of 11 victories against the islanders (in contrast the West Indies have won 30 times), only four of them have come since 2002.

⊙ MOST CATCHES

No player in the history of India–West Indies Test matches has taken more catches than Viv Richards. The legendary Antiguan claimed 39 victims in 28 Tests against India between 1974 and 1989.

⊙ MOST PRODUCTIVE PARTNERSHIP

The most productive partnership in all Tests between India and the West Indies is that of Gordon Greenidge and Desmond Haynes. The formidable opening pair combined to score 1,325 runs in 30 innings between 1983 and 1989 at an average of 45.68.

⊙ DUJON HEADS THE DISMISSALS LIST

The most successful West Indian wicketkeeper in Test history (with 270 dismissals to his name), Jeff Dujon also heads the list in matches between the West Indies and India. In 19 Tests against the Indians between 1983 and 1989, he claimed 60 scalps (with 58 catches and two stumpings).

⊙ MAGNIFICENT MARSHALL LEADS THE WAY

Malcolm Marshall played a significant role in the West Indies' 3–0 series victory in India in 1983–84. The Barbados paceman took two five-wicket hauls, the best being 6 for 37 in the Fifth Test, played at Kolkata, to end the series with 33 wickets – an all-time series record between the two countries.

⊙ MAGICAL DEBUT FOR HIRWANI

It was the most remarkable bowling performance by a debutant in Test history. In the Fourth Test against the West Indies at Chennai in January 1988, India's leg-spinner Narendra Hirwani took 8 for 61 in the first innings and 8 for 75 in the second to bowl his side to a 255-run victory. His match figures of 16 for 136 – the best by a Test debutant in history – are the best in all matches between the two countries.

⊙ INDIA LOSE THE INITIATIVE IN RECORD-BREAKING STYLE

India made the worst possible start to the 1987–88 home series against the West Indies in November 1987. Having won the toss and elected to bat, they would have been planning to compile a first-innings total in the region of 400 and put the islanders under pressure; instead they folded to 75 all out – the lowest total in all matches between the two sides – and went on to lose the match by five wickets.

⊙ A MAIDEN CENTURY TO REMEMBER

A regular in a strong West Indies batting line-up for 16 years, Rohan Kanhai had to wait until his 13th Test, 19 months after making his debut, to record his first three-figure score in international cricket, but rarely has a wait been so worthwhile. In the Third Test of the 1958–59 series at Kolkata, the diminutive right-hander plundered a magnificent 256 – the highest individual score in all matches between the two countries – and the West Indies went on to win the match by an innings and 336 runs.

⊙ A RECORD-BREAKER IN A LOSING CAUSE

The West Indies eventually emerged victorious in the Third Test against India at Ahmedabad in November 1983 (winning the match by 138 runs), but only after being on the receiving end of a record-breaking effort by Kapil Dev. The greatest fast bowler India has ever produced took 9 for 83 in the West Indies' second innings – the best single-innings figures in all Tests between the two countries – to haul his side back into the match, only to see India's batsmen (chasing 242 for victory) slip to a sorry 103 all out in 47.1 overs.

⊙ 644 IS THE LIMIT

Both sides have recorded totals of 644 in Tests between the two countries: India achieved the total (for the loss of seven wickets) in the Sixth and final Test of the 1978–79 series at Kanpur – a match which they drew to secure a 1–0 series victory; the West Indies achieved the same total (for the loss of eight wickets) in the Fifth and final Test of the 1958–59 series in Delhi – that match also ended in a draw, which was enough to see the islanders claim the series 3–0.

⊙ GAVASKAR AND VENGSARKAR MAKE HAY IN THE KOLKATA SUN

Taking advantage of a lifeless pitch, Sunil Gavaskar (with his 182 not out, following on from 107 in the first innings, he became the first batsman in history to score two hundreds in a Test on three occasions) and Dilip Vengsarkar (157 not out) prospered in record-breaking style in the second innings of the Third Test against the West Indies at Kolkata in 1978–79. The pair added 344 for the second wicket – an all-time record in matches between the two countries – to set the West Indies 335 runs for victory. The men from the Caribbean hung on in nervous style, however, finishing on 197 for 9 to secure a draw.

⊙ WONDERFUL WEEKES PROSPERS AGAINST INDIA

Rarely has a batsman enjoyed such a continued streak of fine form in Test cricket's long history. In the West Indies' 1–0 series win in India, in 1948–49, Everton Weekes produced successive scores of 152, 194, 162, 101, 90, 56 and 48 to end the series with 779 runs to his name – an all-time record for a series between India and the West Indies – at an average of 111.28. Weekes's career average against the Indians (106.78 in ten Tests between 1948 and 1953) is also a record.

OVERALL SERIES RECORDS
(82 Tests between 1948 and 2006)

	W	L	T	D	W/L	%W	%L	%D
India	11	30	0	41	0.36	13.42	36.58	50.00
West Indies	30	11	0	41	2.72	36.58	13.42	50.00

First match: 10–14 November 1948, Delhi, India)

MOST WICKETS: TOP 10

Pos	Wkts	Player (Team, Span)
1	89	Kapil Dev (India, 1978–89)
2	76	Malcolm Marshall (West Indies, 1978–89)
3	74	Anil Kumble (India, 1994–2006)
4	68	Srinivas Venkataraghavan (India, 1966–83)
5	67	Andy Roberts (West Indies, 1974–83)
6	65	Wes Hall (West Indies, 1958–67)
=	65	Bhagwath Chandrasekhar (India, 1966–79)
=	65	Courtney Walsh (West Indies, 1987–97)
9	63	Lance Gibbs (West Indies, 1958–75)
10	62	Bishan Bedi (India, 1966–79)

⊙ MOST SUCCESSFUL CAPTAIN

Clive Lloyd is the most successful captain in the history of Test matches between India and the West Indies. The legendary leader recorded ten wins in 20 Tests against India between 1974 and 1983.

MOST RUNS: TOP 10

Pos	Runs	Player (Team, Span)
1	2,749	Sunil Gavaskar (India, 1971–83)
2	2,344	Clive Lloyd (West Indies, 1966–83)
3	1,927	Viv Richards (West Indies, 1974–89)
4	1,920	Garfield Sobers (West Indies, 1958–71)
5	1,693	Rohan Kanhai (West Indies, 1958–71)
6	1,678	Gordon Greenidge (West Indies, 1974–89)
7	1,596	Dilip Vengsarkar (India, 1976–89)
8	1,581	Shivnarine Chanderpaul (W. Indies, 1994–2006)
9	1,495	Everton Weekes (West Indies, 1948–53)
10	1,455	Gundappa Viswanath (India, 1971–79)

NEW ZEALAND v WEST INDIES

Few contests in Test cricket demonstrate more clearly how much fortunes can change than those between New Zealand and the West Indies. Having previously won just two of 23 Tests against the islanders over a period of 35 years, New Zealand have now not lost a Test match against the West Indies since April 1996.

⊙ DOWN AND OUT IN DUNEDIN

New Zealand's early struggles against the West Indies were epitomized in the First Test at Dunedin in February 1956. Having won the toss and elected to bat, the home side's batsmen could find no answer to the spin bowling of Sonny Ramadhin (who took 6 for 23) and were dismissed for a paltry 74 all out – the lowest total in all Test matches between the two countries.

⊙ MOST SUCCESSFUL CAPTAIN

The most successful captain in the history of Test matches between New Zealand and the West Indies is Stephen Fleming. The former New Zealand captain led his side to five wins in seven Tests between 1999 and 2006.

MOST RUNS: TOP 10

Pos	Runs	Player (Team, Span)
1	882	Gordon Greenidge (West Indies, 1980–87)
2	855	Glenn Turner (New Zealand, 1969–72)
3	843	Desmond Haynes (West Indies, 1980–87)
4	820	Chris Gayle (West Indies, 2002–08)
5	764	Bev Congdon (New Zealand, 1969–72)
6	729	Shivnarine Chanderpaul (W. Indies, 1995–2008)
7	715	Nathan Astle (New Zealand, 1996–2006)
8	704	Brian Lara (West Indies, 1995–2006)
9	703	Stephen Fleming (New Zealand, 1995–2006)
10	598	Sherwin Campbell (West Indies, 1995–99)
=	598	Lawrence Rowe (West Indies, 1972–80)

⊙ CAIRNS TURNS MATCH ON ITS HEAD

With the West Indies cruising on 276 for 0 towards the end of the first day's play in the First Test against New Zealand at Hamilton in December 1999, the chances of a home victory seemed remote. However, they ended up winning the match by nine wickets, and it was largely thanks to the second-innings bowling display of Chris Cairns. The all-rounder bagged 7 for 27 off 22.5 overs – the best figures in New Zealand–West Indies Tests and the best figures by any New Zealand bowler other than Richard Hadlee in history – to help dismiss the West Indies for 97 and pave the way for an unlikely victory.

⊙ THE TURNER AND JARVIS SHOW

Having seen the West Indies reach 365 for 7 declared in their first innings in the Fourth Test against New Zealand at Georgetown, Guyana, in April 1972, Glenn Turner (259) and Terry Jarvis (182) ensured New Zealand's reply got off to the perfect start. The opening pair added 387 runs for the first wicket – an all-time record in New Zealand–West Indies matches – to help their side to 543 for 3 declared. The game, however, petered out into a bore draw.

⊙ WEST INDIES BATSMEN FIND THEIR FORM WHEN IT MATTERS

There is no better way of putting an opponent under pressure than compiling a huge first-innings total, and certainly no better time to do so than in a series-deciding Test match. That is exactly what the West Indies did in the Second Test against New Zealand at Wellington in February 1995, as centuries from Jimmy Adams (151), Brian Lara (147) and Junior Murray (101 not out) propelled them to 660 for 5 declared – the highest score in all Tests between the two countries – en route to an innings-and322-run victory and a 1–0 series success.

⊙ COURTNEY ENSURES NEW ZEALAND CRUMBLE

With his batsmen having put his side in a commanding position in the Second Test against New Zealand at Wellington in February 1995, amassing a mighty first-innings total of 660 for 5 declared, it was time for West Indies captain Courtney Walsh to turn the screw. He took 7 for 37 in New Zealand's first innings and 6 for 18 in their second to lead his side to a series-clinching innings-and-332-run victory. His match figures of 13 for 55 are the best in all Tests between the two countries.

OVERALL SERIES RECORDS
(37 Tests between 1952 and 2008)

	W	L	T	D	W/L	%W	%L	%D
New Zealand	9	10	0	18	0.90	24.32	27.03	49.65
West Indies	10	9	0	18	1.11	27.03	24.32	49.65

First match: 8–12 February 1952, Christchurch, New Zealand

⊙ TURNER'S CARIBBEAN TRIUMPH

Glenn Turner was outstanding for New Zealand in the country's first-ever tour to the Caribbean in 1971–72. In a drawn five-match series – a result considered a huge triumph for New Zealand at the time – the straight-batted, dogged opener hit two memorable double-centuries, with a best of 259 (the highest individual score in all matches between the two countries) in the Fourth Test at Georgetown, Guyana, and ended the series with 672 runs (at an average of 96.00). It is the highest series haul in the history of New Zealand–West Indies Test matches.

⊙ A RECORD SHARED

The record for the most wickets in a series between the two countries is 27, a feat achieved by two bowlers: New Zealand's Bruce Taylor in the 1971–72 series in the Caribbean; and Malcolm Marshall of the West Indies in the 1984–85 series in New Zealand.

MOST WICKETS: TOP 10

Pos	Wkts	Player (Team, Span)
1	51	Richard Hadlee (New Zealand, 1980–87)
2	43	Courtney Walsh (West Indies, 1985–99)
3	36	Joel Garner (West Indies, 1980–87)
4	36	Malcolm Marshall (West Indies, 1985–87)
5	33	Daniel Vettori (New Zealand, 1999–2008)
6	32	Bruce Taylor (New Zealand, 1969–72)
=	32	Sonny Ramadhin (West Indies, 1952–56)
8	23	Alf Valentine (West Indies, 1952–56)
=	23	Ewen Chatfield (New Zealand, 1985–87)
10	20	Shane Bond (New Zealand, 2002–06)
=	20	Gary Troup (New Zealand, 1980–85)

INDIA v PAKISTAN

Given the historically uneasy relationship between the two countries – they were born out of India's partition in 1947 – this is the most tension-fuelled and politically driven fixture in international cricket. Since the contest was first played back in 1952, Pakistan lead the way with 12 wins to India's nine.

⊙ WASIM BARI HEADS THE KEEPERS LIST

A veteran of 81 Test matches for Pakistan, Wasim Bari has claimed more dismissals than any other wicketkeeper in Tests between India and Pakistan. In 18 matches against India between 1978 and 1983, the greatest keeper his country has ever produced bagged 55 victims (with 50 catches and five stumpings).

⊙ INDIA ALL AT SEA AS THEY TAKE THEIR BOW IN PAKISTAN

India's batsmen played like fish out of water on the jute-matting pitch used for the first-ever Test match between the two countries to be played in Pakistan. Having won the toss and elected to bat, India slipped to 106 all out in 55.1 overs in 3 hours and 20 minutes – still the lowest-ever team total in matches between India and Pakistan – and went on to lose by an innings and 43 runs.

⊙ A SAFE PAIR OF HANDS

The record for the most catches in matches between India and Pakistan is 19, a feat achieved by two players: Sunil Gavaskar (India) in 24 Tests between 1978 and 1987; and Rahul Dravid (India) in 15 Tests between 1999 and 2007.

⊙ PRIORITY LIES IN BUILDING A BIG SCORE

The fear of defeat lies at the very heart of this fixture: as a result, 38 of the 59 Tests contested between the two countries have been drawn, and the overriding mentality appears to be to bat yourself into a position of absolute safety before even thinking about trying to win the game. As a result, there have been nine scores of 600 plus in matches between the two countries, the highest of which was 699 for 5 declared, achieved by Pakistan in the Third Test at Lahore in December 1989 – a match that, not surprisingly, ended in a draw.

⊙ KUMBLE PUTS PAKISTAN IN A SPIN

It will go down in history as one of the best single-innings bowling performances in Test history, bettered, indeed, only by Jim Laker's remarkable effort against Australia at Old Trafford in 1956. Having taken 4 for 75 in Pakistan's first innings in the Second Test at Delhi in February 1999, Anil Kumble became only the second bowler in Test history to take ten wickets in an innings (10 for 74) to bowl India to a 212-run victory. Kumble's match figures of 14 for 149 are the best in all Tests between the two countries.

MOST WICKETS: TOP 10

Pos	Wkts	Player (Team, Span)
1	99	Kapil Dev (India, 1978–89)
2	94	Imran Khan (Pakistan, 1978–89)
3	81	Anil Kumble (India, 1999–2007)
4	45	Wasim Akram (Pakistan, 1987–99)
5	44	Fazal Mahmood (Pakistan, 1952–61)
6	43	Danish Kaneria (Pakistan, 2004–07)
7	39	Mahmood Hussain (Pakistan, 1952–61)
8	37	Vinoo Mankad (India, 1952–55)
9	36	Sarfraz Nawaz (Pakistan, 1978–83)
10	34	Subhash Gupte (India, 1952–61)
=	34	Iqbal Qasim (Pakistan, 1978–87)

⊙ MOST PRODUCTIVE PARTNERSHIP

The most productive partnership in all Tests between India and Pakistan is that of Younis Khan and Mohammad Yousuf. The pair have combined to score 1,372 runs in nine innings between 2005 and 2007 at an average of 171.50.

⊙ IMRAN'S RECORD-BREAKING HAUL SPARKS PAKISTAN

Where Mudassar Nazar excelled with the bat in Pakistan's stunning 3–0 series victory over arch-rivals India in 1982–83, Imran Khan was the star of the show with the ball. The Pakistan captain took four five-wicket hauls (with a best of 8 for 60 in the Second Test at Karachi) and two ten-wicket match hauls to end the victorious series with 40 wickets – an all-time record series haul in all matches between India and Pakistan.

⊙ IMRAN IS THE MOST SUCCESSFUL LEADER

In a fixture not renowned for producing a result – only 35.59 per cent of matches between India and Pakistan have produced a victory for either side – Pakistan's Imran Khan is the most successful captain in contests between the two countries, recording four wins in 15 Tests between 1982 and 1989.

⊙ MAGICAL MUDASSAR PILES ON THE RUNS

Mudassar Nazar laid the foundations for Pakistan's 3–0 series victory over India in 1982–83. The opener was in sensational form with the bat, hitting four centuries – with a highest score of 231 in the Fourth Test at Hyderabad – and ending the series with 761 runs to his name (at an average of 126.83), an all-time record haul in Test matches between the two countries.

MOST RUNS: TOP 10

Pos	Runs	Player (Team, Span)
1	2,228	Javed Miandad (Pakistan, 1978–89)
2	2,089	Sunil Gavaskar (India, 1978–87)
3	1,740	Zaheer Abbas (Pakistan, 1978–84)
4	1,431	Mudassar Nazar (Pakistan, 1978–84)
5	1,321	Younis Khan (Pakistan, 2005–07)
6	1,284	Dilip Vengsarkar (India, 1978–87)
7	1,276	Virender Sehwag (India, 2004–06)
8	1,247	Mohammad Yousuf (Pakistan, 1999–2007)
9	1,236	Rahul Dravid (India, 1999–2007)
10	1,091	Imran Khan (Pakistan, 1978–89)

⊙ LEADING PAKISTAN TO SAFETY IN RECORD-BREAKING STYLE

With Pakistan losing two wickets in successive deliveries to fall to 60 for 2 and into potential danger against India in the Fourth Test at Hyderabad in January 1983, Mudassar Nazar (231, and in the form of his life) and Javed Miandad (280 not out) steadied the ship in spectacular style. The pair added 451 for the third wicket – the highest partnership in all matches between the two countries – paving the way to Pakistan's 581 for 3 declared and an eventual innings-and-119-run victory.

OVERALL SERIES RECORDS
(59 Tests between 1952 and 2007)

	W	L	T	D	W/L	%W	%L	%D
India	9	12	0	38	0.75	15.25	20.34	64.41
Pakistan	12	9	0	38	1.33	20.34	15.25	64.41

First match: 16–18 October 1952, Delhi, India

⊙ SUPER SEHWAG AT HIS BRILLIANT BEST

A stunning innings by Virender Sehwag was at the heart of India's innings-and-52-run victory over Pakistan in the First Test at Multan in March–April 2004. The free-scoring opener smashed a sensational 309 runs off 375 balls (with 39 fours and six sixes) – the highest individual score in all matches between the two countries – to help his side to a mighty first-innings total of 675 for 5 declared. And this was far from an isolated case of success against Pakistan: Sehwag's career average against them of 91.14 – in nine Tests between 2004 and 2006 (which includes three double-centuries) – is the highest of any player to have completed ten or more innings in India–Pakistan matches.

ENGLAND v PAKISTAN

Test matches between England and Pakistan have never been short of drama – who could forget Mike Gatting's finger-pointing rant at umpire Shakoor Rana at Faisalabad in December 1987, Pakistan's refusal to play after the tea interval following ball-tampering allegations at The Oval in August 2006 or the alleged spot-fixing scandal in 2010? But they are closely fought affairs, with England recording 22 wins to Pakistan's 13.

⊙ MOST SUCCESSFUL CAPTAIN
England's Andrew Strauss is the most successful captain in the history of matches between England and Pakistan. He has recorded six wins in eight Tests against Pakistan between 2006 and 2010.

⊙ MOST DISMISSALS
Wasim Bari, Pakistan's most successful wicketkeeper of all time, is the most prolific keeper in all Tests between England and Pakistan. In 24 matches against England between 1967 and 1982 he claimed 54 dismissals, with 50 catches and four stumpings.

⊙ DEXTER SAVES HIS BEST FOR PAKISTAN
Ted Dexter enjoyed good times with the bat against Pakistan. In ten innings he recorded his highest Test score, 205 in the Third Test at Faisalabad in February 1962, and compiled 749 runs at an average of 93.62 – the highest of any batsman to have completed ten or more innings in Tests between the two countries.

⊙ MOST CATCHES
Javed Miandad holds the record for the most catches taken by a fielder in England–Pakistan Tests. The former Pakistan captain took 20 catches in 22 Tests against England between 1977 and 1992.

⊙ RECORD-BREAKING EFFORT IN A LOSING CAUSE FOR PAKISTAN

For the time being, at least, it was a partnership that kept Pakistan in the Second Test at Headingley in August 2006. Pakistan were trailing 1–0 in the series, and having seen England compile a healthy first-innings total of 515 all out, and then both openers fall in quick succession, the visitors needed senior players Mohammad Yousuf and Younis Khan to stand up and deliver. They did so in magnificent style, putting on 363 for the third wicket (Yousuf with 192 and Khan with 173) – the highest partnership in all matches between the two countries – to help Pakistan to 538 all out. But their effort was all in vain: Pakistan's second-innings collapse (155 all out) saw England win the game by 167 runs.

⊙ MOST PRODUCTIVE PARTNERSHIP

The most productive partnership in all Tests between England and Pakistan is that of Mohammad Yousuf and Inzamam-ul-Haq. The pair combined to score 901 runs in nine innings between 2000 and 2006 at an impressive average of 112.62.

⊙ COMPTON CASHES IN AGAINST UNCERTAIN PAKISTAN

Denis Compton made the most of Pakistan's problems in adjusting to both the cold weather and a damp wicket in the Second Test at Trent Bridge in July 1954. The Middlesex star crashed his highest Test score of 278 (with 34 fours and one six) – also the highest score in matches between the two countries – to help England to a massive first-innings total of 558 for 6 declared and an eventual innings-and-129-run victory.

⊙ BATSMEN POWER PAKISTAN TO HISTORIC SERIES WIN

It was some feat to secure a first-ever series victory on English soil. Holding a 1–0 lead going into the fifth and final Test at The Oval in August 1987, Pakistan won a crucial toss, elected to bat, and soon extinguished any hopes England might have had of winning the match when they compiled a massive 708 all out, with centuries from Javed Miandad (260), Saleem Malik (102) and Imran Khan (118 not out). It is the highest total in all matches between the two countries.

⊙ PAKISTAN FLATTENED AT EDGBASTON

One-nil down in the four-match series going into the Second Test against England at Edgbaston in August 2010, Pakistan won the toss, elected to bat and, in the face of some fine seam bowling from James Anderson (4 for 20) and Stuart Broad (4 for 38), collapsed in spectacular fashion to 72 all out – the lowest score in all Tests between the two countries. England went on to record a comfortable nine-wicket win to take a 2–0 series lead.

⊙ UNDERWOOD THRIVES AT A RAIN-SODDEN LORD'S

There has been no more destructive bowler on a rain-affected wicket in Test history than "Deadly" Derek Underwood, and the Kent left-arm spinner took full advantage of the damp conditions in the Second Test against Pakistan at Lord's in August 1974. He took 5 for 20 in the first innings and 8 for 51 in the second to end with match figures of 13 for 71 – the best in all Tests between England and Pakistan. The weather had the final say in the match, however, and it ended in a draw.

⊙ QADIR'S BOX OF TRICKS TOO MUCH FOR ENGLAND

England's 1987 tour to Pakistan is best remembered, sadly, for the on-the-field tensions and arguments between the English players and the match officials – all of which completely overshadowed Abdul Qadir's stunning performances with the ball throughout the series. In the First Test at Lahore, the leg-spinner got Pakistan off to the perfect start, taking 9 for 56 to help dismiss England for 175 – the best single-innings figures in all matches between the two countries and a vital factor in Pakistan's eventual innings-and-87-run victory. Two further five-wicket hauls followed and Qadir ended the three-match series, which Pakistan won 1–0, with 30 wickets to his name – an all-time record in England–Pakistan matches.

OVERALL SERIES RECORDS
(71 Tests between 1954 and 2010)

	W	L	T	D	W/L	%W	%L	%D
England	22	13	0	36	1.69	30.99	18.31	50.70
Pakistan	13	22	0	36	0.59	18.31	30.99	50.70

First match: 10–15 June 1954, Lord's

MOST RUNS: TOP 10

Pos	Runs	Player (Team, Span)
1	1,584	Inzamam-ul-Haq (Pakistan, 1992–2006)
2	1,554	Mushtaq Mohammad (Pakistan, 1961–74)
3	1,499	Mohammad Yousuf (Pakistan, 2000–10)
4	1,396	Saleem Malik (Pakistan, 1984–96)
5	1,329	Javed Miandad (Pakistan, 1977–92)
6	1,185	David Gower (England, 1978–92)
7	1,086	Zaheer Abbas (Pakistan, 1971–84)
8	1,039	Hanif Mohammad (Pakistan, 1954–69)
9	994	Alec Stewart (England, 1992–2001)
10	943	Tom Graveney (England, 1954–69)

⊙ YOUSUF'S LONE RESISTANCE

Although England, the hosts, won the four-match series 3–0, many of the headlines during the 2006 series against Pakistan were reserved for the sensational batting performances of Mohammad Yousuf. The Pakistan middle-order batsman hit three centuries, with a highest score of 202 in the First Test at Lord's. He ended the series with 631 runs at an average of 90.14 – no batsman in the history of England–Pakistan Tests has scored more runs in a series.

MOST WICKETS: TOP 10

Pos	Wkts	Player (Team, Span)
1	82	Abdul Qadir (Pakistan, 1977–87)
2	57	Wasim Akram (Pakistan, 1987–2001)
3	50	Waqar Younis (Pakistan, 1992–2001)
4	49	Intikhab Alam (Pakistan, 1961–74)
5	47	Imran Khan (Pakistan, 1971–87)
6	40	Ian Botham (England, 1978–92)
7	37	Sarfraz Nawaz (Pakistan, 1969–84)
8	36	Derek Underwood (England, 1967–74)
9	34	Bob Willis (England, 1974–84)
10	33	Mushtaq Ahmed (Pakistan, 1992–2000)

PAKISTAN v NEW ZEALAND

Pakistan's innings-and-one-run victory in their first-ever Test match against New Zealand at Karachi in October 1955 seemed to set the tone for contests between these two countries, which Pakistan have dominated, winning 23 of the 50 matches played as opposed to New Zealand's seven.

⊙ RECORD-BREAKING PARTNERSHIP AT DUNEDIN

Mushtaq Mohammad (201) and Asif Iqbal (175) made the most of a placid wicket in the Second Test match of the 1972–73 series at Dunedin to take Pakistan into a dominant position. The pair added 350 runs for the fourth wicket (the highest partnership in the history of Tests between Pakistan and New Zealand) to lead their side to a commanding 507 for 6 declared and an eventual innings-and-166-run victory.

⊙ PAKISTAN POWER TO HUGE VICTORY

A massive first-innings score by Pakistan in the First Test against New Zealand at Lahore in May 2002 laid the foundations for the fifth-largest margin of victory in Test history. A century from Imran Nazir (127), playing in his first Test match in 17 months, and a magnificent triple-century from captain Inzamam-ul-Haq (329), propelled the home side to 643 all out – the largest total in all matches between the two countries – and an eventual innings-and-324-run victory.

⊙ MOST SUCCESSFUL CAPTAIN

Javed Miandad is the most successful captain in the history of Test matches between Pakistan and New Zealand, leading Pakistan to four wins in seven Tests against the Kiwis between 1985 and 1993.

⊙ INZAMAM DEFIES INJURY TO PRODUCE RECORD-BREAKING KNOCK

Inzamam-ul-Haq scored more than half of his team's runs (51.17 per cent) as Pakistan compiled the highest score in all matches between the two countries (643 all out) in the First Test at Lahore in May 2002. Crippled by cramp that prevented him from running between the wickets in the latter stages of his innings (New Zealand captain Stephen Fleming controversially had denied him a runner, given that he had sustained the injury while batting), he resorted to a boundary-only policy on the way to a magnificent 329 off 436 balls (with 38 fours and nine sixes) – it is the 13th highest score in Test history and the highest individual score in all Pakistan–New Zealand matches.

⊙ WAQAR TOO GOOD FOR NEW ZEALAND

While Shoaib Mohammad laid the foundations with his bat for Pakistan's 3–0 home series victory over New Zealand in 1990–91, hitting a series record 507 runs, Waqar Younis was the chief destroyer with the ball. The paceman took three five-wicket innings hauls and two ten-wicket match hauls (with a best of 12 for 130 in the third and final Test at Faisalabad – the best match haul in all Tests between the two countries) and ended the series with 29 wickets (another record in Pakistan–New Zealand Test matches).

MOST WICKETS: TOP 10

Pos	Wkts	Player (Team, Span)
1	70	Waqar Younis (Pakistan, 1990–2002)
2	60	Wasim Akram (Pakistan, 1985–95)
3	54	Intikhab Alam (Pakistan, 1965–76)
4	51	R.J. Hadlee (New Zealand, 1973–89)
5	45	Pervez Sajjad (Pakistan, 1965–73)
6	35	Mushtaq Ahmed (Pakistan, 1993–2001)
=	35	Chris Martin (New Zealand, 2001–11)
8	32	D.R. Tuffey (New Zealand, 2001–09)
9	31	Imran Khan (Pakistan, 1976–89)
=	31	D.K. Morrison (New Zealand, 1989–95)

⊙ JAVED KING OF THE FIELDERS

No player has taken more catches in Test matches between Pakistan and New Zealand than Javed Miandad. The former Pakistan captain bagged 20 catches in 18 Tests against the Kiwis between 1976 and 1993.

⊙ ALL-TIME LOW FOR NEW ZEALAND IN DRAWN TEST

The first-ever series between Pakistan and New Zealand, in 1955, was a one-sided affair, but not a whitewash. However, it was only the heavy rain that fell over the first three days of the Third Test in Dhaka (now in Bangladesh), and not the tourists' batting, that prevented Pakistan from securing a 3–0 series victory, and even then the home side came very close. On a soaked matting wicket, they dismissed New Zealand for 70 all out in their first innings – the lowest team total in all Tests between the two countries – and had the Kiwis reeling on 69 for 6 in the second innings (still 56 runs adrift) before play was finally brought to a halt.

MOST RUNS: TOP 10

Pos	Runs	Player (Team, Span)
1	1,919	Javed Miandad (Pakistan, 1976–93)
2	1,113	Asif Iqbal (Pakistan, 1965–79)
3	1,059	Inzamam-ul-Haq (Pakistan, 1993–2003)
4	973	Martin Crowe (New Zealand, 1984–90)
5	946	Saleem Malik (Pakistan, 1984–96)
6	936	Majid Khan (Pakistan, 1965–79)
7	854	Shoaib Mohammad (Pakistan, 1984–90)
8	779	Mushtaq Mohammad (Pakistan, 1969–79)
9	753	Mark Burgess (New Zealand, 1969–79)
10	747	Mohammad Yousuf (Pakistan, 2001–09)

⊙ BEST BOWLING IN AN INNINGS

The best single-innings bowling figures in matches between the two countries is 7 for 52, a feat achieved by two bowlers: Intikhab Alam (Pakistan) in the Second Test at Dunedin in February 1973; and Chris Pringle (New Zealand) in the Third Test at Faisalabad in October 1990.

OVERALL SERIES RECORDS
(50 Tests between 1955 and 2011)

	W	L	T	D	W/L	%W	%L	%D
Pakistan	23	7	0	20	3.28	46.00	14.00	40.00
New Zealand	7	23	0	20	0.30	14.00	46.00	40.00

First match: 13–17 October 1955, Karachi, Pakistan

⊙ PROLIFIC KEEPER HEADS DISMISSALS LIST

Wasim Bari, Pakistan's most prolific and most capped wicketkeeper of all time, leads the all-time dismissals list in Pakistan–New Zealand Test matches. He claimed 32 scalps (27 catches and five stumpings) in 11 Tests against New Zealand between 1969 and 1979.

⊙ MOST PRODUCTIVE PARTNERSHIP

The most productive partnership in all Tests between Pakistan and New Zealand is that of Majid Khan and Sadiq Mohammad. The pair combined to score 811 runs in ten innings between 1973 and 1976 at an average of 90.11.

⊙ SHOAIB SHINES

Shoaib Mohammad was Pakistan's star with the bat as they trounced New Zealand 3–0 in the home series in 1990–91. The opening batsman scored three centuries in the three matches with a highest score of 203 not out in the First Test at Karachi and ended the series with 507 runs to his name (the highest haul by any batsman in a Pakistan–New Zealand series), some 357 runs more than Pakistan's next highest scorer (Javed Miandad, with 150 runs). His career average against New Zealand of 106.75 is the highest of any batsman to have completed 10 or more innings in Test matches between the two countries.

INDIA v NEW ZEALAND

New Zealand did not get off to the best of starts in Tests against India – it took them ten Test matches to record their first-ever victory (at Christchurch in February 1968) – but since that time Tests between the two countries have been reasonably even affairs, with India recording 16 victories to New Zealand's nine.

⊙ DOWLING STEERS NEW ZEALAND TO HISTORIC WIN

Captain Graham Dowling produced a record-breaking performance as New Zealand won the Second Test at Christchurch by six wickets in February 1968 to record their first-ever victory over India. Leading from the front in the first innings, the opener faced 519 balls to score 239 runs. It remains the highest individual score in all matches between the two countries.

⊙ VENKAT SPINS INDIA TO SERIES SUCCESS

It took a record-breaking performance from Srinivas Venkataraghavan for India to edge to a seven-wicket victory in the Fourth and final Test against New Zealand in 1964–65 at Delhi. Bowling with accuracy and penetration, the off-spinner took 8 for 72 in the first innings (the best single-innings figures in all Tests between the two countries) and 4 for 80 in the second to finish with match figures of 12 for 152 (another India–New Zealand Test record).

⊙ MOST SUCCESSFUL CAPTAIN

The prime beneficiary of India's early dominance over New Zealand, the Nawab of Pataudi (India) is the most successful captain in all Tests between India and New Zealand. He led his side to five victories in 11 Tests against the Kiwis between 1965 and 1969.

⊙ SMITH THE LEADING GLOVEMAN

A regular behind the stumps for New Zealand for nearly a decade, Ian Smith holds the record for the most dismissals in India–New Zealand Test matches. He pouched 29 victims (all catches) in nine Tests against India between 1981 and 1990.

⊙ MANKAD AND ROY LEAD INDIA TO COMPREHENSIVE VICTORY

India's Vinoo Mankad (231) and Pankaj Roy (173) dashed any hopes New Zealand might have had of squaring the 1955–56 series (India held a 1–0 lead) in the Fourth and final Test at Chennai. After India had won the toss and elected to bat, the pair put on an opening stand of 413 to help their side to a daunting first-innings total of 537 for 3 declared and an eventual innings-and-109-run victory. It remains the highest partnership in all Tests between the two countries.

⊙ MOST PRODUCTIVE PARTNERSHIP

The most productive partnership in all India–New Zealand Tests is that of India's Sachin Tendulkar and Rahul Dravid. The pair have combined to score 860 runs in 16 innings against New Zealand between 1999 and 2010 at an average of 53.75.

MOST WICKETS: TOP 10

Pos	Wkts	Player (Team, Span)
1	65	Richard Hadlee (New Zealand, 1976–90)
2	57	Bishan Bedi (India, 1968–76)
3	55	Erapalli Prasanna (India, 1968–76)
4	50	Anil Kumble (India, 1994–2003)
5	44	Srinivas Venkataraghavan (India, 1965–76)
6	43	Harbhajan Singh (India, 1998–2010)
7	40	Daniel Vettori (New Zealand, 1998–2010)
8	36	Bhagwath Chandrasekhar (India, 1965–76)
9	35	Zaheer Khan (India, 2002–10)
10	34	Subhash Gupte (India, 1955–56)

⊙ SUTCLIFFE SHINES

The outstanding New Zealand batsman of the post-war period, Bert Sutcliffe stood tall while others around him wilted during the 1955–56 series in India. Although the Kiwis lost the series 2–0, the opener scored two centuries, with a highest score of 203 in the Third Test at Delhi, to end the series with 611 runs – a record in any India–New Zealand series. He seemed to prosper against the Indians: in 16 innings against them, he scored 885 runs at an average of 68.07 – the highest by any batsman to have completed ten innings or more in all Tests between the two countries.

⊙ NEW ZEALAND PILE ON THE RUNS AT MOHALI

Following New Zealand's match-saving heroics to deny India victory in the First Test at Ahmedabad, there was still everything to play for when the two sides met at Mohali for the second and final Test of the 2002–03 series. New Zealand won the toss and put themselves in a position of impregnability when – thanks to centuries from Mark Richardson (145), Lou Vincent (106), Scott Styris (119) and Craig McMillan (100 not out) – they amassed a mighty 630 for 6 declared, the highest team total in all matches between the two countries. On a placid wicket, however, New Zealand's bowlers failed to push home the advantage and the match ended in a draw.

⊙ FLEMING IS THE CATCHING KING

Stephen Fleming, by some distance, is the most prolific fielder in New Zealand's history – he claimed 171 catches in 111 Tests; in second place on the all-time list is Martin Crowe with 71. Fleming also holds the record for the most catches in India–New Zealand Tests: he bagged 20 catches in 13 matches against India between 1994 and 2003.

MOST RUNS: TOP 10

Pos	Runs	Player (Team, Span)
1	1,659	Rahul Dravid (India, 1998–2010)
2	1,532	Sachin Tendulkar (India, 1990–2010)
3	964	Graham Dowling (New Zealand, 1965–69)
4	885	Bert Sutcliffe (New Zealand, 1955–65)
5	818	V.V.S. Laxman (India, 2002–10)
6	804	John Wright (New Zealand, 1981–90)
7	796	Mohammad Azharuddin (India, 1988–99)
8	755	Virender Sehwag (India, 2002–10)
9	725	Mark Burgess (New Zealand, 1968–76)
10	713	Bev Congdon (New Zealand, 1965–76)

OVERALL SERIES RECORDS
(50 Tests between 1955 and 2010)

	W	L	T	D	W/L	%W	%L	%D
India	16	9	0	25	1.77	32.00	18.00	50.00
New Zealand	9	16	0	25	0.56	18.00	32.00	50.00

First match: 19–24 November 1955, Hyderabad, India

PAKISTAN v AUSTRALIA

Australia got off to a bad start against Pakistan, losing the first-ever match played between the two countries by nine wickets at Karachi in October 1956, but their overall record against them in subsequent years has been impressive: of the 57 Test matches played, Australia have recorded 28 wins to Pakistan's 12.

⊙ SUPER SHANE'S MAGIC TOO MUCH FOR PAKISTAN

Shane Warne was Pakistan's chief destroyer as Australia romped to a 3–0 series victory in 2002–03. With all the Tests played at neutral venues for safety reasons, the legen dary leg-spinner took two five-wicket hauls in three Tests – with a best return of 7 for 94 in the First Test at Colombo, Sri Lanka. He ended the series with 27 wickets, an all-time record in Australia–Pakistan matches.

⊙ SENSATIONAL SARFRAZ STUNS AUSTRALIA

With Australia, seven wickets in hand, needing only 77 runs for victory on the fifth day of the First Test at Melbourne in March 1979, Sarfraz Nawaz produced one of the greatest bowling performances in Test history. The experienced fast bowler took seven wickets for one run in 33 deliveries to help Pakistan to a stunning 71-run victory and ended with figures of 9 for 86 – the best by any bowler in Australia–Pakistan Test matches.

⊙ TAYLOR LEADS THE WAY

Mark Taylor holds the highest average of all batsmen to have completed ten or more innings in Pakistan–Australia Test matches. The former captain averaged 79.23 (with 1,347 runs) against Pakistan in 20 innings between 1990 and 1998.

⊙ MOST DISMISSALS

Rod Marsh leads the all-time dismissals list in Australia–Pakistan Test matches. The legendary gloveman pouched 68 victims (66 catches and two stumpings) in 20 Tests against Pakistan between 1972 and 1984.

⊙ CAPTAIN TAYLOR HITS AN ALL-TIME HIGH IN PESHAWAR

With Australia 1–0 up in the three-match series going into the Second Test at Peshawar in October 1998, Australian captain Mark Taylor led from the front in record-breaking style. By the end of the second day, after occupying the crease for 12 hours and facing 564 balls, Taylor stood unbeaten on 334 not out – to equal Donald Bradman's all-time highest Test score for an Australian batsman and to leave himself within sight of Brian Lara's world record 375. To the surprise of everyone, however, he made one of Test cricket's most magnanimous gestures: placing his team's need to win the game above any personal glory, he declared. The match ended in a draw, but Taylor's effort is still the highest score by any batsman in Tests between the two countries.

⊙ MAGICAL MALIK STEERS PAKISTAN TO VICTORY

Captain Saleem Malik was the star performer as Pakistan edged to a 1–0 home series victory over Australia in 1994–95. Following a modest performance in the victorious First Test at Lahore (he scored 26 and 43 in the course of Pakistan's one-wicket victory), he proceeded to prosper, saving Pakistan in both the drawn Second Test at Rawalpindi (hitting 237 in the second innings as his side was forced to follow on 261 runs in arrears) and again in the Third and final Test at Karachi (where knocks of 75 and 143 did much to secure a draw and, with it, a series victory). His series haul of 557 runs (at the impressive average of 92.83) is an all-time record in Tests between the two countries.

⊙ MOST SUCCESSFUL CAPTAIN

Ricky Ponting is the most successful captain in the history of Test matches between Australia and Pakistan. He led Australia to seven victories in eight Tests as Australia captain against Pakistan between 2004 and 2010.

⊙ PERFECT PARTNERS

With Australia already holding an unassailable 2–0 lead in the three-match series going into the Third and final Test against Pakistan at Hobart in January 2010, Michael Clarke joined Ricky Ponting at the crease with their side placed on a precarious 71 for 3 and proceeded to put Pakistan's bowlers to the sword. By the time Clarke (166) departed 102.4 overs later, the pair had added 352 runs for the fourth wicket – an all-time record partnership in Australia–Pakistan Test matches. Australia ended up on 519 for 8 (with Ponting reaching 209) and went on to win the match by 231 runs to secure a 3–0 series whitewash.

⊙ PAKISTAN'S SHOCKER IN SHARJAH

Forced to play their three-match series against Australia in October 2002 at neutral venues as a result of safety concerns in their home country, Pakistan played like a fish out of water in the Second Test at Sharjah. After winning the toss and electing to bat, they crashed to 59 all out in their first innings (in 31.5 overs), the lowest score ever made in matches between the two countries. The record did not last for long, however: in the second innings Pakistan fared even worse, subsiding to a sorry 53 all out to lose by an innings and 198 runs.

MOST RUNS: TOP 10

Pos	Runs	Player (Team, Span)
1	1,797	Javed Miandad (Pakistan, 1976–90)
2	1,666	Allan Border (Australia, 1979–90)
3	1,581	Greg Chappell (Australia, 1972–84)
4	1,537	Ricky Ponting (Australia, 1998–2010)
5	1,411	Zaheer Abbas (Pakistan, 1972–84)
6	1,347	Mark Taylor (Australia, 1990–98)
7	1,139	Justin Langer (Australia, 1994–2005)
8	1,106	Saleem Malik (Pakistan, 1983–98)
9	1,085	Ijaz Ahmed (Pakistan, 1988–99)
10	1,016	Kim Hughes (Australia, 1979–84)

⊙ MOST CATCHES

Mark Waugh is the most successful fielder in all Tests between Australia and Pakistan: he took 23 catches in 15 matches against Pakistan between 1994 and 2002.

OVERALL SERIES RECORDS
(57 Tests between 1956 and 2010)

	W	L	T	D	W/L	%W	%L	%D
Pakistan	12	28	0	17	0.42	21.05	49.12	29.83
Australia	28	12	0	17	2.33	49.12	21.05	29.83

First match: 11–17 October 1956, Karachi, Pakistan

⊙ PAKISTAN'S BATSMEN FULFIL THEIR SIDE OF THE BARGAIN

Trailing 1–0 in the five-match series, and having seen Australia compile a competitive first-innings score of 465 all out at Adelaide in December 1983, Pakistan knew their only hope of winning the game was to compile a monumental first-innings score and then to bowl out Australia cheaply in their second innings. They fulfilled the first requirement, as centuries from Mohsin Khan (149), Qasim Umar (113) and Javed Miandad (131) propelled them to a mighty 624 all out (the highest team total in all matches between the two countries) and a lead of 159. Their bowlers failed to deliver, however, and the match ended in a draw.

MOST WICKETS: TOP 10

Pos	Wkts	Player (Team, Span)
1	90	Shane Warne (Australia, 1994–2005)
2	80	Glenn McGrath (Australia, 1994–2005)
3	71	Dennis Lillee (Australia, 1972–84)
4	64	Imran Khan (Pakistan, 1976–90)
5	57	Iqbal Qasim (Pakistan, 1976–88)
6	52	Sarfraz Nawaz (Pakistan, 1972–84)
7	50	Wasim Akram (Pakistan, 1990–99)
8	45	Abdul Qadir (Pakistan, 1982–88)
9	35	Mushtaq Ahmed (Pakistan, 1990–99)
10	34	Danish Kaneria (Pakistan, 2002–10)

WEST INDIES v PAKISTAN

Having won eight of the last 13 matches played between the two countries, one could easily assume that Pakistan have enjoyed an unrelenting supremacy over the West Indies, but this is only a recent phenomenon: despite the historic ebb and flow of a team's fortunes, matches between Pakistan and the West Indies have, for the most part, been closely fought affairs.

⊙ MOST DISMISSALS

A solid if not spectacular performer behind the stumps for the West Indies in a 25-Test career, Gerry Alexander holds the record for the most dismissals in Pakistan–West Indies Test matches. In eight games against Pakistan between 1958 and 1959, the former West Indies captain captured 29 victims, with 25 catches and four stumpings.

⊙ WINDIES PUT ON BATTING MASTERCLASS UNDER THE JAMAICAN SUN

There were four main factors in the West Indies' crushing victory over Pakistan at Kingston, Jamaica, in February–March 1958: Pakistan's depleted and toothless bowling attack; Garfield Sobers's monumental innings of 365 not out (a new world record); the support Sobers received from Conrad Hunte, who scored 260 (the pair's partnership of 446 for the second wicket is an all-time record in matches between the two countries); and the home side's colossal first-innings total of 790 for 3 declared (the highest team total in Tests between the two countries). Trailing by 462 runs after the first innings, Pakistan wilted to 288 all out.

⊙ RICH PICKINGS AGAINST THE WEST INDIES

Mohammad Yousuf has enjoyed some good times against the West Indies. In eight Tests against the islanders since 2000 he has scored 1,214 runs, with seven centuries (a highest of 192 in the First Test of the 2006–07 series at Lahore) at an average of 101.16 – the highest of any batsman to complete ten or more innings in matches between the two sides.

⊙ MOST CATCHES

Viv Richards holds the record for the most catches in Test matches between Pakistan and the West Indies. The "Master Blaster" from Antigua bagged 23 catches in 16 Tests against Pakistan between 1975 and 1988.

⊙ SOBERS ACHIEVES SUPERSTAR STATUS

The outstanding performance of a 21-year-old left-handed batsman overshadowed all other events in the Third Test between the West Indies and Pakistan at Kingston, Jamaica, in February–March 1958. Garfield Sobers (still waiting to score his first century and playing in his 17th Test match) compiled a peerless innings of 365 not out to break Len Hutton's world record score of 364 against Australia at The Oval in 1938 to prompt 20,000 ecstatic supporters to invade the pitch in wild celebration. He wasn't finished there: in the Fourth Test at Georgetown, Guyana, he scored 125 and 109 not out and ended the series with 824 runs to his name at an imposing average of 137.33 – the highest in any series between Pakistan and the West Indies in history.

OVERALL SERIES RECORDS
(44 Tests between 1958 and 2006)

	W	L	T	D	W/L	%W	%L	%D
West Indies	14	15	0	15	0.93	31.82	34.09	34.09
Pakistan	15	14	0	15	1.07	34.09	31.82	34.09

First match: 17–23 January 1958, Bridgetown, Barbados

MOST RUNS: TOP 10

Pos	Runs	Player (Team, Span)
1	1,173	Brian Lara (West Indies, 1990–2006)
2	1,214	Mohammad Yousuf (Pakistan, 2000–06)
3	1,124	Inzamam-ul-Haq (Pakistan, 1993–2006)
4	1,091	Viv Richards (West Indies, 1975–88)
5	998	Carl Hooper (West Indies, 1988–2002)
6	984	Garfield Sobers (West Indies, 1958–59)
7	928	Desmond Haynes (West Indies, 1980–93)
8	923	Shivnarine Chanderpaul (West Indies, 1997–2006)
9	919	Wasim Raja (Pakistan, 1975–81)
10	861	Gordon Greenidge (West Indies, 1977–90)

⊙ WEST INDIES FELLED TO RECORD LOW IN FAISALABAD

The West Indies may not have enjoyed the best of times on Pakistani soil – winning only four times in 21 attempts – but they slipped to a record-breaking low in the First Test of the 1986–87 series between the two countries at Faisalabad. Set an achievable 240 for victory, they capitulated in the face of fine bowling from Imran Khan (4 for 30) and Abdul Qadir (6 for 16), subsiding to a miserable 53 all out and a 186-run defeat. It is the lowest team total in all matches between the two countries

MOST WICKETS: TOP 10

Pos	Wkts	Player (Team, Span)
1	80	Imran Khan (Pakistan, 1977–90)
2	79	Wasim Akram (Pakistan, 1986–2000)
3	63	Courtney Walsh (West Indies, 1986–2000)
4	55	Waqar Younis (Pakistan, 1990–2002)
5	50	Colin Croft (West Indies, 1977–81)
=	50	Malcolm Marshall (West Indies, 1980–90)
7	42	Abdul Qadir (Pakistan, 1980–90)
=	42	Curtly Ambrose (West Indies, 1988–2000)
9	41	Fazal Mahmood (Pakistan, 1958–59)
10	35	Joel Garner (West Indies, 1977–81)

⊙ CROFT CRUSHES PAKISTAN

Perhaps the most feared of all the legendary West Indian fast bowlers over the years, owing to his penchant for, and skill at, unleashing a barrage of high-speed, short-pitched deliveries, Colin Croft flattened Pakistan's batsmen into submission in the 1976–77 series in the Caribbean. In the Second Test at Port of Spain, Trinidad, the paceman took 8 for 29 in the second innings (still the best bowling figures by a West Indian in Test history, and a record in matches between the countries) to lead his side to a six-wicket victory. He ended the series, which the West Indies won 2–1, with 33 wickets to his name, another record in Tests between the two sides.

⊙ MOST PRODUCTIVE PARTNERSHIP

The most productive partnership in all Tests between the West Indies and Pakistan is that between Conrad Hunte and Garfield Sobers. The pair combined to score 723 runs in five innings in the 1957–58 series (with a highest of 446 at Kingston, Jamaica) at an average of 144.60.

PAKISTAN v SRI LANKA

Sri Lanka have played Pakistan on more occasions than they have played against any other Test nation and, despite losing five of their first seven Tests against them, have enjoyed considerable success against their subcontinental near-neighbours. Pakistan still lead the overall series (with 15 wins to Sri Lanka's nine) but, in recent times, matches between the two are regularly competitive.

⊙ THE POSITIVE SIDE OF A SERIES THAT ENDED IN DISASTER

Sri Lanka's 2008–09 tour to Pakistan will always be remembered for the terror attack on the Sri Lanka team bus in Lahore that left eight people dead and the Sri Lanka players, seven of whom had been injured, scrambling aboard a helicopter in a hastily arranged evacuation. One of the injured, Thilan Samaraweera (who had suffered a shrapnel wound to the thigh), had been in the form of his life with the bat. The talented middle-order batsman's risk-free approach to his trade paid dividends as he scored 231 in the drawn First Test in Karachi and 214 in the curtailed Second Test in Lahore. His series haul of 469 runs (at an average of 234.50) is an all-time Pakistan–Sri Lanka record in Test cricket.

⊙ SILKY SANGAKKARA TOPS AVERAGES LIST

A highly talented left-handed stroke player, Kumar Sangakkara has been an integral member of Sri Lanka's batting line-up from the moment he made his debut in 2000. He has enjoyed considerable success against Pakistan over the years, hitting five of his 21 Test centuries in ten matches against them – with a highest score of 230 at Lahore in March 2002 – and scoring 1,314 runs at an average of 77.29, the highest of any player to have completed ten or more innings in Pakistan–Sri Lanka Tests.

⊙ MOST CATCHES

Mahela Jayawardene holds the record for the most catches by a fielder in matches between Pakistan and Sri Lanka: the Sri Lankan has bagged 26 catches in 18 Tests against Pakistan between 1999 and 2009.

⊙ MURALITHARAN IS STAR OF THE SHOW

Not for the first time in his record-breaking career, Muttiah Muralitharan was at the heart of Sri Lanka's 2–1 away series victory over Pakistan in 1999–2000. The wily off-spinner took a series record 29 wickets in the three Tests, with a best of 6 for 71 during Sri Lanka's 57-run, series-clinching victory in the Second Test at Peshawar.

OVERALL SERIES RECORDS
(37 Tests between 1982 and 2009)

	W	L	T	D	W/L	%W	%L	%D
Pakistan	15	9	0	13	1.66	40.54	24.32	35.14
Sri Lanka	9	15	0	13	0.60	24.32	40.54	35.14

First match: 5–10 March 1982, Karachi, Pakistan

MOST WICKETS: TOP 10

Pos	Wkts	Player (Team, Span)
1	80	Muttiah Muralitharan (Sri Lanka, 1994–2009)
2	63	Wasim Akram (Pakistan, 1985–2000)
3	56	Waqar Younis (Pakistan, 1991–2002)
4	47	Chaminda Vaas (Sri Lanka, 1994–2009)
5	46	Imran Khan (Pakistan, 1982–92)
6	35	Danish Kaneria (Pakistan, 2004–09)
7	34	Saqlain Mushtaq (Pakistan, 1995–2000)
8	30	Pramodya Wickramasinghe (Sri Lanka, 1991–2000)
9	28	Ashantha de Mel (Sri Lanka, 1982–86)
10	26	Tauseef Ahmed (Pakistan, 1982–86)
=	26	Abdul Razzaq (Pakistan, 2000–06)
=	26	Rangana Herath (Sri Lanka, 2000–09)

⊙ MOST DISMISSALS

A veteran of 69 Test matches for Pakistan, Moin Khan is the leading wicketkeeper in Pakistan–Sri Lanka Test matches. The former captain claimed 40 victims (35 catches and five stumpings) in 16 matches against Sri Lanka between 1991 and 2004.

⊙ PAKISTAN GRIND OUT THE RUNS IN KARACHI

There have been few more turgid stalemates in Test history. On a desperately flat track – the scourge of the modern game – at Karachi in the First Test of the 2008–09 series, Sri Lanka won the toss, elected to bat, and cruised to 644 for 7 declared. Confident Sri Lanka may have been – defeat was now out of the equation – but the Pakistan batsmen, also thriving on the lifeless surface, responded in style. Aided by a magnificent 313 from captain Younis Khan (the highest individual score in Pakistan–Sri Lanka matches) and an unbeaten 158 from Kamran Akmal, Pakistan powered to 765 for 6 declared – the highest total in all matches between the two countries. To the surprise of no one, the match ended in a draw.

⊙ PERFECT PARTNERS

Mahela Jayawardene (240) and Thilan Samaraweera (231) were Sri Lanka's driving force in the First Test against Pakistan at Karachi in February 2009. The pair added 437 runs for the fourth wicket to power Sri Lanka to 644 for 7 declared in their first innings and a position of impregnability. It is the highest partnership in all Tests between the two countries. The pair also hold the record for being the most productive partnership in Pakistan–Sri Lanka Tests: they have combined to score 883 runs in 16 innings against Pakistan between 2002 and 2009.

MOST RUNS: TOP 10

Pos	Runs	Player (Team, Span)
1	1,559	Inzamam-ul-Haq (Pakistan, 1994–2006)
2	1,490	Sanath Jayasuriya (Sri Lanka, 1991–2006)
3	1,475	Aravinda de Silva (Sri Lanka, 1985–2000)
4	1,314	Kumar Sangakkara (Sri Lanka, 2002–09)
5	1,210	Arjuna Ranatunga (Sri Lanka, 1982–2000)
6	1,135	Younis Khan (Pakistan, 2000–09)
7	1,115	Mahela Jayawardene (S. Lanka, 1999–2009)
8	941	Thilan Samaraweera (Sri Lanka, 2002–09)
9	919	Saeed Anwar (Pakistan, 1994–2000)
10	820	Hashan Tillakaratne (Sri Lanka, 1991–2002)

INDIA v SRI LANKA

While India have enjoyed a prolonged period of success in Test matches against Sri Lanka on home soil – winning ten of 17 Tests and not registering a single defeat – matches in Sri Lanka have always been closer affairs, with India recording only four victories to Sri Lanka's six.

⊙ NEW KID ON THE BLOCK

Ajantha Mendis burst on to the Test cricket scene in spectacular style against India in 2008. Bowling a mixture of leg-spinners, googlies, top-spinners, flippers and speciality "caroms" (released from an unusual snap of the fingers), the Sri Lankan sensation bamboozled India's batsmen. In the First Test at Colombo he became the first Sri Lankan in history to take eight wickets on debut, and he ended the series with 26 wickets – a series record in matches between India and Sri Lanka (and also the best return for a bowler in a three-match debut series, beating Alec Bedser's record haul against India in 1946 by two).

⊙ SEHWAG SPARKLES AGAINST SRI LANKA

A scintillating opening batsman for India with a penchant for compiling huge scores, Virender Sehwag has often been in prime form against Sri Lanka: in 18 innings against them he has scored 1,239 runs – including two double-centuries (201 not out at Galle in July 2008, and 293 at Mumbai in December 2009) – at an average of 72.88. It is the highest by any player to have completed ten or more innings in India–Sri Lanka Test matches.

OVERALL SERIES RECORDS
(32 Tests between 1982 and 2010)

	W	L	T	D	W/L	%W	%L	%D
India	14	6	0	15	2.33	40.00	17.14	52.86
Sri Lanka	6	14	0	15	0.42	17.14	40.00	52.86

First match: 17–22 September 1982, Chennai, India

MOST RUNS: TOP 5

Pos	Runs	Player (Team, Span)
1	1,995	Sachin Tendulkar (India, 1990–2010)
2	1,882	Mahela Jayawardene (Sri Lanka, 1997–2010)
3	1,508	Rahul Dravid (India, 1997–2010)
4	1,257	Kumar Sangakkara (Sri Lanka, 2001–10)
5	1,252	Aravinda de Silva (Sri Lanka, 1985–99)

⊙ SRI LANKA'S BATTING FUN IN THE COLOMBO SUN

The First Test between Sri Lanka and India at Colombo in August 1997 turned into yet another Test match in the subcontinent in which the bat completely dominated, but at least it was a record-breaking one. Having seen India compile 537 for 8 in their first innings, Sri Lanka, helped by sublime innings from both Sanath Jayasuriya (340) and Roshan Mahanama (225), produced a mammoth response, compiling a mighty 952 for 6 declared – the highest team total in Test history – as the match petered out into an inevitable draw.

MOST WICKETS: TOP 5

Pos	Wkts	Player (Team, Span)
1	105	Muttiah Muralitharan (Sri Lanka, 1993–2010)
2	74	Anil Kumble (India, 1993–2008)
3	52	Harbhajan Singh (India, 1999–2010)
4	45	Kapil Dev (India, 1982–94)
5	34	Ajantha Mendis (Sri Lanka, 2008–10)

SRI LANKA v ENGLAND

Even from the first Test matches between the two countries, England have failed to dominate Sri Lanka – perhaps it was this that prompted a seeming reluctance from the ECB to schedule fixtures against the islanders (the two countries played just five Tests between 1982 and 1993) – and in the 21 Tests played have won only eight to Sri Lanka's six.

⊙ SRI LANKA SHOW ENGLAND HOW IT'S DONE IN COLOMBO

Having seen England compile an under-par first-innings 265 all out in the decisive Third and final Test at Colombo in December 2003 (the series was locked at 0–0 as it reached its finale), Sri Lanka's batsmen put a toothless England attack to the sword, compiling a massive 628 for 8 declared – the highest team total in all matches between the two countries – en route to a comprehensive and series-clinching innings-and-215-run victory.

⊙ LOWEST SCORE

The lowest team score in the history of England–Sri Lanka matches is 81 all out, a fate that has been suffered on two occasions: by Sri Lanka at Colombo in March 2001 and by England at Galle in December 2007.

MOST RUNS: TOP 5

Pos	Runs	Player (Team, Span)
1	1,581	Mahela Jayawardene (Sri Lanka, 1998–2007)
2	1,007	Kumar Sangakkara (Sri Lanka, 2001–07)
3	957	Marcus Trescothick (England, 2001–06)
4	819	Sanath Jayasuriya (Sri Lanka, 1991–2007)
5	755	Michael Vaughan (England, 2001–07)

⊙ HIGHEST INDIVIDUAL SCORE

The record for the highest individual score in Test matches between England and Sri Lanka is 213, a feat achieved by two Sri Lankan batsmen: Sanath Jayasuriya (213 at The Oval in August 1998) and Mahela Jayawardene (213 not out at Galle in December 2007). Jayawardene has prospered against England: in 27 innings against them between 1998 and 2007 he has scored 1,581 runs at an average of 65.87 – the highest average of any batsman to have completed ten or more innings in England–Sri Lanka Test matches.

⊙ BEST BOWLING IN AN INNINGS/ MATCH/SERIES

The magical Muttiah Muralitharan, Test cricket's all-time leading wicket-taker, holds every major bowling record in the book in England–Sri Lanka matches: he is the only bowler to take more than 100 wickets (112); he recorded the best single-innings bowling figures (9 for 65 at The Oval in August 1998); the best match figures (16 for 220 in the same Test at The Oval); and the most wickets in a series (26 in Sri Lanka's victorious 2003–04 series against England).

OVERALL SERIES RECORDS
(21 Tests between 1982 and 2007)

	W	L	T	D	W/L	%W	%L	%D
Sri Lanka	6	8	0	7	0.75	28.57	38.10	33.33
England	8	6	0	7	1.33	38.10	28.57	33.33

First match: 17–21 February 1982, Colombo, Sri Lanka

NEW ZEALAND v SRI LANKA

That it took nine years and 11 Tests for Sri Lanka to record their first win in matches between the two countries suggests that New Zealand have a firm hold over the Sri Lankans, but while that may have been the case in early clashes, the pendulum has certainly swung back in recent times. Sri Lanka have won five of their last ten Test matches against New Zealand (losing twice) since July 1998.

⊙ VETTORI'S RECORD-BREAKING EFFORTS ALL IN VAIN

If only New Zealand's batsmen could have displayed with the bat the skill levels Daniel Vettori showed with the ball, the outcome might well have been different. With New Zealand already in trouble in the Second Test against Sri Lanka at Wellington in December 2006 (they were 138 runs behind as Sri Lanka started their second innings), the Kiwi slow left-armer did all he could to bring his side back into the match, taking 7 for 130 – the best single-innings bowling figures in New Zealand-Sri Lanka Tests – to help dismiss the visitors for 365. Set an improbable 504 runs for victory, however, New Zealand slipped to 286 all out and a heavy 217-run defeat.

OVERALL SERIES RECORDS
(26 Tests between 1983 and 2009)

	W	L	T	D	W/L	%W	%L	%D
New Zealand	9	7	0	10	1.28	34.62	26.92	38.46
Sri Lanka	7	9	0	10	0.77	26.92	34.62	38.46

First match: 4–6 March 1983, Christchurch, New Zealand

⊙ NOBODY CAN KEEP UP WITH JONES

One of the pillars upon which New Zealand built their record-breaking recovery against Sri Lanka at Wellington in January–February 1991, hitting 186 (his highest Test score), Andrew Jones continued to enjoy good times against Sri Lanka. In six Tests against them he scored 625 runs (with two further centuries) at an average of 62.50 – the highest by any batsman to complete ten or more innings in New Zealand-Sri Lanka Test matches.

⊙ VAAS A CUT ABOVE THE REST

It was a performance that propelled Sri Lanka to an unexpected victory on a wicket tailored for New Zealand's fast bowlers and which confirmed Chaminda Vaas's status as the finest fast bowler Sri Lanka has ever produced. In the First Test at Napier in March 1995, the left-arm paceman took 5 for 47 in the first innings and 5 for 43 in the second to lead Sri Lanka to a hefty 241-run victory. His match figures of 10 for 90 are the best in all New Zealand-Sri Lanka Tests.

MOST RUNS: TOP 5

Pos	Runs	Player (Team, Span)
1	1,166	Stephen Fleming (New Zealand, 1995–2006)
2	928	Mahela Jayawardene (Sri Lanka, 1998–2009)
3	824	Arjuna Ranatunga (Sri Lanka, 1984–98)
4	819	Hashan Tillakaratne (Sri Lanka, 1991–2003)
5	785	Aravinda de Silva (Sri Lanka, 1991–98)

MOST WICKETS: TOP 5

Pos	Wkts	Player (Team, Span)
1	82	Muttiah Muralitharan (Sri Lanka, 1992–2009)
2	51	Daniel Vettori (New Zealand, 1997–2009)
3	42	Chaminda Vaas (Sri Lanka, 1995–2006)
4	37	Richard Hadlee (New Zealand, 1983–87)
5	24	Vinothen John (Sri Lanka, 1983–84)

SRI LANKA v AUSTRALIA

Sri Lanka have not enjoyed the best of times in Tests against Australia since the two sides met for the first time in Kandy in 1983. They have won only once in 20 attempts and, sensationally at Melbourne in 1995, saw their leading bowler, Muttiah Muralitharan, become one of only 11 players in Test history (and the only Sri Lankan) to be no-balled for throwing.

⊙ SRI LANKA DOWN AND OUT IN DARWIN

Before the Test it was thought that the soft, seaming wicket prepared at Darwin for the First Test of the two-match 2004 series in Australia was unlikely to bring the best out of the Sri Lankan batsmen, and so it proved. Having dismissed Australia comparatively cheaply for 207 in the first innings, Sri Lanka wilted on the unfamiliar surface to 97 all out – the lowest team total in Australia-Sri Lanka Tests. The tourists fared little better second time round: set 312 for victory, they limped to 162 all out – with Michael Kasprowicz taking 7 for 37 (the best single-innings figures in all Tests between the two countries) – and a 149-run defeat.

⊙ HAPPY TIMES FOR WAUGH

The most capped player in Test history (he appeared in 168 Test matches), Steve Waugh enjoyed some fine moments against Sri Lanka. In eight Tests against them between 1988 and 1999, he scored 701 runs (with three centuries – and a highest score of 170 at Adelaide in January 1996) at an average of 87.62 – the highest of any batsman to complete ten or more innings in matches between the two countries.

MOST RUNS: TOP 5

Pos	Runs	Player (Team, Span)
1	851	Ricky Ponting (Australia, 1995–2007)
2	803	Aravinda de Silva (Sri Lanka, 1988–99)
3	701	Steve Waugh (Australia, 1988–99)
4	686	Sanath Jayasuriya (Sri Lanka, 1992–2007)
5	673	Arjuna Ranatunga (Sri Lanka, 1983–99)

MOST WICKETS: TOP 5

Pos	Wkts	Player (Team, Span)
1	59	Shane Warne (Australia, 1992–2004)
2	54	Muttiah Muralitharan (Sri Lanka, 1992–2007)
3	38	Chaminda Vaas (Sri Lanka, 1995–2007)
4	37	Glenn McGrath (Australia, 1995–2004)
5	27	Craig McDermott (Australia, 1988–96)

⊙ AUSTRALIA PROSPER AGAINST FALTERING SRI LANKA

Australia's batsmen took full advantage of an underperforming Sri Lankan bowling attack dogged by accusations of ball-tampering (Sri Lanka became the first team in Test history to be charged with the offence, although the ICC reversed the decision two weeks later) in the First Test of the 1995–96 series at Perth. Led by centuries from Michael Slater, whose 219 is the highest individual score in Australia-Sri Lanka Tests, and Mark Waugh (111), they amassed a colossal 617 for 5 declared – the highest team total in all matches between the two countries – en route to an innings-and-36-run victory.

OVERALL SERIES RECORDS
(20 Tests between 1983 and 2007)

	W	L	T	D	W/L	%W	%L	%D
Sri Lanka	1	13	0	6	0.07	5.00	65.00	30.00
Australia	13	1	0	6	13.00	65.00	5.00	30.00

First match: 22–26 April 1983, Kandy, Sri Lanka

WEST INDIES v SOUTH AFRICA

As the two countries first met only in 1992, by which time the shameful policy of apartheid had started to unravel, South Africa, for the most part, have played only against a troubled West Indian side whose glory days seemed far behind them. As a result, South Africa have dominated proceedings, winning 14 of the 22 Tests played to the West Indies' three.

⊙ A RUN-FEST IN ANTIGUA

The Antigua Recreation Ground confirmed its reputation as possessing the most benign strip in world cricket when the West Indies met South Africa in the Fourth and final Test of the 2004–05 series. South Africa, holding an impregnable 2–0 series lead, won the toss and batted the West Indies out of the game with 588 for 6 declared. But the West Indies, playing for nothing more than pride, responded bravely. Led by an imperious 317 from Chris Gayle (the highest individual score in all matches between the two countries) and three centuries from Ramnaresh Sarwan (127), Shivnarine Chanderpaul (127) and Dwayne Bravo (107), they amassed a colossal 747 all out – the 11th highest team total in Test history and the highest in West Indies-South Africa clashes – as the match meandered towards an inevitable draw.

MOST RUNS: TOP 5

Pos	Runs	Player (Team, Span)
1	2,356	Jacques Kallis (South Africa, 1998–2010)
2	1,715	Brian Lara (West Indies, 1992–2005)
3	1,619	Shivnarine Chanderpaul (West Indies, 1998–2010)
4	1,593	Graeme Smith (South Africa, 2003–10)
5	1,403	Herschelle Gibbs (South Africa, 1998–2008)

MOST WICKETS: TOP 5

Pos	Wkts	Player (Team, Span)
1	70	Shaun Pollock (South Africa, 1998–2008)
2	63	Makhaya Ntini (South Africa, 2001–08)
3	52	Andre Nel (South Africa, 2003–08)
=	52	Jacques Kallis (South Africa, 1998–2010)
5	51	Courtney Walsh (West Indies, 1992–2001)

⊙ DEADLY DE VILLIERS FINDS HIS FORM

A.B. de Villiers has enjoyed some of the finest moments of his already impressive Test career against the West Indies. The right-handed middle-order batsman has hit four of his ten Test centuries against the men from the Caribbean (with a best of 178 at Bridgetown, Barbados, in April 2005) and has hit 1,037 runs in 18 innings at an average of 79.76 – the highest by any batsman to have completed ten innings or more in matches between the two countries.

⊙ GETTING OFF TO THE WORST OF STARTS

The West Indies have endured a miserable sequence of results against South Africa in recent times (losing 5–0 in 1998–99, 2–1 in 2001 and winning only one of 11 Tests against them between 2003 and 2008), so a good start was essential for both their confidence and morale when the two sides met for the First Test (of three) at Port of Spain in June 2010. South Africa won the toss, elected to bat and reached 352 all out. In reply, the West Indies slumped to 102 all out – the lowest total in all Tests between the two countries – and went on to lose the match by 163 runs.

⊙ MOST WICKETS IN A SERIES

The record for the most wickets in a West Indies-South Africa series is 29, a feat achieved by two South African players: Shaun Pollock, in South Africa in 1998–99; and Makhaya Ntini, in South Africa in 2003–04.

OVERALL SERIES RECORDS
(25 Tests between 1992 and 2010)

	W	L	T	D	W/L	%W	%L	%D
West Indies	3	16	0	6	0.18	12.00	64.00	24.00
South Africa	16	3	0	6	5.33	64.00	12.00	24.00

First match: 18–23 April 1992, Bridgetown, Barbados

ZIMBABWE v INDIA

Apart from a pair of unexpected defeats in Harare (in October 1998 and June 2001, when Zimbabwe cricket was at its strongest), India dominated the few Tests they played against Zimbabwe between 1992 and 2005, winning seven out of 11 and drawing two.

⊙ DISAPPOINTMENT IN DELHI FOR ZIM

Trailing India by a mere 25 runs after the completion of the first innings in the Second Test of the two-match 2001–02 series at Delhi, and still very much in the game, Zimbabwe failed to cope with the dual spin threat of Harbhajan Singh and Anil Kumble. The former took 6 for 62 and the latter 4 for 58 as Zimbabwe slipped to 146 all out the lowest team total in Tests between the two countries and an eventual four-wicket defeat.

OVERALL SERIES RECORDS
(11 Tests between 1992 and 2005)

	W	L	T	D	W/L	%W	%L	%D
Zimbabwe	2	7	0	2	0.28	18.18	63.64	18.18
India	7	2	0	2	3.50	63.64	18.18	18.18

First match: 18–22 October 1992, Harare, Zimbabwe

MOST RUNS: TOP 5

Pos	Runs	Player (Team, Span)
1	1,138	Andy Flower (Zimbabwe, 1992–2002)
2	979	Rahul Dravid (India, 1998–2005)
3	918	Sachin Tendulkar (India, 1992–2002)
4	565	Grant Flower (Zimbabwe, 1992–2002)
5	560	Shiv Sander Das (India, 2000–02)

⊙ RECORDS TUMBLE IN NAGPUR

One-nil up in the series when going into the Second and final Test at Nagpur in November 2000, India won the toss and batted Zimbabwe out of the game as centuries from Shiv Sunder Das (110), Rahul Dravid (162) and Sachin Tendulkar (201) propelled them to a mighty 609 for 6 declared – the highest team score in matches between the two sides. When, having dismissed Zimbabwe for 382, they enforced the follow-on, an Indian victory seemed the most probable outcome. In stepped Andy Flower, however, hitting an unbeaten 232 – the highest individual score in Zimbabwe-India Tests – to rescue the draw.

⊙ THE WALL STANDS FIRM

Although Andy Flower may have outgunned him as the all-time leading run-scorer in Zimbabwe-India Tests, no batsman played with more consistency than Rahul Dravid. In 13 innings against Zimbabwe between 1998 and 2005, the man nicknamed "The Wall" hit 979 runs, including five half-centuries and three centuries (with a highest score of 200 not out at Delhi in November 2000), at an average of 97.90 – the highest by any batsman to complete ten or more innings in matches between the two countries.

⊙ PATHAN PROSPERS UNDER THE AFRICAN SUN

India's comprehensive 2–0 series win over a weak Zimbabwe side in 2005–06 was a personal triumph for Irfan Pathan. Swinging the ball prodigiously, the medium-fast bowler took 5 for 58 and 4 for 53 in India's innings-and-90-run victory in the First Test at Bulawayo, and 7 for 59 (the best single-innings bowling figures in Zimbabwe-India Tests) and 5 for 67 in India's ten-wicket win in the Second Test at Harare. His match figures of 12 for 156 at Harare and his series haul of 21 wickets are both records in matches between the two countries.

ZIMBABWE v NEW ZEALAND

Matches between Zimbabwe and New Zealand have been one-way affairs ever since the two sides met for the first time in Bulawayo in 1992, with New Zealand winning seven of the 13 Test matches played and Zimbabwe failing to record a single victory.

⊙ ASTLE TOPS THE BATTING CHARTS

A free-scoring middle-order batsman and a veteran of 81 Test matches for his country, Nathan Astle has been the outstanding batsman in matches between Zimbabwe and New Zealand. The Canterbury star is the leading run-scorer – with 813 runs in 11 Tests between 1996 and 2003 (including three centuries and a highest score of 141 at Wellington in December 2000) – and has the highest average of any batsman to have completed ten or more innings in matches between the two countries (50.81).

⊙ HUCKLE'S SPELL IN THE LIMELIGHT

The brightest moments in Adam Huckle's brief eight-Test career came in the drawn two-match series against New Zealand in 1997–98. In the Second Test at Bulawayo, the leg-spinner took 6 for 109 in the first innings and 5 for 146 in the second as New Zealand, chasing 286 for victory, hung on at 275 for 8 to force a hard-fought, if nervous, draw. Huckle's match haul of 11 for 255 is the best in Zimbabwe-New Zealand Tests, and his series haul of 16 wickets is another record in matches between the two countries.

OVERALL SERIES RECORDS
(13 Tests between 1992 and 2005)

	W	L	T	D	W/L	%W	%L	%D
Zimbabwe	0	7	0	6	0.00	0.00	53.85	46.15
New Zealand	7	0	0	6	-	53.85	0.00	46.15

First match: 1–5 November 1992, Bulawayo, Zimbabwe

⊙ EVERY CLOUD HAS A SILVER LINING

In the end, a flat lifeless pitch was the winner as New Zealand and Zimbabwe played out a predictable draw in the one-off Test at Wellington in December 2000, but, in spite of the result's inevitability, at least New Zealand's batsmen created a slice of history: their first-innings score of 487 for 7 declared was the highest in all Test matches between the two countries.

⊙ HOPES OF RETURN TO FORM DASHED

After a series of disastrous results following the player rebellion in 2004, Zimbabwe hoped that the return of a handful of the rebels for the First Test against New Zealand at Harare in August 2005 would signal a change of fortune. Instead, Zimbabwe sank to a new low. Having seen New Zealand compile an impressive 452 for 9 declared in their first innings, the home side slumped to 59 all out in 29.4 overs – the lowest total in all Zimbabwe-New Zealand Test matches – and an eventual innings-and-294-run defeat (the heaviest defeat in Zimbabwe's history).

MOST RUNS: TOP 5

Pos	Runs	Player (Team, Span)
1	813	Nathan Astle (New Zealand, 1996–2005)
2	780	Grant Flower (Zimbabwe, 1992–2000)
3	721	Andy Flower (Zimbabwe, 1992–2000)
4	647	Guy Whittall (Zimbabwe, 1996–2000)
5	640	Stephen Fleming (New Zealand, 1996–2005)

MOST WICKETS: TOP 5

Pos	Wkts	Player (Team, Span)
1	39	Chris Cairns (New Zealand, 1996–2000)
2	32	Heath Streak (Zimbabwe, 1996–2005)
3	29	Paul Strang (Zimbabwe, 1996–2000)
4	23	Dipak Patel (New Zealand, 1992–96)
=	23	Daniel Vettori (New Zealand, 1997–2005)

SOUTH AFRICA v INDIA

Ever since South Africa edged the historic 1992 home series against India (the first team they played against in the post-apartheid era), they have enjoyed a measure of supremacy over them, both at home and away, recording 12 victories in the 27 Tests played to India's six.

⊙ INDIA SIEZE THEIR CHANCE

Having lost the First Test of the two-match series against South Africa in February 2010 (by an innings and 6 runs in Nagpur), it was win or bust for the home side when the two teams faced off in Kolkata a week later. And when South Africa slipped to an under-par 296 all out in their first innings, India were handed their chance. They grabbed it with both hands as centuries from Virender Sehwag (165), Sachin Tendulkar (106), V.V.S. Laxman (143 not out) and captain Mahendra Singh Dhoni (132 not out) propelled them to a mighty 643 for 6 declared – the highest total in all Tests between the two countries – and an eventual innings-and-57-run victory.

⊙ KALLIS IS MR CONSISTENCY

India's batting legend Sachin Tendulkar has scored the most runs (1,741), but no batsman has performed with more consistency in South Africa-India Tests than Jacques Kallis. South Africa's legendary all-rounder has scored 1,585 runs in 16 Tests against India since 2000 – with a highest score of 201 not out at Pretoria in December 2010 – at an average of 72.04, the highest by any batsman to complete ten or more innings in matches between these two formidable countries.

⊙ DOWN AND OUT IN DURBAN

India's batsmen failed to cope either with an electric performance from South Africa fast bowler Allan Donald (who took 9 for 54 in the match) or with a lively Durban wicket in the First Test of the 1996–97 series. Set an unlikely 395 runs to win the low-scoring match, they crashed to 66 all out – the lowest team total in Tests between the countries – and a 328-run defeat.

⊙ KLUSENER'S CRACKING DEBUT

Lance Klusener produced one of the most scintillating debut performances in Test history to lead South Africa to a comprehensive victory over India in the Second Test of the 1996–97 series at Kolkata. With the home side set an unlikely 467 runs to win both the match and the series, the all-rounder took 8 for 64. They are the best figures by a debutant in South Africa's history and the best single-innings figures in the history of Tests between South Africa and India. Remarkably, this remained the only five-wicket haul of Klusener's 49-Test career.

MOST RUNS: TOP 5

Pos	Runs	Player (Team, Span)
1	1,741	Sachin Tendulkar (India, 1992–2011)
2	1,585	Jacques Kallis (South Africa, 2000–11)
3	1,306	Virender Sehwag (India, 2001–11)
4	1,252	Rahul Dravid (India, 1996–2011)
5	1,164	Hashim Amla (South Africa, 2004–11)

OVERALL SERIES RECORDS
(27 Tests between 1992 and 2011)

	W	L	T	D	W/L	%W	%L	%D
South Africa	12	7	0	8	1.71	44.44	25.93	26.93
India	7	12	0	8	0.58	25.93	44.44	26.93

First match: 13–17 November 1992, Durban, South Africa

MOST WICKETS: TOP 5

Pos	Wkts	Player (Team, Span)
1	84	Anil Kumble (India, 1992–2008)
2	64	Javagal Srinath (India, 1992–2001)
3	60	Harbhajan Singh (India, 2001–11)
4	57	Allan Donald (South Africa, 1992–2000)
5	53	Dale Steyn (South Africa, 2006–11)

SRI LANKA v SOUTH AFRICA

The difficulties faced by both sides to adapt to alien conditions have had a major bearing on matches between South Africa and Sri Lanka: South Africa, with a tendency to struggle on spin-friendly, slow, low surfaces, have won only twice in ten attempts in Sri Lanka; the islanders, exposed to fast bowling on livelier South African wickets, have drawn one and lost six of the seven Test matches.

⊙ SRI LANKA ON CRUISE CONTROL IN COLOMBO

Sri Lanka crushed South Africa in comprehensive and record-breaking style in the First Test of the 2006 series in Colombo. In the first innings, having dismissed South Africa for an under-par 169 and then slipped to a worrying 14 for 2 in reply, Sri Lanka needed something magical – and their two most gifted batsmen duly obliged. Mahela Jayawardene (374 – the fourth highest score in Test history, and the highest in Sri Lanka-South Africa Tests) and Kumar Sangakkara (287) added 624 runs for the third wicket (the highest partnership for any wicket in Test history) to propel Sri Lanka to a mighty 756 for 5 declared – the highest team total in all matches between the two countries – and an eventual innings-and-153-run victory.

OVERALL SERIES RECORDS
(17 Tests between 1993 and 2006)

	W	L	T	D	W/L	%W	%L	%D
Sri Lanka	4	8	0	5	0.50	23.53	47.06	29.41
South Africa	8	4	0	5	2.00	47.06	23.53	29.41
First match: 25–30 August 1993, Moratuwa, Sri Lanka								

MOST RUNS: TOP 5

Pos	Runs	Player (Team, Span)
1	1,472	Mahela Jayawardene (Sri Lanka, 2000–06)
2	1,182	Kumar Sangakkara (Sri Lanka, 2000–06)
3	917	Darryl Cullinan (South Africa, 1993–2001)
4	857	Sanath Jayasuriya (Sri Lanka, 1993–2006)
5	700	Mark Boucher (South Africa, 1998–2006)

MOST WICKETS: TOP 5

Pos	Wkts	Player (Team, Span)
1	104	Muttiah Muralitharan (Sri Lanka, 1993–2006)
2	48	Shaun Pollock (South Africa, 1998–2006)
3	35	Makhaya Ntini (South Africa, 1998–2006)
4	34	Nicky Boje (South Africa, 2000–06)
5	29	Allan Donald (South Africa, 1993–2001)

⊙ STANDOUT PERFORMER

Quite apart from his headline-grabbing innings of 374 in Colombo in 2006, Mahela Jayawardene has excelled against South Africa. In 12 Tests against them since 2000 he has scored 1,472 runs (the most by any batsman in Tests between the two countries), with five centuries (all of them in home matches), at an average of 70.09 – the highest by any batsman to have completed ten or more innings in Sri Lanka-South Africa clashes.

⊙ MURALI PUTS SOUTH AFRICA IN A SPIN

A legion of South African batsmen have failed to fathom the wristy guile of Muttiah Muralitharan over the years: of his world record 792 Test wickets, 104 have come against South Africa (only against England has he taken more, 112). And Murali was at his spellbinding best in the First Test of the 2000 series against South Africa at Galle, taking 7 for 84 in the second innings to end the match with 13 for 171 (each return a record in Sri Lanka-South Africa Tests) as Sri Lanka won the match by an innings and 15 runs. He ended the series with 26 wickets, another record in a series between Sri Lanka and South Africa.

SRI LANKA v WEST INDIES

Aided by a near-impeccable home record against the West Indies (that has seen them win five and draw one of the six Tests played), Sri Lanka have been the dominant force in matches played between the two countries since they met for the first time in 1993, registering six wins to the West Indies' three.

OVERALL SERIES RECORDS
(15 Tests between 1993 and 2010)

	W	L	T	D	W/L	%W	%L	%D
Sri Lanka	6	3	0	6	2.00	40.00	20.00	40.00
West Indies	3	6	0	6	0.50	20.00	40.00	40.00

First match: 8–13 December 1993, Moratuwa, Sri Lanka

⊙ BEST CAREER AVERAGE
Of all the batsmen to complete ten or more innings in matches between Sri Lanka and the West Indies, Hashan Tillakaratne has the best average – 89.20 in ten innings between 1993 and 2003, including a career-best 204 not out at Colombo in November–December 2001.

⊙ MURALI DASHES WEST INDIAN HOPES
Given that Sri Lanka had amassed 375 in their second innings, it was not inconceivable that the West Indies could chase down a victory target of 378 to win the Second Test at Kandy in July 2005 and square the series. But Muttiah Muralitharan had other ideas, hitting top form to take 8 for 46 – the best single-innings figures in Sri Lanka–West Indies Tests – to help dismiss the West Indies for 137 and lead his side to a 240-run win and a 2–0 series victory.

MOST RUNS: TOP 5

Pos	Runs	Player (Team, Span)
1	1,125	Brian Lara (West Indies, 1993–2003)
2	918	Kumar Sangakkara (Sri Lanka, 2001–10)
3	749	Ramnaresh Sarwan (West Indies, 2001–08)
4	748	Mahela Jayawardene (Sri Lanka, 2001–10)
5	644	Thilan Samaraweera (Sri Lanka, 2001–10)

MOST WICKETS: TOP 5

Pos	Wkts	Player (Team, Span)
1	82	Muttiah Muralitharan (Sri Lanka, 1993–2008)
2	55	Chaminda Vaas (Sri Lanka, 2001–08)
3	14	Curtly Ambrose (West Indies, 1993–97)
=	14	Corey Collymore (West Indies, 2003)
5	13	Daren Powell (West Indies, 2005–08)
=	13	Jermaine Taylor (West Indies, 2003–08)

⊙ THE COLOMBO RUN-FEST

Already holding an unassailable 2–0 lead in the three-match 2001–02 series going into the final Test at Colombo, Sri Lanka responded in style to the West Indies first-innings score of 390 (of which Brian Lara contributed 221 – the highest individual score in all Tests between the two countries). Led by an unbeaten 204 from Hashan Tillakaratne, they compiled 627 for 9 declared – the highest team total in Sri Lanka-West Indies clashes – en route to a ten-wicket win and a 3–0 series whitewash.

⊙ WEST INDIES CRAWL TO RECORD-BREAKING LOW

Holding a 58-run first-innings lead and very much in the driving seat in the First Test of the 2005 series at Colombo, the West Indies then capitulated to Sri Lanka in disappointing style. Unable to withstand fine bowling from Chaminda Vaas (4 for 15) and Muttiah Muralitharan (6 for 36), they limped to 113 all out in 60 overs – the lowest team total in matches between the two countries – and an eventual six-wicket defeat.

ZIMBABWE v SRI LANKA

Sri Lanka may have been forced to work harder to achieve a victory on Zimbabwean soil – they won three of the eight Tests played there and drew five – but at home against the southern Africans they were invincible, recording seven wins out of seven, and most of them in dominant style.

⊙ MARVELLOUS MARVAN HEADS AVERAGES LIST

A veteran of 90 Test matches for Sri Lanka over a period of 17 years, Marvan Atapattu was a useful opening batsman who seemed to reserve his best performances for matches against Zimbabwe. In ten Test matches against them between 1998 and 2004, he scored 1,145 runs, with five centuries, at an average of 95.41 – the highest by any batsman to complete ten or more innings in matches between the two countries.

⊙ SRI LANKA CASH IN AGAINST WEAK ZIMBABWE

By 2004, what was effectively the reserve Zimbabwe team had been exposed as being completely out of its depth in international cricket, and when Sri Lanka played against them at Bulawayo in May 2004 they took full advantage. Having seen Zimbabwe struggle to 228 all out, they made the most of the batting-friendly surface. Bolstered by centuries from captain Marvan Atapattu (249), Kumar Sangakkara (270 – the highest individual score in Zimbabwe-Sri Lanka Tests) and Mahela Jayawardene (100 not out), they reached 713 for 3 declared (the highest team total in all Tests between the two countries) before bowling out Zimbabwe for 231 second time round to win the match by an innings and 254 runs.

⊙ ZIMBABWE GUNNED OUT AT GALLE

In truth, few thought Zimbabwe capable of chasing down a target of 395 runs from 125 overs to win the Third and final Test of the 2001–02 series – in which Sri Lanka already held a 2–0 lead – but their spectacular collapse still came as a surprise. Failing to come to terms with the dual spin threat of Sanath Jayasuriya (4 for 31) and Muttiah Muralitharan (4 for 24), they folded to 79 all out – the lowest team total in Tests between the countries – and defeat by 315 runs.

OVERALL SERIES RECORDS
(15 Tests between 1994 and 2004)

	W	L	T	D	W/L	%W	%L	%D
Zimbabwe	0	10	0	5	0.00	0.00	66.67	33.33
Sri Lanka	10	0	0	5	0.50	66.67	0.00	33.33

First match: 11–16 October 1994, Harare, Zimbabwe

MOST RUNS: TOP 5

Pos	Runs	Player (Team, Span)
1	1,145	Marvan Atapattu (Sri Lanka, 1998–2004)
2	778	Andy Flower (Zimbabwe, 1994–2002)
3	730	Sanath Jayasuriya (Sri Lanka, 1994–2004)
4	536	Kumar Sangakkara (Sri Lanka, 2001–04)
5	527	Grant Flower (Zimbabwe, 1994–2002)

MOST WICKETS: TOP 5

Pos	Wkts	Player (Team, Span)
1	87	Muttiah Muralitharan (Sri Lanka, 1994–2004)
2	48	Chaminda Vaas (Sri Lanka, 1994–2004)
3	33	Heath Streak (Zimbabwe, 1994–2002)
4	20	Sanath Jayasuriya (Sri Lanka, 1994–2004)
=	20	Ravindra Pushpakumara (Sri Lanka, 1994–99)

SOUTH AFRICA v PAKISTAN

South Africa have played only 18 Test matches against Pakistan since the two sides met for the first time in 1995, but they have already gained a degree of mastery over the men from the subcontinent, recording eight wins to Pakistan's three, with seven of the Tests drawn.

⊙ MOST WICKETS IN A SERIES

The record for the most wickets in a South Africa-Pakistan series is 19, a feat achieved by two bowlers: South Africa's Makhaya Ntini in South Africa in 2006–07; and Pakistan's Mohammad Asif also in South Africa in 2006–07.

⊙ SOUTH AFRICA ON CRUISE CONTROL IN CAPE TOWN

One–nil up in the two-match series against Pakistan, South Africa got off to a flying start in the Second Test at Cape Town in January 2003. Graeme Smith (151) and Herschelle Gibbs (228 – the highest individual score in South Africa-Pakistan clashes) put on 368 runs for the first wicket to propel the home side to 620 for 7 declared (the highest team total in matches between the two countries). Pakistan wilted under the pressure and lost the match by an innings and 142 runs.

⊙ PAKISTAN IN FREEFALL IN FAISALABAD

Pakistan capitulated in spectacular style in the Third and final Test of the 1997–98 series to hand South Africa their first taste of victory on Pakistani soil and an unexpected series win. Set a mere 146 runs for victory, the home side slipped to 92 all out in 37.3 overs – the lowest team total in all matches between the two countries.

⊙ KALLIS PROSPERS AGAINST PAKISTAN

One of the most effective batsmen of modern times – some claim he is the best – Jacques Kallis has forged a glittering career out of grinding opponents into submission and scoring a massive number of "dirty" runs. Against no other team has he grafted more successfully than Pakistan: in 15 Tests against them since 1997 he has scored 1,472 runs (including six centuries, with a highest score of 155 at Karachi in October 2007) at an average of 66.90 – the best by any batsman.

OVERALL SERIES RECORDS
(18 Tests between 1995 and 2010)

	W	L	T	D	W/L	%W	%L	%D
South Africa	8	3	0	7	2.66	44.44	16.97	38.89
Pakistan	3	8	0	7	0.37	16.67	44.44	38.89

First match: 19–23 January 1995, Johannesburg, South Africa

TOP RUNS: TOP 5

Pos	Runs	Player (Team, Span)
1	1,472	Jacques Kallis (South Africa, 1997–2010)
2	849	Graeme Smith (South Africa, 2002–10)
3	838	Gary Kirsten (South Africa, 1995–2003)
4	750	Younis Khan (Pakistan, 2002–10)
5	730	Taufeeq Umar (Pakistan, 2002–10)

MOST WICKETS: TOP 5

Pos	Wkts	Player (Team, Span)
1	45	Shaun Pollock (South Africa, 1997–2007)
2	41	Makhaya Ntini (South Africa, 2002–07)
3	36	Danish Kaneria (Pakistan, 2003–07)
4	29	Mushtaq Ahmed (Pakistan, 1997–2003)
5	27	Allan Donald (South Africa, 1995–98)

PAKISTAN v ZIMBABWE

It may not have been an iron grip, but Pakistan certainly held the upper hand in the 14 Test matches they played against Zimbabwe between 1993 and 2002, winning eight, drawing four and losing only two of them.

⊙ WAQAR EXTINGUISHES ZIMBABWE CHALLENGE

Zimbabwe were unfortunate to run into Waqar Younis bowling at the peak of his prodigious powers when they faced Pakistan for the first time in a three-match series in 1993–94. The paceman took 7 for 91 and 6 for 44 in the First Test at Karachi (his match haul of 13 for 135 is an all-time Pakistan-Zimbabwe record), 5 for 88 and 4 for 50 in the Second Test at Rawalpindi, and 5 for 100 in the fog-and bad light-affected Third Test at Lahore. Waqar ended the series, which Pakistan won 2–0, with 27 wickets – another all-time record in matches between the two countries.

⊙ WASIM'S RECORD-BREAKING RESCUE ACT AT SHEIKHUPURA

For a short while, with Pakistan struggling on 237 for 7, still 138 runs behind their first-innings score in the First Test of the 1996–97 series at Sheikhupura, Zimbabwe must have felt they stood a reasonable chance of winning the game. But a sensational batting performance from Wasim Akram, who hit an unbeaten 257 (the highest score by a No. 8 in Test history and the highest in Pakistan-Zimbabwe clashes), propelled the home side to 553 all out – still the highest team total in all matches between the two countries. Wasim's efforts were not enough to win the match, however, which ended in a draw.

OVERALL SERIES RECORDS
(14 Tests between 1993 and 2002)

	W	L	T	D	W/L	%W	%L	%D
Pakistan	8	2	0	4	4.00	57.14	14.29	28.57
Zimbabwe	2	8	0	4	0.25	14.29	57.14	28.57

First match: 1–6 December 1993, Karachi, Pakistan

MOST RUNS: TOP 5

Pos	Runs	Player (Team, Span)
1	961	Grant Flower (Zimbabwe, 1993–2002)
2	931	Andy Flower (Zimbabwe, 1993–2002)
3	772	Inzamam-ul-Haq (Pakistan, 1993–2002)
4	616	Mohammad Yousuf (Pakistan, 1998–2002)
5	612	Alistair Campbell (Zimbabwe, 1993–2002)

MOST WICKETS: TOP 5

Pos	Wkts	Player (Team, Span)
1	62	Waqar Younis (Pakistan, 1993–2002)
2	47	Wasim Akram (Pakistan, 1993–98)
3	44	Heath Streak (Zimbabwe, 1993–98)
4	28	Saqlain Mushtaq (Pakistan, 1996–2002)
5	23	Guy Whittall (Zimbabwe, 1993–2002)

⊙ SPIN-FRIENDLY SURFACE SUITS SAQLAIN

Saqlain Mushtaq took full advantage of a wicket that offered spin from the first afternoon of the Second Test at Bulawayo, in November 2002, to lay the foundations for Pakistan's ten-wicket victory over Zimbabwe to claim a 2–0 series win. The off-spinner took 7 for 66 in the first innings (the best single-innings figures in matches between the two countries) to help dismiss Zimbabwe for 178, a position from which the home side failed to recover.

SOUTH AFRICA v ZIMBABWE

Given their geographical situation as southern African neighbours, it seems strange that South Africa and Zimbabwe contested only seven Test matches in ten years between 1995 and 2005. What is less strange, however, is that South Africa dominated the matches that were played: winning all but one of the matches played and drawing the other.

⊙ HAPPY TIMES IN HARARE

South Africa's batsmen prospered on a friendly, even surface against a weak Zimbabwe attack in the First Test of the two-match 2001–02 series at Harare. After winning the toss and electing to bat, South Africa's top three batsmen all passed three figures – Herschelle Gibbs (147), Gary Kirsten (220, the highest individual score in South Africa-Zimbabwe Tests) and Jacques Kallis (157 not out) – to propel their side to a substantial 600 for 3 declared (the highest team total in all Tests between the two countries) and an eventual nine-wicket win.

MOST RUNS: TOP 5

Pos	Runs	Player (Team, Span)
1	679	Jacques Kallis (South Africa, 1999–2005)
2	566	Andy Flower (Zimbabwe, 1995–2001)
3	330	Gary Kirsten (South Africa, 1995–2001)
4	278	Hamilton Masakadza (Zimbabwe, 2001–05)
5	276	Herschelle Gibbs (South Africa, 2001–05)

OVERALL SERIES RECORDS
(7 Tests between 1995 and 2005)

	W	L	T	D	W/L	%W	%L	%D
South Africa	6	0	0	1	-	85.71	0.00	14.29
Zimbabwe	0	6	0	1	0.00	0.00	85.71	14.29

First match: 13–16 October 1995, Harare, Zimbabwe

⊙ DONALD AT HIS DESTRUCTIVE BEST

A blistering performance from Allan Donald with the ball in Zimbabwe's second innings paved the way for South Africa's victory in October 1995 at Harare. The legendary fast bowler took 8 for 71 (the best single-innings figures in South Africa-Zimbabwe Tests) to skittle Zimbabwe out for 283 and leave South Africa requiring a mere 108 runs for victory, a target they achieved for the loss of three wickets. Donald's match haul (11 for 113) is also a record in South Africa-Zimbabwe matches.

⊙ ANDY FLOWER BLOSSOMS AGAINST SOUTH AFRICA

A truly outstanding performer for his country in a 63-Test, decade-long international career, Andy Flower seemed, at times, to provide the sole resistance for Zimbabwe in matches against South Africa. In five Tests against them between 1995 and 2001 he scored 566 runs (with two centuries, two half-centuries and a highest score of 199 not out, at Harare in September 2001) at an average of 70.75 – the highest by any batsman to complete ten or more innings in matches between the two countries.

MOST WICKETS: TOP 5

Pos	Wkts	Player (Team, Span)
1	23	Shaun Pollock (South Africa, 1999–2005)
2	21	Jacques Kallis (South Africa, 1999–2005)
3	14	Allan Donald (South Africa, 1995–99)
4	11	Claude Henderson (South Africa, 2001)
5	9	Bryan Strang (Zimbabwe, 1995–99)
=	9	Andre Nel (South Africa, 2001–05)
=	9	Monde Zondeki (South Africa, 2005)

ZIMBABWE v ENGLAND

A record of three victories by an innings and no defeats in the six Test matches they played against Zimbabwe between 1996 and 2000 suggests a complete English dominance over Zimbabwe, but, on occasion, particularly in home Tests, the southern Africans more than held their own.

⊙ JOHNSON'S HEADLINE-GRABBING DEBUT

Richard Johnson made a sensational debut for England against Zimbabwe in the first ever Test match played at Chester-le-Street in June 2003: he took two wickets in his first over and ended up with figures of 6 for 33 – the best single-innings figures in all England-Zimbabwe matches – as the home side went on to win the match by a innings and 69 runs.

⊙ ENGLAND CASH IN AT LORD'S

An undisciplined performance in the field by Zimbabwe allowed England to lay the foundations for an impressive victory inside three days in the First Test of the 2003 series at Lord's. Aided by Mark Butcher's 256-ball 137, and some unforgivably loose bowling from the visitors, the home side reached 472 all out – the highest team total in all matches between the two countries. They then bowled out Zimbabwe twice (for 147 and 233) to win the match by an innings and 92 runs.

⊙ GOODWIN SHOWS ZIMBABWE THE WAY

Following a comprehensive defeat at Lord's in the first match of the 2000 series, Zimbabwe showed considerable fight in the rain-affected and drawn Second Test at Trent Bridge, and no one more so than Murray Goodwin. The middle-order batsman hit 148 not out in Zimbabwe's first innings, the highest individual score in all Tests between the two countries.

MOST RUNS: TOP 5

Pos	Runs	Player (Team, Span)
1	483	Alec Stewart (England, 1996–2003)
2	259	Michael Atherton (England, 1996–2000)
3	248	Nick Knight (England, 1996–2000)
4	200	Andy Flower (Zimbabwe, 1996–2000)
5	198	Nasser Hussain (England, 1996–2003)

MOST WICKETS: TOP 5

Pos	Wkts	Player (Team, Span)
1	24	Heath Streak (Zimbabwe, 1996–2003)
2	16	Darren Gough (England, 1996–2000)
3	13	Guy Whittall (Zimbabwe, 1996–2000)
4	11	James Anderson (England, 2003)
5	10	Paul Strang (Zimbabwe, 1996)

OVERALL SERIES RECORDS
(6 Tests between 1996 and 2003)

	W	L	T	D	W/L	%W	%L	%D
Zimbabwe	0	3	0	3	0.00	0.00	50.00	50.00
England	3	0	0	3	-	50.00	0.00	50.00

First match: 18–22 December 1996, Bulawayo, Zimbabwe

⊙ ALL AT SEA AT THE HOME OF CRICKET

Lord's has been a far from happy hunting ground for Zimbabwe – they have played there twice over the years and lost both matches by an innings – but their first visit to the home of cricket, in May 2000, will revive particularly painful memories for the southern Africans. After losing the toss and being put in to bat, they collapsed to 83 all out in 30.3 overs (the lowest-ever total in Zimbabwe-England matches).

ZIMBABWE v AUSTRALIA

Australia simply proved too strong for Zimbabwe: the two countries contested only three Test matches between 1999 and 2003 and the Australians won them all, producing some record-breaking performances along the way.

⊙ HAYDEN HEROICS LIGHT UP PERTH

Matthew Hayden grabbed the headlines in the First Test against Zimbabwe at Perth in October 2003. The Queensland opener, who was nursing a sore back, occupied the crease for 10 hours and 22 minutes, faced 437 balls and celebrated wildly as he hit 380 runs to break Brian Lara's record for the highest score in Test cricket (a record Lara would regain seven months later). Hayden's dismissal prompted an Australian declaration: on 735 for 6 – the second-highest team total in Australia's history and the highest in all Australia-Zimbabwe matches.

⊙ ZIMBABWE'S HIGHS AND LOWS

The root of Zimbabwe's problems in Test matches against Australia has been their batsmen's inability to amass a total of any real significance: their highest total (321) came after Australia had smashed 735 runs of their own at Perth in October 2003; their lowest effort (194) came in the first-ever match between the two sides at Harare in October 1999.

OVERALL SERIES RECORDS
(3 Tests between 1999 and 2003)

	W	L	T	D	W/L	%W	%L	%D
Zimbabwe	0	3	0	0	0.00	0.00	100.00	0.00
Australia	3	0	0	0	-	100.00	0.00	0.00

First match: 14–17 October 1999, Harare, Zimbabwe

MOST RUNS: TOP 5

Pos	Runs	Player (Team, Span)
1	501	Matthew Hayden (Australia, 2003)
2	290	Ricky Ponting (Australia, 1999–2003)
=	290	Steve Waugh (Australia, 1999–2003)
4	179	Trevor Gripper (Zimbabwe, 1999–2003)
5	166	Mark Vermeulen (Zimbabwe, 2003)

⊙ PART-TIME BOWLER STEALS THE SHOW

He went on to become an established presence at the top of the Australian order, but early in his Test career Simon Katich hit the headlines not for his batting but for his part-time left-arm leg-break bowling. In the Second Test against Zimbabwe at Sydney in October 2003, he took 6 for 65 in the second innings (the best bowling figures in Tests between the two countries) to help set up a nine-wicket victory for Australia. Katich also holds the record for the best match figures (6 for 90) – shared with Glenn McGrath, who achieved the feat at Harare in October 1999.

MOST WICKETS: TOP 5

Pos	Wkts	Player (Team, Span)
1	10	Andy Bichel (Australia, 2003)
2	7	Heath Streak (Zimbabwe, 1999–2003)
3	6	Glenn McGrath (Australia, 1999)
=	6	Shane Warne (Australia, 1999)
=	6	Simon Katich (Australia, 2003)
=	6	Brett Lee (Australia, 2003)
=	6	Ray Price (Zimbabwe, 2003)

WEST INDIES v ZIMBABWE

Despite their ever-increasing woes against the strongest cricketing nations since the turn of the new millennium, the West Indies enjoyed playing against Zimbabwe. In the six matches between the two countries since they met for the first time in 2000, the men from the Caribbean proved too strong for the southern Africans, winning four of them and drawing the other two.

⊙ BATTING MASTERCLASS FROM LARA

An imperious innings by Brian Lara ultimately proved the difference between the two sides in the Second Test between Zimbabwe and the West Indies at Bulawayo in November 2003. The masterful left-hander crafted a brilliant 191 off 203 balls – the highest individual score in West Indies- Zimbabwe Tests – in a match the West Indies went on to win by 128 runs.

⊙ PRICE IS SPOT ON

An impressive left-arm spinner who played 18 Tests for Zimbabwe between 1999 and 2004, Ray Price was at his best in the two-match series against the West Indies in November 2003. He took 6 for 73 (the best single-innings figures in West Indies-Zimbabwe matches) and 4 for 88 in the drawn First Test at Harare (his match figures of 10 for 161 are also a record in Tests between the two countries), and 5 for 199 and 4 for 36 in a losing cause in the Second Test at Bulawayo. His series haul of 19 wickets is another West Indies-Zimbabwe record.

⊙ RECORD-BREAKING RESCUE ACT

Trailing by 216 runs at the start of their second innings, Zimbabwe needed to produce an innings of huge proportions to avoid crashing to a second successive heavy defeat in the two-Test 2001 series at Harare. And they did: led by Hamilton Masakadza's 316-ball 119, and bolstered by late-order contributions from Heath Streak (83 not out) and Andy Blignaut (92), Zimbabwe battled to 563 for 9. The highest team total in all matches between the two countries enabled Zimbabwe to evade defeat for the first time against the West Indies.

OVERALL SERIES RECORDS
(6 Tests between 1996 and 2003)

	W	L	T	D	W/L	%W	%L	%D
West Indies	4	0	0	2	-	66.67	0.00	33.33
Zimbabwe	0	4	0	2	0.00	0.00	66.67	33.33

First match: 16–20 March 2000, Port of Spain, Trinidad

MOST RUNS: TOP 5

Pos	Runs	Player (Team, Span)
1	353	Chris Gayle (West Indies, 2000–03)
2	331	Craig Wishart (Zimbabwe, 2001–03)
3	297	Ramnaresh Sarwan (West Indies, 2001–03)
4	288	Heath Streak (Zimbabwe, 2000–03)
5	281	Wavell Hinds (West Indies, 2000–03)

⊙ THE WORST OF STARTS

Zimbabwe crashed to a morale-crushing defeat in their first-ever Test match against the West Indies, at Port of Spain, Trinidad, in March 2000. Chasing a mere 99 runs for victory, they slumped to 63 all out – the lowest-ever total in West Indies-Zimbabwe Tests.

MOST WICKETS: TOP 5

Pos	Wkts	Player (Team, Span)
1	23	Ray Price (Zimbabwe, 2001–03)
2	21	Heath Streak (Zimbabwe, 2000–03)
3	16	Reon King (West Indies, 2000–01)
4	12	Neil McGarrell (West Indies, 2001)
=	12	Colin Stuart (West Indies, 2001)

BANGLADESH v INDIA

India, Bangladesh's first-ever opponents in Test cricket, have dominated the few Test matches played against their subcontinental neighbours, winning six of the seven Tests played (all of them in Bangladesh) and drawing just once.

⊙ INDIA PROSPER IN DHAKA

Having suffered the ignominy of drawing the first of the two Tests in Bangladesh in May 2007, India bounced back in style in the Second Test at Dhaka. Bolstered by centuries from each of their top four batsmen – Dinesh Karthik (129), Wasim Jaffer (138), Rahul Dravid (129) and Sachin Tendulkar (122 not out) – they reached 610 for 3 declared (the highest team total in Bangladesh-India Tests) and went on to win by an innings and 239 runs – their largest-ever Test victory.

⊙ BANGLADESH LET IT SLIP

A sorry second-innings batting display by Bangladesh saw them crash to a six-wicket defeat in the first-ever Test against India at Dhaka in December 2004. The home side crashed to 91 all out – the lowest-ever total in Bangladesh-India clashes.

OVERALL SERIES RECORDS
(7 Tests between 2000 and 2010)

	W	L	T	D	W/L	%W	%L	%D
Bangladesh	0	6	0	1	0.00	0.00	85.71	14.29
India	6	0	0	1	-	85.71	0.00	14.29

First match: 10–13 November 2000, Dhaka, Bangladesh

MOST RUNS: TOP 5

Pos	Runs	Player (Team, Span)
1	820	Sachin Tendulkar (India, 2000–10)
2	560	Rahul Dravid (India, 2000–10)
3	386	Mohammad Ashraful (Bangladesh, 2004–10)
4	381	Gautham Gambhir (India, 2004–10)
5	371	Sourav Ganguly (India, 2000–07)

MOST WICKETS: TOP 5

Pos	Wkts	Player (Team, Span)
1	31	Zaheer Khan (India, 2000–10)
2	18	Irfan Pathan (India, 2004)
3	15	Mohammad Rafique (Bangladesh, 2000–07)
=	15	Anil Kumble (India, 2004–07)
5	12	Shahadat Hossain (Bangladesh, 2007–10)

⊙ PATHAN PLAGUES BANGLADESH

Despite Sachin Tendulkar's star turn with the bat in the First Test against Bangladesh at Dhaka in December 2004, India would not have achieved their massive innings-and-140-run victory without Irfan Pathan's considerable efforts with the ball. The young pace bowler, considered by many to have the potential to become the best Indian fast bowler since Kapil Dev, took 5 for 45 in the first innings and 6 for 51 in the second to end the match with 11 for 96 – the best match figures in all Tests between the two countries. Seven wickets in the Second Test at Chittagong saw Pathan end the series with 18 wickets – another all-time Bangladesh-India record.

⊙ TENDULKAR TOP OF THE BILL IN DHAKA

It may have come against the weakest opponents he has encountered in his illustrious Test career, but Sachin Tendulkar cashed in with style in the First Test against Bangladesh at Dhaka in December 2004 to record the highest score of his career (and the best individual score in Bangladesh-India matches). The "Little Master" faced 379 balls (hitting 35 fours) to compile an unbeaten 248 in a match that India went on to win by an innings and 140 runs.

PAKISTAN v BANGLADESH

India, Bangladesh's first-ever opponents in Test cricket, have dominated the few Test matches played against their subcontinental neighbours, winning six of the seven Tests played (all of them in Bangladesh) and drawing just once.

⊙ KANERIA CASHES IN

One of only four Pakistan bowlers in history to take more than 250 Test wickets (254), Danish Kaneria has enjoyed some fine moments against Bangladesh. In the first-ever Test between the two countries at Multan in August 2001 he took 6 for 42 in the first innings and 6 for 52 in the second – his match haul of 12 for 94 is the best in all matches between the two countries – as Pakistan cruised to an innings-and-264-run victory; five months later, in Dhaka, he took 7 for 77 – the best single-innings figures in Pakistan-Bangladesh Tests.

⊙ YOUSUF SHOWS HOW IT'S DONE

Mohammad Yousuf was in prime batting form for Pakistan in the Second Test of the 2001–02 series against Bangladesh at Chittagong, producing a masterful innings of 204 not out – the highest individual total in matches between the two countries – as Pakistan cruised to 465 for 9. In contrast, Bangladesh's batsmen were woeful, slipping to 148 all out in both innings to lose the match by an innings and 169 runs.

⊙ BANGLADESH LOSE THEIR NERVE

Leading Pakistan by 66 runs after the first innings of the Second Test at Peshawar in August 2003, Bangladesh were in a strong position to win the match. But instead of pushing on to gain a first-ever victory over their subcontinental cousins, Bangladesh's batmen lost their nerve and crashed to 96 all out – the lowest total in all matches between the two sides – and a Test match they should have won was eventually lost by nine wickets.

OVERALL SERIES RECORDS
(6 Tests between 2001 and 2003)

	W	L	T	D	W/L	%W	%L	%D
Pakistan	6	0	0	0	-	100.00	0.00	0.00
Bangladesh	0	6	0	0	0.00	0.00	100.00	0.00

First match: 29–31 August 2001, Multan, Pakistan

MOST RUNS: TOP 5

Pos	Runs	Player (Team, Span)
1	554	Habibul Bashar (Bangladesh, 2001–03)
2	503	Mohammad Yousuf (Pakistan, 2001–03)
3	404	Inzamam-ul-Haq (Pakistan, 2001–03)
4	373	Yasir Hameed (Pakistan, 2003)
5	364	Taufeeq Umar (Pakistan, 2001–03)

MOST WICKETS: TOP 5

Pos	Wkts	Player (Team, Span)
1	34	Danish Kaneria (Pakistan, 2001–03)
2	18	Waqar Younis (Pakistan, 2001–02)
3	17	Shabbir Ahmed (Pakistan, 2003)
=	17	Shoaib Akhtar (Pakistan, 2002–03)
=	17	Mohammad Rafique (Bangladesh, 2003)

⊙ MOST WICKETS IN A SERIES

The record for the most wickets in a Pakistan-Bangladesh series is 17, a feat achieved by two bowlers: Shabbir Ahmed (Pakistan) and Mohammad Rafique (Bangladesh), both in the 2003 series in Pakistan.

NEW ZEALAND v BANGLADESH

New Zealand have dominated Bangladesh in comprehensive fashion since the two countries met for the first time at Hamilton in December 2001, winning seven of the eight matches played – five of them by an innings – while the other was a rain-affected draw.

⊙ SHAKIB PUTS NEW ZEALAND IN A SPIN

That New Zealand won the First Test of the 2008–09 series at Chittagong by just three wickets shows both how much Bangladesh have improved in Test cricket and how much pressure New Zealand were under following a fine spell of bowling from Shakib Al Hasan. The Bangladesh left-arm spinner took 7 for 36 in New Zealand's first innings – the best single-innings figures in all Tests between the two countries – to guide his side to a 74-run first-innings lead, a position which, ultimately, they ended up squandering.

⊙ FLEMING LEADS FROM THE FRONT

Having seen his side brush aside Bangladesh in the First Test of the 2004–05 series (New Zealand won the match at Dhaka by an innings and 90 runs), Stephen Fleming ensured his side carried the momentum into the Second Test at Chittagong. Leading from the front in imperious fashion, the Kiwi captain smashed 202 off 318 balls (the highest individual score in New Zealand-Bangladesh Tests) to help his side reach 545 for 6 declared (the highest team total in matches between the two countries) en route to a comprehensive innings-and-101-run victory.

OVERALL SERIES RECORDS
(9 Tests between 2001 and 2010)

	W	L	T	D	W/L	%W	%L	%D
New Zealand	8	0	0	1	-	88.88	0.00	11.12
Bangladesh	0	8	0	1	0.00	0.00	88.88	11.12

First match: 18–22 December 2001, Hamilton, New Zealand

⊙ THE WORST OF STARTS

Bangladesh's batsmen were all at sea on a bowler-friendly surface at Hamilton against New Zealand in December 2001 – the first-ever Test between the two countries. Having seen the home side scramble to 365 for 9 declared in just 77.1 overs in an attempt to force a result, Bangladesh fell for 205 in the first innings and, following on, 108 in the second (the lowest total in New Zealand-Bangladesh matches) to lose by an innings and 52 runs.

⊙ BANGLADESH BOW TO VETTORI

Where Stephen Fleming, with his 202, was the star with the bat in the Second Test at Chittagong in October 2004, Daniel Vettori was New Zealand's hero with the ball. The slow left-armer took 6 for 70 in Bangladesh's first innings and 6 for 100 in their second to help bowl his side to an innings-and-101-run victory. His match figures of 12 for 170 are a record in New Zealand-Bangladesh Tests.

MOST WICKETS: TOP 5

Pos	Wkts	Player (Team, Span)
1	51	Daniel Vettori (New Zealand, 2001–10)
2	19	Chris Martin (New Zealand, 2001–10)
=	15	Ian O'Brien (New Zealand, 2008)
4	14	Mashrafe Mortaza (Bangladesh, 2001–08)
5	13	Chris Cairns (New Zealand, 2001)

MOST RUNS: TOP 5

Pos	Runs	Player (Team, Span)
1	504	Brendon McCullum (New Zealand, 2004–10)
2	397	Stephen Fleming (New Zealand, 2001–08)
3	358	Shakib Al Hasan (Bangladesh, 2008–10)
4	325	Tamim Iqbal (Bangladesh, 2008–10)
=	325	Daniel Vettori (New Zealand, 2001–10)

SRI LANKA v BANGLADESH

Those who argue that Bangladesh's elevation to Test status was premature could point to their performances against Sri Lanka. They have played 12 Tests against the Sri Lankans (more than against any other country) and have lost every one of them – seven of them by an innings.

⊙ SUPER SANGAKKARA CASHES IN

Sri Lanka's complete dominance with the ball in matches against Bangladesh (Test cricket's new boys have posted only one 350-plus score against Sri Lanka in 24 attempts) has given their batsmen both the time and a free rein to craft a big innings. And, in the Third Test of the 2007 series at Kandy, Kumar Sangakkara was only too keen to take advantage of the situation. The talented left-hander hit an unbeaten 222 – the highest individual score in Sri Lanka-Bangladesh matches – to help his side reach 500 for 4 declared (in response to Bangladesh's paltry 131 all out) en route to an innings-and-193-run victory.

⊙ BANGLADESH SPELLBOUND BY MURALI MAGIC

One of the arguments against Muttiah Muralitharan being the greatest spin bowler ever to play the game – despite his standing as Test cricket's all-time leading wicket-taker (with 792) – will be that he played the majority of his matches in favourable conditions and, in the case of Bangladesh, against favourable opposition. Murali has simply been too good for the Bangladesh batsmen – in 11 Tests he has claimed 89 wickets – and holds all manner of bowling records in matches between the two countries, including: the best bowling in an innings (6 for 18 at Colombo in September 2005); the best bowling in a match (12 for 82 at Kandy in July 2007); and the most wickets in a series (26 in 2007).

⊙ SRI LANKA CRUISE IN COLOMBO

Sri Lanka swept aside Bangladesh with ease in the First Test of a three-match series at Colombo in June 2007. After winning the toss and electing to bowl, they felled Bangladesh for 89 and then – aided by centuries from Michael Vandort (117), Mahela Jayawardene (127), Prasanna Jayawardene (120 not out) and Chaminda Vaas (100 not out) – piled on a massive 577 for 6 declared (the highest team total in Sri Lanka-Bangladesh Tests) and went on to win the match by an innings and 234 runs.

⊙ COLOMBO CAPITULATION

Bangladesh's lowest point against Sri Lanka came in the First Test of the three-match 2007 series at Colombo: they fell to 61 all out in the first innings – the lowest total in all matches between the two countries.

OVERALL SERIES RECORDS
(12 Tests between 2001 and 2009)

	W	L	T	D	W/L	%W	%L	%D
Sri Lanka	12	0	0	0	-	100.00	0.00	0.00
Bangladesh	0	12	0	0	0.00	0.00	100.00	0.00

First match: 6–8 September 2001, Colombo, Sri Lanka

MOST RUNS: TOP 5

Pos	Runs	Player (Team, Span)
1	876	Kumar Sangakkara (Sri Lanka, 2001–09
2	860	Mahela Jayawardene (Sri Lanka, 2001–09
3	858	Mohammad Ashraful (Bangladesh, 2001–09
4	771	Tillakaratne Dilshan (Sri Lanka, 2005–09
5	600	Thilan Samaraweera (Sri Lanka, 2001–09

MOST WICKETS: TOP 5

Pos	Wkts	Player (Team, Span)
1	89	Muttiah Muralitharan (Sri Lanka, 2001–09)
2	28	Dilhara Fernando (Sri Lanka, 2002–09)
3	27	Lasith Malinga (Sri Lanka, 2005–07)
4	23	Shahadat Hossain (Bangladesh, 2005–09)
5	19	Chaminda Vaas (Sri Lanka, 2001–09)

SOUTH AFRICA v BANGLADESH

Bangladesh have enjoyed no success in matches against South Africa: in eight matches played between the two countries since they met for the first time at East London in October 2002 they have lost every time – and on seven of those occasions they have lost by an innings.

⊙ DREAMS DASHED IN DHAKA

After restricting South Africa to 330 all out in the Second Test of the 2003 series at Dhaka, Bangladesh were very much in the game, but any aspirations they may have had to win the match were soon dashed. In reply, they slipped to 102 all out – the lowest total in South Africa-Bangladesh Tests – and went on to lose by an innings and 18 runs.

⊙ ADAMS SPINS SOUTH AFRICA TO VICTORY

Paul Adams was South Africa's star with the ball as they crushed Bangladesh by an innings and 60 runs in the First Test at Chittagong in April 2003. The unconventional leg-spinner took 5 for 37 in the first innings and 5 for 59 in the second to record match figures of 10 for 106 – a record in South Africa-Bangladesh Test matches.

⊙ HOSSEIN GIVES BANGLADESH CAUSE FOR HOPE

Although South Africa ultimately won the First Test of the 2007–08 series by five wickets, they did so only after Shahadat Hossain caused them to post their lowest-ever total against Bangladesh. The promising young fast bowler took 6 for 27 in the first innings – the best single-innings figures in matches between the two countries – to help dismiss the visitors for 170.

OVERALL SERIES RECORDS
(8 Tests between 2002 and 2008)

	W	L	T	D	W/L	%W	%L	%D
South Africa	8	0	0	0	-	100.00	0.00	0.00
Bangladesh	0	8	0	0	0.00	0.00	100.00	0.00

First match: 18–21 October 2002, East London, South Africa

MOST RUNS: TOP 5

Pos	Runs	Player (Team, Span)
1	743	Graeme Smith (South Africa, 2002–08)
2	317	Jacques Kallis (South Africa, 2002–08)
3	310	Gary Kirsten (South Africa, 2002)
4	306	Neil McKenzie (South Africa, 2003–08)
5	301	Habibul Bashar (Bangladesh, 2002–08)

MOST WICKETS: TOP 5

Pos	Wkts	Player (Team, Span)
1	35	Makhaya Ntini (South Africa, 2002–08)
2	22	Dale Steyn (South Africa, 2008)
3	17	Jacques Kallis (South Africa, 2002–08)
4	15	Shahadat Hossain (Bangladesh, 2008)
5	14	Morne Morkel (South Africa, 2008)

⊙ SOUTH AFRICA CRUSH BANGLADESH AT CHITTAGONG

Having won the First Test of the 2007–08 series against Bangladesh only by five wickets (thus losing their record of having won every match against them by an innings), South Africa would have been keen to reassert their total supremacy over Test cricket's newest nation in the Second Test at Chittagong. And so they did: Graeme Smith hit 232 (the highest individual score in South Africa–Bangladesh Tests) and Neil McKenzie 226 (the pair put on 415 runs for the opening wicket) to send South Africa on their way to a total of 583 for 7 declared (the highest in all matches between the two countries). South Africa went on to win the match by an innings and 205 runs.

BANGLADESH v WEST INDIES

Bangladesh have enjoyed more success against the West Indies than against any other nation since their elevation to Test status in 2001, winning two of the six Test matches played – both times, admittedly, against a much-weakened West Indies outfit.

⊙ SARWAN SPEARHEADS WEST INDIES VICTORY

The West Indies crushed Bangladesh in the first-ever Test between the two countries at Kingston, Jamaica, in June 2004. A brilliant unbeaten 261 from Ramnaresh Sarwan (the highest individual score in Bangladesh-West Indies Tests) led his side to 559 for 9 declared (another Bangladesh-West Indies record) and an eventual innings-and-99-run victory.

OVERALL SERIES RECORDS
(6 Tests between 2002 and 2009)

	W	L	T	D	W/L	%W	%L	%D
Bangladesh	2	3	0	1	0.66	33.33	50.00	16.67
West Indies	3	2	0	1	1.50	50.00	33.33	16.67

First match: 8–10 December 2002, Dhaka, Bangladesh

MOST RUNS: TOP 5

Pos	Runs	Player (Team, Span)
1	450	Ramnaresh Sarwan (West Indies, 2002–04)
2	347	Chris Gayle (West Indies, 2002–04)
3	284	Habibul Bashar (Bangladesh, 2002–04)
4	203	Khaled Mashud (Bangladesh, 2002–04)
5	197	Tamim Iqbal (Bangladesh, 2009–09)

MOST WICKETS: TOP 5

Pos	Wkts	Player (Team, Span)
1	26	Pedro Collins (West Indies, 2002–04)
2	13	Jermaine Lawson (West Indies, 2002–04)
=	13	Kemar Roach (West Indies, 2009)
=	13	Shakib Al Hasan (Bangladesh, 2009)
5	12	Mahmudullah (Bangladesh, 2009)
=	12	Darren Sammy (West Indies, 2009)

AUSTRALIA v BANGLADESH

In Test matches played between the two countries, both at home and away, Bangladesh have proved no match for Australia, losing four Tests out of four, three of them by an innings.

⊙ GILLESPIE'S GOLDEN INNINGS

It was the most unexpected performance in Test cricket in recent memory. Coming in as a nightwatchman, Jason Gillespie ended the first day of the Second Test against Bangladesh at Chittagong in April 2006 on 5 not out. Three days later, remarkably, he was still batting, reaching 201 not out (the highest score by a nightwatchman in Test history and the highest individual score in Bangladesh-Australia clashes) before Australia declared on 581 for 4. Gillespie's performance was a match-winning one: the visitors went on to win the match by an innings and 80 runs.

OVERALL SERIES RECORDS
(4 Tests between 2003 and 2006)

	W	L	T	D	W/L	%W	%L	%D
Australia	4	0	0	0	-	100.00	0.00	0.00
Bangladesh	0	4	0	0	0.00	0.00	100.00	0.00

First match: 18–20 July 2003, Darwin, Australia

MOST RUNS: TOP 5

Pos	Runs	Player (Team, Span)
1	287	Darren Lehmann (Australia, 2003)
2	282	Habibul Bashar (Bangladesh, 2003–06)
3	260	Ricky Ponting (Australia, 2003–06)
4	256	Steve Waugh (Australia, 2003)
5	250	Shahriar Nafees (Bangladesh, 2006)

MOST WICKETS: TOP 5

Pos	Wkts	Player (Team, Span)
1	33	Stuart MacGill (Australia, 2003–06)
2	19	Jason Gillespie (Australia, 2003–06)
3	11	Shane Warne (Australia, 2006)
=	11	Mohammad Rafique (Bangladesh, 2006)
5	8	Brett Lee (Australia, 2003–06)

BANGLADESH v ENGLAND

Such has been England's dominance over Bangladesh – they have won all six of the Test matches played with ease – that they now see matches against Test cricket's new boys as an opportunity to rest some of their star players in what has become an increasingly congested international schedule.

⊙ HIGHS AND LOWS
Highest score (team): 599 for 6 declared – England v Bangladesh at Chittagong in March 2010
Lowest score (team): 104 all out – Bangladesh v England at Chester-le-Street in June 2005

⊙ TROTT TEARS INTO BANGLADESH
Jonathan Trott produced the standout performance in a masterful commanding display by England against Bangladesh in the First Test of the 2010 series at Lord's. Coming to the crease with England, batting first after being put into bat, the Warwickshire No.3 batted beautifully, hitting 226 – the highest individual score in Bangladesh-England clashes – to lead his side to an imposing 505 all out. England went on to win the match by eight wickets to take a 1–0 series lead.

OVERALL SERIES RECORDS
(8 Tests between 2003 and 2010)

	W	L	T	D	W/L	%W	%L	%D
Bangladesh	0	8	0	0	0.00	0.00	100.00	0.00
England	8	0	0	0	-	100.00	0.00	0.00

First match: 21–25 October 2003, Dhaka, Bangladesh

MOST WICKETS: TOP 5

Pos	Wkts	Player (Team, Span)
1	23	M.J. Hoggard (England, 2003–05)
2	22	G.P. Swann (England, 2010)
3	19	S.J. Harmison (England, 2003–05)
=	19	Steven Finn (England, 2010)
5	17	Shakib Al Hasan (Bangladesh, 2010)

MOST RUNS: TOP 5

Pos	Runs	Player (Team, Span)
1	633	Ian Bell (England, 2005–10)
2	551	Marcus Trescothick (England, 2003–05)
3	505	Tamim Iqbal (Bangladesh, 2010)
4	401	Alistair Cook (England, 2010)
=	401	Jonathan Trott (England, 2010)

⊙ BOWLING BESTS

Innings: 5 for 35 – Steve Harmison (England), England v Bangladesh at Dhaka in October 2003
Match: 10 for 217 – Graeme Swann (England), England v Bangladesh at Chittagong in March 2010
Series: 16 – Graeme Swann (England), England in Bangladesh in 2009–10

PART 2: ONE-DAY INTERNATIONAL CRICKET

It was thought merely to have been a one-off arrangement, a means of appeasing a cricket-hungry public following a Boxing Day Test washout, but when Australia played England in a 40-over match at Melbourne on 5 January 1971, one-day international cricket was born. The public loved it, with 46,000 paying spectators turning up to watch this new phenomenon, and, over the years, the limited-overs game has gone on to form an increasing part of a cricket fan's diet. Cricket's World Cup is based on the formula, with the first being won in 1975 by the West Indies.

Detractors would suggest a cricket fan is force-fed limited-overs cricket: in the first five years of the 1980s, 402 one-day internationals were played, as opposed to 1,382 between 2000 and 2004 – more than three times as many. But one-day international cricket, particularly in the subcontinent, has become an essential asset for the game's finances – its continued popularity has made it international cricket's cash cow. How long that situation lasts, with the meteoric rise of the Twenty20 game, remains to be seen.

Those who don't like the format also point out that the abbreviated form of the game brings out the worst in players; that the need for quick runs leads to the breakdown of technique. Its enduring popularity, however, suggests the one-day international game is a platform upon which the best players can dazzle. The following pages consist of those whose stars have shone the brightest in the first of the game's limited-overs formats.

ICC WORLD CUP

The fourth most watched sporting event on the planet, the ICC World Cup is international cricket's premier 50-over tournament. It has grown in stature over the years: the first edition, held in England in 1975, featured eight pre-invited teams; the 2007 edition, staged in the Caribbean, featured 16 nations, including six teams that had come through a qualifying tournament.

⊙ LARGEST VICTORIES

By runs: by 257 runs – India v Bermuda at Port of Spain, Trinidad, on 19 March 2007 (India 413 for 5 off 50 overs; Bermuda 156 all out in 43.1 overs).
By wickets: by ten wickets on seven occasions.

⊙ SMALLEST VICTORIES

By runs: by one run on two occasions – Australia v India at Chennai, India, on 9 October 1987; and Australia v India at Brisbane on 1 March 1992.
By wickets: by one wicket on four occasions – West Indies v Pakistan at Birmingham on 11 June 1975; Pakistan v West Indies at Lahore on 16 October 1987; South Africa v Sri Lanka at Providence, Guyana, on 28 March 2007; and England v West Indies at Bridgetown, Barbados, on 21 April 2007.

⊙ INDIA TOO HOT TO HANDLE FOR BERMUDA

One of the consequences of the ICC's commendable drive to expand the World Cup and hand cricket's lesser nations a chance to compete on the international stage has been a growing number of mismatches. When India met Bermuda at Port of Spain, Trinidad, in the 2007 tournament, they eased to 413 for 5 off their 50 overs – the highest total in World Cup history – en route to a colossal 257-run victory.

⊙ MOST MATCHES LOST

No side has lost more World Cup matches than Zimbabwe. In 45 matches between 1983 and 2007, the southern Africans have lost 33 matches and won just eight of them (with one tie and three no-results).

⊙ THAT WINNING FEELING

Three-time winners Australia are the most successful side in World Cup history: in 69 matches between 1975 and 2007, the men from Down Under have won a record 51 matches – 15 more than second-placed England (with 36).

ICC WORLD CUP WINNERS

Season	Winner	Host
1975	West Indies	(England)
1979	West Indies	(England)
1983	India	(England)
1987	Australia	(India/Pakistan)
1992	Pakistan	(Australia/New Zealand)
1996	Sri Lanka	(India/Pakistan/Sri Lanka)
1999	Australia	(England/Ireland/Netherlands/Scotland)
2003	Australia	(Kenya/South Africa/Zimbabwe)
2007	Australia	(West Indies)

⊙ TIED MATCHES

There have been three tied matches in World Cup history: Australia v South Africa at Edgbaston on 17 June 1999; South Africa v Sri Lanka at Durban in March 2003; and Ireland v Zimbabwe at Kingston, Jamaica, on 15 March 2007.

⊙ HIGHEST TEAM TOTAL IN A LOSING CAUSE

Pukekura Park in New Plymouth, New Zealand, is one of the most picturesque grounds in world cricket, but not one of the largest, and when Zimbabwe met Sri Lanka there in the group stages of the 1992 World Cup, the match turned into a run-fest. Zimbabwe batted first and compiled 312 for 4 off their 50 overs but still lost, with Sri Lanka reaching the target with four balls and three wickets to spare. At the time this record may have been no consolation, but Zimbabwe's total remains the highest losing total in World Cup history.

⊙ RUNS GALORE AT BASSETERRE

For spectators wishing to see runs in the 2006–07 World Cup, Australia's Group A clash against South Africa at Basseterre, St Kitts and Nevis, was the match to watch. Batting first, Australia, helped by scintillating knocks from Matthew Hayden (101), Ricky Ponting (91) and Michael Clarke (92), eased to a commanding 377 for 6. South Africa fell short in reply – dismissed for 294 in 48 overs – but the total of 671 runs scored in the match remains an all-time World Cup record.

⊙ COMING BACK FROM THE DEAD

When Zimbabwe crashed to 134 all out in 46.1 overs in their group match against England at Albury in 1992, only the most optimistic of their players would have harboured any hopes that they could end their 18-match losing streak in the World Cup stretching back to 1983. But, aided by a bowler-friendly surface, the southern Africans struck back in headline-grabbing fashion, bowling England out for 125 to win the match by nine runs. Their total is the lowest winning total by any side batting first in World Cup history.

ICC WORLD CUP LEAGUE TABLE (RANKED BY WIN-LOSS RATIO)

Pos	Team (Span)	W/L	Mat	Won	Lost	Tied	NR
1	Australia (1975–2007)	3.00	69	51	17	1	0
2	South Africa (1992–2007)	1.92	40	25	13	2	0
3	West Indies (1975–2007)	1.66	57	35	21	0	1
4	England (1975–2007)	1.63	59	36	22	0	1
5	New Zealand (1975–2007)	1.34	62	35	26	0	1
6	India (1975–2007)	1.28	58	32	25	0	1
7	Pakistan (1975–2007)	1.25	56	30	24	0	2
8	Sri Lanka (1975–2007)	0.83	57	25	30	1	1
9	Kenya (1996–2007)	0.37	23	6	16	0	1
10	Bangladesh (1999–2007)	0.35	20	5	14	0	1
11	Ireland (2007)	0.33	9	2	6	1	0
12	United Arab Emirates (1996)	0.25	5	1	4	0	0
13	Zimbabwe (1983–2007)	0.24	45	8	33	1	3
14	Netherlands (1996–2007)	0.16	14	2	12	0	0
15	Canada (1979–2007)	0.09	12	1	11	0	0
16	Bermuda (2007)	0.00	3	0	3	0	0
=	East Africa (1975)	0.00	3	0	3	0	0
=	Namibia (2003)	0.00	6	0	6	0	0
=	Scotland (1999–2007)	0.00	8	0	8	0	0

BATTING RECORDS

MOST RUNS: TOP 10

Pos	Runs	Player (Team, Span)
1	1,796	Sachin Tendulkar (India, 1992–2007)
2	1,537	Ricky Ponting (Australia, 1996–2007)
3	1,225	Brian Lara (West Indies, 1992–2007)
4	1,165	Sanath Jayasuriya (Sri Lanka, 1992–2007)
5	1,085	Adam Gilchrist (Australia, 1999–2007)
6	1,083	Javed Miandad (Pakistan, 1975–96)
7	1,075	Stephen Fleming (New Zealand, 1996–2007)
8	1,067	Herschelle Gibbs (South Africa, 1999–2007)
9	1,064	Aravinda de Silva (Sri Lanka, 1987–2003)
10	1,013	Viv Richards (West Indies, 1975–87)

⊙ KLUSENER CRASHES HIS WAY INTO THE RECORD BOOKS

In his early forays in first-class cricket, Lance Klusener was considered nothing more than a fast bowler who would bat at No. 11. However, he developed into an all-rounder of true international class and he was at his best in one-day cricket, where his clean ball-striking often gave his side late-order impetus. In 11 World Cup innings for South Africa between 1999 and 2003, Klusener scored 372 runs at an average of 124.00 with a strike-rate of 121.17 runs per 100 balls. Both are World Cup records.

⊙ MOST WORLD CUP CENTURIES

The record for the most centuries hit in World Cup matches is four, a feat achieved by four players: Sachin Tendulkar (India, 1992–2007); Mark Waugh (Australia, 1992–99); Ricky Ponting (Australia, 1996–2007); and Sourav Ganguly (India, 1999–2007).

⊙ KING OF THE BIG HITTERS

Renowned for the artful manner in which he constructs an innings and guaranteed to go down in history as one of the greatest batsmen cricket has seen, Ricky Ponting could also mix it with the game's biggest hitters in one-day cricket. In 39 World Cup matches for Australia between 1996 and 2007, the Tasmanian star has struck a tournament record 30 sixes, including a record eight against India in the 2003 World Cup final at Johannesburg.

⊙ MOST WORLD CUP CAREER DUCKS

The record for the most World Cup ducks is five, held by two players – Nathan Astle (in 22 matches for New Zealand between 1996 and 2003); and Ijaz Ahmed (in 29 matches for Pakistan between 1987 and 1999).

⊙ FASTEST WORLD CUP CENTURY

Matthew Hayden ensured Australia got off to a spectacular start in their Group A clash against South Africa at St Kitts at the 2007 World Cup. The left-handed opener smashed 101 off 66 balls – the fastest century in the tournament's history – as Australia romped to an 83-run victory.

⊙ SIX SIXES IN AN OVER

The 29th over of South Africa's 2007 World Cup Group A encounter against Netherlands at St Kitts provided a moment of cricket history. Herschelle Gibbs became only the fourth man in the history of the game – and the first in either a World Cup match or a one-day international – to hit six sixes in an over. The unfortunate bowler was Daan van Bunge.

⊙ MOST SIXES IN AN INNINGS

The most sixes hit in a single innings by a player is eight, a feat achieved by three players: Ricky Ponting (Australia) against India at Johannesburg on 23 March 2003; Imran Nazir (Pakistan) against Zimbabwe at Kingston, Jamaica, on 21 March 2007; and by Adam Gilchrist (Australia) against Sri Lanka at Bridgetown, Barbados, on 28 April 2007.

⊙ KIRSTEN CASHES IN

Gary Kirsten made a mockery of pre-match predictions that the wicket at Rawalpindi for South Africa's 1997 Group B match against United Arab Emirates, having remained under covers for four days because of rain, would be a bowler-friendly surface. The left-handed opener smashed an unbeaten 188 off 159 balls – the highest individual score in World Cup history – as South Africa romped to a 169-run victory.

⊙ GIBBS GLORIOUS IN DEFEAT

It was one of the most scintillating batting performances of the 2003 World Cup. Herschelle Gibbs thrilled the partisan Johannesburg crowd with a scintillating innings of 143 to help South Africa to an imposing 306 for 6 in their Pool B encounter with New Zealand. But then the rain came and, with its arrival, South Africa's fortunes changed. New Zealand, chasing a revised target of 226 from 39 overs, and propelled by an unbeaten 134 from captain Stephen Fleming – an innings that contained the most fours in World Cup history (21) – eased to victory with 13 balls to spare. Gibbs's effort is the highest score in a losing cause in World Cup history.

⊙ THE RECORD BREAKER

One of the greatest batsmen ever to play the game, India's Sachin Tendulkar has shone in World Cup matches. Having played 36 matches in the tournament between 1992 and 2007, he holds the record for the most runs (1,796), the most balls faced (2,036), the most centuries (4, a record shared with three other players – Sourav Ganguly, Mark Waugh and Ricky Ponting), the most half-centuries (17), and the most runs scored in a single tournament (673 at the 2003 World Cup).

⊙ FASTEST WORLD CUP 50

Although Lou Vincent, with his 101, made the headlines after New Zealand's comfortable 114-run victory over Canada in the two sides' Group C encounter at St Lucia in the 2007 World Cup, it was Brendon McCullum, with his late display of power hitting towards the end of New Zealand's innings of 363 for 5, who found a way into the record books. The Kiwi keeper smashed a 20-ball half-century to close his side's innings – it was the fastest 50 in World Cup history.

BOWLING RECORDS

MOST WICKETS

Pos	Wkts	Player (Team, Span)
1	71	Glenn McGrath (Australia, 1996–2007)
2	55	Wasim Akram (Pakistan, 1987–2003)
3	53	Muttiah Muralitharan (Sri Lanka, 1996–2007)
4	49	Chaminda Vaas (Sri Lanka, 1996–2007)
5	44	Javagal Srinath (India, 1992–2003)
6	38	Allan Donald (SA, 1992–2003)
7	34	Brad Hogg (Australia, 2003–07)
=	34	Imran Khan (Pakistan, 1975–92)
9	32	Shane Warne (Australia, 1996–99)
=	32	Chris Harris (New Zealand, 1992–2003)

⊙ SNEDDEN FEELS THE HEAT

New Zealand's Martin Snedden felt the full force of a blistering England batting display during the two countries' Group A encounter at The Oval in the 1983 World Cup. The medium-pace bowler took two wickets but went for 105 runs off his 12 overs – the most runs conceded in an innings in World Cup history – as England compiled 322 for 6 (off 60 overs) en route to a comprehensive 106-run victory.

⊙ BOND'S HEROICS ALL IN VAIN

At the halfway stage of New Zealand's Super Six match against Australia at Port Elizabeth on 11 March 2003, the Kiwis were firmly in the driving seat after Shane Bond's magnificent 6 for 23 – the best one-day international return for New Zealand – had reduced Australia to 208 for 9. But where Bond had prospered with the ball, his team-mates floundered with the bat, crashing to 112 all out in 30.1 overs – the Kiwis' lowest-ever World Cup total – to lose the match by 96 runs. Bond's return is the best spell by any bowler in World Cup history to end up on the losing side.

⊙ SUPER GLENN MCGRATH

Glenn McGrath is the most successful bowler in World Cup history. The Australian paceman holds the record for the best figures in an innings (7 for 15 v Namibia at Potchefstroom on 27 February 2003), the best average (18.19), the best strike-rate (27.5), the most wickets in a single tournament (26 in the 2003 World Cup in South Africa), the most maidens bowled in a World Cup career (42), and for the most overs bowled (325.5).

⊙ MOST FIVE-WICKET HAULS

The record for the most five-wicket hauls in World Cup history is two, a feat achieved by four players: Gary Gilmour (Australia) in two matches in the 1975 World Cup; Vasbert Drakes (West Indies) in six matches in the 2003 World Cup; Ashantha de Mel (Sri Lanka) in nine matches in the 1983 and 1987 World Cups; and Glenn McGrath (Australia) in 39 matches between 1996 and 2007.

⊙ MOST FOUR-WICKET HAULS

The greatest leg-spinner of all time, Shane Warne appeared in only two World Cups (he was sensationally dumped from Australia's squad for the 2003 tournament, and subsequently banned from all cricket for a year, after failing a drug test), but when he did play, he more than made his mark. in 17 World Cup matches between 1996 and 1999 he took a record four four-wicket hauls, with a best of 4 for 29 in Australia's epic semi-final clash against South Africa at Edgbaston on 17 June 1999.

⊙ BEST ECONOMY RATE IN AN INNINGS BY A BOWLER

It was the crowning performance of a commanding bowling display by England before rain robbed them of certain victory against Pakistan in the two sides' group match at Adelaide in the 1992 World Cup. As Pakistan floundered to 74 all out, England all-rounder Dermot Reeve bowled five overs for a mere two runs: his economy rate of 0.40 is the best in a single innings by any bowler to bowl five overs or more in World Cup history.

⊙ LETHAL WEAPON

Poker-faced he may have been, but Andy Roberts was arguably the meanest and most deadly of all the great West Indian fast bowlers of the late 1970s and early '80s and played an integral role in his team's World Cup successes in 1975 and 1979. In a World Cup career spanning 16 matches between 1975 and 1983, the Antiguan paceman conceded 552 runs off 170.1 overs (taking 26 wickets) – his economy rate of 3.24 is the best by any bowler in the tournament's history.

⊙ HARRIS'S HEROICS SEE KIWIS THROUGH TO NEXT STAGE

New Zealand travelled to Edinburgh to face Scotland in their final group match at the 1999 World Cup knowing they not only needed to win, but win well if they wanted to overhaul the West Indies to qualify for the Super Sixes. And Chris Harris duly rose to the occasion, taking 4 for 7 off 3.1 overs (the best strike-rate in a single innings – a wicket every 4.7 balls – by any bowler to take four wickets or more in World Cup history) as Scotland slumped to 121 all out. New Zealand reached the victory target with six wickets and 193 balls to spare to progress to the next stage of the competition.

WORLD CUP HAT-TRICKS

Player	For	Against	Venue	Date
Chetan Sharma	India	New Zealand	Nagpur	31 October 1987
Saqlain Mushtaq	Pakistan	Zimbabwe	The Oval	11 June 1999
Chaminda Vaas	Sri Lanka	Bangladesh	Pietermaritzburg	14 February 2003*
Brett Lee	Australia	Kenya	Durban	15 March 2003
Lasith Malinga	Sri Lanka	South Africa	Georgetown	28 March 2007

Remarkably, Vaas's hat-trick came in the first three deliveries of the match.

OTHER RECORDS

HIGHEST PARTNERSHIP BY WICKET

Wkt	Runs	Partners	Team	Opposition	Venue	Date
1st	194	Saeed Anwar/Wajahatullah Wasti	Pakistan	New Zealand	Manchester	16 June 1999
2nd	318	S.C. Ganguly/R. Dravid	India	Sri Lanka	Taunton	26 May 1999
3rd	237*	R. Dravid/S.R. Tendulkar	India	Kenya	Bristol	23 May 1999
4th	204	M.J. Clarke/B.J. Hodge	Australia	Netherlands	Basseterre	18 March 2007
5th	148	R.G. Twose/C.L. Cairns	New Zealand	Australia	Cardiff	20 May 1999
6th	161	M.O. Odumbe/A.V. Vadher	Kenya	Sri Lanka	Southampton	30 May 1999
7th	98	R.R. Sarwan/R.D. Jacobs	West Indies	New Zealand	Port Elizabeth	13 February 2003
8th	117	D.L. Houghton/I.P. Butchart	Zimbabwe	New Zealand	Hyderabad	10 October 1987
9th	126*	Kapil Dev/S.M.H. Kirmani	India	Zimbabwe	Tunbridge Wells	18 June 1983
10th	71	A.M.E. Roberts/J. Garner	West Indies	India	Manchester	9 June 1983

⊙ MOST CATCHES IN AN INNINGS

The record for the most catches in an innings is four, by Mohammad Kaif in India's Super Six match against Sri Lanka at Johannesburg on 10 March 2003. The feat helped India to victory by 183 runs.

⊙ MOST WORLD CUP CATCHES

No fielder has taken more World Cup catches than Australia's Ricky Ponting. In 39 matches between 1996 and 2007 the Tasmanian has pouched 25 victims. He also holds the record for the most catches in a single tournament (11 at the 2003 World Cup in South Africa).

⊙ MOST DISMISSALS BY A WICKETKEEPER

Adam Gilchrist was an outstanding performer with the bat for Australia during their period of World Cup dominance between 1999 and 2007 (they claimed three successive tournament wins), and his destructive hitting at the top of the order often propelled his side into an unassailable position. Gilchrist was also a mightily effective, and often underrated, performer behind the stumps. He holds the World Cup record for the most dismissals (52), the most dismissals in an innings (six v. Namibia at Potchefstroom on 27 February 2003) and for the most dismissals in a single tournament (21 in the 2003 World Cup in South Africa).

⊙ DRAVID AND GANGULY SHOW EASES INDIA TO VICTORY

Taking advantage of some undisciplined bowling, a batsman-friendly surface and some favourably short boundaries, Rahul Dravid and Sourav Ganguly were in record-breaking form in India's Group A encounter with Sri Lanka at Taunton in the 1999 World Cup. The pair added 318 runs in 45 overs for the second wicket – an all-time record for any wicket in one-day international cricket – to help their side to a comfortable 157-run win.

⊙ BEST ATTENDED WORLD CUP

The best attended World Cup in history was the 2003 tournament held in Kenya, Zimbabwe and South Africa. A total of 626,845 spectators flocked through the turnstiles during the 52 matches played.

⊙ FIRST WORLD CUP MATCH PLAYED UNDER LIGHTS

The first day-night match to be played in World Cup history was the pool match between England and India at Perth during the 1992 World Cup. For the record, England won the closely fought match by nine runs.

⊙ MOST EXTRAS CONCEDED IN AN INNINGS

As expected, Scotland were comfortably outclassed by Pakistan in the two sides' Group A encounter at Chester-le-Street in the 1999 World Cup, losing the match by 94 runs, but indiscipline with the ball did little to help their cause. During Pakistan's innings, the Scots conceded a World Cup record 59 extras – five byes, six leg-byes, 33 wides and 15 no-balls.

⊙ MOST MATCHES PLAYED

The highest number of World Cup appearances by any player is 39, a record shared by two men: Glenn McGrath and Ricky Ponting, both representing Australia between 1996 and 2007.

⊙ MOST MATCHES AS CAPTAIN

Stephen Fleming led his side into World Cup battle on more occasions than any other captain. The Kiwi skipper captained his country 27 times in World Cup matches between 1999 and 2007.

⊙ MOST MATCHES AS AN UMPIRE

Much-loved English umpire David Shepherd, whose death in October 2009 saddened the entire cricket world, holds the record for the most World Cup appearances as an umpire. The former Gloucestershire batsman officiated in 46 matches in the tournament, including the 1996, 1999 and 2003 World Cup finals.

⊙ MOST WORLD CUP MATCHES STAGED

Headingley, in Leeds, England, has hosted more World Cup matches than any other ground in history. The home of Yorkshire CCC has staged 12 matches in the tournament between 1975 and 1999.

⊙ MOST HUNDREDS IN A TOURNAMENT

Big scores were the order of the day at the 2003 World Cup in Kenya, South Africa and Zimbabwe. The tournament saw a tournament record 21 centuries in the 52 matches played – the highest score was Craig Wishart's unbeaten 172 for Zimbabwe against Namibia at Harare on 10 February 2003.

MOST WINS AS CAPTAIN: TOP 5

Pos	Wins	Player (Team, Span)
1	22	Ricky Ponting (Australia, 2003–07)
2	16	Stephen Fleming (New Zealand, 1999–2007)
3	15	Clive Lloyd (West Indies, 1975–83)
4	14	Imran Khan (Pakistan, 1983–92)
5	11	Allan Border (Australia, 1987–92)
=	11	Hansie Cronje (South Africa, 1996–99)
=	11	Kapil Dev (India, 1983–87)

ICC CHAMPIONS TROPHY

Played on a bi-annual basis and considered the second most important one-day competition in world cricket, the ICC Champions Trophy was first contested in Bangladesh in 1998 and has been held on six occasions. Australia are the tournament's only two-time winners.

ICC CHAMPIONS TROPHY WINNERS

Year	Winner	Host
1998	South Africa	Bangladesh
2000	New Zealand	Kenya
2002	India/Sri Lanka*	Sri Lanka
2004	West Indies	England
2006	Australia	India
2009	Australia	South Africa**

The trophy was shared after the final was washed out by rain.
**The tournament was scheduled to be played in Pakistan but was moved to South Africa because of security fears.*

⊙ MAHAROOF MESMERIZES WEST INDIANS

Bowling full and straight on a low, slow wicket at the Brabourne Stadium in Mumbai, Sri Lanka's Farveez Maharoof proved too much for the West Indies batsmen in the two sides' qualifying group encounter at the 2002 ICC Champions Trophy. The paceman took 6 for 14 off nine overs – the best bowling figures in the tournament's history – as the West Indies slipped to 80 all out. Sri Lanka eased to victory in 13.2 overs with nine wickets in hand.

⊙ HIGHEST INDIVIDUAL SCORES

Two players hold the record for the highest individual score in ICC Champions Trophy history: New Zealand's Nathan Astle, 145 not out v USA at The Oval on 10 September 2004; and Zimbabwe's Andy Flower, 145 v India at Colombo on 14 September 2002.

⊙ MOST SUCCESSFUL CAPTAIN

The only captain in the tournament's history to lift the cup on two occasions, Australia's Ricky Ponting is the most successful captain in ICC Champions Trophy history. The Australian skipper has led his side to 12 wins in 16 matches between 2002 and 2009.

⊙ NEW ZEALAND TAKE ADVANTAGE OF UNCLE SAM

New Zealand cruelly exposed a lack of depth in the USA's bowling attack in the Americans' first-ever match in the ICC Champions Trophy at The Oval on 10 September 2004. Batting first, the Kiwis – propelled by big innings from Nathan Astle (145 not out), Scott Styris (75) and Craig McMillan (64 not out) – amassed a mighty 347 for 4 off their 50 overs (the highest total in the tournament's history) en route to a crushing 210-run win – the largest in ICC Champions Trophy history.

⊙ WATSON AND PONTING CRUSH HUMBLED ENGLAND

Propelled to a commendable 257 all out (after being on 101 for 6) by a battling 76-ball 80 from Tim Bresnan, England would have had high hopes of containing Australia in the two sides' ICC Champions Trophy tie at Centurion on 2 October 2009. But those hopes were soon dashed: Shane Watson (136 not out) and Ricky Ponting (111 not out) put on 252 runs for the second wicket – the highest partnership in the tournament's history – to ease Australia past the winning post with 8.1 overs to spare.

⊙ MOST CATCHES

Sri Lanka's Mahela Jayawardene is the leading fielder in all ICC Champions Trophy matches. He has bagged 13 catches in 18 matches between 2000 and 2009.

⊙ MOST DISMISSALS BY A WICKETKEEPER

Kumar Sangakkara holds the ICC Champions Trophy record for the most dismissals by a wicketkeeper. The Sri Lankan gloveman has pouched 28 victims (24 caught and four stumped) in 18 matches in the tournament between 2000 and 2009.

⊙ SORRY USA COLLAPSE AGAINST AUSTRALIA

On paper, the match between the USA and Australia at Southampton in the 2004 ICC Champions Trophy was always going to be a mismatch, and so it proved. Put in to bat, the USA were skittled for a paltry 65 all out in 24 overs – the lowest total in the tournament's history. Australia eased to the victory target with nine wickets and a colossal 42.1 overs to spare.

MOST RUNS: TOP 5

Pos	Runs	Player (Team, Span)
1	695	Chris Gayle (West Indies, 2002–06)
2	665	Sourav Ganguly (India, 1998–2004)
3	653	Jacques Kallis (South Africa, 1998–2009)
4	627	Rahul Dravid (India, 1998–2009)
5	593	Ricky Ponting (Australia, 1998–2009)

MOST WICKETS: TOP 5

Pos	Wkts	Player (Team, Span)
1	24	Muttiah Muralitharan (Sri Lanka, 1998–2009)
2	22	Kyle Mills (New Zealand, 2002–09)
=	22	Brett Lee (Australia, 2000–09)
4	21	Glenn McGrath (Australia, 2000–06)
5	20	Jacques Kallis (South Africa, 1998–2009)

ICC CHAMPIONS TROPHY LEAGUE TABLE

Pos	Team (Span)	Mat	Won	Lost	Tied	NR	%
1	Australia (1998–2009)	18	12	5	0	1	70.58
2	India (1998–2009)	19	10	6	0	3	62.50
3	New Zealand (1998–2009)	18	11	7	0	0	61.11
=	Sri Lanka (1998–2009)	20	11	7	0	2	61.11
5	South Africa (1998–2009)	17	10	7	0	0	58.82
6	West Indies (1998–2009)	21	12	9	0	0	57.14
7	England (1998–2009)	16	8	8	0	0	50.00
8	Pakistan (1998–2009)	15	7	8	0	0	46.66
9	Bangladesh (2000–06)	8	1	7	0	0	12.50
10	Kenya (2000–04)	5	0	5	0	0	0.00
=	Netherlands (2002)	2	0	2	0	0	0.00
=	USA (2004)	2	0	2	0	0	0.00
=	Zimbabwe (1998–2006)	9	0	9	0	0	0.00

⊙ SMALLEST VICTORIES

By runs: by ten runs on two occasions – India v South Africa at Colombo on 25 September 2002; and West Indies v Australia at Mumbai on 18 October 2006.

By wickets: by two wickets on three occasions – South Africa v West Indies at Colombo on 13 September 2002; West Indies v England at The Oval on 25 September 2004; and Australia v Pakistan at Centurion on 30 September 2009.

ODI CRICKET

The first one-day international, a hastily arranged affair after rain washed out the Fifth Test of the 1970–71 Ashes series, was played between Australia and England at Melbourne on 5 January 1971. One-day internationals may not be universally popular, but since then they have become a mainstay of modern cricket: in 2009 alone there were 150 one-day internationals compared to 41 Test matches.

⊙ LARGEST VICTORIES
By runs: by 290 runs – New Zealand v Ireland at Aberdeen on 1 July 2008.
By wickets: by ten wickets on 38 occasions.
By balls remaining: 277 – England v Canada at Old Trafford on 13 June 1979.

⊙ NARROWEST VICTORIES
By runs: by one run on 24 occasions. By wickets: by one wicket on 38 occasions.
By balls remaining: off the last ball of the match on 30 occasions.

⊙ NAMIBIA SLUMP TO RECORD DEFEAT
It was the biggest mismatch of the 2003 ICC World Cup. Batting first, defending champions Australia cruised to 301 for 6 off the 50-over allocation; in reply, Namibia, in the face of some fine bowling from Glenn McGrath (7 for 15), wilted to 45 all out in 14 overs – their innings, which lasted a mere 84 balls, is the shortest completed innings (by balls received) in one-day international cricket history.

TEAM RECORDS: ONE-DAY INTERNATIONAL
RESULT SUMMARY (BY COUNTRY)

Team (span)	Mat	Won	Lost	Tied	NR	%
Afghanistan (2009–10)	16	9	7	0	0	56.25
Africa XI (2005–07)	6	1	4	0	1	20.00
Asia XI (2005–07)	7	4	2	0	1	66.66
Australia (1971–2011)	758	470	256	8	24	64.57
Bangladesh (1986–2011)	239	64	173	0	2	27.00
Bermuda (2006–09)	35	7	28	0	0	20.00
Canada (1979–2011)	61	16	43	0	1	27.11
East Africa (1975)	3	0	3	0	0	0.00
England (1971–2011)	549	264	262	5	18	50.18
Hong Kong (2004–08)	4	0	4	0	0	0.00
ICC World XI (2005)	4	1	3	0	0	25.00
India (1974–2011)	765	374	354	3	34	51.36
Ireland (2006–10)	58	28	26	1	6	51.81
Kenya (1996–2011)	137	38	94	0	5	28.78
Namibia (2003)	6	0	6	0	0	0.00
Netherlands (1996–2010)	57	23	32	0	2	41.81
New Zealand (1973–2011)	604	259	308	5	32	45.71
Pakistan (1973–2011)	734	390	322	6	16	54.73
Scotland (1999–2010)	50	15	32	0	3	31.91
South Africa (1991–2011)	452	282	153	5	12	64.65
Sri Lanka (1975–2011)	619	290	300	3	25	49.15
United Arab Emirates (1994–2008)	11	1	10	0	0	9.09
USA (2004)	2	0	2	0	0	0.00
West Indies (1973–2011)	640	335	276	5	24	54.78
Zimbabwe (1983–2010)	387	101	272	5	9	27.38

HIGHEST TEAM TOTAL: TOP 5

Pos	Score	Team	Opposition	Venue	Date
1	443–9	Sri Lanka	Netherlands	Amstelveen	4 Jul 2006
2	438–9	South Africa	Australia	Johannesburg	12 Mar 2006
3	434–4	Australia	South Africa	Johannesburg	12 Mar 2006
4	418–5	South Africa	Zimbabwe	Potchefstroom	20 Sep 2006
5	414–7	India	Sri Lanka	Rajkot	15 Dec 2009

LOWEST TEAM TOTAL: TOP 5

Pos	Score	Team	Opposition	Venue	Date
1	35	Zimbabwe	Sri Lanka	Harare	25 Apr 2004
2	36	Canada	Sri Lanka	Paarl	19 Feb 2003
3	38	Zimbabwe	Sri Lanka	Colombo	8 Dec 2001
4	43	Pakistan	West Indies	Cape Town	25 Feb 1993
5	44	Zimbabwe	Banngladesh	Chittagong	3 Nov 2009

⊙ AUSTRALIA'S RECORD-BREAKING STREAK

Australia hold the all-time record for the most consecutive one-day international victories. Between 11 January 2003 (a seven-run victory over England at Hobart) and 24 May 2003 (a 67-run win against the West Indies at Port of Spain, Trinidad) they racked up 21 successive victories – a run that included success at the 2003 ICC World Cup. The record-breaking streak came to an end when they slipped to a 39-run defeat by the West Indies at Port of Spain on 25 May 2003.

⊙ RUNS GALORE AT JOHANNESBURG

With the five-match series evenly poised at 2–2, South Africa and Australia put on a dynamic show of batting brilliance in the fifth and final one-day international at Johannesburg on 12 March 2006. Batting first, Australia romped to a mighty, and apparently match-winning, 434 for 4 off their 50 overs, helped by an innings of 164 from captain Ricky Ponting. Undaunted by the colossal total, however, South Africa, inspired by a sublime, stroke-filled, 111-ball 175 from Herschelle Gibbs, sensationally reached the victory target with one ball to spare. The total of 872 runs scored in the match is an all-time record in one-day international cricket.

⊙ MOST CONSECUTIVE DEFEATS

Bangladesh's early struggles in the Test arena – they had to wait 35 Tests and four years and three months before notching up their first victory – were replicated in one-day internationals. Between 8 October 1999 (a 73-run loss to the West Indies at Dhaka) and 9 October 2002 (a seven-wicket defeat by South Africa at Kimberley), they crashed to a record 23 consecutive defeats. Rain, rather than good play, finally brought the run to an end: their match against the West Indies at Chittagong on 29 November 2002 ended up as a no-result.

⊙ TIED MATCHES

There have been 23 tied matches in one-day international cricket, most famously when Australia tied with South Africa in the 1999 World Cup semi-final to progress to the final.

⊙ MOST SIXES IN AN INNINGS

The record for the most sixes in an innings is 18, a feat achieved on four occasions: by South Africa (v Netherlands at Basseterre, St Kitts and Nevis, on 16 March 2007 – a game in which Herschelle Gibbs hit six sixes in an over); twice by India (v Bermuda at Port of Spain, Trinidad, on 19 March 2007 and v New Zealand at Christchurch on 8 March 2009); and by New Zealand (v Ireland at Aberdeen on 1 July 2008).

⊙ MOST FOURS IN AN INNINGS

Irritated at being asked by the ICC to contest two one-day internationals against the Netherlands hot on the heels of a tough tour of England, Sri Lanka unleashed their frustration in record-breaking fashion in the first of the two matches, played at Amstelveen on 4 July 2006. They smashed a one-day international record 443 for 9 off their 50 overs, an innings that included a remarkable 56 fours (50.56 per cent of their total runs) – another one-day record. Sanath Jayasuriya hit 24 of them in an innings of 157.

⊙ MOST DUCKS IN A MATCH

The headlines following the West Indies 92-run victory over England in the 1979 ICC World Cup final at Lord's were reserved for Viv Richards's stunning innings of 138 not out, but the match was also remarkable because eight batsmen in the match failed to score – an all-time record in one-day international cricket.

⊙ CHAPPELL AND COSIER'S EFFORTS ALL IN VAIN

Greg Chappell (5 for 20) and Gary Cosier (5 for 18) created history against England at Edgbaston on 4 June 1977 – it is the only occasion in which two bowlers have taken five wickets in the same innings – but their efforts weren't enough to win Australia the match. England's bowlers rallied in spectacular style to dismiss Australia for 70 and secure a 101-run victory.

⊙ CRASHING TIMBERS

Having set New Zealand 260 to win the third one-day international at Albion, Guyana, on 14 April 1985, the West Indies bowlers used the maxim "If you miss, I'll hit" to supreme effect: a record eight Kiwi batsmen were out bowled as the visitors slipped to 129 all out and a 130-run defeat.

⊙ MOST RUNS FROM FOURS AND SIXES IN AN INNINGS

The record for the most runs from boundaries in a one-day international is 256, a feat achieved by two teams: Sri Lanka (43 fours and 14 sixes) v Kenya at Kandy on 6 March 1996; and Australia (43 fours and 14 sixes) v South Africa at Johannesburg on 12 March 2006. Ricky Ponting was South Africa's chief destroyer, hitting a majestic 164 with 13 four and nine sixes.

⊙ RUNS GALORE IN LAHORE

When Pakistan, bolstered by centuries from Ijaz Ahmed (111) and Yousuf Youhana (100), posted 315 for 8 off their 50-over allocation against Australia in the third and final one-day international at Lahore on 10 November 1998, they must have felt as though they had done enough to avoid a series whitewash. But Australia had other ideas: propelled by centuries from Adam Gilchrist (103) and Ricky Ponting (124 not out), the tourists reached the victory target with seven balls and four wickets to spare. The four centuries struck in the match set an all-time record in one-day international cricket.

⊙ HISTORY-MAKING MOMENT IN MULTAN

Mohsin Khan (117 not out) and Zaheer Abbas (118) created a slice of history during Pakistan's 37-run victory over India in the second one-day international at Multan on 17 December 1982: it was the first time in one-day international history that two players from the same side had passed 100 in the same innings. The feat has since been repeated on 82 occasions.

⊙ ASSORTED BOWLING RECORDS

Most bowlers used: 9 – on 12 occasions
Most bowlers taking wickets in a match: 12 – on four occasions
Most ducks in an innings: 6 – on four occasions

⊙ ASSORTED BATTING RECORDS

Most batsmen reaching double figures: 10 – on four occasions
All 11 batsmen failing to reach double figures: on two occasions
Most batsmen caught in an innings: 10 – on 14 occasions
Most batsmen lbw in an innings: 6 – on two occasions
Most batsmen run out in an innings: 5 – on nine occasions
Most batsmen stumped in an innings: 3 – on 13 occasions

⊙ OPENERS EFFORTS NOT ENOUGH FOR AUSTRALIA

Geoff Marsh (104) and David Boon (111) created history against India at Jaipur on 7 September 1986 – it was the first time in one-day international cricket history that both openers had scored a century in an innings (there have been 20 subsequent instances) – but it wasn't enough to win Australia the match. Chasing 251 for victory, India, thanks in no small part to Kris Srikkanth's 102, won by seven wickets with six overs to spare.

⊙ MOST WIDES IN AN INNINGS

The West Indies bowlers' radars were clearly malfunctioning in their Benson and Hedges World Series match against Pakistan at Brisbane on 7 January 1989: during the course of Pakistan's 258 for 7, they delivered a one-day international record 37 wides. And their batsmen fared little better: they were dismissed for 203 in 40.4 overs to lose the match by 55 runs.

⊙ MOST NO-BALLS IN AN INNINGS

A record number of no-balls (20) ultimately cost Pakistan victory against arch-rivals India in the first one-day international (of seven) at Karachi on 13 March 2004. Chasing 350 for victory, they ultimately fell six runs short.

BATTING RECORDS

MOST CAREER RUNS: TOP 10

Pos	Runs	Player (Team, Span)
1	17,629	Sachin Tendulkar (India, 1989–2011)
2	13,428	Sanath Jayasuriya (Asia/Sri Lanka, 1989–2009)
3	13,082	Ricky Ponting (ICC/Australia, 1995–2011)
4	11,739	Inzamam-ul-Haq (Asia/Pakistan, 1991–2007)
5	11,363	Sourav Ganguly (Asia/India, 1992–2007)
6	11,002	Jacques Kallis (Africa/ICC/South Africa, 1996–2011)
7	10,765	Rahul Dravid (Asia/ICC/India, 1996–2009)
8	10,405	Brian Lara (ICC/West Indies, 1990–2007)
9	9,720	Mohammad Yousuf (Asia/Pakistan, 1998–2010)
10	9,619	Adam Gilchrist (ICC/Australia, 1996–2008)

⊙ DHONI PUTS ON BATTING MASTERCLASS

It was an innings that confirmed India's Mahendra Singh Dhoni as a batsman of the highest class. With his side chasing an imposing 299 for victory against Sri Lanka in the third one-day international at Jaipur on 31 October 2005, Dhoni, batting at No. 3, struck an imperious, chanceless 183 not out in 145 balls to ease his side to a six-wicket victory with 23 balls to spare. It is the highest score by a wicketkeeper in one-day international history.

⊙ THE ONE-DAY INTERNATIONAL BATTING KING

Sachin Tendulkar, known as the "Little Master", has truly lived up to his reputation in one-day cricket. A veteran of 444 matches (no player in history has played more), he has scored the most runs (17,629), has recorded the most centuries (46), the most scores of 50-plus (139), the most 90s (18), has been dismissed on 99 more times than any other batsman (3), holds the record for the most runs in a calendar year (1,894) and the record for the most centuries in a calendar year (9).

⊙ MOST RUNS IN A CAREER WITHOUT A HUNDRED

Feared for his bowling, but admired in equal measure for his hard-hitting, late-order exploits with the bat, Pakistan's Wasim Akram holds the all-time one-day international cricket record for the most runs scored without ever recording a century. The all-rounder notched up 3,717 runs in 356 matches for Pakistan between 1984 and 2003, with a highest score of 86 coming against Australia at Melbourne on 26 February 1990.

HIGHEST CAREER BATTING AVERAGE (MINIMUM OF 20 INNINGS): TOP 5

Pos	Ave	Player (Team, Span)
1	68.55	Ryan ten Doeschate (Netherlands, 2006–10)
2	59.88	Hashim Amla (South Africa, 2008–11)
3	53.58	Michael Bevan (Australia, 1994–2004)
2	51.96	Micheal Hussey (Australia, 2004–11)
5	49.22	Vinod Kohli (India, 2008–11)

⊙ THERE'S NO PLACE LIKE HOME FOR JAYASURIYA

The second-most experienced one-day international cricketer of all time (444 matches) and the second-leading all-time run-scorer in the 50-over format of the game (with 13,428 runs), Sri Lanka's Sanath Jayasuriya has enjoyed considerable success at the R. Premadasa Stadium in Colombo. In 70 innings there between 1992 and 2009, the left-hander has scored 2,514 runs (with four centuries and a highest score of 130) – the most scored by a player at a single ground in one-day international cricket history.

⊙ HOTTEST BATTING STREAKS

The record for the most centuries posted in consecutive innings is three, a feat achieved by four players: Zaheer Abbas (Pakistan) against India between 17 December 1982 and 21 January 1983; Saeed Anwar (Pakistan) against Sri Lanka, West Indies, Sri Lanka between 30 October and 2 November 1993; Herschelle Gibbs (South Africa) against Kenya, India, Bangladesh between 20 September and 3 October 2002; and A.B. de Villiers (South Africa) against India (twice) and the West Indies between 24 February and 22 May 2010.

⊙ BOOM BOOM AFRIDI

A compulsive shot-maker, often to his own detriment, and one of the cleanest strikers of a cricket ball ever to play the game, Pakistan's Shahid Afridi is tailor-made for the shorter formats of the game. In 312 one-day internationals for his country between 1996 and 2011 he has scored 6,583 runs (at an average of 22.93 with four centuries) off 5,787 deliveries – the highest career strike-rate of any player to complete 50 innings in one-day international history (113.75). He also holds the record for the highest strike-rate (runs per hundred balls faced) in an innings: 305.55 – 55 not out off 18 balls against Netherlands at Colombo on 21 September 2002.

⊙ HITTING NEW HEIGHTS

By 2010, Sachin Tendulkar held almost every cricket batting record in the book: he had scored the most runs in Test matches (13,447), the most runs in ODIs and had hit more centuries in both forms of the game (47 in Tests and 46 in ODIs) than any other batsman in history. But if any criticism could be directed towards the "Little Master", it would be that he has consistently failed to push on and gather huge scores. That perception changed on 24 February 2010 when India played South Africa in the second one-day international at Gwalior. Opening the batting, Tendulkar smashed an unbeaten 200 off 147 balls (with 25 fours – the most by any batsman in one-day international history – and three sixes) to become the first batsman in one-day international cricket history to pass the 200-mark.

SCORING 100 ON DEBUT

Player (team)	Runs	Opposition	Venue	Date
Dennis Amiss (England)	103	Australia	Manchester	24 Aug 1972
Desmond Haynes (West Indies)	148	Australia	St John's	22 Feb 1978
Andy Flower (Zimbabwe)	115*	Sri Lanka	New Plymouth	23 Feb 1992
Saleem Elahi (Pakistan)	102*	Sri Lanka	Gujranwala	29 Sep 1995
Martin Guptill (New Zealand)	122*	West Indies	Auckland	10 Jan 2009

⊙ AFRIDI'S SPECTACULAR ENTRANCE ON TO WORLD STAGE

Pakistan's Shahid Afridi took the cricket world by storm. Playing in only his second one-day international, but batting for the first time (against Sri Lanka at Nairobi, Kenya, on 4 October 1996) in his fledgling career, the young star (aged just 16 years 217 days at the time) struck 102 off a mere 37 deliveries to record the fastest one-day international century of all time and become the youngest player in history to hit a century in the game's 50-over format.

HIGHEST SCORE: PROGRESSIVE RECORD HOLDERS

Runs	Player (country)	Opposition	Venue	Date
82	John Edrich (England)	Australia	Melbourne	5 Jan 1971
103	Dennis Amiss (England)	Australia	Manchester	24 Aug 1972
105	Roy Fredericks (West Indies)	England	The Oval	7 Sep 1973
116*	David Lloyd (England)	Pakistan	Nottingham	31 Aug 1974
171*	Glenn Turner (New Zealand)	East Africa	Birmingham	7 Jun 1975
175*	Kapil Dev (India)	Zimbabwe	Tunbridge Wells	18 Jun 1983
189*	Viv Richards (West Indies)	England	Manchester	31 May 1984
194	Saeed Anwar (Pakistan)	India	Chennai	21 May 1997
194*	Charles Coventry (Zimbabwe)	Bangladesh	Bulawayo	16 Aug 2009
200*	SouthTendulkar (India)	South Africa	Gwalior	24 Feb 2010

⊙ AGE NO DETERRENT FOR JAYASURIYA

Sri Lanka's Sanath Jayasuriya, the most capped one-day international cricketer of all time, proved age was no barrier when, on 28 January 2009, aged 39 years and 212 days, he struck 107 against India at Dambulla to become the oldest centurion in one-day
international cricket history. Sadly for the veteran, it did not turn out to be a match-winning contribution, as India cantered to victory with six wickets and 11 balls to spare.

⊙ TROUBLING THE SCORERS

Kumar Dharmasena became an integral part of Sri Lanka's one-day set-up through his unorthodox, but highly effective, off-spin bowling (playing in 141 one-day internationals between 1994 and 2004), but it was his exploits with the bat that forced him into the record books: the right-hander went 72 innings before recording his first duck – an all-time record in one-day international cricket.

⊙ TURNER'S ONE-DAY MARATHON

It was as much of a marathon innings as you could ever wish to see in a one-day international. Opening the batting for New Zealand against East Africa in the two countries' Group A encounter at Edgbaston in the 1975 World Cup, Glenn Turner batted through the entire 60-over innings to reach 171 not out – the 201 balls he faced is a record in one-day international cricket.

CARRYING BAT THROUGH A COMPLETED INNINGS

Player (country)	Runs	Total	Opposition	Venue	Date
Grant Flower (Zimbabwe)	84	205	England	Sydney	15 Dec 1994
Saeed Anwar (Pakistan)	103	219	Zimbabwe	Harare	22 Feb 1995
Nick Knight (England)	125	246	Pakistan	Nottingham	1 Sep 1996
Ridley Jacobs (West Indies)	49	110	Australia	Manchester	30 May 1999
Damien Martyn (Australia)	116	191	New Zealand	Auckland	3 Mar 2000
Herschelle Gibbs (South Africa)	59	101†	Pakistan	Sharjah	28 Mar 2000
Alec Stewart (England)	100	192	West Indies	Nottingham	20 Jul 2000
Javed Omar (Bangladesh)	33	103	Zimbabwe	Harare	8 Apr 2001

† not all ten wickets fell in the innings

FASTEST TO...

Runs	Innings	Player (country)
1,000	21	Viv Richards (West Indies)
	21	Kevin Pietersen (ICC/England)
2,000	40	Hashim Amla (South Africa)
3,000	69	Viv Richards (West Indies)
4,000	88	Viv Richards (West Indies)
5,000	114	Viv Richards (West Indies)
6,000	141	Viv Richards (West Indies)
7,000	174	Sourav Ganguly (India)
8,000	200	Sourav Ganguly (India)
9,000	228	Sourav Ganguly (India)
10,000	259	Sachin Tendulkar (India)
11,000	276	Sachin Tendulkar (India)
12,000	300	Sachin Tendulkar (India)
13,000	321	Sachin Tendulkar (India)
14,000	350	Sachin Tendulkar (India)
15,000	377	Sachin Tendulkar (India)
16,000	399	Sachin Tendulkar (India)
17,000	424	Sachin Tendulkar (India)

BOWLING RECORDS

MOST WICKETS: TOP 10

Pos	Wkts	Player (Team, Span)
1	519	Muttiah Muralitharan (Asia/ICC/Sri Lanka, 1993–2011)
2	502	Wasim Akram (Pakistan, 1984–2003)
3	416	Waqar Younis (Pakistan, 1989–2003)
4	400	Chaminda Vaas (Asia/Sri Lanka, 1994–2008)
5	393	Shaun Pollock (Africa/ICC/South Africa, 1996–2008)
6	381	Glenn McGrath (ICC/Australia, 1993–2007)
7	337	Anil Kumble (Asia/India, 1990–2007)
8	335	Brett Lee (Australia, 2000–11)
9	322	Sanath Jayasuriya (Asia/Sri Lanka, 1989–2009)
10	315	Javagal Srinath (India, 1991–2003)

⊙ IMRAN STANDS TALL AS PAKISTAN FALTER

A magnificent spell of bowling from Pakistan's Imran Khan (he took 6 for 14 off his ten-over allocation) saw India crash to 125 all out in the opening match of the Four Nations Cup at Sharjah on 22 May 1985. But his magical performance was not enough to win his side the game: in reply, Pakistan slipped to 87 all out to lose the match by 38 runs. Imran's figures are the best by any bowler to end up on the losing side in one-day international cricket history.

⊙ BIG BIRD PUTS THE BREAKS ON OPPOSITION BATSMEN

There has perhaps been no more fearful sight for batsmen in cricket history: the 6ft 8in Joel Garner tearing into the bowling crease ready to unleash an array of searing, fast-paced deliveries from out of the clouds. And the man they called "Big Bird" was at his most potent in one-day cricket: in 98 matches for the West Indies between 1977 and 1987 he took 146 wickets for 2,752 runs at an economy rate of 3.09 runs per over – the best rate by any bowler to have bowled 1,000 deliveries or more in one-day international cricket history.

⊙ AT THE PEAK OF HIS POWERS

Pakistan's most effective spin bowler of recent times, Saqlain Mushtaq enjoyed considerable success in the one-day arena. He reached the 100-, 150-, 200- and 250-wicket landmarks faster than any other bowler in history and enjoyed magical years in both 1996 (in which he took 65 one-day international wickets) and 1997 (in which he took 69 wickets – an all-time record number of wickets in a calendar year in one-day international cricket).

⊙ TEN DOESCHATE CATCHES THE EYE

The most admired cricketer from a non-Test-playing country currently appearing in one-day international cricket, South Africa-born Ryan ten Doeschate has been a revelation with both bat and ball for the Netherlands since he made his debut against Sri Lanka on 4 July 2006. In 27 matches he has scored 1,234 runs (at the impressive average of 68.55) and taken 48 wickets at a strike-rate of a wicket every 26.4 balls – the best by any bowler to have bowled 1,000 balls or more in one-day international cricket history.

⊙ RECORD-BREAKING SUCCESS AT SHARJAH

No fast bowler in history has taken more wickets in one-day international cricket than Wasim Akram (502 wickets in 356 matches), and the Pakistan paceman was supremely effective in his country's matches at Sharjah. 77 matches in the emirate between 1985 and 2002 he took 122 wickets – the most wickets by any bowler at a single ground in ODI history.

⊙ MAGICAL MCGRATH PROPELS AUSTRALIA TO VICTORY

Glenn McGrath was in blistering form with the ball during Australia's successful campaign in the 1998–99 Carlton and United triangular series (which also involved England and Sri Lanka). The fast bowler took 27 wickets in 11 matches – the best by any bowler in history in a one-day tournament – at an average of 15.62 runs per wicket, with a best haul of 5 for 40 against Sri Lanka at Adelaide on 24 January 1999.

⊙ MISERLY SIMMONS EASES WEST INDIES TO VICTORY

Phil Simmons's medium-pace swing bowling proved too much for Pakistan at Sydney on 17 December 1992: the West Indies all-rounder took 4 for 3 off his ten overs – the most economical figures ever recorded in a full spell of bowling in one-day international cricket – in a match the West Indies went on to win by 133 runs.

⊙ WORST ECONOMY RATE IN AN INNINGS

The worst economy rate in an innings in one-day international cricket (having bowled a minimum of 30 balls) is 12.42, an unfortunate feat achieved by two bowlers: Bangladesh's Tapash Baisya (7.0-0-87-0 v England at Trent Bridge on 21 June 2005) and Australia's Stuart Clark (7.0-0-87-0 v West Indies at Kuala Lumpur on 18 September 2006).

⊙ WORST CAREER ECONOMY RATE

Sahfiul Islam made his first-class debut for Ranjashi Division in December 2007 aged 18, took five wickets in an innings and soon caught the eye of Bangladesh's selectors. Within three years he made his one-day international debut – against Sri Lanka in Dhaka in January 2010 – and has been an ever-present in the squad ever since. Not with the greatest success, however: his economy rate (6.42) is the worst by any bowler to have bowled 1,000 balls or more in one-day international cricket history.

⊙ LACKING THE KILLER PUNCH

A bowler who lacked the pace to make his mark in international cricket, Zimbabwe's Pommie Mbangwa holds the dubious record of having the worst career strike-rate of any bowler to have bowled 1,000 balls or more in one-day international cricket history. The medium-pace swing bowler took 11 wickets for his country in 29 matches between 1996 and 2002 at a strike-rate of a wicket every 124.4 deliveries

⊙ VAAS RIPS THROUGH ZIMBABWE

Sri Lanka's Chaminda Vaas was inspirational against Zimbabwe at Colombo on 8 December 2001. The left-arm paceman took a wicket with the first delivery of the match and never let up, helping to rout the visitors for the third lowest score in 50-over cricket (38 all out) and become the first, and to date only, bowler in one-day international cricket history to take eight wickets in an innings.

He finished with the astonishing figures of 8 for 19 off eight overs.

BEST CAREER BOWLING AVERAGE: TOP 5 (QUALIFICATION: 50 WICKETS)

Pos	Ave	Player (Team, Span)
1	18.84	Joel Garner (West Indies, 1977–87)
1	19.57	Ajantha Mendis (Sri Lanka, 2008–11)
3	20.11	Len Pascoe (Australia, 1977–82)
4	20.35	Andy Roberts (West Indies, 1975–83)
5	20.82	Dennis Lillee (Australia, 1972–83)

DEADLIEST BOWLER–BATSMAN COMBINATION: TOP 5

Pos	Wkts	Bowler (country)	Victim (country)	Span
1	13	Waqar Younis (Pak)	Sanath Jayasuriya (SL)	1989–2002
2	12	Wasim Akram (Pak)	Desmond Haynes (WI)	1985–93
=	12	Shaun Pollock (ICC/SA)	Adam Gilchrist (Aus)	1997–2007
4	11	Chaminda Vaas (Asia/SL)	Stephen Fleming (ICC/NZ)	1994–2007
=	11	Chaminda Vaas (SL)	Saeed Anwar (Pak)	1994–2002

⊙ WAQAR PROVIDES GLIMPSE INTO A GLORIOUS FUTURE

It did not take long for Waqar Younis to give notice of the talent that would see him become one of the most successful fast bowlers ever to play in the 50-over format of the game. Playing in his 21st match for Pakistan (against Sri Lanka at Sharjah on 29 April 1990), he took 6 for 26 to become, aged 18 years and 164 days, the youngest player to take five wickets in an innings in one-day international cricket history.

⊙ A POOR DAY AT THE OFFICE

Australia's Mick Lewis had a day to forget as South Africa chased down a victory target of 435 to win by one wicket at Johannesburg on 12 March 2006. The fast-medium bowler went for 113 runs off his 10 overs – the most ever conceded by a bowler to bowl his full allocation of overs in an ODI.

⊙ MOST BALLS BOWLED IN AN ODI CAREER

No bowler has bowled more deliveries in one-day international cricket than Muttiah Muralitharan, who has bowled 18,439 balls for Sri Lanka in 342 matches between 1993 and 2011. The spin wizard has also conceded the most runs in one-day internationals (12,073).

⊙MAGIC MALINGA CARVES THROUGH SOUTH AFRICA

There have been 27 hat-tricks in the history of one-day international cricket, but there has been only one case of a bowler taking four wickets in four balls: Lasith Malinga dismissed Shaun Pollock (bowled), Andrew Hall (caught), Jacques Kallis (caught) and Makhaya Ntini (bowled) in successive deliveries during Sri Lanka's World Cup Super Eight match against South Africa at Providence, Guyana, on 28 March 2007, but still saw his side lose by one run.

⊙ AGE NO BARRIER FOR DHANIRAM

Sunil Dhaniram created a slice of history during Canada's match against Bermuda at Ontario on 29 June 2008. The Canadian slow left-armer, playing in his 26th one-day international, took 5 for 32 to become, aged 39 years and 256 days, the oldest player in history to take five wickets in an innings in a 50-over international. Sadly for Dhaniram, his record-breaking effort did not turn out to be a match-winning one: Bermuda went on to win the rain-affected match by 11 runs.

⊙ BREAKING THE MOULD

With his late reverse swing that was as likely to crash into the base of the stumps as it was to cannon into a batsman's foot, Waqar Younis set a new trend for fast bowlers. He was mightily effective in all formats of the game, but his record in one-day international cricket was truly exceptional: in 262 matches for Pakistan between 1989 and 2003 he took 416 wickets and broke the records for the most five-wicket hauls (13) and the most four wickets plus (27). He is also the only bowler in one-day international cricket history to take three successive five-wicket hauls and the only player in ODI history to take two consecutive five-wicket hauls on three occasions.

⊙ EDWARDS ENJOYS DEVASTATING DEBUT

Fidel Edwards got his one-day international career for the West Indies off to a blistering start against Zimbabwe at Harare on 29 November 2003. He took a wicket with his first delivery – uprooting Barney Rogers's off stump with a stunning yorker – and ended up with figures of 6 for 22 off seven overs (the best by any bowler making his one-day international debut) as the West Indies went on to win the match by 72 runs.

⊙ MOST WICKETS TAKEN...

Bowled: 176 – Wasim Akram (Pakistan, 1984–2003)
Caught: 281 – Muttiah Muralitharan (Sri Lanka, 1993–2011)
Caught and bowled: 34 – Muttiah Muralitharan (Sri Lanka, 1993–2011)
Caught by a fielder: 238 – Muttiah Muralitharan (Sri Lanka, 1993–2011)
Caught by a wicketkeeper: 93 – Wasim Akram (Pakistan, 1984–2003)
LBW: 92 – Wasim Akram (Pakistan, 1984–2003)
Stumped: 55 – Muttiah Muralitharan (Sri Lanka, 1993–2011)
Hit wicket: 3 – Courtney Walsh (West Indies, 1985–2000); and Wasim Akram (Pakistan, 1984–2003)

⊙ BEST BOWLER-FIELDER COMBINATION

The most successful bowler fielder combination in one-day international cricket history is that between South Africa's Makhaya Ntini and Mark Boucher. The pair combined for 75 dismissals in 164 matches between 1998 and 2009.

FASTEST TO...

Wkts	Matches	Player (country)
50	19	Ajantha Mendis (Sri Lanka)
100	53	Saqlain Mushtaq (Pakistan)
150	78	Saqlain Mushtaq (Pakistan)
200	104	Saqlain Mushtaq (Pakistan)
250	138	Saqlain Mushtaq (Pakistan)
300	171	Brett Lee (Australia)
350	218	Waqar Younis (Pakistan)
400	252	Waqar Younis (Pakistan)
450	295	Muttiah Muralitharan (Asia/ICC/Sri Lanka)
500	324	Muttiah Muralitharan (Asia/ICC/Sri Lanka)

OTHER RECORDS

⊙ A DAY TO FORGET BEHIND THE STUMPS FOR ASHRAF ALI

Forced to play second fiddle to Wasim Bari for most of his career, Ashraf Ali eventually played 16 one-day internationals for Pakistan between 1980 and 1985 but got his international career off to the worst possible start. In his debut match, against the West Indies at Sialkot on 5 December 1980, he conceded 20 byes – the most by any wicketkeeper in an innings in one-day international cricket – in a game the West Indies went on to win by seven wickets.

MOST CATCHES IN A CAREER: TOP 5

Pos	Ct	Player (Team, Span)
1	170	Mahela Jayawardene (Asia/Sri Lanka, 1998–2011)
2	156	Mohammad Azharuddin (India, 1985–2000)
3	152	Ricky Ponting (ICC/Australia, 1995–2010)
4	134	Sachin Tendulkar (India, 1989–2011)
5	133	Stephen Fleming (ICC/New Zealand, 1994–2007)

⊙ ELECTRIC RHODES IS THE GREATEST FIELDER OF THEM ALL

South Africa's Jonty Rhodes in full flight in the field was as majestic a sight as a bowler or batsman at the very top of his game: in short, he was the greatest fielder to play the game and a record-breaking one, too. In South Africa's match against the West Indies at Mumbai on 14 November 1993 he took five catches – the most catches in an innings by a fielder in one-day international cricket history.

⊙ MOST DISMISSALS IN A CAREER FOR GILCHRIST

The player who perhaps contributed more than any other to Australia's three successive World Cup triumphs between 1999 and 2007, Adam Gilchrist was as colossal behind the stumps as he was destructive at the top of the batting order. In 287 one-day internationals for his country between 1996 and 2008, he claimed a record 472 dismissals, with 417 catches and 55 stumpings.

⊙ CAPTAINCY RECORDS

Ricky Ponting has led Australia in a record 221 one-day internationals between 2002 and 2010 and also holds the record for the most wins as captain – with 160 (a win percentage of 76.66). South Africa's Hansie Cronje holds the record for the most consecutive matches as captain: 130 between 6 December 1994 and 27 March 2000.

HIGHEST PARTNERSHIP BY WICKET

Wkt	Runs	Partners	Team	Opposition	Venue	Date
1st	286	W.U. Tharanga/S.T. Jayasuriya	Sri Lanka	England	Leeds	1 Jul 2006
2nd	331	S.R. Tendulkar/R. Dravid	India	New Zealand	Hyderabad	8 Nov 1999
3rd	237*	R. Dravid/S.R. Tendulkar	India	Kenya	Bristol	23 May 1999
4th	275*	M. Azharuddin/A. Jadeja	India	Zimbabwe	Cuttack	9 Apr 1998
5th	223	M. Azharuddin/A. Jadeja	India	Sri Lanka	Colombo (RPS)	17 Aug 1997
6th	218	D.P.M.D. Jayawardene/M.S. Dhoni	Asia XI	Africa XI	Chennai	10 Jun 2007
7th	130	A. Flower/H.H. Streak	Zimbabwe	England	Harare	7 Oct 2001
8th	138*	J.M. Kemp/A.J. Hall	South Africa	India	Cape Town	26 Nov 2006
9th	132	A.D. Mathews/S.L. Malinga	Sri Lanka	Australia	Melbourne	3 Nov 2010
10th	106*	I.V.A. Richards/M.A. Holding	West Indies	England	Manchester	31 May 1984

⊙ THE LITTLE MASTER'S OTHER RECORDS

The leading run-scorer in one-day international cricket, Sachin Tendulkar also holds the record for the most consecutive matches played in the 50-over format of the game. The "Little Master" appeared in 185 consecutive games for India between 25 April 1990 and 24 April 1998. Tendulkar also holds the record for the most man of the match awards, with 61.

⊙ TENDULKAR AND DRAVID STEAL THE SHOW

Sachin Tendulkar (186 not out) and Rahul Dravid (153) combined to stunning and record-breaking effect as India thrashed New Zealand by 174 runs in the second one-day international of the five-match series between the two countries at Hyderabad on 8 November 1999. The pair added 331 for the second wicket – the highest partnership in one-day international cricket history.

⊙ PERFECT PARTNERS

The most productive partnership in the history of one-day international cricket is that between India's Sachin Tendulkar and Sourav Ganguly. The pair combined to score 8,227 runs in 176 innings for their country between 1992 and 2007, with 26 century stands at an average of 47.55 runs per partnership.

ICC TROPHY

First contested in 1979, the ICC Trophy is a one-day match tournament for non-Test-playing nations. In recent years it has gained extra significance: it serves as a qualifying tournament for the ICC World Cup – the 2009 edition of the tournament saw Ireland, Canada, Netherlands and Kenya qualify for the 2011 World Cup – and the top five finishing teams are awarded ODI status for a four-year period.

ICC TROPHY WINNERS

Year	Winners	Host
1979	Sri Lanka	England
1982	Zimbabwe	England
1986	Zimbabwe	England
1990	Zimbabwe	Netherlands
1994	United Arab Emirates	Kenya
1997	Bangladesh	Malaysia
2001	Netherlands	Canada
2005	Scotland	Ireland
2009	Ireland	South Africa

⊙ MAGIC MYLES HITS TOURNAMENT BEST

Simon Myles was the standout performer during Hong Kong's 144-run demolition of Gibraltar in the one-sided Group 2 encounter in the 1986 ICC World Cup, played at Bridgnorth. The Hong Kong batsman smashed a tournament best 172 out of his side's total of 324 for 5. Gibraltar were 180 all out in reply.

⊙ MOST WICKETS IN SERIES

The Netherlands' seam bowler Ronnie Elferink was the pick of the bowlers at the 1986 ICC Trophy. In ten matches he took two five-wicket hauls – with a best return of 6 for 14 against Fiji at Gloucester – and ended the tournament with 23 wickets (a record in a single tournament) at an average of 9.82.

⊙ NETHERLANDS POWER PAST EAST AND CENTRAL AFRICA

It took just 20.5 overs for the Netherlands to dismiss the challenge of East and Central Africa in the two sides' match at the 1997 ICC Trophy in Kuala Lumpur. After winning the toss and electing to bowl, the Netherlands dismissed East and Central Africa for a paltry 26 all out in 15.2 overs – the lowest team total in the tournament's history. The Netherlands reached the minimal victory target in 5.3 overs for the loss of two wickets.

⊙ TAU AO HIT TO ALL PARTS OF THE GROUND

Papua New Guinea's Tau Ao bore the brunt of Canada's onslaught during the two sides' Group 2 encounter at Walsall in the 1986 ICC Trophy. As Canada reached an imposing 356 for 5, the Papua New Guinea opening bowler went for 116 off his 12-over allocation – the most runs conceded in an innings by a bowler in the tournament's history.

⊙ LONGEVITY THE KEY FOR LEFEBVRE

A player who performed with distinction in county cricket for a number of years (he played for Somerset and Glamorgan between 1990 and 1995), Roland Lefebvre put his skills to good use in the ICC Trophy for the Netherlands between 1986 and 2001. He holds the record for the most wickets in the tournament's history (71) and also for the most matches played (43).

⊙ LARGEST MARGIN OF VICTORY

By runs: by 369 runs – Papua New Guinea v Gibraltar at Cannock on 18 June 1986.
By wickets: by ten wickets on 12 occasions.
By balls remaining: 337 balls remaining – Canada v Gibraltar at Swindon on 20 June 1986

⊙ KENYA PAY HEAVY PRICE FOR INDISCIPLINE IN THE FIELD

Perhaps the principal reason for Kenya's surprise 37-run loss to Papua New Guinea, at The Hague in the two sides' 1990 ICC Trophy encounter, was their record-breaking indiscipline in the field. During Papua New Guinea's innings (230 all out), the Kenyans conceded a massive 54 extras (16 leg-byes, 35 wides and three no-balls) – the most in the tournament's history. In reply, the Kenyans slipped to 193 all out.

⊙ MORTENSEN MAKES WAVES WITH THE BALL

A burly seam bowler who performed with great success in county cricket with Derbyshire for over a decade, Ole Mortensen was an outstanding performer in the ICC Trophy for Denmark in 26 matches in the tournament between 1979 and 1994 he set the all-time records for the best average (10.41), the most four-wicket-plus hauls (seven) and the best strike-rate (taking a wicket every 25.4 deliveries).

MOST RUNS: TOP 5

Pos	Runs	Player (Team, Span)
1	1,173	Maurice Odumbe (Kenya, 1990–97)
2	1,040	Nolan Clarke (Netherlands, 1990–94)
3	772	Rupert Gomes (Netherlands, 1986–90)
4	761	Minhajul Abedin (Bangladesh, 1986–97)
5	747	Paul Prashad (Canada, 1986–94)

MOST WICKETS: TOP 5

Pos	Wkts	Player (Team, Span)
1	71	Roland Lefebvre (Netherlands, 1986–2001)
2	63	Ole Mortensen (Denmark, 1979–94)
3	48	Aasif Karim (Kenya, 1986–97)
4	44	Anthony Edwards (Bermuda, 1986–94)
5	42	Noel Gibbons (Bermuda, 1979–94)

⊙ GOOD THINGS COME TO THOSE WHO WAIT

A star performer for Barbados against the England tourists in 1973–74 (a match in which he hit an imperious 158), Nolan Clarke may not have reached the dizzy heights that many at the time predicted he would, but he did go on to enjoy a lengthy and successful career with the Netherlands. In 18 ICC Trophy matches for them between 1990 and 1994 he scored 1,040 runs (with a highest score of 154 against Israel at Amstelveen on 4 June 1990) at an average of 74.28 – the highest by any batsman to have scored 500 runs or more in ICC Trophy history. He also holds the tournament record for the most hundreds scored (five).

⊙ PRASHAD PROSPERS AS CANADA FALL SHORT

Although his team failed to progress beyond the group stages of the 1986 ICC Trophy held in England, for Canada's Paul Prashad it was a tournament to remember. In eight innings he hit three centuries (with a highest score of 164 not out against Papua New Guinea at Walsall) and finished with 533 runs to his name – a record for a single ICC Trophy tournament – at an average of 88.83.

⊙ DUTCH OFF TO A FLYING START

Rene Schoonheim (117) and R.E. Lifmann (155 not out) provided the perfect platform for the Netherlands during their 125-run victory over Malaysia in the two sides' Group 2 encounter at Redditch in the 1982 ICC Trophy. The pair put on 257 runs for the opening wicket – the highest partnership in the tournament's history.

⊙ PNG HIT THE HEIGHTS

Papua New Guinea were simply too strong for Gibraltar when the two sides met at Cannock in the 1986 ICC Trophy. Batting first, Papua New Guinea amassed a colossal 455 for 9 (off 60 overs), with B. Harry top-scoring with 127. In reply, Gibraltar wilted to a sorry 86 all out to lose the match by 369 runs.

⊙ KHAN RECORDS BEST SINGLE INNINGS BOWLING FIGURES

Asim Khan was the main destroyer when East and Central Africa slipped to a record-breaking low of 26 all out against the Netherlands at Kuala Lumpur in the 1997 ICC Trophy. The Dutch paceman produced figures of 7 for 9 off 7.2 overs – the best in the tournament's history.

ODI RECORDS: BY TEAM

One-day international cricket is played more in some parts of the world than in others. For example, Kevin Pietersen (England) and M.S. Dhoni (India) both made their one-day international debuts towards the end of 2004 and have been regulars ever since. But in February 2011, however, Pietersen had appeared in 110 ODIs compared to Dhoni's 178. The relative chances of a player featuring among the list of one-day international cricket's all-time cumulative record-holders depend very much on which country he plays for. To be an all-time ODI leading performer for your country, though, is a completely different matter and is always a coveted honour.

AUSTRALIA

Australia are the most successful team in the history of one-day international cricket: they have won the most matches (470), have won the ICC World Cup more times than any other country (in 1987, 1999, 2003 and 2007) and are the only team to have won the ICC Champions Trophy on two occasions (emerging victorious in 2006 and 2009).

⊙ McGRATH LEADS THE WAY

The most successful one-day bowler in Australia's history (with 380 wickets in 249 matches), Glenn McGrath also holds the record for the best figures ever recorded by an Australian bowler in one-day international cricket, with 7 for 15 against Namibia at Potchefstroom in the 2003 World Cup (also a World Cup best).

RESULT SUMMARY

Opposition (Span)	Mat	Won	Lost	Tied	NR	%
Bangladesh (1990–2008)	16	15	1	0	0	93.75
Canada (1979)	1	1	0	0	0	100.00
England (1971–2009)	101	59	38	2	2	60.60
ICC World XI (2005)	3	3	0	0	0	100.00
India (1980–2009)	103	61	34	0	8	64.21
Ireland (2007)	1	1	0	0	0	100.00
Kenya (1996–2003)	4	4	0	0	0	100.00
Namibia (2003)	1	1	0	0	0	100.00
Netherlands (2003–07)	2	2	0	0	0	100.00
New Zealand (1974–2010)	123	84	34	0	5	71.18
Pakistan (1975–2010)	85	52	29	1	3	64.02
Scotland (1999–2009)	3	3	0	0	0	100.00
South Africa (1992–2009)	77	39	35	3	0	52.59
Sri Lanka (1975–2008)	68	46	20	0	2	69.69
USA (2004)	1	1	0	0	0	100.00
West Indies (1975–2009)	120	59	57	2	2	50.84
Zimbabwe (1983–2004)	27	25	1	0	1	96.15

⊙ A TRUE LEGEND OF THE GAME

A true rock upon which Australia have built their considerable success in one-day international cricket in recent years, Ricky Ponting will go down in history as one of cricket's greatest players, and his record in one-day international cricket is among the best of all time. He holds the Australian all-time records for: the most runs (12,967), the most centuries (28 – with a highest of 164 against South Africa at Johannesburg on 12 March 2006), the most catches (151) and the most matches (351). He is also the most successful one-day captain in Australia's history, notching up 160 wins in 221 matches as captain between 2002 and 2010.

⊙ HAYDEN HEROICS NOT ENOUGH FOR AUSTRALIA

Matthew Hayden was in inspirational form with the bat for Australia in the one-day international against New Zealand at Hamilton on 20 February 2007. The lefthanded opener smashed an unbeaten 181 – the highest score by an Australian batsman in one-day international cricket history – off 166 balls with 11 fours and ten sixes. It wasn't enough to win the game, however. New Zealand scraped to the 347-run victory target with one wicket and three balls to spare.

MOST RUNS: TOP 5

Pos	Runs	Player (span)
1	12,967	Ricky Ponting (1995–2010)
2	9,595	Adam Gilchrist (1996–2008)
3	8,500	Mark Waugh (1988–2002)
4	7,569	Steve Waugh (1986–2002)
5	6,912	Michael Bevan (1994–2004)

MOST WICKETS: TOP 5

Pos	Wkts	Player (span)
1	380	Glenn McGrath (1993–2007)
2	335	Brett Lee (2000–11)
3	291	Shane Warne (1993–2003)
4	203	Craig McDermott (1985–96)
5	195	Steve Waugh (1986–2002)

ENGLAND

Although they have been runners-up three times in the ICC World Cup (in 1979, 1987 and 1992), England have always struggled to hit the heights in one-day international cricket. In 549 matches played since their opening one-day international against Australia in 1971 they have notched up 264 victories – of all the current Test-playing nations, only Bangladesh and New Zealand have recorded fewer.

RESULT SUMMARY

Opposition (Span)	Mat	Won	Lost	Tied	NR	%
Australia (1971–2011)	113	42	67	2	2	38.73
Bangladesh (2000–10)	14	13	1	0	0	92.85
Canada (1979–2007)	2	2	0	0	0	100.00
East Africa (1975)	1	1	0	0	0	100.00
India (1974–2008)	70	30	38	0	2	44.11
Ireland (2006–09)	3	3	0	0	0	100.00
Kenya (1999–2007)	2	2	0	0	0	100.00
Namibia (2003)	1	1	0	0	0	100.00
Netherlands (1996–2003)	2	2	0	0	0	100.00
New Zealand (1973–2009)	70	29	35	2	4	45.45
Pakistan (1974–2010)	68	38	28	0	2	57.57
Scotland (2008–10)	2	1	0	0	1	100.00
South Africa (1992–2009)	44	18	23	1	2	44.04
Sri Lanka (1982–2009)	44	23	21	0	0	52.27
UAE (1996)	1	1	0	0	0	100.00
West Indies (1973–2009)	82	37	41	0	4	47.43
Zimbabwe (1992–2004)	30	21	8	0	1	72.41

⊙ DAZZLING DARREN GUNS HIS WAY INTO THE RECORD BOOKS

England's best strike bowler since Bob Willis and, with his ability to reverse-swing the ball at pace, an extremely effective "death" bowler, Darren Gough is the most successful English bowler in one-day international cricket history (with 235 wickets in 159 matches between 1994 and 2006). He also holds the English record for the most four-wicket-plus innings hauls, with 12.

⏵ SMITH PUTS ON A SHOW AT EDGBASTON

Australia eventually won the match (and with it the series) against England at Edgbaston on 21 May 1993, but not before they had encountered one of the most destructive one-day innings ever seen on English soil. Robin Smith powered his way to a 163-ball unbeaten 167 – the highest score by an England player in one-day international cricket history – as the home side reached 277 for 5. Australia reached the target for the loss of four wickets with nine balls to spare.

⏵ PIETERSEN POWERS HIS WAY INTO LIMELIGHT

Few players have made a more immediate impact on international cricket than Kevin Pietersen. Having shunned South Africa's quota system to qualify for England, he returned to the country of his birth with his adopted nation in 2005, hit three centuries in six one-day internationals using a wide array of powerful, unconventional strokes and has been viewed as one of the world's leading batsmen ever since. In 108 one-day internationals between 2004 and 2011 he has hit 3,499 runs (with seven centuries) at an average of 42.15 – the highest by any England batsman to have completed 20 innings or more in one-day international cricket history.

MOST RUNS: TOP 5

Pos	Runs	Player (span)
1	5,031	Paul Collingwood (2001–11)
2	4,677	Alec Stewart (1989–2003)
3	4,335	Marcus Trescothick (2000–06)
4	4,290	Graham Gooch (1976–95)
5	4,010	Allan Lamb (1982–92)

MOST WICKETS: TOP 5

Pos	Wkts	Player (span)
1	234	Darren Gough (1994–2006)
2	186	James Anderson (2002–11)
3	168	Andrew Flintoff (1999–2009)
4	145	Ian Botham (1976–92)
5	124	Stuart Broad (2006–10)

INDIA

Cricket-mad India has developed a taste for the one-day game like no other country on earth, playing more matches (765) than any other cricketing nation. And they have enjoyed considerable success, too: sensationally they won the ICC World Cup in 1983 and have notched up 374 victories – only Australia (with 470 wins) and Pakistan (with 390) have more.

RESULT SUMMARY

Opposition (span)	Mat	Won	Lost	Tied	NR	%
Australia (1980–2010)	104	35	61	0	8	36.45
Bangladesh (1988–2011)	23	21	2	0	0	91.30
Bermuda (2007)	1	1	0	0	0	100.00
East Africa (1975)	1	1	0	0	0	100.00
England (1974–2008)	70	38	30	0	2	55.88
Hong Kong (2008)	1	1	0	0	0	100.00
Ireland (2007)	1	1	0	0	0	100.00
Kenya (1996–2004)	13	11	2	0	0	84.61
Namibia (2003)	1	1	0	0	0	100.00
Netherlands (2003)	1	1	0	0	0	100.00
New Zealand (1975–2010)	88	46	37	0	5	55.42
Pakistan (1978–2010)	119	46	69	0	4	40.00
Scotland (2007)	1	1	0	0	0	100.00
South Africa (1991–2011)	65	24	39	0	2	38.09
Sri Lanka (1979–2010)	128	67	50	0	11	57.26
UAE (1994–2004)	2	2	0	0	0	100.00
West Indies (1979–2009)	95	38	54	1	2	41.39
Zimbabwe (1983–2010)	51	39	10	2	0	78.43

⊙ KUMBLE IS INDIA'S ODI KING OF SPIN

India's leading wicket-taker in one-day international cricket (with 334 wickets in 269 matches between 1990 and 2007), Anil Kumble also produced the best-ever bowling display by an Indian in the 50-over format of the game, taking 6 for 12 (off 6.1 overs) against the West Indies at Kolkata on 27 November 1993 – a match India won by 102 runs.

⊙ DASHING DHONI LEADS AVERAGES LIST

Mahendra Singh Dhoni, who has been a steady performer behind the stumps for India since making his debut against South Africa in December 2004, has more dismissals to his name – 225 (171 catches and 54 stumpings) – than any other India wicketkeeper in one-day international history, and has been captain of the national side since September 2007. It is Dhoni's swashbuckling performances with the bat, however, that have marked him out as an all-round player of the highest calibre. In 174 one-day internationals he has scored 5,634 runs (with a highest score of 183 not out against Sri Lanka at Jaipur on 31 October 2005) at an average of 48.15 – it is the highest average by any Indian batsman who has completed 25 innings or more in one-day international cricket history.

MOST RUNS: TOP 5

Pos	Runs	Player (span)
1	17,629	Sachin Tendulkar (1989–2011)
2	11,221	Sourav Ganguly (1992–2007)
3	10,644	Rahul Dravid (1996–2009)
4	9,378	Mohammad Azharuddin (1985–2000)
5	4,704	Yuvraj Singh (2000–11)

MOST WICKETS: TOP 5

Pos	Wkts	Player (span)
1	334	Anil Kumble (1990–2007)
2	315	Javagal Srinath (1991–2003)
3	288	Ajit Agarkar (1998–2007)
4	253	Kapil Dev (1978–94)
5	242	Harbhajan Singh (1998–2011)

⊙ TENDULKAR'S MARCH TO CRICKET GREATNESS

The most complete batsman of his generation, possessing a game without any apparent weaknesses, Sachin Tendulkar has become a serial record-breaker in one-day international cricket. In 444 matches for India between 1989 and 2011, he has set all-time records for the most runs (17,629) and the most centuries (46), and was the fastest to reach every target from 10,000 to 17,000 runs. On 24 February 2010, against South Africa at Gwalior, he smashed 200 not out to become the first and to date only player to hit a double-century in one-day international cricket.

NEW ZEALAND

From the moment they played their first-ever one-day international in 1973, New Zealand, five-time semi-finalists in the ICC World Cup, have provided dogged opposition in the shortened format of the game and have evolved into one of the most consistent sides on the one-day circuit: the Black Caps are capable of beating anyone on their day.

RESULT SUMMARY

Opposition (Span)	Mat	Won	Lost	Tied	NR	%
Australia (1974–2010)	123	34	84	0	5	28.81
Bangladesh (1990–2010)	21	16	5	0	0	76.19
Canada (2003–07)	2	2	0	0	0	100.00
East Africa (1975)	1	1	0	0	0	100.00
England (1973–2009)	70	35	29	2	4	54.54
India (1975–2010)	88	37	46	0	5	44.57
Ireland (2007–08)	2	2	0	0	0	100.00
Kenya (2007–11)	2	2	0	0	0	100.00
Netherlands (1996)	1	1	0	0	0	100.00
Pakistan (1973–2011)	88	34	51	1	2	40.11
Scotland (1999–2008)	2	2	0	0	0	100.00
South Africa (1992–2009)	51	17	30	0	4	36.17
Sri Lanka (1979–2010)	72	35	32	1	4	52.20
UAE (1996)	1	1	0	0	0	100.00
USA (2004)	1	1	0	0	0	100.00
West Indies (1975–2009)	51	20	24	0	7	45.45
Zimbabwe (1987–2005)	28	19	7	1	1	72.22

⊙ MOST CENTURIES

There is a strong case for regarding the free-scoring Nathan Astle as the finest one-day player New Zealand has ever produced. In 223 one-day internationals for his country between 1995 and 2007 he scored 7,090 runs at an average of 34.92 and hit 16 centuries – the most by any New Zealand batsman in one-day international cricket – with a highest score of 145 not out against the United States at The Oval on 10 September 2004.

⊙ ONE OF THE BEST IN THE BUSINESS

His career may have been blighted by a succession of injuries – many of which kept him out of the game for lengthy periods – but, when fit, Shane Bond proved he was one of the finest fast bowlers of his generation. He holds several all-time records for New Zealand in one-day international cricket: the best bowling in an innings (6 for 19 against India at Bulawayo on 26 August 2005); the best career average (20.87); and for the most four-wicket-plus hauls (ten in 77 matches between 2002 and 2009).

MOST RUNS: TOP 5

Pos	Runs	Player (span)
1	8,007	Stephen Fleming (1994–2007)
2	7,090	Nathan Astle (1995–2007)
3	4,881	Chris Cairns (1991–2006)
4	4,707	Craig McMillan (1997–2007)
5	4,704	Martin Crowe (1982–95)

MOST WICKETS: TOP 5

Pos	Wkts	Player (span)
1	271	Daniel Vettori (1997–2011)
2	203	Chris Harris (1990–2004)
3	200	Chris Cairns (1991–2006)
4	186	Kyle Mills (2001–09)
5	158	Richard Hadlee (1973–90)

⊙ SERIAL RECORD-BREAKER

Stephen Fleming was a prolific run-scorer for New Zealand in one-day international cricket over a 13-year career stretching from 1994 to 2007 (his 8,007 career runs is the most ever by any New Zealand batsman in one-day international cricket). The left-handed batsman is most successful captain his country has ever produced (notching up 98 wins in 218 matches as captain between 1997 and 2007). Fleming also holds the all-time New Zealand records for the most one-day international matches played (279) and for the most catches taken (132).

⊙ BIGGEST VICTORIES

By runs: by 290 runs against Ireland at Aberdeen on 1 July 2008.
By wickets: by ten wickets on four occasions.
By balls remaining (in the second innings): with 264 balls remaining against Bangladesh at Queenstown on 31 December 2007.

PAKISTAN

There is no team in world cricket quite like Pakistan, a frustrating blend of sparkling brilliance and overt ordinariness. Their ability to hit heady heights one day and almost laughable lows the next is reflected in their ODI performances. In 1992 their star shone brightly when they won the ICC World Cup; in 2007, however, they failed to progress beyond the group stages.

RESULT SUMMARY

Opposition (Span)	Mat	Won	Lost	Tied	NR	%
Australia (1975–2010)	85	29	52	1	3	35.97
Bangladesh (1986–2008)	26	25	1	0	0	96.15
Canada (1979)	1	1	0	0	0	100.00
England (1974–2010)	68	28	38	0	2	42.42
Hong Kong (2004–08)	2	2	0	0	0	100.00
India (1978–2010)	119	69	46	0	4	60.00
Ireland (2007)	1	0	1	0	0	0.00
Kenya (1996–2004)	5	5	0	0	0	100.00
Namibia (2003)	1	1	0	0	0	100.00
Netherlands (1996–2003)	3	3	0	0	0	100.00
New Zealand (1973–2011)	88	51	34	1	2	59.88
Scotland (1999–2006)	2	2	0	0	0	100.00
South Africa (1992–2010)	57	18	38	0	1	32.14
Sri Lanka (1975–2010)	120	70	46	1	3	60.25
UAE (1994–96)	2	2	0	0	0	100.00
West Indies (1975–2009)	114	48	64	2	0	42.98
Zimbabwe (1992–2008)	40	36	2	1	1	93.58

⊙ THE ASIAN BRADMAN

Dubbed the "Asian Bradman" in his prime for the single-minded consistency with which he accumulated runs, Zaheer Abbas was a refined stroke player who compiled big scores with an array of shots all around the wicket. In 62 one-day internationals for his country between 1974 and 1985 he scored 2,572 runs (with a highest score of 123 against Sri Lanka at Lahore on 29 March 1982) at an average of 47.62 – the highest by any Pakistan player to have completed 20 innings or more in one-day international cricket history.

⊙ WONDERFUL WAQAR WALTZES INTO THE RECORD BOOKS

Along with Wasim Akram, Waqar Younis formed one half of the most destructive new-ball bowling attacks in one-day international cricket history. In 262 one-day matches for his country between 1989 and 2003 he took 416 wickets and set his country's all-time records for the best bowling performance in an innings (7 for 36 against England at Headingley on 17 June 2001) and for the most four-wicket-plus innings hauls (27).

⊙ THE MASTER OPENER

A sweet timer of the ball and a graceful stroke-maker, Saeed Anwar stood tall at the top of the Pakistan batting order in all forms of the game for over a decade, but some of his performances in one-day international cricket (he played in 247 matches between 1989 and 2003) were particularly eye-catching. On 21 May 1997, against India at Chennai, he smashed an imperious 194 off 146 balls to break Viv Richards's record for the highest ever individual score in a one-day international. It was one of 20 one-day centuries compiled in his career – an all-time record for a Pakistan batsman

MOST RUNS: TOP 5

Pos	Runs	Player (span)
1	11,701	Inzamam-ul-Haq (1991–2007)
2	9,554	Mohammad Yousuf (1998–2010)
3	8,824	Saeed Anwar (1989–2003)
4	7,381	Javed Miandad (1975–96)
5	7,170	Saleem Malik (1982–99)

MOST WICKETS: TOP 5

Pos	Wkts	Player (span)
1	502	Wasim Akram (1984–2003)
2	416	Waqar Younis (1989–2003)
3	290	Shahid Afridi (1996–2011)
4	288	Saqlain Mushtaq (1995–2003)
5	261	Abdul Razzaq (1996–2011)

⊙ HIGHEST AND LOWEST

Highest score: 385 for 7 against Bangladesh at Dambulla on 21 June 2010.
Lowest score: 43 all out against the West Indies at Cape Town on 25 February 1993.

SOUTH AFRICA

Ever since their return to the international cricket fold after 21 years in the wilderness – their first match back was an ODI against India at Kolkata on 10 November 1991 – South Africa have proved they are a considerable force in the 50-over game. They have the highest winning percentage of any of the current Test-playing nations, with 64.65 per cent.

⊙ MAGIC MAKHAYA DESTROYS AUSTRALIA

A devastating spell of bowling from Makhaya Ntini helped South Africa to their biggest-ever victory over Australia at Cape Town on 3 March 2006. Making the most of the seamer-friendly conditions under the Newlands lights, the Mdingi-born paceman took 6 for 22 – the best bowling figures by a South African in one-day international cricket history – to reduce Australia to 93 all out and set up South Africa's crushing 196-run victory.

RESULT SUMMARY

Opposition (span)	Mat	Won	Lost	Tied	NR	%
Australia (1992–2009)	77	35	39	3	0	47.40
Bangladesh (2002–08)	13	12	1	0	0	92.30
Canada (2003)	1	1	0	0	0	100.00
England (1992–2009)	44	23	18	1	2	55.95
India (1991–2011)	65	39	24	0	2	61.90
Ireland (2007)	2	2	0	0	0	100.00
Kenya (1996–2008)	10	10	0	0	0	100.00
Netherlands (1996–2007)	2	2	0	0	0	100.00
New Zealand (1992–2009)	51	30	17	0	4	63.82
Pakistan (1992–2010)	57	38	18	0	1	67.85
Scotland (2007)	1	1	0	0	0	100.00
Sri Lanka (1992–2009)	46	22	22	1	1	50.00
UAE (1996)	1	1	0	0	0	100.00
West Indies (1992–2010)	50	37	12	0	1	75.51
Zimbabwe (1992–2010)	32	29	2	0	1	93.54

⊙ GLORIOUS GIBBS HEADS CENTURIES LIST

One of the most electric stroke-players in the modern game – at times it appears no shot is beyond him – Herschelle Gibbs has hit more one-day international centuries than any other South Africa player in history (21). The highlight of his glittering career came when he smashed a 111-ball 175 against Australia at Johannesburg on 12 March 2006 to help his side chase down a seemingly unattainable 435-run victory target.

⊙ RECORD-BREAKING POLLOCK

A bowler who relied on metronomic accuracy rather than express pace, Shaun Pollock (South Africa's most capped one-day international player of all time, with 294 appearances between 1996 and 2008) has taken more four-wicket-plus hauls for his country (17) and more wickets (387) than any other player in history. His best performance came when he took 6 for 35 against the West Indies at East London on 24 January 1999.

⊙ KIRSTEN RUNS RIOT AT RAWALPINDI

The opposition may not have been the strongest, but Gary Kirsten made a mockery of pre-match predictions that the wicket for South Africa's 1996 ICC World Cup Group B encounter against the United Arab Emirates at Rawalpindi would be a bowler-friendly surface. The left-handed opener batted through the innings to compile a 159-ball unbeaten 188 – the highest score in the tournament's history and the highest-ever score by a South Africa batsman in one-day international cricket.

MOST RUNS: TOP 5

Pos	Runs	Player (span)
1	10,973	Jacques Kallis (1996–2011)
2	8,094	Herschelle Gibbs (1996–2010)
3	6,798	Gary Kirsten (1993–2003)
4	6,097	Graeme Smith (2002–11)
5	5,935	Jonty Rhodes (1992–2003)

MOST WICKETS: TOP 5

Pos	Wkts	Player (span)
1	387	Shaun Pollock (1996–2008)
2	272	Allan Donald (1991–2003)
3	265	Makhaya Ntini (1998–2009)
4	255	Jacques Kallis (1996–2011)
5	192	Lance Klusener (1996–2004)

SRI LANKA

Following their elevation to Test status in 1982, for many years Sri Lanka were considered to be the minnows of world cricket, but they used the one-day international arena to propel themselves into the world's elite. In 1996, spectacularly, they shocked Australia in the final to capture the ICC World Cup and have been treated with the greatest respect ever since.

RESULT SUMMARY

Opposition (span)	Mat	Won	Lost	Tied	NR	%
Australia (1975–2010)	71	22	47	0	2	31.88
Bangladesh (1986–2010)	29	27	2	0	0	93.10
Bermuda (2007)	1	1	0	0	0	100.00
Canada (2003–11)	2	2	0	0	0	100.00
England (1982–2009)	44	21	23	0	0	47.72
India (1979–2010)	128	50	67	0	11	42.73
Ireland (2007)	1	1	0	0	0	100.00
Kenya (1996–2003)	5	4	1	0	0	80.00
Netherlands (2002–06)	3	3	0	0	0	100.00
New Zealand (1979–2010)	72	32	35	1	4	47.79
Pakistan (1975–2010)	120	46	70	1	3	39.74
South Africa (1992–2009)	46	22	22	1	1	50.00
UAE (2004–08)	2	2	0	0	0	100.00
West Indies (1975–2011)	49	20	26	0	3	43.47
Zimbabwe (1992–2010)	46	38	7	0	1	84.44

⊙ SPECTACULAR FOR MORE THAN 20 YEARS

After Sachin Tendulkar, the most capped one-day international player of all time (appearing in a staggering 440 matches between 1989 and 2009), Sanath Jayasuriya started the trend of modern pinch-hitters at the top of the batting order and did much to help Sri Lanka towards the most glorious moment of their cricket history – winning the ICC World Cup in 1996. Over a decade and a half later he is still one of the most destructive hitters in the modern game, and has set numerous all-time records for his country. He has scored the most runs (13,362), holds the record for the highest score (189 against India at Sharjah on 29 October 2000), has hit the most centuries (28) and has the best strike-rate (91.28 runs per 100 balls).

MOST RUNS: TOP 5

Pos	Runs	Player (span)
1	13,362	Sanath Jayasuriya (1989–2009)
2	9,284	Aravinda de Silva (1984–2003)
3	8,850	Mahela Jayawardene (1998–2011)
4	8,529	Marvan Atapattu (1990–2007)
5	8,440	Kumar Sangakkara (2000–11)

MOST WICKETS: TOP 5

Pos	Wkts	Player (span)
1	508	Muttiah Muralitharan (1993–2011)
2	399	Chaminda Vaas (1994–2008)
3	319	Sanath Jayasuriya (1989–2009)
4	176	Dilhara Fernando (2001–11)
5	151	Upul Chandana (1994–2007)

⊙ PATIENCE THE KEY TO ATAPATTU'S SUCCESS

Marvan Atapattu's steady approach to building an innings provided the perfect foil for his opening partner Sanath Jayasuriya's more cavalier contributions at the top of the Sri Lankan order. In 268 matches for his country between 1990 and 2007 he scored 8,529 runs (with 11 centuries and a highest score of 132 not out against England at Lord's on 20 August 1998) at an average of 37.57 – the best average by a Sri Lankan batsman to complete 20 innings or more in one-day international cricket.

⊙ MURALI SILENCES DETRACTORS IN RECORD-BREAKING FASHION

The first and only Tamil of Indian origin to play for Sri Lanka, Muttiah Muralitharan has brushed aside the repeated controversies regarding his action that have remained throughout his career (the ICC has investigated the mechanics of his action twice) by taking wicket after wicket. An integral part of Sri Lanka's 1996 ICC World Cup-winning outfit, the history-making spin bowler has set numerous all-time records for his country. In 341 matches between 1993 and 2011 he has taken the most wickets (508); holds the record for the best average (23.18); and has taken the most four-wicket-plus innings hauls (24, with a best of 7 for 30 against India at Sharjah on 27 October 2000).

WEST INDIES

They were the kings of Test and one-day cricket in the 1970s and early '80s, years which saw them rule the roost in the five-day game and appear in three successive ICC World Cup finals (winning two of them). Since then the cricket gods have been less kind to the West Indies in the Test arena, but the men from the Caribbean have more than held their own in one-day cricket.

RESULT SUMMARY

Opposition (Span)	Mat	Won	Lost	Tied	NR	%
Australia (1975–2010)	125	57	63	2	3	47.54
Bangladesh (1999–2009)	16	11	3	0	2	78.57
Bermuda (2008)	1	1	0	0	0	100.00
Canada (2003–10)	4	4	0	0	0	100.00
England (1973–2009)	82	41	37	0	4	52.56
India (1979–2009)	95	54	38	1	2	58.60
Ireland (2007–10)	3	2	0	0	1	100.00
Kenya (1996–2003)	6	5	1	0	0	83.33
Netherlands (2007)	1	1	0	0	0	100.00
New Zealand (1975–2009)	51	24	20	0	7	54.54
Pakistan (1975–2009)	114	64	48	2	0	57.01
Scotland (1999–2007)	2	2	0	0	0	100.00
South Africa (1992–2010)	50	12	37	0	1	24.48
Sri Lanka (1975–2011)	49	26	20	0	3	56.52
Zimbabwe (1983–2010)	41	31	9	0	1	77.50

⊙ BORN TO PLAY ONE-DAY CRICKET

In June 1975, Viv Richards became the fastest player to reach 1,000 one-day international runs (in 21 matches, a record equalled by Kevin Pietersen) and went on to set numerous West Indian all-time records in the one-day game. He recorded the highest score (189 not out against England at Old Trafford on 31 May 1984); holds the record for the best average (47.00); and, despite never lifting the ICC World Cup (unlike Clive Lloyd who lifted it twice), was the most successful West Indian captain in one-day history, leading his side to 67 wins in 125 matches as captain between 1980 and 1991.

⊙ THE MEANEST SIGHT IN MODERN CRICKET

An ability to propel the ball with searing pace from a 6ft 7in frame made Curtly Ambrose the most feared sight for batsmen for over a decade. He was a magnificent performer both in Test matches (where he took 405 wickets in 98 matches) and in one-day internationals, with 225 wickets in 176 matches between 1988 and 2000, including ten four-wicket-plus hauls – a West Indies record – and a best return of 5 for 17 against Australia at Melbourne on 15 December 1988.

⊙ GAYLE FORCES HIS WAY INTO THE RECORD BOOKS

When Chris Gayle is on his A game, there are few finer sights in world cricket. A bully at the crease in the Viv Richards mould, he has the ability to destroy the opposition's attack, off both the front foot and the back. In 212 one-day internationals for the West Indies between 1999 and 2010 he has scored 7,702 runs (at an average of 40.11) including a West Indies record 19 centuries (with a highest score of 153 not out, against Zimbabwe at Bulawayo on 22 November 2003).

MOST RUNS: TOP 5

Pos	Runs	Player (span)
1	10,348	Brian Lara (1990–2007)
2	8,664	Shivnarine Chanderpaul (1994–2011)
3	8,648	Desmond Haynes (1978–94)
4	7,862	Chris Gayle (1999–2011)
5	6,721	Viv Richards (1975–91)

MOST WICKETS: TOP 5

Pos	Wkts	Player (span)
1	227	Courtney Walsh (1985–2000)
2	225	Curtly Ambrose (1988–2000)
3	193	Carl Hooper (1987–2003)
4	157	Malcolm Marshall (1980–92)
5	156	Chris Gayle (1999–2011)

⊙ DAVIS DEMOLISHES AUSTRALIA

Winston Davis produced a devastating spell of fast bowling on an unpredictable Headingley pitch to catapult the West Indies to a 101-run victory over Australia in the two sides' 1983 ICC World Cup Group B encounter. The St Vincent-born paceman took 7 for 51 – the best bowling figures by a West Indies player in one-day international cricket.

BANGLADESH

Considered the best of the rest following their victory in the ICC Trophy in Malaysia in 1997, Bangladesh were granted Test status in 2000 and soon found life with cricket's big boys a harsher proposition in all formats of the game. Having won just 64 of 238 one-day internationals, Bangladesh have the worst record of any of the current Test-playing nations.

OVERALL ONE-DAY INTERNATIONAL RECORD

Opposition	Span	Mat	Won	Lost	Tied	NR	%
All opponents	1986–2010	221	55	164	0	2	25.11

⊙ HIGHEST AND LOWEST

Highest score: 320 for 8 against Zimbabwe at Bulawayo on 11 August 2009.
Lowest score: 58 all out against West Indies at Dhaka on 4 March 2011.

⊙ THE BEST IS STILL TO COME

Still waiting to fulfil, on a consistent basis, the enormous potential that saw him become Test cricket's youngest centurion (he hit 114, aged 17 years and 61 days, against Sri Lanka at Colombo on 6 September 2001), Mohammad Ashraful has been a regular member of Bangladesh's one-day side for the best part of a decade. He holds two national records, for the most runs scored (3,360 at an average of 23.49) and for the most matches played (162 between 2001 and 2010).

⊙ TAMIL IQBAL SECURES UNLIKELY VICTORY

Having watched Charles Coventry compile a world record 194 not out to lead Zimbabwe to a massive total of 312 for 8 in Bulawayo on 16 August 2009, it would have been easy for Bangladesh to slide to a despondent defeat. To their great credit, they chased down the total with relish. Tamim Iqbal's 154 off 138 balls – a record high score for a Bangladesh player in a one-day international – was the foundation as Bangladesh reached the victory target for the loss of six wickets.

IRELAND

Granted one-day international status in 2005, Ireland have gone on to earn a reputation as the giantkillers of world cricket. At the 2007 ICC World Cup they roduced some headline-grabbing results – a tie with Zimbabwe and a sensational three-wicket victory over Pakistan – to reach the Super Eights. They ended the tournament ranked tenth in the world, above Kenya and Zimbabwe.

OVERALL ONE-DAY INTERNATIONAL RECORD

Opposition	Span	Mat	Won	Lost	Tied	NR	%
All opponents	2006–10	58	28	26	1	3	48.28

⊙ HIGHEST AND LOWEST

Highest score: 329 for 7 against England at Bangalore on 2 March 2011.
Lowest score: 77 all out against Sri Lanka at St George's, Grenada, on 18 April 2007.

⊙ MR CONSISTENCY

William Porterfield has been Ireland's most consistent run-scorer in one-day international cricket. In 44 matches between 2006 and 2010, the current national captain has scored 1,371 runs (with a highest of 112 not out against Bermuda at Nairobi, Kenya, on 31 January 2007) and a total of five centuries – both records for Ireland in the 50-over format of the game.

⊙ AGE NO BARRIER FOR JOHNSTON

An Australian by birth, whose career developed at New South Wales alongside the likes of Brett Lee, Mark Taylor and Michael Slater before he switched his allegiance to Ireland, Trent Johnston has been a mainstay of his country's bowling attack in one-day international cricket despite his advancing years. On 19 April 2009 (ten days before his 35th birthday), he enjoyed his best moments in the international arena, taking an Irish record 5 for 14 against Canada at Centurion. He is also Ireland's leading wicket-taker in one-day internationals, with 46 wickets.

KENYA

Kenya caused one of the greatest shocks in ODI cricket history when they reached the semi-finals of the 2003 ICC World Cup, but that performance remains the exception in the Africans' encounters at the top table of international cricket. They remain very much among the second tier of world cricket.

OVERALL ONE-DAY INTERNATIONAL RECORD

Opposition	Span	Mat	Won	Lost	Tied	NR	%
All opponents	1996–2010	136	38	93	0	5	27.94

⊙ ALL-ROUND ASSET

Thomas Odoyo's wholehearted all-round performances have made him a key member of Kenya's side from the moment he made his debut as a 17-year-old at the 1996 ICC World Cup. The first non-Test player to achieve the 1,500-run, 100-wicket double in one-day international cricket, he has scored 2,262 runs with the bat (with a highest score of 111 not out against Canada at Nairobi on 18 October 2007) in 124 matches, but it is his performances with the ball that are more noteworthy: he holds his country's all-time records for the most wickets (134) and for the most four-wicket-plus hauls (five – with a best of 4 for 25 against Bermuda at Mombasa on 12 November 2006).

⊙ KENYA'S FINEST

The poster-boy of Kenyan cricket for over a decade, Steve Tikolo is regarded as the finest player in history to emerge from the non-Test-playing nations. He holds numerous all-time records for Kenya in one-day international cricket: he has played in the most matches (129 between 1996 and 2010); has scored the most runs (3,377 at the respectable average of 29.88); and has recorded the most centuries (three – with a highest score of 111 against Bermuda at Mombasa on 14 November 2006).

NETHERLANDS

Winners of the ICC Trophy in 2001, the Netherlands have not made the transition from second-tier standouts to minor members of world cricket's elite. Regular qualifiers for the ICC World Cup (they appeared in 1996, 2003 and 2007 and qualified for the 2011 tournament), they have not yet won a one-day international match against a Test-playing nation in 16 attempts.

OVERALL ONE-DAY INTERNATIONAL RECORD

Opposition	Span	Mat	Won	Lost	Tied	NR	%
All opponents	1996–2010	57	23	32	0	2	40.35

⊙ A SERIOUS TALENT

The Netherlands' big-name player – and fast developing a reputation as being the best player outside the Test game (South African born, but of Dutch descent), Ryan ten Doeschate has produced some outstanding performances for his country with both bat and ball since making his debut in July 2006. In 27 one-day internationals he has set Netherlands records for the most runs scored (1,234, at a hefty average of 68.55), for the most centuries (three, with a highest score of 109 not out against Bermuda at Nairobi on 4 February 2007) and also for the most wickets (48, at an average of 20.93).

⊙ BREAKING THE WORLD CUP DUCK

Revelling in the chance to play against opponents of whom they had the measure on the one-day game's greatest stage, Feiko Kloppenburg (121) and Klaas-Jan von Noortwijk (134 not out – the highest individual score by a Netherlands player in one-day international cricket) produced a performance of the highest class to propel their side to a first-ever victory in the ICC World Cup. The pair put on a record 228 for the second wicket to lead the Dutch charge to 314 for 4 against Namibia at Bloemfontein on 3 March 2003; they then bowled out Namibia for 250 to win the match by 64 runs.

SCOTLAND

Scotland have been a standout team in world cricket's second tier in recent years, but have failed to find the ingredients required to move to the next level. ICC Trophy winners for the first time in 2005, they have qualified for two of the last four ICC World Cups, but have still to record their first victory in the tournament and have never beaten a Test-status side in a one-day international.

OVERALL ONE-DAY INTERNATIONAL RECORD

Opposition	Span	Mat	Won	Lost	Tied	NR	%
All opponents	1999–2010	50	15	32	0	3	30.00

⊙ BIGGEST VICTORIES

By runs: by 77 runs against Kenya at Nairobi on 4 February 2007.
By wickets: by six wickets on two occasions – against the Netherlands at Dublin on 29 July 2008; and against Afghanistan at Ayr on 17 August 2010.

⊙ CAREER CHANGE LEADS TO NATIONAL SUCCESS

John Blain, who, in his youth, switched from life as a footballer with Falkirk FC to that of a professional cricketer, has been a key member of the Scotland bowling attack for over a decade. After playing in 33 matches between 1999 and 2009 he holds the Scotland records in one-day international cricket for: the most wickets (41); the best bowling in an innings (5 for 22 against the Netherlands at Dublin on 29 July 2008); and the most four-wicket-plus innings hauls (two).

⊙ MOST CENTURIES

Gavin Hamilton holds the Scotland record for the most centuries in one-day international cricket. The former Yorkshire and England player has registered two centuries in 38 matches for his country between 1999 and 2010, with a highest score of 119 against Canada at Aberdeen on 7 July 2009.

ZIMBABWE

Zimbabwe was a cricket nation on the up. They appeared in nine successive ICC World Cups between 1983 and 2007, causing several upsets along the way, and by the turn of the 21st century could call upon a core of players of real international class. But as the country crumbled politically, so did its cricket team and, once again, Zimbabwe stands among the second tier of world cricket.

⊙ LEADER OF THE BOWLING PACK

The finest fast bowler Zimbabwe has produced, lion-hearted Heath Streak shone in both Test cricket (the first and only Zimbabwe bowler to take 100 Test wickets, he ended up with 216 scalps in a 65-Test career) and in one-day international cricket (in 187 matches between 1993 and 2005 he took 237 wickets, with a Zimbabwe record eight four-wicket-plus hauls and a best bowling performance of 5 for 32 against India at Bulawayo on 15 February 1997).

OVERALL ONE-DAY INTERNATIONAL RECORD

Opposition	Span	Mat	Won	Lost	Tied	NR	%
All opponents	1983–2010	387	101	272	5	9	26.10

⊙ OLONGA OUTCLASSES ENGLAND

Henry Olonga produced the best bowling figures by a Zimbabwe bowler in one-day international cricket at Cape Town on 28 January 2000 – and the best by any bowler on African soil – to send England crashing to their sixth defeat in eight meetings against Zimbabwe. The paceman took 6 for 19 to send England (chasing 212) tumbling to 107 all out and a 104-run defeat.

⊙ MOST MATCHES

A top-order batsman capable of churning out big scores and a slow left-arm bowler with wicket-taking capabilities, Grant Flower has played in more one-day internationals for Zimbabwe than any other player: 219 between 1992 and 2004.

OTHER TEAMS

The ICC's decision in recent years to allocate one-day international status to matches between world cricket's second-tier nations has led to a surge in the number of matches: in 1990, 61 one-day internationals were played throughout the world; but, by 2009, that number had risen to 150. Here are some of the outstanding performances from the best of the rest.

OVERALL RESULTS SUMMARY (AGAINST ALL OPPONENTS)

Opposition	Span	Mat	Won	Lost	Tied	NR	%
Afghanistan	2009–10	16	9	7	0	0	56.25
Africa XI	2005–07	6	1	4	0	1	16.67
Asia XI	2005–07	7	4	2	0	1	57.14
Bermuda	2006–09	35	7	28	0	0	20.00
Canada	1979–2011	61	16	44	0	1	26.66
East Africa	1975	3	0	3	0	0	0.00
Hong Kong	2004–08	4	0	4	0	0	0.00
ICC World XI	2005	4	1	3	0	0	25.00
Namibia	2003	6	0	6	0	0	0.00
UAE	1994–2008	11	1	10	0	0	9.09
USA	2004	2	0	2	0	0	0.00

Hong Kong, Israel, Wales and others appeared in 1970s/80s World Cups or qualifiers.

⊙ BAGAI THE PICK OF THE BATSMEN

Alongside the Netherlands' Ryan ten Doeschate, Canada's Ashish Bagai is the only player from one of cricket's minor nations to have scored 1,000 runs in ODIs. The Delhi-born wicketkeeper batsman has scored 1,736 runs in 54 matches between 2003 and 2011, with a highest score of 137 not out against Scotland at Nairobi on 31 January 2007.

⊙ FIRST FORFEIT OF ODI

Canada forfeited their one-day international at Mombasa on 20 January 2007 owing to player illness; Kenya thus won the match without a ball being bowled – the only instance of such a case in the history of one-day international cricket.

LEADING BATSMEN (BY TEAM)

Team	Runs	Player
Afghanistan	643	Mohammad Shahzad (2009–10)
Africa XI	326	Shaun Pollock (2005–07)
Asia XI	269	Mahela Jayawardene (2005–07)
Bermuda	783	Irving Romaine (2006–09)
Canada	1,736	Ashish Bagai (2003–10)
East Africa	57	Frasat Ali (1975)
Hong Kong	101	Tabarak Dar (2004–08)
ICC World XI	138	Kumar Sangakkara (2005)
Namibia	199	Jan-Berrie Burger (2003)
UAE	179	Mazhar Hussain (1994–96)
USA	39	Clayton Lambert (2004)

⊙ CROWD-PLEASING PERFORMANCE

In a match hastily arranged to raise funds for victims of the 2004 Boxing Day tsunami, the ICC World XI put on a blistering batting display against an Asia XI at Melbourne on 10 January 2005. Propelled by a 102-ball 115 from Ricky Ponting and a belligerent 47-ball 69 from Chris Cairns, they reached 344 for 8 off their 50 overs. The Asia XI slipped to 232 all out in reply to lose the match by 112 runs.

LEADING BOWLERS (BY TEAM)

Team	Wkts	Player
Afghanistan	22	Hameed Hasan (2009–10)
Africa XI	8	Morne Morkel (2007)
Asia XI	13	Zaheer Khan (2005–07)
Bermuda	34	Dwayne Leverock (2006–09)
Canada	41	Sunil Dhaniram (2006–10)
East Africa	4	Zulfiqar Ali (1975)
Hong Kong	4	Ilyas Gull (2004); Afzaal Haider (2004–08)
ICC World XI	8	Daniel Vettori (2005)
Namibia	8	Rudi van Vuuren (2003)
UAE	7	Khurram Khan (2004–08)
USA	2	Richard Staple (2007)

⊙ CODRINGTON MAKES HISTORY FOR CANADA

Canada's first-ever ICC World Cup campaign got off to a headline-grabbing start when they beat Bangladesh by 60 runs at Durban on 11 February 2003 to become the only "minor" cricket nation to record a victory over a Test-playing nation. The star of the show was Austin Codrington, a 27-year-old, Jamaican-born apprentice plumber who took 5 for 27 with his medium-pace bowling to help reduce Bangladesh (chasing 181) to 120 all out.

PART 3: TWENTY20 CRICKET

Given the staggering manner in which Twenty20 cricket has been received by fans around the world, it seems strange to remember that when first Twenty20 international was staged on 17 February 2005 it was taken less than seriously, with New Zealand players adorned with retro 1970s wigs and moustaches.

It took a hastily arranged World Cup in South Africa in 2007 to change all that. The 2007 ICC World Twenty20 was a spectacular success. When India faced off against Pakistan in the final, the match was beamed across 100 countries worldwide and became the tenth most-watched sports event of the year. India's five-run victory, and the ecstatic manner in which it was received, led to the subsequent establishment of the Indian Premier League and assured Twenty20 cricket's status on the domestic scene.

The success of the 2009 and 2010 ICC World Twenty20 tournaments, hosted by England and the West Indies, respectively, has ensured international Twenty20 cricket is here to stay. For now, it may have been sidelined by existing television contracts committed to showing one-day internationals, but do not be too surprised if the 20-over game starts to form an increasing part of the cricket calendar in the years to come.

ICC WORLD TWENTY20

It took some time, but the ICC finally realized that Twenty20 cricket not only provided great entertainment, but could also be a considerable money-spinner. The first three ICC World Twenty20s, held in South Africa, England and the West Indies respectively, have all been a spectacular success and the tournament looks set to become a permanent fixture on the international cricket calendar.

ICC WORLD TWENTY20 WINNERS

Year	Winner	Host
2007	India	South Africa
2009	Pakistan	England
2010	England	West Indies

⊙ AUSTRALIA CRUISE INTO FINAL FOUR

With both sides needing to win to progress to the semi-finals of the 2007 ICC World Twenty20, the match between Australia and Sri Lanka at Cape Town on 20 September 2007 was rightly billed as a high-stakes, winner-takes-all encounter. It certainly wasn't a nail-biting one, however. Australia dismissed Sri Lanka for 101 and reached the victory target without losing a wicket – Matthew Hayden (58 not out) and Adam Gilchrist (31 not out) took 10.2 overs to record the first, and to date only, ten-wicket victory in ICC World Twenty20 history.

⊙ INDISCIPLINE WITH BALL COSTS WEST INDIES

When the West Indies looked back to see how they failed to defend a target of 205 against South Africa in the opening match of the 2007 ICC World Twenty20 at Johannesburg, they would have looked no further than the extras column. The men from the Caribbean delivered an astonishing 23 wides (a tournament record) as South Africa cruised to an eight-wicket victory with 14 balls to spare.

ICC WORLD TWENTY20 LEAGUE TABLE
(RANKED BY WIN PERCENTAGE)

Pos	Team	(Span)	Mat	Won	Lost	Tied	NR	%
1	South Africa	2007–10	16	11	5	0	0	68.75
2	Sri Lanka	2007–10	18	12	6	0	0	66.66
3	Pakistan	2007–10	20	12	7	0	0	62.50
4	Australia	2007–10	15	9	6	1	0	60.00
5	India	2007–10	17	8	7	0	1	53.12
6	England	2007–10	17	8	8	1	1	50.00
=	Netherlands	2009	2	1	1	0	0	50.00
=	New Zealand	2007–10	16	8	8	0	0	50.00
9	West Indies	2007–10	13	6	7	0	0	46.15
10	Zimbabwe	2007–10	4	1	3	0	0	25.00
11	Ireland	2009–10	7	1	5	0	1	16.66
12	Bangladesh	2007–10	9	1	8	0	0	11.11
13	Afghanistan	2010	2	0	2	0	0	0.00
=	Kenya	2007	2	0	2	0	0	0.00
=	Scotland	2007–09	4	0	3	0	1	0.00

⊙ MINNOW-BASHING AT ITS BEST

Sri Lanka pulverized Kenya in the two sides' Group C meeting at
Johannesburg in the 2007 ICC World Twenty20. Batting first, they
blitzed the Kenyan bowling attack to all parts of the ground in
amassing a gargantuan 260 for 6 off their 20 overs – the highest
score by any team in any Twenty20 match – with Sanath Jayasuriya
top-scoring with 88. Overwhelmed, Kenya crept to 88 for 9.
Sri Lanka's 172-run margin of victory is the highest (by runs) in
international Twenty20 history.

⊙ RUNS GALORE AT DURBAN

India and England's Group E encounter at Durban in the 2007 ICC
World Twenty20 captured the very essence of all that is good about
the shortest format of the game – hard hitting and plenty of runs.
India, boosted by six sixes from Yuvraj Singh in a Stuart Broad over,
reached 218 for 4. England reached a spirited 200 for 6 in reply to
lose the match by 18 runs. The match aggregate of 418 runs is the
highest in the tournament's history.

⊙ MOST DEFEATS

The record for most defeats in the history of the ICC World Twenty20
is eight, a feat achieved by three teams: Bangladesh (in nine
matches), England (in 17 matches) and New Zealand (in 16 matches).

⊙ NARROWEST VICTORY (BY WICKETS)

The smallest margin of victory (by wickets) in ICC World Twenty20 competition is a win by two wickets, which occurred when New Zealand beat Sri Lanka at Providence, Guyana, on 30 April 2010.

⊙ KENYA SLUMP TO RECORD DEFEAT

Kenya got their 2007 ICC World Twenty20 campaign off to the worst possible start against New Zealand at Durban on 12 September 2007. Put in to bat on a lively surface, they lost their first three batsmen in the first seven balls of the match without registering a run, slipped to 1 for 4 by the end of the second over and scrambled to 73 all out. New Zealand cantered to a nine-wicket victory with 74 balls remaining – the largest margin (by balls remaining) in international Twenty20 cricket history.

⊙ MOST VICTORIES

The record for the most victories recorded in ICC World Twenty20 matches is 12, recorded by two teams: Pakistan (champions in 2009, runners-up in 2007 and semi-finalists in 2010) and Sri Lanka (runners-up in 2009 and semi-finalists in 2010).

⊙ FINE LINE BETWEEN VICTORY AND DEFEAT

New Zealand have made a habit of being involved in ICC World Twenty20 games that have been resolved by the slenderest of margins. In their Group D encounter against South Africa at Lord's in 2009, they fell to defeat by one run; eleven months later, in their Super Eight match against Pakistan at Bridgetown, Barbados, they won by one run. They are the only two instances of one-run victories in ICC World Twenty20 history.

⊙ LAST-BALL SUCCESSES

It was the most spectacular upset in the tournament's history as the Netherlands, making their first-ever appearance, shocked hosts England at the home of cricket, Lord's, in the two sides' opening Group B encounter at the 2009 ICC World Twenty20. Chasing 163 for victory, the men in orange squeaked over the winning line off the last ball of the match to record a memorable four-wicket victory. There has only been one other last-ball success in ICC World Twenty20 history: Sri Lanka beat India (by five wickets) off the final ball of the match at Gros Inlet on 11 May 2010.

BATTING RECORDS

MOST RUNS: TOP 10

Pos	Runs	Player (country, span)
1	615	Mahela Jayawardene (Sri Lanka, 2007–10)
2	580	Kevin Pietersen (England, 2007–10)
3	453	Tillakaratne Dilshan (Sri Lanka, 2007–10)
4	444	Guatham Gambhir (India, 2007–10)
5	442	Chris Gayle (West Indies, 2007–09)
6	420	Kumar Sangakkare (Sri Lanka, 2007–10)
7	412	Kamran Akmal (Pakistan, 2007–10)
8	409	Jacques Kallis (South Africa, 2009–10)
9	389	A.B. de Villiers (South Africa, 2007–10)
10	375	Yuvraj Singh (Ind, 2007–10)

⊙ GAMBHIR COMES OF AGE

He is now widely regarded as one of the best openers in world cricket but, when he looks back, Gautam Gambhir will see the 2007 ICC World Twenty20 as the moment when his career took off. Handed yet another chance to establish himself in a much-changed India side following the country's poor showing at the 2007 ICC World Cup, Gambhir grabbed it with both hands, hitting three half-centuries in the tournament, including a high-class knock of 75 in the pressure-cooker atmosphere of the final against Pakistan, which India won by five runs. Gambhir's effort remains the highest score yet recorded in an ICC World Twenty20 final.

⊙ TALK OF THE TOWN

Tillakaratne Dilshan was the talk of world cricket during the 2009 ICC World Twenty20. Not only did he bring a new shot to the game (an audacious paddle scoop over his left shoulder, described in various quarters as the "flick shot", the "genuflector" or simply the "Dilshan"), he also kept on piling up the big scores. His tournament record 317 runs (with a highest score of 96 not out against the West Indies at The Oval) played a pivotal role in Sri Lanka's progress to the final, where they lost to Pakistan, and were enough to earn him the player of the tournament award.

⊙ MOST DUCKS

It seems to be boom or bust for Sanath Jayasuriya as he reaches the twilight of his international career. The veteran opener may have recorded three half-centuries for Sri Lanka in 18 ICC World Twenty20 matches, but he has also recorded four ducks – the most by any individual player in the tournament's history.

HIGHEST SCORES BY BATTING POSITION

Pos	Score	Player (team)	Against	Venue	Date
1/2	117	C.H. Gayle (West Indies)	South Africa	Johannesburg	11 Sep 2007
1/2	100	D.P.M.D. Jayawardene (Sri Lanka)	Zimbabwe	Providence	3 May 2010
3	101	S.K. Raina (India)	South Africa	Gros Inlet	2 May 2010
4	89*	J.M. Kemp (South Africa)	New Zealand	Durban	19 Sep 2007
5	59	D.J. Hussey (Australia)	England	Bridgetown	16 May 2010
6	85*	C.L. White (Australia)	Sri Lanka	Bridgetown	9 May 2010
7	60*	M.E.K. Hussey (Australia)	Pakistan	Gros Inlet	14 May 2010
8	35*	A.D. Mathews (Sri Lanka)	Pakistan	Lord's	21 Jun 2009
9	28	Naeem Islam (Bangladesh)	India	Trent Bridge	6 Jun 2009
10	22	Hamid Hassan (Afghanistan)	South Africa	Bridgetown	5 May 2010
11	13*	J.D. Nel (Scotland)	Pakistan	Durban	12 Sep 2007

⊙ SIX SIXES IN AN OVER

Yuvraj Singh is rightly regarded as one of the cleanest and most destructive strikers of the ball in world cricket, as Stuart Broad found out. In the 18th over of India's Group E match against England at Durban on 19 September 2007, the left-hander smashed the hapless English bowler for six consecutive sixes to become the first player in Twenty20 cricket (and the fourth in senior cricket) to achieve the feat.

⊙ AKMAL SETS A TOURNAMENT BEST

Defending champions Pakistan got their 2010 ICC World Twenty20 campaign off to the best of starts when they won their opening match against Bangladesh by 21 runs at Gros Inlet, St Lucia, on 1 May 2010. And for that, they had their openers to thank: Salman Butt scored 73 off 46 balls (with eight fours and two sixes) and Kamran Akmal scored 73 off 55 balls (with eight fours and one six) – the highest score by a designated wicketkeeper in the tournament's history.

BOWLING RECORDS

⊙ PATHAN PILES ON THE PRESSURE

Where Gautam Gambhir (75) starred with the bat during India's five-run victory over Pakistan in the 2007 ICC World Twenty20 final, Irfan Pathan was the hero with the ball: the left-arm medium-fast bowler took 3 for 16 in the middle of the innings to pile on the pressure under which the Pakistan batsmen would ultimately crack. They remain the best bowling figures recorded in an ICC World Twenty20 final.

MOST WICKETS: TOP 10

Pos	Wkts	Player (Team, Span)
1	27	Shahid Afridi (Pakistan, 2007–10)
2	26	Umar Gul (Pakistan, 2007–09)
3	25	Lasith Malinga (Sri Lanka, 2007–10)
4	23	Saeed Ajmal (Pakistan, 2009–10)
5	20	Mitchell Johnson (Australia, 2007–10)
6	19	Stuart Broad (England, 2007–10)
7	18	Daniel Vettori (New Zealand, 2007–10)
8	17	Morne Morkel (South Africa, 2007–10)
9	16	Ajantha Mendis (Sri Lanka, 2009–10)
10	15	Dirk Nannes (Australia/Netherlands, 2009–10)

⊙ STANDOUT PERFORMER WITH THE BALL

A mainstay of Pakistan's bowling attack since making his international debut as a 19-year-old in 2003 (having made just nine prior first-class appearances), Umar Gul is the perfect death bowler, capable of bowling high-speed reverse-swinging yorkers in the closing overs of an innings. He played a pivotal role in Pakistan's success in the 2009 competition and holds the all-time tournament records for: the best bowling figures in an innings (5 for 6 against New Zealand at The Oval on 13 June 2009, a performance that saw him break the record for the best economy rate in an innings – 2.00); and for the most four-wicket-plus hauls in an innings (two, a record he shares with Pakistan team-mates Shahid Afridi and Saeed Amjal and South Africa's Morne Morkel).

⊙ KEEPING IT TIGHT

There has been no more miserly bowler in ICC World Twenty20 matches than Nikita Miller. The Jamaican slow left-arm bowler has bowled 12.0 overs for 63 runs in three matches at an economy rate of 5.25 runs per over – the lowest by any bowler to have delivered ten overs or more in the tournament's history.

⊙ PACE OR SPIN?

Twenty20 cricket has confounded the critics who predicted a crash-bang-wallop game in which spin bowlers were little more than lambs to the slaughter. As statistics for ICC World Twenty20 matches show, spin bowlers not only play an integral part in games, they can be equally as effective as pace bowlers, with both a better average and economy rate:

Type	Overs	Mdns	Runs	Wkts	BBI	Ave	Econ	SR	4	5
Pace	1862.4	24	14,467	607	5/6	23.83	7.76	18.4	15	1
Spin	1018.4	7	7,259	314	4/11	23.11	7.12	19.4	7	0

⊙ MOST MAIDENS BOWLED

Given the nature of the game, a maiden over is a particularly rare feat in international Twenty20 cricket. The record for the most career maidens bowled in ICC World Twenty20 matches is three, set by Dilhara Fernando. The Sri Lankan paceman achieved the feat in 17 overs in five matches in the 2007 edition of the tournament held in South Africa.

⊙ NO ORDINARY CRICKETER

A globe-trotter, a Japanese speaker and a saxophone player who represented Australia in World Cup skiing events, Dirk Nannes is not your run-of-the-mill cricketer, but he is certainly a talented one. Of Dutch parentage, he played for the Netherlands at the 2009 ICC World Twenty20, after missing out on a place in Australia's squad, and performed with such distinction that he caught the Australian selectors' eyes and was rapidly drafted into Australia's squad for the 2010 edition of the tournament. Bowling with precision and raw pace, his 14 wickets in the tournament, which did much to propel Australia to the final, are the most by any bowler at a single ICC World Twenty20.

OTHER RECORDS

HIGHEST PARTNERSHIPS: TOP 10

Pos	Runs	Partners	Wkt	Team	Against	Venue	Date
1	166	D.P.M.D. Jayawardene, K.C Sangakkara	2nd	SL	WI	Bridgetown	7 May 2010
2	145	C.H. Gayle, D.S. Smith	1st	WI	SA	Johannesburg	11 Sep 2007
3	142	Kamran Akmal, Salman Butt	1st	Pak	Bang	Gros Islet	1 May 2010
4	136	G. Gambhir, V. Sehwag	1st	Ind	Eng	Durban	19 Sep 2007
5	133	C.H. Gayle, A.D.S. Fletcher	1st	WI	Aus	The Oval	6 Jun 2009
6	124	T.M. Dilshan, S.T. Jayasuriya	1st	SL	WI	Nottingham	10 Jun 2009
7	120*	H.H. Gibbs, J.M. Kemp	3rd	SA	WI	Johannesburg	11 Sep 2007
8	119*	Shoaib Malik, Misbah-ul-Haq	5th	Pak	Aus	Johannesburg	18 Sep 2007
9	111	C. Kieswetter, K.P. Pietersen	2nd	Eng	Aus	Bridgetown	16 May 2010
10	109	Aftab Ahmed, Mohammad Ashraful	3rd	Bang	WI	Johannesburg	13 Sep 2007

⊙ SRI LANKAN STARS PUT WEST INDIES TO THE SWORD

Two sublime innings from the team's two best batsmen helped Sri Lanka ease to a comfortable victory over hosts West Indies in the two sides' Super Eight encounter at Bridgetown, Barbados, on 7 May 2010. Mahela Jayawardene (98 not out) and Kumar Sangakkara (68) added 166 runs off 16.3 overs for the second wicket – the highest partnership in the tournament's history – to lead Sri Lanka to an imposing 195 for 3. In response, the West Indies slipped to 138 for 8 and defeat by 57 runs.

⊙ DE VILLIERS LEADS THE WAY IN THE FIELD

South Africa's A.B. de Villiers is fast developing a reputation for being the best fielder in world cricket. Positioned for the most part at backward point – a regular spot for many of the 20-over game's best fielders – he has taken more catches in ICC World Twenty matches than any other player (11 in 11 matches between 2007 and 2009). He also shares the record – with Pakistan's Younis Khan (in 2007) and the West Indies' Andre Fletcher (in 2009) for the most catches in a single tournament, with six in 2007.

⊙ MOST CATCHES IN AN INNINGS BY A FIELDER

The record for the most catches in an innings by a fielder is four, by Darren Samy, for the West Indies against Ireland at Providence, Guyana, on 30 April 2010.

HIGHEST PARTNERSHIPS: BY WICKET

Wkt	Runs	Partners	Team	Against	Venue	Date
1st	145	C.H. Gayle, D.S. Smith	WI	SA	Johannesburg	11 Sep 2007
2nd	166	D.P.M.D. Jayawardene, K.C. Sangakkara	SL	WI	Bridgetown	7 May 2007
3rd	120*	H.H. Gibbs, J.M. Kemp	SA	WI	Johannesburg	11 Sep 2007
4th	101	Younis Khan, Shoaib Malik	Pak	SL	Johannesburg	17 Sep 2007
5th	119*	Shoaib Malik, Misbah-ul-Haq	Pak	Aus	Johannesburg	18 Sep 2007
6th	101*	C.L. White, M.E.K. Hussey	Aus	SL	Bridgetown	9 May 2010
7th	74	M.E.K. Hussey, S.P.D. Smith	Aus	Ban	Bridgetown	5 May 2010
8th	53	M.E.K. Hussey, M.G. Johnson	Aus	Pak	Gros Inlet	14 May 2010
9th	36	R.G. Sharma, Z Khan	Ind	Aus	Bridgetown	7 May 2010
10th	20	N.O. Miller, S.J. Benn	WI	Aus	Gros Inlet	11 May 2010

ICC WORLD TWENTY20 PLAYER OF THE TOURNAMENT WINNERS

2007	Shahid Afridi	Pakistan
2009	Tillakaratne Dilshan	Sri Lanka
2010	Kevin Pietersen	England

⊙ MOST WICKETKEEPING DISMISSALS IN AN INNINGS

The ICC World Twenty20 record for the most dismissals in an innings by a keeper is four, a feat achieved by five players: Adam Gilchrist, for Australia against Zimbabwe at Cape Town on 12 September 2007 (4ct); Matt Prior, for England against South Africa at Cape Town on 16 September 2007 (4ct); Kamran Akmal, for Pakistan against the Netherlands at Lord's on 9 June 2009 (4st); Niall O'Brien, for Ireland against Sri Lanka at Lord's on 14 June 2009 (3ct, 1st); and Mahendra Singh Dhoni, for India against Afghanistan at Gros Inlet on 1 May 2010 (4ct).

⊙ MOST WICKETKEEPER DISMISSALS

Kumar Sangakkara is the most successful wicketkeeper to appear in the ICC World Twenty20. Sri Lanka's wicketkeeper-batsman-captain has bagged 13 victims in 12 matches in the tournament (7ct, 6st). He also holds the record for the most dismissals in a single tournament with nine in 2009 – a record he shares with Australia's Adam Gilchrist (in 2007).

INTERNATIONAL TWENTY20

It took a comprehensive 100-run victory for England over Australia at the Rose Bowl in June 2005 before international Twenty20 cricket was taken seriously. Since then, as the ICC has tried to work out how best to integrate the new format into the international cricket calendar, matches – with the exception of ICC World Twenty20 tournaments – have been few and far between.

RESULT SUMMARY

Team (Span)	Mat	Won	Lost	Tied	NR	%
Afghanistan (2010)	8	4	4	0	0	50.00
Australia (2005–11)	41	22	17	1	1	56.25
Bangladesh (2006–10)	16	3	13	0	0	18.75
Bermuda (2008)	3	0	3	0	0	0.00
Canada (2008–10)	11	3	7	1	0	31.81
England (2005–11)	36	18	16	0	2	52.94
India (2006–11)	28	15	11	1	1	57.40
Ireland (2008–10)	17	7	8	0	2	46.66
Kenya (2007–10)	12	4	8	0	0	33.33
Netherlands (2008–10)	10	6	3	0	1	66.66
New Zealand (2005–10)	43	19	21	3	0	47.65
Pakistan (2006–10)	45	27	17	1	0	61.11
Scotland (2007–10)	12	2	9	0	1	18.18
South Africa (2005–11)	38	25	13	0	0	65.78
Sri Lanka (2006–10)	34	20	14	0	0	58.82
West Indies (2006–10)	28	11	15	2	0	42.85
Zimbabwe (2006–10)	14	3	10	1	0	25.00

⊙ OFF TO A GALLOPING START

A forthright opening stand from Graeme Smith (88) and Loots Bosman (94) placed South Africa in a match-winning position in their international Twenty20 match against England at Centurion on 15 November 2009. The pair added 170 runs for the opening wicket – a record partnership in international Twenty20 cricket – to lead South Africa to an impressive 241 for 6. England wilted to a distant 157 for 8 in reply.

⊙ MCCULLUM A BIG HIT IN TWENTY20

There have been numerous cases of Twenty20 cricket enhancing a player's reputation, but perhaps the best example is that of New Zealand's Brendon McCullum. The wicketkeeper-batsman ensured the Indian Premier League got off to a blistering start when he smashed 158 not out in the tournament's first-ever game – still the highest score in any 20-over match. He has since carried that form into international matches: he is the only batsman to have scored more than 1,000 runs in Twenty20 internationals (1,100 runs) and also holds the record for the most sixes in Twenty20 internationals (with 39).

⊙ MADE FOR THE GAME

Andrew Symonds is a big-hitting batsman with a simple approach to the game – his mantra often seems to be "see ball, hit ball". Indiscretions both on and off the pitch have seen him in and out of the Australia side in all formats of the game since he made his international debut back in 1998, but on his day there is no finer batsman in Twenty20 cricket. In 14 Twenty20 internationals for Australia between 2004 and 2009 he has scored 337 runs (with a top score of 85 not out against New Zealand at Perth on 11 December 2007) at an average of 48.14 and compiled at a strike-rate of 169.34 runs per 100 balls faced – his career average and strike-rate are both all-time highs in international Twenty20 cricket.

MOST RUNS: TOP 5

Pos	Runs	Player (Team, Span)
1	1,100	Brendon McCullum (New Zealand, 2005–10)
2	958	Graeme Smith (South Africa, 2005–10)
3	937	Kevin Pietersen (England, 2005–11)
4	784	Mahela Jayawardene (Sri Lanka, 2006–10)
5	777	Kumar Sangakkara (Sri Lanka, 2006–10)

MOST WICKETS: TOP 5

Pos	Wkts	Player (Team, Span)
1	53	Shahid Afridi (Pakistan, 2006–10)
2	47	Umar Gul (Pakistan, 2007–10)
3	41	Saeed Ajmal (Pakistan, 2009–10)
4	35	D.L. Vettori (New Zealand, 2007–10)
=	35	S.C.J. Broad (England, 2006–10)
=	35	Lasith Malinga (Sri Lanka, 2006–10)

⊙ HIGHEST AND LOWEST

Highest score: 260 for 6 – Sri Lanka v Kenya at Johannesburg on 14 September 2007.

Lowest score: 67 all out – Kenya v Ireland at Belfast on 4 August 2008.

⊙ BIGGEST VICTORIES

By runs: by 172 runs – Sri Lanka v Kenya at Johannesburg on 14 September 2007.

By wickets: by ten wickets on five occasions.

By balls remaining: with 74 balls remaining – New Zealand v Kenya at Durban on 12 September 2007.

⊙ SMALLEST VICTORIES

By runs: by one run – on five occasions.

By wickets: by one wicket – England v Australia at Adelaide on 12 January 2011.

By balls remaining: off the last ball of the match on four occasions.

⊙ MOST CAREER MAIDENS

Zimbabwe's Ray Price is fast developing a reputation as being one of the most miserly bowlers on the international circuit. The slow left-arm bowler has delivered four maidens in nine Twenty20 international matches – the most by any bowler.

⊙ HAT-TRICKS

There have been three hat-tricks in international Twenty20 cricket: by Australia's Brett Lee, against Bangladesh at Cape Town on 16 September 2007 – Shakib Al Hasan (caught), Mashrafe Mortaza (bowled) and Alok Kapali (lbw); by New Zealand's Jacob Oram, against Sri Lanka at Colombo on 2 September 2009 – Angelo Mathews (caught and bowled), Malinga Bandara (caught) and Nuwan Kulasekara (caught); and by New Zealand's Tim Southee, against Pakistan at Auckland on 26 December 2010 – Younis Khan (caught), Mohammad Hafeez (caught) and Umar Akmal (lbw).

PART 4: DOMESTIC CRICKET RECORDS

Domestic cricket is the lifeblood of the game, the breeding ground where cricket's future stars will learn their trade and the format through whose ranks every one of the game's greatest names has passed. It includes first-class cricket (timed matches), limited-overs cricket (matches of 40 to 60 overs per side) and Twenty20 cricket.

The term "first-class" dates back to May 1894, but records of matches between two representative sides go back much further than that. In 1709, Kent and Surrey staged the first-known inter-county match; in 1825, Kent and Sussex contested home-and-away fixtures (a forerunner to the county championship, which was constituted in 1890); in Australia, the first first-class match (between Tasmania and Victoria) took place in 1850–51; and by the early years of the 20th century, first-class cricket competitions were being contested throughout the world. The majority of cumulative first-class records (most career runs/wickets, etc.) belong to English cricketers of the game's Golden Age, directly as a result of the sheer volume of games in which they played: Wilfred Rhodes, for example, played 1,110 first-class matches in a 32-year career; in contrast, Graeme Hick, who retired in 2008 after 25 years in the county game, played just 526.

Limited-overs cricket in the domestic game is a more modern phenomenon that kicked off in England with the launch of the Gillette Cup in 1963. Twenty20 cricket has been played domestically since 2003, first in England, then South Africa and now throughout the world, including the Indian Premier League – the richest tournament in the game.

FIRST-CLASS TEAM RECORDS

HIGHEST INNINGS TOTALS: TOP 10

Pos	Total	For	Against	Venue	Season
1	1,107	Victoria	New South Wales	Melbourne	1926–27
2	1,059	Victoria	Tasmania	Melbourne	1922–23
3	952–6d	Sri Lanka	India	Colombo	1997–98
4	951–7d	Sind	Baluchistan	Karachi	1973–74
5	944–6d	Hyderabad	Andhra Pradesh	Hyderabad	1993–94
6	918	New South Wales	South Australia	Sydney	1900–01
7	912–8d	Holkar	Mysore	Indore	1945–46
=	912–6d	Tamil Nadu	Goa	Panjim	1988–89
9	910–6d	Railways	Dera Ismail Khan	Lahore	1964–65
10	903–7d	England	Australia	The Oval	1938

⊙ ESSEX PEAK TOO SOON

When they were finally dismissed for 642 on the second day of their County Championship Division Two match against Glamorgan at Chelmsford in September 2004, Essex would no doubt have thought they had done enough, at the very least, to avoid defeat. But how fortunes can change: Glamorgan made 587 in reply; bowled out Essex for 165 second time around; and chased down the 221 runs required for victory for the loss of six wickets. Essex's first innings total is the highest by a losing side in first-class cricket history.

⊙ PAKISTAN RAILWAYS STEAM TO VICTORY

It was the most one-sided game in first-class history. In Pakistan's 1964–65 domestic season, Pakistan Railways won the toss, batted and, thanks to centuries from Ijaz Hussain (124), Javed Babar (200), Pervez Akhtar (337 not out) and Mohammad Sharif (106 not out), reached a massive 910 for 6 declared. They then dismissed Dera Ismail Khan for 32 and 27 to win the match by an innings and 851 runs – the largest victory (by an innings) in first-class cricket history.

⊙ THRILLER AT TAUNTON

Set 454 runs to win the game, Somerset fell agonizingly short in a thrilling encounter against West Indies A at Taunton in July 2002. Bolstered by a fine innings of 140 from Peter Trego, they finally fell for 453 to tie the game. It is the highest fourth-innings score by a team that has gone on to tie a game in first-class cricket history.

LOWEST INNINGS TOTALS: TOP 10

Pos	Total	For	Against	Venue	Season
1	12	Oxford University	MCC	Oxford	1877
=	12	Northamptonshire	Gloucestershire	Gloucester	1907
3	13	Auckland	Canterbury	Auckland	1877–78
=	13	Nottinghamshire	Yorkshire	Nottingham	1901
5	14	Surrey	Essex	Chelmsford	1983
6	15	MCC	Surrey	Lord's	1839
=	15	Victoria	MCC	Melbourne	1903–04
=	15	Northamptonshire	Yorkshire	Northampton	1908
=	15	Hampshire	Warwickshire	Birmingham	1922
10	16	MCC	Surrey	Lord's	1872
=	16	Derbyshire	Nottinghamshire	Nottingham	1879
=	16	Surrey	Nottinghamshire	The Oval	1880
=	16	Warwickshire	Kent	Tonbridge	1913
=	16	Trinidad	Barbados	Bridgetown	1942–43

⊙ HIGHEST FOURTH INNINGS TOTAL

The highest fourth-innings total in first-class cricket history was achieved during the England v South Africa Test match at Durban in 1938–39 – the last of the timeless Tests. Set 696 runs for victory, England had reached 654 for 5 when, at tea on the tenth day, following repeated interruptions for rain, the two sides agreed to call the match a draw – principally to allow the England players time to travel to Cape Town to catch the mail boat home.

⊙ NSW BOOSTED BY BRADMAN TOWARDS RECORD-BREAKING VICTORY

By the time both sides had completed the first innings of the Sheffield Shield Match at Sydney in 1929–30, New South Wales held a slender eight-run lead over Queensland. Then Donald Bradman came to the party, hitting a then world record 452 not out to lead his side to 761 for 8 declared. Bewildered by the prospect of chasing 770 to win the match, Queensland folded to 84 all out. New South Wales's victory – by 675 runs – is the largest (by runs) in first-class cricket history.

⊙ LOWEST COMPLETED FIRST-CLASS INNINGS TOTAL TO INCLUDE A CENTURY

143 all out – Nottinghamshire against Hampshire at Bournemouth in 1981, of which Clive Rice made 105 not out (73.40 per cent of his team's total); his team-mates contributing 35 runs, with three extras.

FIRST-CLASS BATTING RECORDS

HIGHEST INDIVIDUAL SCORE: TOP 10

Pos	Total	Player (team)	Against	Venue	Season
1	501*	Brian Lara (Warwickshire)	Durham	Edgbaston	1994
2	499	Hanif Mohammad (Karachi)	Bahawalpur	Karachi	1958–59
3	452*	Donald Bradman (New South Wales)	Queensland	Sydney	1929–30
4	443*	Bhausaheb Nimbalkar (Maharashtra)	Kathiawar	Poona	1948–49
5	437	Bill Ponsford (Victoria)	Queensland	Melbourne	1927–28
6	429	Bill Ponsford (Victoria)	Tasmania	Melbourne	1922–23
7	428	Aftab Baloch (Sind)	Baluchistan	Karachi	1973–74
8	424	Archie MacLaren (Lancashire)	Somerset	Taunton	1895
9	405*	Graeme Hick (Worcestershire)	Somerset	Taunton	1988
10	400*	Brian Lara (West Indies)	England	Antigua	2003–04

⊙ HUNDREDS IN CONSECUTIVE INNINGS

The record for the most hundreds in consecutive innings
in first-class cricket is six, a feat achieved by three players:
Donald Bradman (in 1938–39), C.B. Fry (in 1901) and Mike
Procter (in 1970–71).

⊙ TURNER PLAYS LONE HAND IN SURVIVAL

A magnificent performance from overseas player Glenn Turner
single-handedly ensured that Worcestershire emerged from their
1977 County Championship encounter with Glamorgan at Swansea
having suffered nothing worse than a draw. After the home side
hit 309 for 4 in their first innings, only the New Zealand Test star
stood tall for the visitors, hitting an unbeaten 141 out of a team
total of 169 all out, a remarkable 83.43 per cent of his team's runs.
It remains the highest percentage of runs scored in a completed
innings in first-class cricket history

⊙ SIX SIXES IN AN OVER FOR SOBERS

It was a true milestone in the game and it was achieved, fittingly,
by the best player of his generation. Playing for Nottinghamshire
against Glamorgan at Swansea in the final match of the 1968
County Championship season, Garfield Sobers became the first
player in almost a century of first-class cricket to hit six sixes in
an over (the unfortunate bowler was Malcolm Nash). The feat
has only been repeated once in first-class cricket: by Ravi Shastri
(Mumbai v Baroda at Mumbai in 1984–85, off the bowling of
Tilak Rak).

⊙ COMPTON'S YEAR OF YEARS

1947 was the year in which Denis Compton's star shone at its brightest. He scored six centuries for England (including two in a failed Ashes campaign), and ended the year with 1,159 Test runs to his name (at an average of 82.78) to break Clem Hill's record for the most Test runs in a calendar year (1,060) that had stood since 1902. Compton was equally prolific in county cricket that year: in 50 innings for Middlesex and England during the 1947 English domestic season he hit 3,816 runs (at an average of 90.85) – an all-time record in first-class cricket.

⊙ WHITE'S ONE-MAN SHOW FOR SOMERSET AT DERBY

Set an unlikely 579 runs to win their County Championship Division Two match against Derbyshire at Derby in August 2006, Somerset owed it to their overseas player Cameron White that their eventual margin of defeat (by 80 runs) was not even larger. The Victoria batsman, captaining the side, led from the front, hitting an unbeaten 260 (off 246 balls) as his team-mates capitulated to 498 all out around him. His effort is the highest-ever score by a batsman in the fourth innings of a match in first-class cricket history.

MOST CAREER RUNS: TOP 10

Pos	Runs	Player (span)
1	61,760	Jack Hobbs (1905–34)
2	58,959	Frank Woolley (1906–38)
3	57,611	Patsy Hendren (1907–37)
4	55,061	Phil Mead (1905–36)
5	54,211	W.G. Grace (1865–1908)
6	50,670	Herbert Sutcliffe (1919–45)
7	50,551	Walter Hammond (1920–51)
8	48,426	Geoffrey Boycott (1962–86)
9	47,793	Tom Graveney (1948–72)
10	44,846	Graham Gooch (1973–2000)

⊙ BRILLIANT BRADMAN LEADS THE WAY

The most prolific batsman to play the game, Donald Bradman not only holds the all-time record for the highest career average in Tests (99.94), but also in first-class cricket: in 234 first-class matches for New South Wales, South Australia and Australia between 1927 and 1949 he scored 28,067 runs with 117 centuries, 69 fifties and a highest score of 452 not out, at an average of 95.14.

⊙ LARA'S RECORD-BREAKING RUN CONTINUES

Brian Lara was on the hottest batting streak in cricket history. Less than two months after breaking Garfield Sobers's world record Test score (Lara hit 375 not out against England at St John's in Antigua on 18 April 1994), he was at it again, this time for Warwickshire in their County Championship match against Durham at Edgbaston. The left hander hit 501 not out to break Hanif Mohammad's record for the highest score in first-class cricket. His 427-ball innings contained ten sixes and 62 fours – a record number of boundaries by a batsman in a first-class innings.

HIGHEST CAREER AVERAGE: TOP 10

Pos	Ave	Player (span)
1	95.14	Donald Bradman (1927–49)
2	71.64	Vijay Merchant (1929–51)
3	69.86	George Headley (1927–54)
4	67.72	Ajinkya Rahane (2007–11)
5	67.46	Ajay Sharma (1984–2001)
6	65.18	Bill Ponsford (1920–34)
7	64.99	Bill Woodfull (1921–34)
8	63.10	Shantanu Sugwekar (1987–2002)
9	62.31	Subramaniam Badrinath (2000–11)
10	61.24	K.C. Ibrahim (1938–50)

MOST CENTURIES IN A CAREER: TOP 10

Pos	100s	Player (span)
1	199	Jack Hobbs (1905–34)
2	170	Patsy Hendren (1907–37)
3	167	Walter Hammond (1920–51)
4	153	Chil Mead (1905–36)
5	151	Geoffrey Boycott (1962–86)
=	151	Herbert Sutcliffe (1919–45)
7	145	Frank Woolley (1906–38)
8	136	Graeme Hick (1983–2008)
9	129	Len Hutton (1934–55)
10	128	Graham Gooch (1973–2000)

⊙ MOST CENTURIES FOR ONE TEAM

The most prolific run-scorer in the history of the first-class game (with an astonishing 61,760 career runs), Jack Hobbs also holds the all-time record for the most centuries scored for a single team: he hit 144 centuries for Surrey in a career that stretched from 1905 to 1934.

⊙ FOR SURREY, READ RAMPRAKASH

One man and one man alone was the reason for Surrey's fourth-place finish in the 2007 County Championship. Mark Ramprakash, in his 38th year, was in the form of his life, hitting a staggering 30.02 per cent of his team's runs (excluding extras) during the course of the season. The classy right-hander hit 2,026 runs in 16 matches (at an average of 101.30), while his team-mates managed 4,721 runs between them (at an average of 26.08).

HIGHEST PARTNERSHIPS: BY WICKET

Wkt	Runs	Partners (team)	Against	Venue	Season
1st	561	Waheed Mirza/Mansoor Akhtar (Karachi Whites)	Quetta	Karachi	1976–77
2nd	580	Rafatullah Mohmand/Aamer Sajjad (WPDA)	Sui SGC	Sheikhupura	2009–10
3rd	624	K.C. Sangakkara/D.P.M.D. Jayawardene (Sri Lanka)	South Africa	Colombo	2006
4th	577	V.S. Hazare/Gul Mohammad (Baroda)	Holkar	Baroda	1946–47
5th	520*	C.A. Pujara/R.A. Jadeja (Saurashtra)	Orissa	Rajkot	2008–09
6th	487*	G.A. Headley/C.C. Passailaigue (Jamaica)	Lord Tennyson's XI	Kingston	1931–32
7th	460	Bhupinder Singh/P. Dharmani (Punjab)	Delhi	Delhi	1994–95
8th	433	A. Sims/V.T. Trumper (Australians)	Canterbury	Christchurch	1913–14
9th	283	A. Warren/J. Chapman (Derbyshire)	Warwickshire	Blackwell	1910
10th	307	A.F. Kippax/J.E.H. Hooker (New South Wales)	Victoria	Melbourne	1928–29

⊙ DEADLY DEREK LOSES HIS BITE WITH THE BAT

The best spin bowler England has ever produced (he took 297 wickets in 86 Tests for his country between 1966 and 1982), "Deadly" Derek Underwood was far less lethal with the bat. In a 24-year first-class career (between 1963 and 1987), he registered just one century – 111, for Kent against Sussex at Hastings in 1984. The 591 matches it took him to reach the landmark is an all-time record in first-class cricket.

⊙ ENDING THE LONG WAIT

Renowned as a tall off-spinner who used his height and unerring accuracy, rather than any great amount of spin imparted on the ball, to forge a successful 16-year career with Lancashire (between 1948 and 1964) and also play in 16 Tests for England, Roy Tattersall was resolute in defence with the bat, but not a prolific run-scorer. He holds the all-time first-class record for the most matches played before scoring a maiden half-century (306). The magic moment came when he scored 58 against Leicestershire at Old Trafford in 1958.

FIRST-CLASS BOWLING RECORDS

MOST CAREER WICKETS: TOP 10

Pos	Wkts	Player (span)
1	4,204	Wilfred Rhodes (1898–1930)
2	3,776	"Titch" Freeman (1914–36)
3	3,278	Charlie Parker (1903–35)
4	3,061	Jack Hearne (1888–1923)
5	2,979	Tom Goddard (1922–52)
6	2,874	Alex Kennedy (1907–36)
7	2,857	Derek Shackleton (1948–69)
8	2,844	Tony Lock (1946–71)
9	2,830	Fred Titmus (1949–82)
10	2,809	W.G. Grace (1865–1908)

⊙ BEST FIGURES IN A MATCH

No bowler has ever managed to better Jim Laker's Ashes-winning feat for England against Australia at Old Trafford in 1956. The Yorkshire off-spin bowler took 9 for 37 in the first innings and a Test-best 10 for 53 in the second to record the best match figures in the history of the game – 19 for 90.

⊙ A DAY TO REMEMBER

The second, and ultimately final, day of Kent's County Championship match against Northamptonshire at Northampton, on 31 May 1907, has gone down as one of the most unusual in first-class cricket history and, for Kent slow left-arm bowler Colin "Charlie" Blythe, as the most remarkable of his career. Batting first, Kent made a below-par 254. Enter Blythe: on the second day he took 10 for 30 as the home side fell to 60 all out in their first innings; in the second innings he took 7 for 18 as Northamptonshire, following on, folded to a miserable 31 all out and an innings-and-155-run defeat. Blythe's morning efforts had yielded figures of 17 for 48 – the best in a single day in first-class cricket history.

⊙ ANOTHER ODDITY

In their match against England at The Oval in 1863, Surrey lost four wickets in the course of a four-ball over from George Bennett. It is the only instance in first-class history of a bowler succeeding with every delivery of an over, albeit an abbreviated one.

⊙ LETHAL LILLYWHITE MARCHES INTO HISTORY BOOKS

William Lillywhite, one of the early exponents of round-arm bowling, enjoyed a remarkable 28-year first-class career for Cambridge Town Club, Hampshire, Middlesex, Surrey and Sussex. In 237 matches between 1825 and 1853, the 5ft 4in fast bowler took 1,576 wickets at an astonishing average of 1.54 runs per wicket – the best average of any bowler in the history of first-class cricket.

⊙ MASTER OF HIS TRADE

With his smooth, well balanced run-up, high action and controlled, almost calculated variation, slow left-arm bowler Hedley Verity was a true master of his trade. In 378 matches for Yorkshire in the 1930s (he also played in 40 Tests for England) he took an astonishing 1,956 wickets, including a best of 10 for 10 against Nottinghamshire at Headingley in 1932 – the best figures ever recorded in first-class cricket

⊙ LAWRENCE REGISTERS AN ALL-TIME LOW

A slow left-arm bowler for Oxford University between 1982 and 1986, Mark Lawrence holds the unusual distinction of having the worst career average of any bowler to have bowled 5,000 balls or more in first-class cricket. In 30 matches for the varsity side he took 2 wickets at an average of 70.92 runs per wicket.

BEST CAREER AVERAGE: TOP 10

Pos	Ave	Player (span)
1	1.54	William Lillywhite (1825–53)
2	5.43	William Clarke (1826–55)
3	6.19	Jemmy Dean Sr (1835–61)
4	6.66	John Wisden (1845–63)
5	7.73	Thomas Sherman (1846–70)
6	9.71	George Freeman (1865–80)
7	11.43	John Jackson (1855–67)
8	11.69	Arnold Rylott (1870–88)
9	11.82	Stephen Draai (1973–87)
10	11.95	Vincent Barnes (1978–95)

OUTSTANDING ANALYSIS (QUALIFICATION: SEVEN WICKETS FOR TEN RUNS OR FEWER)

Figures	Player (team)	Against	O-M-R-W	Venue	Season
10 for 10	H. Verity (Yorkshire)	Nottinghamshire	19.4-16-10-10	Headingley	1932
9 for 2	G. Elliott (Victoria)	Tasmania	19-17-2-9	Launceston	1857–58
9 for 7	Ahad Khan (Railways)	Dera Ismail Khan	6.3-4-7-9	Lahore	1964–65
8 for 2	J.C. Laker (England)	The Rest	14-12-2-8	Bradford	1950
8 for 4	D. Shackleton (Hampshire)	Somerset	11.1-7-4-8	Weston-s-Mare	1955
8 for 5	E. Peate (Yorkshire)	Surrey	16-11-5-8	Holbeck	1883
7 for 3	F.R. Spofforth (Australians)	England XI	8.3-6-3-7	Edgbaston	1884
7 for 4	W.A. Henderson (NE Transvaal)	Orange Free State	9.3-7-4-7	Bloemfontein	1937–38
7 for 4	Rajinder Goel (Haryana)	Jammu and Kashmir	7-4-4-7	Chandigarh	1977–78

⦿ TEN WICKETS IN AN INNINGS – ALL BOWLED

The best all-round cricketer of his day, who would go on to lend his name to the world's most famous cricket annual, the *Wisden Cricketers' Almanack*, John Wisden made history playing for the South against the North at Lord's in 1850. In the second innings of the match he became the first, and to date only, bowler in first-class cricket to take all ten wickets clean bowled.

⦿ TITCH STANDS TALL WITH THE BALL IN HIS HAND

Standing at a mere 5ft 2in, leg-break bowler Alfred Percy "Titch" Freeman was one of the greatest and most prolific slow bowlers the game has ever seen. A remarkable performer for Kent, for whom he played 592 matches between 1914 and 1936 (although he failed to replicate his county form for England, playing in only 12 Tests between 1924 and 1929), he set all-time first-class records for the most five-wicket hauls in a career (386); the most ten-wicket hauls in matches (140); and the most wickets in a season (a remarkable 304 in 1928).

100 WICKETS IN A SEASON OUTSIDE ENGLAND

Wkts	Player	Season	Country	Runs	Ave
116	Maurice Tate	1926–27	India, Ceylon	1,599	13.78
107	Ijaz Faqih	1985–86	Pakistan	1,719	16.06
106	Charlie Turner	1887–88	Australia	1,441	13.59
106	Richie Benaud	1957–58	South Africa	2,056	19.39
105	Murtaza Hussain	1995–96	Pakistan	1,882	17.92
104	S.F. Barnes	1913–14	South Africa	1,117	10.74
104	Sajjad Akbar	1989–90	Pakistan	2,328	22.38
103	Abdul Qadir	1982–83	Pakistan	2,367	22.98

250 WICKETS IN A SEASON

Wkts	Player	Season
304	"Titch" Freeman	1928
298	"Titch" Freeman	1933
290	Tom Richardson	1895
283	Charlie Turner	1888
276	"Titch" Freeman	1931
275	"Titch" Freeman	1930
273	Tom Richardson	1897
267	"Titch" Freeman	1929
261	Wilfred Rhodes	1900

⊙ MR WICKETS

The most prolific wicket taker the game of cricket has ever seen, Wilfred Rhodes took 4,204 wickets in a 1,110-match first-class career for Yorkshire and England between 1898 and 1930. The slow left-arm bowler also holds the all-time first-class record for registering the most instances of 100 wickets in a season, with 23.

HAT-TRICK ON DEBUT

Player (team)	Opposition	Venue	Season
Henry Hay (South Australia)	Lord Hawke's XI	Adelaide	1902–03
Herbert Sedgwick (Yorkshire)	Worcestershire	Hull	1906
Vasant Ranjane (Maharashtra)	Saurashtra	Poona	1956–57
Joginder Rao (Services)	Jammu & Kashmir	Delhi	1963–64
Roddy Estwick (Barbados)	Guyana	Bridgetown	1982–83
Salil Ankola (Maharashtra)	Gujurat	Poona	1988–89
Javagal Srinath (Karnataka)	Hyderabad	Secunderabad	1989–90
Saradindu Mukherjee (Benga)	Hyderabad	Secunderabad	1989–90
Shane Harwood (Victoria)	Tasmania	Melbourne	2002–03
Peter Connell (Ireland)	Netherlands	Rotterdam	2008
Abhimanyu Mithan (Uttar Pradesh)	Karnataka	Meerut	2009–10

UNDERWOOD SPINS HIS WAY INTO RECORD BOOKS

The record for the most instances of 100 wickets in a season since the reduction of the number of games played in the County Championship in 1969 is five, held by Kent and England's Derek Underwood, who achieved the feat in 1969 (101), 1971 (102), 1978 (110), 1979 (106) and 1983 (106).

FIRST-CLASS OTHER RECORDS

⊙ RECORD-BREAKING WICKETKEEPER

A fine performer behind the stumps who was forced to play second fiddle to Alan Knott in the England set-up for over half a decade before finally getting, and then seizing, his chance (he made just one Test appearance between February 1971 and December 1977 before going on to enjoy a 57-match international career), Bob Taylor was a record-breaker in first-class cricket. In 639 matches for Derbyshire and England between 1960 and 1988 he set the all-time first-class record for the most dismissals – 1,649, with a record 1,473 catchesand 176 stumpings.

⊙ A SAFE PAIR OF HANDS

The second-highest run-scorer in first-class cricket history (he scored 58,959 runs in his career at an average of 40.77), Frank Woolley also possessed the safest pair of hands the game has ever seen. In 979 matches for Kent and England between 1906 and 1938 he took an unbelievable 1,018 catches – and remains the only player in history to have surpassed the milestone of 1,000 catches.

⊙ HAMMOND GIVES GLOS A HELPING HAND

Walter Hammond was the outstanding performer for Gloucestershire in their County Championship match against Surrey at Cheltenham in August 1928. Not only did the England star shine with the bat (hitting 139 in the first innings and 143 in the second), he also played a major role in the field, taking four catches in Surrey's first innings and a sensational six in their second – his ten catches in the match is an all-time record for a fielder in first-class cricket. Gloucestershire went on to win the match by 189 runs.

⊙ GIFFEN'S ONE-MAN SHOW

A solid right-hand batsman and a slow-medium bowler, George Giffen produced perhaps the finest display in first-class cricket history to help South Australia to an innings-and-164-run victory over Victoria at Adelaide in November 1891. The South Australia captain hit 271 with the bat and proceeded to take 9 for 96 and 7 for 70 with the ball to lead his side to a comfortable victory. He is the only player in history to score 200-plus runs in an innings and take 15-plus wickets in a match in first-class cricket

⊙ THE FASTEST HANDS IN WORLD CRICKET

The first genuine wicketkeeper-batsman in world cricket (he scored 2,434 runs at an average of 40.56 and made 97 dismissals in 47 Tests for England between 1929 and 1939), Les Ames was the sharpest gloveman first-class cricket has ever seen. In a career spanning 25 years and 593 matches for Kent and England between 1925 and 1951 he made an all-time record 418 career stumpings.

⊙ MOST MATCHES IN CAREER

No player in history has played in more first-class matches than Wilfred Rhodes, the man who personified Yorkshire when the White Rose county was enjoying its heyday (Yorkshire won 12 County Championships during his time there, including four in a row between 1922 and 1925). He appeared in a mighty 1,110 first-class matches for the Europeans (India), Maharaja of Patiala's XI, Yorkshire and England between 1898 and 1930.

20,000 RUNS AND 2,000 WICKETS IN A CAREER

Player (span)	Runs	Wkts
W.G. Grace (1865–1908)	54,896	2,876
George Hirst (1891–1929)	36,323	2,739
Wilfred Rhodes (1898–1930)	39,802	4,187
Ewart Astill (1906–39)	22,731	2,431
Frank Woolley (1906–38)	58,969	2,068
Maurice Tate (1912–37)	21,717	2,784
Trevor Bailey (1945–67)	28,641	2,082
Fred Titmus (1949–82)	21,588	2,830
Raymond Illingworth (1951–83)	24,134	2,072

⊙ ALL-ROUND PERFECTION FOR HIRST

Yorkshire had George Hirst to thank for their comfortable 389-run County Championship victory over Somerset at Bath in August 1906. Described by Lord Hawke as "the greatest county cricketer of all time", Hirst scored 111 and 117 not out with the bat and took 6 for 70 and 5 for 45 with the ball to become the first, and to date only, player in first-class cricket history to score a century and take five wickets in both innings of a match. He ended the 1906 season with 2,385 runs and 208 wickets to his name to become the only man in cricket history to score 2,000 runs and take 200 wickets in a season.

LIST A MATCHES

According to the ICC's Classification of Official Cricket released in 2006, matches that fall under the List A category are all limited-overs matches that are either one-day internationals, other international limited-over matches, limited-overs matches from premier one-day tournaments in domestic cricket or official one-day matches between touring teams and first-class teams.

HIGHEST INNINGS TOTALS: TOP 5

Pos	Total	Overs	For	Against	Venue	Season
1	496–4	50	Surrey	Gloucestershire	The Oval	2007
2	443–9	50	Sri Lanka	Netherlands	Amstelveen	2006
3	438–5	50	Surrey	Glamorgan	The Oval	2002
4	438–9	49.5	South Africa	Australia	Johannesburg	2005–06
5	434–4	50	Australia	South Africa	Johannesburg	2005–06

LOWEST INNINGS TOTALS: TOP 5

Pos	Total	Overs	For	Against	Venue	Season
1	18	14.3	West Indies U19	Barbados	Guyana	2007–08
2	23	19.4	Middlesex	Yorkshire	Leeds	1974
3	31	13.5	Border	South Western Districts	East London	2007–08
4	34	21.1	Saurashtra	Mumbai	Mumbai	1999–2000
5	35	18	Zimbabwe	Sri Lanka	Harare	2004–05

⊙ ON A HOT STREAK

All-rounder Mike Procter was one of the most naturally talented cricketers ever to play the game. Sadly, owing to South Africa's exclusion from international cricket during the apartheid years, the world was denied the opportunity of seeing Procter perform in his prime on the international stage. When he was at his best, he was simply brilliant: playing for Rhodesia in the 1970–71 South African domestic season, he became the first, and to date only, player in history to hit six consecutive hundreds in List A matches

⊙ THE JOHANNESBURG RUN-FEST

South Africa's rollicking run-chase at Johannesburg on 12 March 2006, which saw them successfully chase down Australia's mighty total of 434 for 4 with one wicket and one ball to spare to clinch the five-match series 3–2, not only provided one of the most highly entertaining one-day international matches in history, but it also ensured the game entered the record books. The 872 runs scored in the match (for the loss of 13 wickets) is an all-time aggregate record in List A cricket.

⊙ KING OF THE ONE DAY GAME

Michael Bevan forged a worldwide reputation out of his exploits in the limited-overs game. Whereas he struggled in the Test arena, particularly against the short ball (he scored 785 runs in 18 Tests at an average of 29.07, with no centuries), he excelled in the shortened format of the game, both in and for Australia and beyond. In 427 List A matches between 1989 and 1996 the left-hander accumulated 15,103 runs at an average of 57.86 – the highest career average in List A matches of all time.

MOST RUNS IN A CAREER: TOP 10

Pos	Runs	Player (span)
1	22,211	Graham Gooch (1973–97)
2	22,059	Graeme Hick (1983–2008)
3	21,209	Sachin Tendulkar (1989–2011)
4	16,995	Viv Richards (1973–93)
5	16,349	Gordon Greenidge (1970–92)
6	16,025	Sanath Jayasuriya (1989–2010)
7	15,658	Allan Lamb (1972–95)
8	15,651	Desmond Haynes (1977–97)
9	15,564	Kim Barnett (1979–2005)
10	15,531	Sourav Ganguly (1989–2010)

⊙ TENDULKAR'S TASTE FOR BIG SCORES

Fast closing in on Graham Gooch's all-time record for the most runs scored in List A matches (22,211 runs compared to 21,150), Sachin Tendulkar has had a greater taste for making three-figure scores than any other batsman in List A cricket history. India's batting maestro has compiled 57 innings of a hundred or more in 529 List A matches between 1989 and 2010, with a highest score of 200 not out for India against South Africa at Gwalior on 24 February 2010.

MOST RUNS IN AN INNINGS: TOP 10

Pos	Runs	Player (team)	Against	Venue	Season
1	268	Ali Brown (Surrey)	Glamorgan	The Oval	2002
2	222*	Graeme Pollock (Eastern Province)	Border	East London	1974–75
3	207	Mohammad Ali (Pakistan Customs)	Defence Housing Authority	Sialkot	2004–05
4	206	Alvin Kallicharran (Warwickshire)	Oxfordshire	Birmingham	1984
5	204*	Khalid Latif (Karachi Dolphins)	Quetta Bears	Karachi	2008–09
6	203	Ali Brown (Surrey)	Hampshire	Guildford	1997
7	202*	Alan Barrow (Natal)	South Africa African XI	Durban	1975–76
8	201	Vince Wells (Leicestershire)	Berkshire	Leicester	1996
=	201*	Ravi Bopara (Essex)	Leicestershire	Leicester	2008
10	200*	Sachin Tendulkar (India)	South Africa	Gwalior	2009–10

⊙ THE ULTIMATE ONE-DAY BOWLER

A left-arm fast-medium bowler who, at the peak of his powers, was good enough to play five Test matches for England between 1964 and 1965 (taking 17 wickets), Fred Rumsey was at his best in the one-day arena, so much so that in the final five years of his career it was the only form of the game he played. In 95 List A matches for Derbyshire, Somerset, Worcestershire and England between 1963 and 1973 his career economy rate was 2.73 runs per over – an all-time record in List A cricket for any bowler who has bowled 2,500 balls or more.

MOST WICKETS: TOP 10

Pos	Wkts	Player (span)
1	881	Wasim Akram (1984–2003)
2	684	Allan Donald (1985–2004)
3	674	John Lever (1968–90)
=	674	Waqar Younis (1988–2004)
5	668	Muttiah Muralitharan (1991–2011)
6	647	John Emburey (1975–2000)
7	612	Ian Botham (1973–93)
8	598	Darren Gough (1990–2008)
9	573	Shaun Pollock (1992–2008)
10	572	Derek Underwood (1963–87)

⊙ MOST RUNS OFF ONE OVER

In the 30th over of South Africa's ICC World Cup Group A match against the Netherlands at St Kitts on 16 March 2007, Herschelle Gibbs showed exactly why he is regarded as one of the most exciting batsmen of modern times. He became only the third man in the game's history (alongside Garfield Sobers and Ravi Shastri) – and the only player in a List A match – to hit six sixes in an over.

BEST FIGURES IN AN INNINGS: TOP 10

Pos	Figures	Player (team)	Against	Venue	Season
1	8–15	Rahul Sanghvi (Delhi Himachal)	Pradesh	Una	1997–98
2	8–19	Chaminda Vaas (Sri Lanka)	Zimbabwe	Colombo	2001–02
3	8–20	Tharaka Kottehewa (Nondescripts CC)	Ragama CC	Colombo	2007–08
4	8–21	Michael Holding (Derbyshire)	Sussex	Hove	1988
5	8–26	Keith Boyce (Essex)	Lancashire	Old Trafford	1971
6	8–30	Romesh Eranga (Burgher RC)	Sri Lanka Army SC	Colombo	2007–08
7	8–31	Derek Underwood (Kent)	Scotland	Edinburgh	1987
8	8–43	Shaun Tait (South Australia)	Tasmania	Adelaide	2003–04
9	8–66	Simon Francis (Somerset)	Derbyshire	Derby	2004
10	7–7	Iqbal Sikander (Karachi Whites)	Peshawar	Karachi	1990–91

⊙ HIGHEST PARTNERSHIP

An all-time record in one-day international cricket, the second-wicket partnership of 331 between Sachin Tendulkar (186 not out) and Rahul Dravid (153) for India against New Zealand at Hyderabad on 8 November 1999 is also the highest-ever partnership in List A matches and one of only three 300-plus partnerships in history – the others being: Ghulam Ali and Sohail Jaffar's unbeaten partnership of 326 for PIA against ADBP at Sialkot in 2000–01, and Tim Curtis and Tom Moody's unbeaten partnership of 309 for Worcestershire against Surrey at The Oval in 1994.

5,000 RUNS AND 500 WICKETS IN A CAREER

Player (span)	Runs	Wkts
Clive Rice (1970–94)	13,474	517
Ian Botham (1973–93)	10,474	612
Imran Khan (1973–92)	10,100	507
Wasim Akram (1984–2003)	6,993	881
Phillip DeFreitas (1985–2004)	5,181	539
Shaun Pollock (1992–2008)	5,494	573

TWENTY20 CRICKET

Introduced first in England in 2003 to arrest the decline in the number of spectators attending domestic cricket, Twenty20 cricket proved enormously popular and soon spread to all parts of the world, providing fans with some scintillating cricket along the way.

HIGHEST TOTALS: TOP 5

Score	Team	Opponent	Venue	Date
260–6	Sri Lanka	Kenya	Johannesburg	14 Sep 2007
250–3	Somerset	Gloucs	Taunton	27 Jun 2006
246–5	Chennai	Rajasthan	Chennai	3 Apr 2010
245–3	Nondescripts	SL Air SC	Colombo	16 Oct 2005
243–2	Dolphins	L Eagles	Lahore	14 Oct 2010

LOWEST TOTALS: TOP 5

Score	Team	Opponent	Venue	Date
30	Tripura	Jharkhand	Dhanbad	20 Oct 2009
47	Titans	Eagles	Centurion	28 Apr 2004
58	Rajasthan	Bangalore	Cape Town	18 Apr 2009
58	Andrha	Hyderabad	Hyderabad	14 Oct 2010
59	SL Army	Sinhalese	Colombo	2 Mar 2007
59	Mountaineers	Eagles	Harare	19 Feb 2010

⊙ WELL WORTH THE WAIT

A right-handed batsman who had to wait until he was 27 years old before making his first-class debut for Rawalpindi in November 2009, Naved Malik has more than made up for any lost time, particularly in Twenty20 cricket. In ten matches for the Rawalpindi Rams he has scored 283 runs from 151 balls faced at a strike-rate of 187.41 runs per 100 balls faced – the best by any player to have faced 150 balls or more in Twenty20 cricket.

⊙ MOST CONSECUTIVE WINS

The power team of domestic Twenty20 cricket in Pakistan, the Sialkot Stallions have produced the longest winning streak in Twenty20 history, stringing together 24 successive victories between 24 February 2006 and 7 March 2010.

⊙ ROYALS RECORD-BREAKING EFFORT ALL IN VAIN

Having watched Chennai amass a mighty 246 for 5 (the third highest score in Twenty20 history) in their Indian Premier League encounter in Chennai on 3 April 2010, many could have forgiven a demoralized Rajastan for accepting defeat as an inevitably. To their great credit, however, they came out with all guns blazing and, although they still lost the match, reached a creditable 223 for 5 – the highest score by a team batting second in Twenty20 cricket.

MOST RUNS: TOP 10

Pos	Runs	Player (span)
1	3,476	David Hussey (2004–11)
2	3,405	Brad Hodge (2003–11)
3	2,716	Brendon McCullum (2005–10)
4	2,607	Ross Taylor (2006–11)
5	2,579	Herschelle Gibbs (2004–11)
6	2,512	David Warner (2007–11)
7	2,320	Owais Shah (2003–11)
8	2,256	Scott Styris (2005–10)
9	2,216	Graeme Smith (2004–10)
10	2,210	J.P. Duminy (2004–10)

HIGHEST SCORES: TOP 5

Pos	Runs	Player (team)	Against	Venue	Date
1	158*	Brendon McCullum (Kolkata)	Bangalore	Bangalore	18 Apr 2008
2	152*	Graham Napier (Essex)	Sussex	Chelmsford	24 Jun 2008
3	141*	Cameron White (Somerset)	Worcs	Worcester	9 Jul 2006
4	127	Murali Vijay (Chennai)	Rajasthan	Chennai	3 Apr 2010
5	124*	Michael Lumb (Hampshire)	Essex	Southampton	4 Jun 2009

⊙ HARVEY'S CENTURY-MAKING HEROICS

A hard-hitting lower-order batsman and a medium-pace bowler with one of the deadliest slower balls in the business, Ian Harvey may have struggled to establish himself in international cricket with Australia (playing 73 one-day internationals over a seven-year period), but he has achieved almost legendary status in county cricket in England (playing for Gloucestershire, Hampshire, Northamptonshire and Yorkshire), particularly for his exploits in Twenty20 cricket. The first player in history to reach three figures in the 20-over game (100 not out for Gloucestershire against Warwickshire at Edgbaston on 23 June 2003), he has passed 100 on a further two occasions.

MOST WICKETS: TOP 10

Pos	Wkts	Player (span)
1	132	Dirk Nannes (2007–11)
2	112	Alfonso Thomas (2004–11)
3	111	Albie Morkel (2004–11)
4	108	Yasir Arafat (2006–11)
5	101	Andrew Hall (2003–10)
6	98	Shahid Afridi (2004–10)
7	95	Muttiah Muralitharan (2005–10)
8	93	Tyrone Henderson (2004–09)
9	92	Charl Langeveldt (2004–11)
=	92	Umar Gul (2005–10)

⊙ A KEEN EYE FOR A WICKET

A pugnacious all-rounder who played in four Tests and 35 one-day internationals for England, Adam Hollioake's medium-pace bowling – and his "knuckle" ball in particular – proved enormously effective in Twenty20 cricket. In 22 matches for Surrey and Essex between 2003 and 2007 he took 40 wickets in 64.1 overs at a strike-rate of one wicket every 9.6 deliveries – the best in history by any player to have bowled 300 balls or more in Twenty20 matches.

⊙ BOTHA BLOOMS IN TWENTY20 CRICKET

A South African by birth, Andre Botha made an immediate impact when he made his one-day international debut for Ireland, against England in June 2006, scoring 52 from 89 balls, but he has since become more renowned for his performances with the ball, establishing a reputation as a neat and tidy off-spinner capable of both keeping it tight and taking wickets. One of only four players to have scored 2,000 runs and taken 100 wickets for Ireland, he has thrived in Twenty20 cricket, taking 26 wickets in 19 matches between 2008 and 2010 at an average of 11.30 – the best by any bowler to have bowled 300 balls or more in Twenty20 cricket.

BEST FIGURES IN AN INNINGS: TOP 5

Pos	Figures	Player (team)	Opponent	Venue	Date
1	6–14	Sohail Tanvir (Rajasthan)	Chennai	Jaipur	4 May 2008
2	6–15	Sanjeewa Roshan (Panadura)	SL Air SC	Colombo	30 Oct 2005
3	6–21	Andrew Hall (Northants)	Worcs	Northampton	13 Jun 2008
4	6–24	Tim Murtagh (Surrey)	Middlesex	Lord's	23 Jun 2005
5	6–25	Irfanuddin (K. Dolphins)	S. Stallions	Karachi	3 Mar 2006
=	6–25	Michael Dighton (Tasmania)	Queensland	Toowoomba	1 Jan 2007

⊙ BADREE SHOWS HIS MEAN STREAK

A leg-spin bowler of early promise who made his first-class debut for Trinidad and Tobago as long ago as the 2001–02 season but then failed to nail down a regular place in the side, Samuel Badree has redefined himself as an extremely effective bowler in the limited-overs formats of the game, particularly Twenty20 cricket. He has played in 23 matches, bowled 436 deliveries and conceded just 334 runs. His economy rate of 4.56 runs conceded per over, is the best by any bowler in Twenty20 history.

⊙ HUSSEY JR IS THE KING OF THE CATCHERS IN TWENTY20 CRICKET

He may have been overshadowed by his elder brother Mike in international cricket, but David Hussey has been a standout performer in domestic cricket over the years and has produced the goods in Twenty20 cricket. In 137 matches for Australia, Australia A, Victoria, Kolkata Knight Riders and Nottinghamshire between 2004 and 2011, he has taken 74 catches – at an average of 0.54 catches per innings. No player has taken more in Twenty20 matches.

⊙ BEST FIGURES IN A LOSING CAUSE

The best-ever figures recorded in Twenty20 cricket by a bowler who has ended up on the losing side are 6 for 25, achieved by two players: Irfanuddin (4.0-0-25-6 for Karachi Dolphins against Sialkot Stallions at Karachi on 3 March 2006 – a match Sialkot won by 29 runs) and Michael Dighton (3.0-0-25-6 for Tasmania against Queensland at Toowoomba on 1 January 2007 – a match Queensland won by 38 runs).

INDIAN PREMIER LEAGUE

First contested in 2008, principally off the back of the surge of enthusiasm in India for the new format of the game following the country's 2007 ICC World Twenty20 triumph, the Indian Premier League (IPL), featuring eight franchises, has been a huge success, attracting vast crowds and the best players from around the world

INDIAN PREMIER LEAGUE WINNERS

2008	Rajasthan Royals
2009	Deccan Chargers
2010	Chennai Super Kings

RESULT SUMMARY

Team (Span)	Mat	Won	Lost	Tied	NR	%
Chennai Super Kings (2008–10)	46	26	19	1	0	57.60
Deccan Chargers (2008–10)	46	19	27	0	0	41.30
Delhi Daredevils (2008–10)	43	24	19	0	0	55.81
Kings XI Punjab (2008–10)	43	20	22	1	0	47.67
Kolkata Knight Riders (2008–10)	40	16	21	1	0	41.25
Mumbai Indians (2008–10)	43	23	20	0	0	53.48
Rajasthan Royals (2008–10)	43	24	18	1	0	56.97
Royal Challengers Bangalore (2008–10)	46	21	25	0	0	45.65

⊙ McCULLUM TAKES CENTRE STAGE

As the entire world looked on with reserved anticipation, a Hollywood scriptwriter could not have come up with a better first act for the first-ever match in the IPL – Kolkata against Bangalore at Bangalore on 18 April 2008. And if the script was sensational, Brendon McCullum's performance with the bat was the star turn. The Kolkata opener bludgeoned the highest individual score in Twenty20 history, 158 not out off 73 deliveries – an innings that contained a tournament record 13 sixes, to lead his side to a mighty 222 for 3 and an eventual 140-run victory.

⊙ CASHING IN IN CHENNAI

Chennai hit their stride in spectacular and record-breaking fashion against Rajasthan at Chennai on 3 April 2010. Having won the toss and elected to bat they put the Royals' bowlers to the sword, with Murali Vijay hitting a 56-ball 127 and Albie Morkel swatting a 34-ball 62 to take them to 246 for 5 – the highest team total in IPL history. The Royals made a creditable 223 for 5 in reply as Chennai went on to win the match by 23 runs.

⊙ RAJASTHAN ROYALS LOSE GRIP OF IPL CROWN

Rajasthan's defence of the IPL crown, which they won in spectacular style in 2007, got off to the worst of starts against Bangalore at Cape Town in 18 April 2009. Having restricted their opponents to an under-par 133 for 8, the Royals batsmen slumped in less than regal fashion to 58 all out – the lowest team total in all IPL matches – and a 75-run defeat

MOST RUNS: TOP 10

Pos	Runs	Player (Team, Span)
1	1,375	Suresh Raina (Chennai, 2008–10)
2	1,220	Adam Gilchrist (Deccan, 2008–10)
3	1,170	Sachin Tendulkar (Mumbai, 2008–10)
=	1,170	Rohit Sharma (Deccan, 2008–10)
5	1,132	Jacques Kallis (Bangalore, 2008–10)
6	1,107	Matthew Hayden (Chennai, 2008–10)
7	1,097	Gautham Gambhir (Delhi, 2008–10)
8	1,033	Mahendra Singh Dhoni (Chennai, 2008–10)
9	1,031	Sourav Ganguly (Kolkata, 2008–10)
10	1,011	Yusuf Pathan (Rajasthan, 2008–10)

⊙ STAR OF THE SHOW

A hefty US$700,000 he may have cost, but Adam Gilchrist has given his all for the Deccan Chargers, leading them to the IPL crown in 2009 (when the tournament was staged in South Africa) and producing some scintillating performances along the way: he has hit more sixes than any other player in the tournament's history (an impressive 64).

HIGHEST INDIVIDUAL SCORE: TOP 10

Pos	Runs	Player (team)	Opponent	Venue	Date
1	158*	Brendon McCullum (Kolkata)	Bangalore	Bangalore	18 Apr 2008
2	127	Murali Vijay (Chennai)	Rajasthan	Chennai	3 Apr 2010
3	117*	Andrew Symonds (Deccan)	Rajasthan	Hyderabad	24 Apr 2008
4	116*	Michael Hussey (Chennai)	Punjab	Mohali	19 Apr 2008
5	115	Shaun Marsh (Punjab)	Rajasthan	Mohali	28 May 2008
6	114*	Sanath Jayasuriya (Mumbai)	Chennai	Mumbai	14 May 2008
=	114*	Manish Pandey (Bangalore)	Deccan	Centurion	21 May 2009
8	110*	Mahela Jayawardene (Punjab)	Kolkata	Kolkata	4 Apr 2010
9	109*	Adam Gilchrist (Deccan)	Mumbai	Mumbai	27 Apr 2008
10	107*	David Warner (Delhi)	Kolkata	Delhi	29 Mar 2010

⊙ LARGEST VICTORIES

By runs: by 140 runs – Kolkata v Bangalore at Bangalore on 18 April 2008.
By wickets: by ten wickets on three occasions.
By balls remaining: with 87 balls remaining – Mumbai v Kolkata at Mumbai on 16 May 2008.

⊙ SMALLEST VICTORIES

By runs: by one run on two occasions – Punjab v Mumbai at Mumbai on 21 May 2008; and Punjab v Deccan at Johannesburg on 17 May 2009.
By wickets: by two wickets – Bangalore v Chennai at Durban on 14 May 2009.
By balls remaining: off the last ball of the match on six occasions.

⊙ MOST SCORES OF 50 OR OVER

Controversially left out of South Africa's side for the inaugural ICC World Twenty20 because the selectors questioned his worth in the 20-over game, Jacques Kallis has shone for Bangalore in the IPL. He has struck 10 half-centuries in 42 matches – an all-time record in the IPL.

⊙ MOST DISMISSALS

Not merely a belligerent performer with the bat (only Suresh Raina has scored more runs in the IPL), Adam Gilchrist has also shone behind the stumps for the Deccan Chargers. He has bagged 38 dismissals (25 catches, 13 stumpings) in 46 matches – an all-time tournament record.

MOST WICKETS: TOP 10

Pos	Wkts	Player (Team, Span)
1	51	R.P. Singh (Deccan, 2008–10)
2	50	Pragyan Ojha (Deccan, 2008–10)
3	47	Irfan Pathan (Punjab, 2008–10)
4	45	Anil Kumble (Bang, 2008–10)
5	44	Shane Warne (Raj, 2008–10)
6	42	Amit Mishra (Delhi, 2008–10)
7	41	Piyush Chawla (Punjab, 2008–10)
=	41	Albie Morkel (Chennai, 2008–10)
9	40	Muttiah Muralitharan (Chennai, 2008–10)
10	37	Ashish Nehra (Delhi, 2008–10)

⊙ JAKATI PRODUCES THE GOODS FOR CHENNAI

Some players have used the Indian Premier League as a platform to launch themselves out of relative obscurity, and one such example is Goa-born Shadab Jakati. After ten relatively unsuccessful seasons in domestic cricket for Goa, the left-arm spinner joined Chennai in 2009 and has shone, taking 26 wickets in 20 matches at a strike-rate of a wicket every 15.4 deliveries – the best in IPL history.He played a major role in Chennai's march to the IPL crown in 2010.

⊙ DECCAN EASE PAST MUMBAI WITH PLENTY TO SPARE

Adam Gilchrist (109 not out) and V.V.S. Laxman (37 not out) made short work of Mumbai's bowling attack to hammer Deccan to a comfortable ten-wicket victory at Mumbai on 27 April 2008. With Gilchrist, in particular, in blitzkrieg form, the pair added an unbeaten 155 for the opening wicket – the highest partnership in IPL history – to ease Deccan past the victory target with 48 balls to spare.

⊙ TERRIFIC TANVIR TAMES THE SUPER KINGS

A scintillating spell of bowling from Sohail Tanvir saw Rajasthan cruise to victory over the Chennai Super Kings at Jaipur on 4 May 2008. The left-arm Pakistan paceman, who cost the Royals US$100,000 at auction, took 6 for 14 IN his four-over stint – the best bowling figures in Twenty20 history (and the competition's only six-wicket haul) – to send Chennai spinning to 109 all out. Rajasthan cantered to victory for the loss of two wickets with 34 balls to spare.

HIGHEST PARTNERSHIP BY WICKET

Wkt	Runs	Partners	Team	Opposition	Venue	Date
1st	155*	A.C. Gilchrist, V.V.S. Laxman	Deccan	Mumbai	Mumbai	27 Apr 2008
2nd	137*	M. Vijay, S.K. Raina	Chennai	Kolkata	Chennai	13 Apr 2010
3rd	152	M. Vijay, J.A. Morkel	Chennai	Rajasthan	Chennai	3 Apr 2010
4th	128	D.A. Warner, P.D. Collingwood	Delhi	Kolkata	Delhi	29 Mar 2010
5th	130*	O.A. Shah, A.D. Mathews	Kolkata	Deccan	Mumbai	12 Mar 2010
6th	104	D.J. Hussey, W.P. Saha	Kolkata	Punjab	Mohali	3 May 2008
7th	60	R.A. Jadeja, S.K. Warne	Rajasthan	Punjab	Cape Town	26 Apr 2009
8th	53*	R. McLaren, Harbhajan Singh	Mumbai	Deccan	Mumbai	28 Mar 2010
9th	36	Harbhajan Singh, A.N. Ahmed	Mumbai	Chennai	Chennai	6 Apr 2010
10th	29*	S.K. Trivedi, M.M. Patel	Rajasthan	Delhi	Bloemfontein	17 May 2009

⊙ CHENNAI'S ASHWIN THE ECONOMY RATE KING

A tall off-spinner whose performances for Chennai in the Indian Premier League have propelled him into the fringes of India's Twenty20 squad, Ravichandran Ashwin is the most miserly bowler in IPL history. Often bowling with the new ball at the start of the innings, he has gone for 306 runs in 52.0 overs bowled – an economy rate of 5.88 runs per over (the best in IPL history).

⊙ MIXED FORTUNES FOR SINGH

Deccan's R.P. Singh, one of the IPL's most expensive players (the Chargers paid US$875,000 to secure his services), found himself on the receiving end of a bashing against Kolkata at Hyderabad on 11 May 2008. As the visitors compiled a mighty 204 for 4 off their 20 overs, Singh's four overs went for 59 runs (the most expensive spell in IPL history). But it hasn't all been bad news for India's 2007 ICC World Twenty20 star: in 2009, when Deccan took the IPL crown, Singh was one of their best performers, taking 23 wickets in the tournament – a single-season record in the IPL.

⊙ MOST SUCCESSFUL CAPTAIN

A revelation for India since he took over the captaincy from Rahul Dravid in all forms of the game after leading his side to the ICC World Twenty20 crown in South Africa in 2007, Mahendra Singh Dhoni has proved equally inspirational for the Chennai Super Kings. He has guided his side to 25 wins in 43 matches – the most by any captain in the tournament's history – and led his side (the most expensive franchise in the competition) to the IPL crown in 2010.

⊙ SHUKLA DEMOLISHES DELHI'S LOWER ORDER

An incisive performance with the ball from Laxmi Shukla swept Kolkata to a comfortable victory over Delhi at Kolkata on 13 May 2008. Brought into the attack in the 18th over, with Delhi on 104 for 7 chasing 134, the right-arm medium-pace bowler took 3 for 6 in five deliveries to hand his side a 23-run win. His innings strike-rate (a wicket every 1.6 deliveries) is the best in IPL history.

⊙ KEEPING IT TIGHT

Wickets are not the be all and end all in Twenty20 cricket; a four-over stint that goes for anything less than six runs per over is a success. Two bowlers have done far better than that, each going for a miserly, tournament-record six runs off their four-over allocations (an economy rate of 1.50): Fidel Edwards (4-1-6-0 for Deccan against Kolkata at Cape Town on 19 April 2009); and Ashish Nehra (4-1-6-1 for Delhi against Punjab at Bloemfontein on 15 May 2009).

⊙ MOST CATCHES

The most exciting young batsman in India (a serial run-scorer in youth cricket and Ranji Trophy matches, he was propelled into India's Test team when he was 19), Suresh Raina has added to his fast-growing reputation with athletic and often dazzling performances in the field. In 46 matches for Chennai in the IPL he has taken 27 catches – no player has taken more.

⊙ POLLARD SHINES FOR MUMBAI

Kieron Pollard had a season to remember for the Mumbai Indians in 2010 – his debut season in the IPL. He smashed 273 runs off 147 balls at a strike-rate of 185.71 runs per 100 balls, a tournament record.

PART 5: OTHER CRICKET

The first women's cricket club – the White Heather Club in Yorkshire – was established in 1887, but it was a further 47 years before the first women's Test match was played (Australia played England in December 1934). Despite its rich history, women's cricket has never achieved the same status as the men's game, even though it has been more innovative.

The first women's World Cup, for example, was contested in 1973, two years before the men's equivalent; they also staged the first Twenty20 international, in August 2004, six months before the men. When the ICC Women's World Twenty20 in England was staged in conjunction with the men's tournament it showed that, even though it has some distance to go, the women's game is making great strides.

Also, the importance of international youth cricket often gets lost amid the sheer weight of games played at a higher level, but many of those who go on to perform with distinction in the upper echelons of the game have passed through its ranks: 17 of the 29 players who took part in the 2009 Ashes series had played in youth Test cricket. The first youth Tests and one-day internationals were played in 1974 and, since 1998, there has been an ICC Under-19 World Cup every two years.

WOMEN'S TEST CRICKET

Anyone who thought that the first-ever women's Test match, played between Australia and England at Brisbane in December 1934, heralded the dawn of a proliferation of women's cricket around the world, has been proved sadly wrong. Since that milestone match (which England won by nine wickets), only 131 further women's Test matches have been played – compared to the 1,720 men's Test matches.

RESULTS SUMMARY

Team (Span)	Mat	Won	Lost	Tied	Draw	W/L	%W	%L	%D
Australia (1934–2011)	69	19	9	0	41	2.11	27.53	13.04	59.43
England (1934–2011)	89	19	12	0	58	1.58	21.34	13.48	65.16
India (1976–2006)	34	3	6	0	25	0.50	8.82	17.64	73.52
Ireland (2000)	1	1	0	0	0	–	100.00	0.00	0.00
Netherlands (2007)	1	0	1	0	0	0.00	0.00	100.00	0.00
New Zealand (1935–2004)	45	2	10	0	33	0.20	4.44	22.22	73.33
Pakistan (1998–2004)	3	0	2	0	1	0.00	0.00	66.66	33.33
South Africa (1960–2007)	11	1	4	0	6	0.25	9.09	36.36	54.54
Sri Lanka (1998)	1	1	0	0	0	–	100.00	0.00	0.00
West Indies (1976–2004)	12	1	3	0	8	0.33	8.33	25.00	66.66

⊙ CONSISTENCY THE KEY FOR ANNETTS

Denise Annetts announced her arrival on the Test stage for Australia, against England at Wetherby in August 1987, in spectacular style. Making her debut in the drawn Second Test, she scored 193 not out and shared a record women's Test partnership of 309 with Lindsay Reeler (110 not out). Although she failed to hit such heady heights again, the Sydney-born right-hander remained a consistent run-gatherer throughout her career: in ten Tests between 1987 and 1992 she scored 819 runs (with two centuries and six half-centuries) at an average of 81.90 – the highest by any player to have completed ten innings or more in women's Test cricket history.

⊙ THE QUEEN OF BATTING

The most capped women's Test cricketer of all time (she played in 27 Tests for England between 1979 and 1998), Jan Brittin was the most prolific run-scorer women's cricket has ever seen, scoring 1,935 runs at an average of 49.61. She set all-time women's Test records for the most centuries (five, with a highest score of 167 against Australia at Harrogate in August 1998) and for the most runs scored in a calendar year (with 531 runs in five innings in 1994).

MOST RUNS: TOP 5

Pos	Runs	Player (Team, Span)
1	1,935	Jan Brittin (England, 1979–98)
2	1,594	Rachael Heyhoe-Flint (England, 1960–79)
3	1,522	Charlotte Edwards (England, 1996–2011)
4	1,301	Debbie Hockley (New Zealand, 1979–96)
5	1,164	Carole Hodges (England, 1984–92)

MOST WICKETS: TOP 5

Pos	Wkts	Player (Team, Span)
1	77	Mary Duggan (England, 1949–63)
2	68	Betty Wilson (Australia, 1948–58)
3	63	Diana Edulji (India, 1976–91)
4	60	Myrtle Maclagan (England, 1934–51)
=	60	Cathryn Fitzpatrick (Australia, 1991–2006)
=	60	Shubhangi Kulkarni (Ind, 1976–91)

⊙ HIGHEST AND LOWEST

Highest team total: 569 for 6 declared – Australia v England at Guildford in August 1998.
Lowest team total: 35 all out – England v Australia at Melbourne in February 1958.

⊙ BIGGEST VICTORIES

By an innings: by an innings and 337 runs – England v New Zealand at Christchurch in February 1935.
By runs: by 309 runs – Sri Lanka v Pakistan at Colombo in April 1998.

⊙ SMALLEST VICTORIES

By runs: by two runs – England v India at Jamshedpur in November 1995.
By wickets: by two wickets – Australia v England at Worcester in June–July 1951.

WOMEN'S ODI CRICKET

It was women, not men, who contested cricket's first-ever World Cup. The 1973 ICC Women's World Cup, held in England (and won by the hosts), heralded the start of one-day international cricket in the women's game, and the format has proved more popular than the Test game: 46 women's one-day internationals were staged around the world in 2009 alone, a year which saw just a single Test.

RESULTS SUMMARY

Team (span)	Mat	Won	Lost	Tied	NR	%
Australia (1973–2011)	243	187	50	1	5	78.78
Denmark (1989–99)	33	6	27	0	0	18.18
England (1973–2011)	254	139	104	2	9	57.14
India (1978–2011)	183	96	82	1	4	53.91
International XI (1973–82)	18	3	14	0	1	17.64
Ireland (1987–2010)	112	35	74	0	3	32.11
Jamaica (1973)	5	1	4	0	0	20.00
Japan (2003)	5	0	5	0	0	0.00
Netherlands (1984–2010)	93	18	75	0	0	19.35
New Zealand (1973–2010)	246	127	112	2	5	53.11
Pakistan (1997–2010)	76	15	60	0	1	20.00
Scotland (2001–03)	8	1	7	0	0	12.50
South Africa (1997–2010)	83	38	40	1	4	48.73
Sri Lanka (1997–2010)	83	41	40	0	2	50.61
Trinidad & Tobago (1973)	6	2	4	0	0	33.33
West Indies (1979–2011)	84	37	44	1	2	45.73
Young England (1973)	6	1	5	0	0	16.60

WORLD CUP WINNERS

Year	Winners	Host	Year	Winners	Host
1973	England	England	1997	Australia	India
1978	Australia	India	2000	New Zealand	New Zealand
1982	Australia	New Zealand	2005	Australia	South Africa
1988	Australia	Australia	2009	England	Australia
1993	England	England			

⊙ SENSATIONAL SHAH SETS TONGUES WAGGING

Ever since she caused a sensation by making her international debut at the age of 12, against Ireland at Dublin on 23 July 2000, Sajjida Shah has been a regular and successful member of the Pakistan side. And her headline-grabbing feats have not been solely restricted to her debut: in Pakistan's ICC Women's Trophy match against Japan at Amsterdam on 21 July 2003, she took 7 for 4 off eight overs of off-spin (as Japan slumped to 28 all out) to record the best bowling figures in women's one-day international cricket history.

MOST CAREER RUNS: TOP 5

Pos	Runs	Player (Team, Span)
1	4,844	Belinda Clark (Australia, 1991–2005)
2	4,814	Karen Rolton (Australia, 1995–2009)
3	4,300	Charlotte Edwards (England, 1997–2011)
4	4,064	Debbie Hockley (New Zealand, 1982–2000)
5	4,007	Mithala Raj (India, 1999–2011)

MOST CAREER WICKETS: TOP 5

Pos	Wkts	Player (Team, Span)
1	180	Cathryn Fitzpatrick (Australia, 1993–2007)
2	141	Neeth David (India, 1995–2008)
3	124	Jhulan Goswami (India, 2002–11)
4	117	Lisa Sthalekar (Australia, 2001–11)
5	102	Clare Taylor (England, 1988–2005)

⊙ PIONEER OF THE WOMEN'S GAME

Rachel Heyhoe-Flint, an integral figure in English women's cricket for over a generation, had done so much to get the ICC Women's World Cup tournament off the ground in the first place, that it seemed more than appropriate when, on 28 July 1973, she became the first woman in history to lift the trophy. A fine all-round batsman, capable of blunting an attack with her defence or destroying it with cavalier strokeplay, she enjoyed a long and successful career. In 23 matches between 1973 and 1982 she scored 643 runs (with a highest score of 114 against Young England at Ilford on 18 July 1973) at an average of 58.45 – the highest in women's one-day international history.

WOMEN'S TWENTY20

As was the case with the 50-over World Cup, the women stole a march on the men in Twenty20 cricket. The first-ever Twenty20 international match was played between England Women and New Zealand Women at Hove on 6 August 2004 – a match New Zealand won by nine runs. Since then, cricket's newest format has become a staple of the women's game.

RESULTS SUMMARY

Team (span)	Mat	Won	Lost	Tied	NR	%
Australia (2005–11)	34	17	15	2	0	52.94
England (2004–11)	37	23	13	1	0	63.51
India (2006–11)	16	8	8	0	0	50.00
Ireland (2008–10)	9	3	6	0	0	33.33
Netherlands (2008–10)	6	0	6	0	0	0.00
New Zealand (2004–11)	34	22	11	1	0	66.17
Pakistan (2009–10)	12	3	9	0	0	25.00
South Africa (2007–10)	18	3	15	0	0	16.66
Sri Lanka (2009–10)	15	4	11	0	0	26.66
West Indies (2008–11)	25	18	7	0	0	72.00

⊙ HITTING NEW HEIGHTS

Shandre Fritz was the star of the show as South Africa compiled 205 for 1 (the highest score in women's Twenty20 international cricket) against Netherlands at Potchefstroom on 14 October 2010. The Cape Town-born right-hander smashed an unbeaten 116 – the highest score by a women in the 20-over format of the game.

⊙ UNLIKELY BOWLING HEROINE

A specialist top-order batsman she may be, but it was Amy Satterthwaite's performance with the ball that grabbed the headlines following the third Twenty20 international between England and New Zealand at Taunton on 16 August 2007. Bowling right-arm medium pace, the 20-year-old New Zealander tore through England's batting line-up, taking 6 for 17 – the best bowling figures ever recorded in women's Twenty20 international cricket – to lead her side to a 38-run victory.

MOST CAREER RUNS: TOP 5

Pos	Runs	Player (Team, Span)
1	966	Charlotte Edwards (England, 2004–11)
2	739	Shelley Nitschke (Australia, 2005–11)
3	714	Aimee Watkins (New Zealand, 2004–10)
4	670	Suzie Bates (New Zealand, 2007–11)
5	640	Sara McGlashan (New Zealand, 2004–11)

MOST CAREER WICKETS: TOP 5

Pos	Wkts	Player (Team, Span)
1	38	Anisa Mohammed (West Indies, 2008–11)
=	38	Shelley Nitschke (Austalia, 2005–11)
3	37	Lisa Sthalekar (Australia, 2005–11)
4	32	Hannah Colvin (England, 2007–11)
5	31	Nicola Browne (New Zealand, 2004–10)

⊙ HIGHEST AND LOWEST

Highest team total: 205 for 1 – South Africa v Netherlands at Potchefstroom on 14 October 2010.
Lowest team total: 60 all out – Pakistan v England at Taunton on 16 June 2009.

⊙ BIGGEST VICTORIES

By runs: by 115 runs – South Africa v Netherlands at Potchefstroom on 14 October 2010.
By wickets: by ten wickets – England v India at Taunton on 11 June 2009.
By balls remaining: with 70 balls remaining – New Zealand v Pakistan at Basseterre, St Kitts, on 10 May 2010.

⊙ SMALLEST VICTORIES

By runs: by one run on two occasions.
By wickets: by two wickets – England v India at Mumbai on 4 March 2010.
By balls remaining: with one ball remaining – England v India at Mumbai on 4 March 2010.

WORLD CUP WINNERS

Year	Winners	Host
2009	England	England
2010	Australia	West Indies

YOUTH TEST CRICKET

Representative youth cricket around the world plays a vital role as the nursery for international cricketers of the future. The vast majority of players who have gone on to enjoy a first-class career and beyond have, at some stage, passed through youth cricket's doors.

RESULT SUMMARY

Team (span)	Mat	Won	Lost	Tied	Draw	W/L	%W	%L	%D
Australia U19 (1979–2009)	68	27	14	0	27	1.92	39.70	20.58	39.70
Bangladesh U19 (2004–09)	12	1	4	0	7	0.25	8.33	33.33	58.33
England U19 (1974–2011)	134	33	38	0	62	0.86	24.81	38.57	46.61
India U19 (1979–2009)	67	20	12	0	35	1.66	29.85	17.91	52.23
New Zealand U19 (1986–2008)	43	11	10	0	22	1.10	25.58	23.25	51.16
Pakistan U19 (1979–2007)	64	10	13	0	41	0.76	15.62	20.31	64.06
South Africa U19 (1995–2008)	23	3	9	0	11	0.33	13.04	39.13	47.82
Sri Lanka U19 (1984–2011)	43	6	14	0	23	0.42	13.95	32.55	53.48
West Indies U19 (1974–2001)	35	12	5	0	18	2.40	34.28	14.28	51.42
Zimbabwe U19 (1996–97)	6	0	4	0	2	0.00	0.00	66.66	33.33

⊙ HIGHEST AND LOWEST

Highest team total: 646 for 9 declared – South Africa U19 v England U19 at Chelmsford in August 2003.
Lowest team total: 47 all out – Zimbabwe U19 v England U19 at Harare in January 1996.

⊙ HIGHEST INDIVIDUAL SCORE

Clinton Peake was the undoubted star for Australia in their drawn second Youth Test match against India at Melbourne in March 1995. With India having amassed 426 all out in their first innings, Peake, a pint-sized left-hander, born in Gelong, led Australia's response in style, hitting an unbeaten 304 – the highest-ever score in Youth Test cricket – to take his side to a result-killing 565 for 8. Peake failed to fulfil his potential in senior cricket, going on to play only nine first-class matches for Victoria.

YOUTH ODI CRICKET

Limited-overs matches have been a regular feature on the youth-international circuit since the first match between the West Indies and England at Trinidad in August 1976. A biennial ICC Youth World Cup was launched in 1998 (although a one-off tournament had previously been held in Australia in 1988). Australia have been the most successful team with three victories (1988, 2002 and 2010).

YOUTH WORLD CUP WINNERS

Year	Winner	Host
1988	Australia	Australia
1998	England	South Africa
2000	India	Sri Lanka
2002	Australia	New Zealand
2004	Pakistan	Bangladesh
2006	Pakistan	Sri Lanka
2008	India	Malaysia
2010	Australia	New Zealand

MOST RUNS: TOP 5

Pos	Runs	Player (Team, Span)
1	1,318	Ahmed Shehzad (Pakistan U19, 2007–10)
2	1,316	Tanmay Srivastava (India U19, 2005–08)
3	1,168	Mahmudul Hasan (Bangladesh U19, 2007–10)
4	1,040	Bhanuka Rajapaska (Sri Lanka U19, 2009–11)
5	999	Ali Asad (Pakistan U19, 2005–08)

MOST WICKETS: TOP 5

Pos	Wkts	Player (Team, Span)
1	73	Imad Wasim (Pakistan U19, 2005–08)
2	71	Piyush Chawla (India U19, 2003–07)
3	66	Mahmudul Hasan (Bangladesh U19, 2007–10)
4	64	Sachitu Pathirana (Sri Lanka U19, 2005–08)
5	59	Chathura Peiris (Sri Lanka U19, 2007–10)